CHILDREN AND SOCIAL STUDIES

Creative Teaching in the Elementary Classroom

Third Edition

CHILDREN AND SOCIAL STUDIES

Creative Teaching in the Elementary Classroom

Third Edition

Murry R. Nelson
Pennsylvania State University

Harcourt Brace College Publishers

Fort Worth   Philadelphia   San Diego   New York   Orlando   Austin   San Antonio
Toronto   Montreal   London   Sydney   Tokyo

Publisher	Earl McPeek
Acquisitions Editor	Jo-Anne Weaver
Marketing Manager	Don Grainger
Project Editor	Sandy Walton
Art Director	Lora Gray
Production Manager	Andrea Johnson

Cover image credit: Mary Thelan, represented by Lorraine and Associates

ISBN: 0-15-505465-1
Library of Congress Catalog Card Number: 97-73574

Address for Orders
Harcourt Brace College Publishers, 6277 Sea Harbor Drive, Orlando, FL 32887-6777
1-800-782-4479

Address for Editorial Correspondence
Harcourt Brace College Publishers, 301 Commerce Street, Suite 3700, Fort Worth, TX 76102

Web Site Address
http://www.hbcollege.com

Printed in the United States of America

7 8 9 0 1 2 3 4 5 6   039   9 8 7 6 5 4 3 2 1

Harcourt Brace College Publishers

To Elizabeth, Rebecca, and Daniel,
and to my students, who have taught me much.

PREFACE

Preparing this edition of *Children and Social Studies* was an exciting challenge because of the tremendous changes that have occurred since the last edition was published. It is truly amazing how much has happened during these years and this edition reflects those rapid changes.

Since 1992, the most noticeable concern has been with standards in the field. Starting in 1994 with the Social Studies Standards produced by the National Council for the Social Studies, five sets have been produced. The others are standards in history, geography, economics, and civics. I address the notion of these standards in Chapter 2, though do not reprint the standards, which run almost 1,000 pages. A second, unprecedented, development has been in the Internet. As recently as 1992, the Internet had almost no impact on the learning of students in the elementary school. Now, there is a desire on the part of many people, including President Clinton, to get every school on line by 2000. The Internet and use of it are addressed in dramatically revised Chapter 10, which also notes the increased use and availability of cable television nationwide, particularly for school use.

I am pleased that during the 1990s multiculturalism has become more and more accepted as part of the school's curricular concerns. What had been less common but needed in schools is rapidly becoming mainstream and that can only benefit the education of all children and the improvement of our American cultural fabric. Part of that concern is expressed by some in their renewed interest in character education and that is addressed in the revision of Chapter 4. This chapter also looks briefly at the paradox of religious practice and non-religious beliefs across nations. Updates on controversial issues (Chapter 13), evaluation, with particular attention to portfolios (Chapter 14), textbook usage (Chapter 7), and conflict resolution in schools (Chapter 13) are some of the other highlights of this edition. Many of the maps and graphics have been replaced to offer new views to the material discussed. I have also updated all of the material in the appendix.

Despite the pessimists and critics, education continues to be the best avenue for advancement both in the United States and abroad. More students graduate from high school and go on to college, and there is so much more to learn. Information continues to multiply at a staggering pace, and education is racing to try and sustain that pace. After more than twenty-five years as an educator, I am optimistic about the future of schools and their ability to "deliver the goods" to students and the public.

There are many people who helped me to compile and produce this book. Among those who have been most helpful are Melissa Butler, my graduate research assistant, and a host of librarians at The Pennsylvania State University, but particularly Steven Herb and Deborah Chaney. Joanna Petrie of the U.S. Department of Transportation provided me with a unique map and regulations that allowed me to update the population/time zone map in Chapter 12. Thomas Dana, my colleague at Penn State, and Genevieve Duque, my graduate assistant, provided suggestions and feedback.

A number of colleagues read the manuscript and provided useful comments for revision and their help is much appreciated. These include Lynn Nielsen, University of Northern Iowa; Etta Hollins, Washington State University; Ben Smith, Kansas State University; Bill Vanderhoof, Texas Christian University.

My team at Harcourt Brace College Publishers included Jo-Anne Weaver, Linda Blundell, Don Grainger, Sandy Walton, Lora Gray, Andrea Johnson, and Audra Laird. I thank them for providing encouragement and for their efforts on my behalf.

I appreciate all the assistance that has been provided to me from those named and unnamed, but what is here still is no one's responsibility but mine. Over the years that I have taught social studies education, I have tried to approach each course and each student as an unique entity. This has contributed to my belief that every student has something to learn and something to teach; I hope that this book contributes to that.

CONTENTS IN BRIEF

DETAILED CONTENTS

PART III
Teaching Strategies   157

Chapter Six   159
INQUIRY, LECTURE, AND GUIDED DISCOVERY

Chapter Seven   179
TEXTBOOKS AND SOCIAL STUDIES TEACHING

Chapter Eleven   *288*
MAP AND GLOBE SKILLS

Chapter Twelve   *315*
CHRONOLOGY, QUESTIONING, AND LANGUAGE SKILLS

CHILDREN AND SOCIAL STUDIES

Creative Teaching in the Elementary Classroom

Third Edition

PART I

Educational Environment

Chapter One

THE SCHOOL SETTING

This book is about social studies education and teaching. Although social studies encompasses many things in our society, we will limit our discussion to school-related social studies education, because the school setting is an important variable in any social study. In this chapter we will first look at what we—that is, society—perceive as school and how our perceptions are consistent or inconsistent with what we consider important to life in a democratic society. At times the chapter may seem to venture beyond social studies concerns. But the social studies curriculum is charged with citizenship training, so it must be viewed in a larger context, not just in terms of classroom practices. Over the past 100 years or more school, curriculum and, more recently, social studies, have been viewed from the same general position, that is, from the viewpoint of a society predominately white and overwhelmingly male-dominated. Thus, those with most of the power have interpreted society and the place of school and school subjects within society from their point of view. Whether or not this point of view has been deliberately perpetrated, it has been highly replicative in interpreting reality and advocating future realities. In many eras this view of dominance has been questioned, but those "in power" have always successfully withstood such scrutiny by relying on traditional views as "the right" views and creating an aura of absoluteness to such ideas. During the past 20 years and especially since 1990 there have been more philosophical attacks on what is termed "the western canon." Questioning the canon implies that one is not wholly satisfied with the "right" answer; in fact, there may be multiple right answers depending upon school, teacher, students, and educational environment. This point of view, referred to by many of today's educators as "constructivism" reflects the notion that

> there is no particular understanding to be acquired by students. Subject mat-
> ter topics are not something to be covered by the teacher and passed on to
> the students but areas of experience and ideas to which students relate their
> own associations and concepts for these topics. (McNeil, 4)

Thus, the school setting and social studies must be viewed from multiple perspectives. Our own views as teachers will vary, and our views may be in marked contrast to that of our students. This may make some new teachers uncomfortable. After all, many of us advance through school seeking the right answers, that is, the answers to those questions shaped by one's teachers. Now I assert that right answers are not the "be all and end all" of school goals. In fact we must recognize early on that answers will be far *less* important than questions. How one forms a question immediately defines the parameters for the answer(s) that can be offered. Thus, it will be important to keep in mind throughout the reading of this text and throughout one's teaching career the notion that reality is not objective; rather, points of view, experience, and autobiographical data combine to shape one's view of what constitutes reality. This should not be feared, but acknowledged. From this acknowledgment can come the acceptance of a community of learners—teachers, students, parents. Together all can learn from and teach each other.

It is important to recognize that American society is undergoing steady, marked changes. Despite the continued majority of Americans being of European descent, the number of non-European Americans is increasing at a much faster pace. This is largely because of the changes in the ethnic backgrounds of immigrants over the past eighty to one hundred years. Whereas European immigrants constituted about 87 percent of the legal immigrants in 1920, today that number is reversed; non-Europeans constituted about 85 percent of the immigrants in 1995.

Clearly it behooves us to recognize that the view of the traditional, white male power structure is just *one* point of view of many possible. One of the overarching themes that I will try to incorporate throughout this book is one of turning traditional views on their heads, so to speak. This will be a multicultural point of view. Such a view recognizes that most decisions that people make reflect their own experiences and conform to their agenda, as noted earlier. A multicultural point of view is not limited to ostensible issues of race, class, color, or gender. In fact, almost all of our curricular or school decisions reflect such issues. It will be my job to try to present other views of what we in social studies have presented as accepted reality for decades. It will be the job of the readers of this book to weigh the perspectives and consider them in light of their own experiences and backgrounds. Together we can reconsider our views of the world and be prepared to help our students to make decisions on the issues and problems that they will face in an ever-changing world.

The next part of the chapter will sketch briefly the historical and contemporary goals of schooling. Finally, we will take a sociological look at the teacher's role. Among the questions to be deliberated are why people teach, what goals they have, and what background they share with other teachers. We will consider a teacher's role as role model, counselor, friend, parent, stranger, bureaucrat, servant, arbiter, researcher, and leader. It is this last role of leader that more teachers must take to heart and act on accordingly.

PERCEPTIONS OF SCHOOL

Each of us brings unique sociocultural "baggage" to school with us. Recognizing and sharing that help one to be alert to how one's point of view is a product of that background. By knowing ourselves better, we can be more honest and caring with our students. I was born and raised in a midwestern metropolis—Chicago—and had parents who took advantage of the artistic and scientific institutions that were, almost literally, at our doorstep. By the time I was 10 I had been a regular visitor to the city's art museums, zoos, science museums, aquarium, and planetarium, not to mention the parks and sports arenas that were in the city. Television was a relatively new phenomenon in the 1950s, but I became an instant acolyte, which explains, to some small degree, my entertainment preferences.

Since we lived in an apartment I found visiting friends or relatives in single-family homes in the city or suburbs a thrilling experience if for no other reason than there were pets allowed. By the time my family joined the exodus to suburbia when I was in junior high school, I had gained an understanding of and a fascination with urban life. After graduating from college I returned to the city to teach and live. My initial views of school, however, were not always very positive.

My first four and a half years of school were spent in a gloomy four-story building in the city of Chicago. The enormity of this building was so overwhelming that finding my way from one end to the other was always an act of faith and luck. The school did not *sit* on the site; it *crouched,* ready to snatch unsuspecting children from the street and force them inside. In architectural design, older schools often are mistaken for jails. Many children would not dispute that. This school had a high iron fence surrounding it, to keep visitors out and students in. In a school of this size the principal was rarely seen and hardly mentioned except in tones of awe. In short, school was scary.

Despite the pleasures of meeting and playing with one's peers, there is no denying that school is a frightening place to many children. So many fears abound—fear of going into the wrong room, fear of being late, fear of being asked to do something you cannot do, fear of being reprimanded, fear of not being allowed to go to the bathroom when you really *really* have to go, fear of being intimidated by an older child, fear of being kept after school, fear of missing the school bus home, fear that your parents will find out about something you did in school. I am not trying to overdramatize; this is the way some kids think. Most times these fears are based on a wild imagination or on the tales of an older child, but, then, it doesn't take much to exploit a child's imagination.

To some people, older schools resemble factories of the same era. This design may have served as a kind of security. For example, Clark University, founded in Worcester, Massachusetts, in 1887, initially held all classes in one building. That building was designed so that, in the event the university failed, the building could be converted into a shoe factory within 30 days.

The analogy between schools and factories has been expanded to include factory jargon and equipment. Time clocks are found in many schools. Students become "products." The turning out of these products is often compared to an assembly line. Much of this philosophy comes from the so-called efficiency movement of the 1890s, which was widely embraced by the business community. At educational conferences during the early 1900s businesses promoted the move toward efficiency as a way to provide the same or better education *and* save money as well.

School administrators were swift to jump on the bandwagon. They advocated maximal use of school facilities through platoon or pontoon systems that allowed for double shifts of classes. Children skipped grades with impunity. The latter practice was not for the benefit of the child, however. Rather, it was believed that it would not harm the children, and by getting them through school as quickly as possible, it would cost the school district less to educate them.[1]

To promote efficiency, schools are run in an orderly fashion, and students are expected to conduct themselves accordingly. For example, one does not get up and go to the bathroom; one asks permission and may have to carry a pass to symbolize that authoritarian power. One also does not talk when one has something to say until the teacher permits it. One does not arrive at school at 9:15 A.M. when school begins at 9:00 A.M. One eats when told it is lunchtime and not before, and so on.

In that same old Chicago school there was an ash pit in the playground area. The school burned coal, and the ashes were dumped into the pit, which was surrounded on three sides by a concrete wall about four feet high. Students were not to play in the ash pit, ostensibly because it was dangerous and

---

[1] This whole thesis is the topic of an excellent book by Raymond Callahan entitled *Education and the Cult of Efficiency* (Chicago: University of Chicago Press, 1962).

Students pledged allegiance to their country in a different manner in the early 1900s.

dirty. It actually was neither; it was crunchy and flexible. In retrospect, the only reason I can see for our not being allowed in the ash pit was that ashes might escape from the pit and look messy. Schools hate mess. To keep students from climbing the concrete wall around the ash pit, a thin layer of grease was put on top of the wall. The lesson was simple: one does not play where one wishes; one plays where one is told. In a society that theoretically uses schools to prepare students for life in a democracy, schools are often decidedly undemocratic and, actually, antidemocratic.

Schools are accused of homogenization, that is, of trying to get all students to think alike in some way. Again, the citizenship function may demand that all students be aware of the responses society expects from its citizens. But it is up to the teacher to help students see this function as one of learning societal norms and not as something designed to inhibit their freedom. This issue will be addressed in Chapter 13 when we discuss law-related education.

Although some of our perceptions of school may be decidedly negative, many are very positive. Schools can unite a community, and the building often serves as the hub of community activity. Often the school was (and may still be) the only place large enough for the community to gather. Even the local churches may have been too small or not flexible enough for town meetings, square dances, quilting bees, or adult education classes, or to serve as polling places, recreation centers, or theaters. In both rural and urban communities the school building offered warmth and pleasure to children and adults alike.

To many children a school is a place to get away from as quickly as possible, rather than a place to get something out of as pleasantly as possible. To many parents a school represents another bureaucracy layered with red tape and ways to catch unsuspecting adults. This may sound irrational, but years away from school can warp one's memories. A school no longer had people inside: it was an entity in itself.

A large number of recent immigrants, particularly those from Mexico and rural Latin America, come to the United States with minimal education. Many have come from countries where there was insufficient funding to support universal schooling. Some immigrants may be coming from war-torn countries where schools were destroyed and education was nearly impossible. Many immigrants come from rural areas where education did not lead to immediate economic improvement, so it may have been eschewed for early vocational training or simply searching for any available way to accumulate financial capital.

To many people, then, the American school may be viewed with a mixture of awe, distrust, and anxiety. School rules may seem totally arbitrary, teachers intimidating, and the tasks difficult. To folks who are illiterate in their own language, becoming literate in a second, spoken language may be daunting. This is not a new reality for schools, however, since there was tremendous illiteracy among Eastern and Southern Europeans who entered the United States in the early 1900s. A difference is that some newcomers may perceive that school represents a threat to their culture. Being American may mean taking on the notions of a white, middle-class power structure and being forced to abandon one's ethnicity in order to be successful. Schools must be part of the solution to this problem rather than an extension of such a problem.

Of course, for many people and cultures a school represents a center of learning, an intellectual island in an unenlightened world. Schools promote learning, and if one stays long enough and works hard enough one will learn something. A corollary to this view is that schools provide a way to better oneself. Among Japanese-Americans and Jewish-Americans, for example, education has been highly valued, because with it one could get a better job, make more money, rise in esteem, and embrace American culture.

So the school has been, and still is, the subject of widely varied perceptions. The goals of many teachers may still not be compatible with those perceptions.

THE GOALS OF SCHOOLING

The goals of educators are not consistent throughout the world, although most are concerned with socializing students, that is, with preparing them to behave in the way society expects its citizens to behave. Some of these societal expectations are based on specific knowledge as well as specific skills. This has not always been the case, however. Schooling in colonial America and in the early years of the United States was for the wealthy, in which case it was quite developed; for the "common" folk, it was quite basic. Common schooling was the impetus for universal education in the United States and had the ultimate goal of universal literacy.

During those early years schooling took place in the one-room schoolhouses of a predominantly rural nation, and much of the teaching was done by itinerant teachers. They traveled from town to town, teaching under town contract for as long as the town or the parents could afford. The goals were simple—the three Rs—although a fourth R, religion, was considered just as vital because the function of reading was to enable people to read the Bible. Before the Republic was founded, and for years afterward, sectarianism was a part of schooling, and the famous *New England Primer* was an integral part of the curriculum. The *Primer* used Bible quotations, allusions, and sections as the most important source of reading material. The major goal of schooling was to promote the Bible and Bible reading. Even after the Constitution prohibited this practice, it continued because of tradition and because most people were members of supportive Christian sects. Waves of immigration, however, began to change that homogeneity, strengthening and shaping the American character.

Closely related to the religious goal was the development of moral character. As the *New England Primer* fell into disuse, it was largely replaced by editions of the *McGuffey Reader.* These volumes included obvious moral lessons. In the *McGuffey* reading selections, issues of morality were clear and were usually inspired by the Judeo-Christian ethical ideas of the Bible. Another goal of schooling, then, was proper value orientation through indoctrination.

These obvious lessons in morality based on Judeo-Christian religion became hidden during the nineteenth century. For various legal and ethical reasons, schools could no longer be so blatant in their proselytizing. Instead, they attempted to teach only content—or at least to *claim* that was what they taught.

The waves of immigrants that came to America during the 1800s altered the functions and goals of the schools considerably. These immigrants, many of whom spoke no English, had to be assimilated into the American mainstream, and the schools were to be the primary instrument in that enterprise. Schools taught children during the day and adults in citizenship classes at night. Part of the new purpose of schools was to teach these immigrants the proper values all citizens should hold.

The citizenship function of schooling has always been important to the operation of schools. Students had to learn how "good" Americans behaved—that is, by voting, obeying laws, paying taxes, paying bills, dealing honestly with others, and supporting their country's decisions. At times some of this citizenship indoctrination was based on mythology. For example, the myth that George Washington cut down a cherry tree and then confessed his ill deed was

These pages from the New England Primer *show the moral messages that accompanied reading and writing in elementary schools.*

seen by some as necessary for promoting good citizenship through hero worship. The founding fathers became larger than life, and all one could hope to do was emulate them by being a good citizen. And what did a good citizen do? Exactly what he or she was *told* to.

Some educational historians, like Michael Katz, felt that teaching good citizenship in the schools was designed to perpetuate a class system in America.[2] Rather than enabling people to improve their position in society, American schools taught them to be comfortable in their particular class. Learning punctuality, authoritarianism, bureaucratic structures, and the like prepared students to work in factories without questioning labor conditions, for example. Some researchers have claimed that this is still true, although somewhat more refined—that whole schools no longer strive toward societal homogeneity but toward class reinforcement.[3]

A larger issue, then, is who benefits from various aspects of schooling. Who wants what from schools and why? One interested party is American business, which often contends that the school curriculum has too many "frills" and that

---

[2] Michael Katz, *The Irony of Early School Reform* (Boston: Beacon Press, 1968) and *Class, Bureaucracy and Schools* (New York: Praeger University Press, 1971).

[3] J. Anyon's work is reflective of this theme, although it has been strongly criticized. See Anyon, "Ideology and United States History Textbooks," *Harvard Educational Review,* Vol. 49, No. 3 (August 1979).

the direction of many schools is vague or wrongheaded. Students, many in business would contend, should be prepared to step into jobs, and most of them are not.

Certainly business people should be concerned about the preparation of the next generation of workers, but it seems a bit fatuous to demand that workers fit into businesses when businesses themselves change their needs so swiftly. Preparing students for a world that *was* runs counter to preparing them for a world that they will live in as adults. As James Moffet notes

> During recent decades, leading companies in every field—pharmaceuticals, chemicals, defense contractors, automobiles, brokerage, savings and loans, insurance—have been convicted or indicted for breaking laws. . . . How much honest public concern can we expect from corporations that fire older employees to avoid paying retirement benefits, keep secret their own unfavorable findings about their products and mount massively expensive campaigns—paid for by the consumer through increased prices of goods—to lobby against environmental protection? (Moffett, 586)

It benefits business to have class distinctions perpetrated in school through tracking, for example, so that students will come into the workplace with beliefs and expectations that will prepare most for working-class or middle-management jobs where one is to do what one is told. The problem with this, however, is that it is shortsighted. If workers are unquestioning, change can not be easily incorporated. And change is everywhere in our society. Schools and businesses would do better to prepare students for uncertainty by emphasizing critical thinking, decision making, and group interaction/discussion skills. Despite the demands of some groups to have schools "get back to basics" in order to compete internationally, the recent Third International Mathematics and Science Study indicates that students in the United States do far *more* homework and have *more* class time on math and science, yet U.S. students scored in the middle range of the 41 countries studied. A big difference is that 83 percent of Japanese teaching time is spent on concepts, with only 17 percent spent on drill and practice, while in the United States the number is reversed, with 22 percent of the time spent on learning concepts and 78 percent on drill and practice. (Wingert, 96)

The goal of schooling for a society, generally is the smooth transition of young people from school to work in order to ensure a continual productive, stable society. But what if the society is racist or sexist? Should schools merely train youngsters to accepts society as it is and enter it as workers? I hope that most teachers would say "no," but I know that many would not. Taking a stand requires courage and many of us fear retaliation, real or imagined.

Parents want their children to be successful young adults, but how do we measure success? If the measure were to be income level, all teachers would be relatively unsuccessful. But we often measure success by what individuals contribute to society. Few would argue the enormous contributions that teachers make to improving society. But many disagree on what the contribution is worth in financial remuneration.

All these notions of the goals of schooling require the cooperation, either active or passive, of the teacher. Probably no profession in our society encompasses so many different roles as that of teacher. The next section will explore some of these roles, as well as the background of a typical teacher.

THE TEACHER'S ROLE

Who becomes a teacher? There are many reasons why people choose teaching careers. The decision may relate to family background, ethnic background, or personal influences. Obviously a complex series of events is involved in the decision to spend one's working life as a teacher. No one should choose a life's career on the spur of the moment. To modify an old saw: "Decide in haste, regret at leisure."

Too often a college student sees a career choice as vital when declaring a major. Avenues of pursuit emerge later. Many people who have elementary education as their major area of concentration will never teach in a classroom, except as student teachers. Conversely, many noneducation majors become lifelong educators, acquiring certification after graduating from college. One should not feel insecure because one has decided on a major and then two years later abandons that field. (This is easier to say, of course, than to practice.) People are constantly changing their jobs, being retrained, or entering a new, "uncharted" field. Teachers are no different from the general populace in that respect. Many people choose teaching as a springboard, to gain knowledge of a field that they will never leave but will continue to reshape. This group includes school administrators, state or federal department of education officials, college professors in various disciplines, attorneys who specialize in school law, and school psychologists, to name a few.

Although no teacher may be considered typical, one can make some rough generalizations about the people in this profession. Most of those who enter teaching like children—or think they like children. At worst, someone might be indifferent toward children but love a subject enough to want to teach it to children. This kind of teacher is more common in secondary than in elementary education. If one proves not to like children, that soon becomes evident to others (superiors, cooperating teachers) when a prospective teacher enters a classroom for practicum experience. At this juncture the person is often counseled out of teaching before the damage to all concerned becomes too great.

Besides liking children, most teachers seem to be quite social; they make friends easily and like to talk and interact with others. Again, this is a generalization, not a requirement.

Sometimes a young teacher will use teaching to escape being social. He or she may be shy and may feel more comfortable speaking and interacting with children than with adults. The notion of escape has entered into many people's decisions to become teachers. During the early years of the Vietnam War

(1962–1967), for example, teaching was a draft-deferred profession. Many young men entered the teaching profession in this benign manner. They initially had little commitment to teaching, but their lack of training caused little harm. In fact, many of them stayed in teaching, providing a better gender balance in elementary teaching and infusing many fine ideas into the field. Admittedly, many left as soon as it was safe to do so, but since teacher turnover rates had been high over the previous 15 years, their departure was not particularly noticeable.

Other people have used teaching to escape personal responsibilities, a particular place, or the exigencies of society at large. This latter rationale may seem odd, because teachers have been expected to promote good citizenship in their young charges. Nevertheless, it is quite possible to close off the outside world in one's classroom and commit oneself to one's students. This unfortunate practice must be recognized as relatively common. Many teachers are horribly ignorant of national and world politics, economic conditions, recent scientific breakthroughs, or best-selling books. This kind of ignorance, however, is antithetical to the idea of a true educator.

Many people enter teaching because their relatives have been teachers or because they are among the first in their families to graduate from college. In either group, teaching is considered a noble, esteemed profession. Clearly, people do not enter teaching for the money. They also do not enter teaching to achieve long-range teaching goals. Teaching is basically a "front-loading" profession—professional rewards such as tenure come early in one's career.

Then why teach? Many like the steady security of teaching. A teacher's hours in the classroom are fixed, preparation can be done flexibly, at a time and place of one's choosing, the job is secure (more or less), and summer vacations are long (unless one wants to work a second job or teach summer school). Working with children has many intrinsic rewards; each day something may happen that indicates to teachers that they have done their job well and are appreciated.

Over the past 10 years teacher education has been the focus of much new research, with Stanford University and Michigan State University in the forefront of this work. Of particular concern to the researchers has been the pedagogical content knowledge of teachers and how this affects their planning and teaching.

A number of researchers have noted the differences between novice and expert teachers. Besides the obvious difference of experience, novice and expert teachers differ in their point of view. The expert has a developed philosophy of education and the subject matter that is taught, while the novice does not. Hillkirk worked with preservice teachers in attempting to develop their philosophy of teaching, but his results were inconclusive. Experts differ from novices in both their opportunities and their abilities to redefine their content knowledge in shaping their knowledge of teaching content. This has helped the expert to see teaching on many more levels than the novice does and has allowed the expert to take many different avenues to reach teaching goals. Experts can see a bigger picture, but novice teachers tend to see only short-range goals—units and lesson plans (Gudmundsdottir and Shulman). This is not surprising, but some teacher training programs are attempting to help students see beyond short-range concerns.

A number of years ago, Len Davidman of California Polytechnical University tried to compile and assess all the different roles assumed by teachers.[4] Here are a few ideas from his fascinating study.

ROLE MODEL

Teachers serve as role models for children. Although many teachers may not wish to accept this responsibility, it goes with the territory. As role models, teachers can affect a student's ideas about a profession, modes of dress, ways of speaking, ideas and practices of tolerance, compassion, or interest.

Because of this responsibility, teachers are often subjected to a higher community standard of behavior; they are scrutinized by the entire community no matter what they do. This is especially true in small or rural communities, where everyone seems to know everyone else and what they are doing. Even if one wishes to avoid such a role, it will be foisted upon one anyway. Awareness of this may save the teacher future surprise or embarrassment. A teacher's expressions, for example, may be imitated by students and found unacceptable by their parents. Students may also imitate a teacher's mannerisms. Long before the teacher realizes it, students are subtly imitating or concentrating on his or her quirks. ("How many 'you knows' *did* he say that hour—fifty-three?") My own seventh-grade social studies teacher was well traveled, had a deep interest in Japanese culture and language, and drove a baby-blue Renault. None of those things were sources of modeled behavior, however. He also had a quick, sly, at times sarcastic wit, a behavior that fit perfectly for this author. The result of this modeled adulation, I found, was that I had to stay after school at least two days a week.

COUNSELOR

A teacher is always being asked to counsel students, prospective teachers, or colleagues. Even one who disavows any training in the field is likely to be appealed to for aid. Students come to teachers with problems about getting along with other students, what to wear for Halloween, or how to avoid parental abuse. These are all at different levels of importance, but they all demand the teacher's seriousness and nonjudgmental advice. Often students go to the teacher as they would to a school counselor for confirmation of a decision that they have already made; what they really want is a supportive, confirming voice. Sometimes a student needs more help than the teacher can provide, as in the case of suspected child abuse, for example. Then a teacher must offer

---

[4] I am grateful to Len Davidman for his insight in this whole discussion.

advice in a way that does not threaten the teacher-student relationship but that nevertheless helps the child deal with the problem.

The teacher as counselor practices reflective listening but must also be able to suggest ideas or options that the student needs to consider. Being a good counselor means not always being just an agreeable person.

As mentioned earlier, the counseling of student teachers is vital. The pre-service teacher needs encouragement ("cheerleading") but also needs honesty if it becomes apparent that he or she has made a mistake in career choice. It should be clearly, humanely conveyed that being a poor teacher is no reflection on one's worth as a person or one's desire to be a good teacher. Desire is not enough.

FRIEND

The teacher-as-friend may overlap with the teacher-as-counselor function. Many people contend that teachers cannot and ought not to be friends with their students. There are many different types of friendship, however, varying with the depth and quality of the relationship. A teacher can be the type of friend who takes a few students to the ball game or the zoo on Saturday, who invites students in for a snack if they drop by after school, who brings in books or magazines that the teacher knows a particular student would like to read. There is no room for baring one's soul to students, however, or for functioning as a surrogate parent. If friendship is maintained, this kind of relationship may be possible when a student leaves the school district, but certainly not before.

With the recent disclosures of child abuse at some day-care centers, teachers may feel wary about taking students anywhere. Caution is certainly called for, but it would be unfortunate if a teacher-student friendship were totally stifled for fear of accusations of abuse.

This fear can be greatly alleviated if the teacher has met a child's parent or parents *outside* of school. The most obvious place is at the teacher's or student's home, but even a park or grocery store encounter that produces discussion and insight can help to build trust between parents and teachers.

Parents must feel comfortable with teachers as peers, not be intimidated by them. It is up to the teacher to work at alleviating parental discomfort. If the effort is not successful, the teacher should probably make no further attempts to befriend the student.

With younger children, the teacher-as-friend function may be one of teacher-as-parent in the nursing of wounds, soothing of hurt feelings, and reminding children of proper manners. In almost every kindergarten, at least once a day some child addresses the teacher as "mommy" without realizing it.

STRANGER, ENEMY

Two other analogous roles are the teacher as stranger or as enemy. As noted earlier, despite the closeness of teacher-student relations, many teachers never allow this relationship to go beyond civility or cordiality. For example, how many elementary school teachers' first names did you know when you went to school? Teachers reinforce that distance by introducing themselves as Ms. _____ or Mr. _____.

The message is, "Hi, glad to meet you, but I'm in charge here and don't you forget it." Obviously a fourth-grade teacher does not give the students a lengthy autobiography, but neither should one attempt to hide harmless details of one's life, such as that one is married, has two children, once traveled to Mexico, and loves the New York Yankees.

The teacher-as-enemy is often the creation of students who see the teacher as someone who keeps them from doing as they wish—the person who prevents them from going outside to play during math class or who restricts the use of various materials so they can be shared. Some students might interpret a teacher's actions as *personally* vindictive, rather than as a generic necessity.

BUREAUCRAT

Anyone in an institutional setting inevitably becomes a paper pusher of sorts. Many teachers lose their zest for teaching because they feel that they spend more time on paperwork than they do teaching. This can be doubly frustrating if it is unexpected. But teaching school involves a lot of paperwork, much of it either silly or inexplicable. For example, taking attendance and noting tardiness are not just internal classroom procedures; such data must be sent daily to the school office, then compiled for report cards or monthly attendance sheets. Similarly, federal- or state-aided lunch or milk subsidy programs have eligibility requirements that occasionally change. Thus teachers must keep track of eligible students for school and classroom figures. Individual Education Programs (IEPs) are required for all special education students and in some states for gifted students. Such IEPs are written by a team of educators with parental counseling. The teacher is part of that school team.

Of course, the ultimate paper pushing is the compilation of grades. Grading tests, papers, and projects, then assessing the cumulative weight of such assignments, often drives teachers a bit wild. Conduct reports may also be required or encouraged for each student. Some schools require weekly pupil anecdotal records to provide fodder for report card conduct reports.

A good bureaucracy keeps track of its material wealth to some extent, and that task, too, falls to the teacher. Recording who has borrowed what textbook and the actual issuing and collecting of those textbooks are the teacher's responsibility. When supplies are scarce, students may have to be issued construction paper, rulers, crayons, and so on, rather than just taking what they need.

Often the teacher has to perform a few janitorial services, too. Even though there is custodial service, most teachers have to keep their rooms moderately clean on their own or the custodian may not stay friendly—analogous to cleaning the house before the cleaning person comes.

Another part of the bureaucracy is differentiated staffing. Since most schools cannot afford to hire people to monitor halls, help load and unload school buses, or supervise at lunchtime, teachers often assume these functions as part of their everyday work load.

SERVANT

A helping hand to students is appreciated, but some students may grow to expect it or almost demand it. To these students, the teacher is there to do their bidding and many parents do little to dispel that belief. These parents may make demands, remind teachers that they are public servants, and state their expectations as to what their children should be capable of doing in school.

The servant function is easily reinforced when teachers spend much of their time picking up candy wrappers, old erasers, and pencil stubs from the floor and operating in a like manner on the playground. With younger children, the teacher as parent overlaps with the servant function. Tying shoes, pulling off boots, zipping coats, wiping noses, tightening scarves, and finding lost mittens all reinforce the belief that this is the teacher's job.

ARBITER

Because teachers are in the middle of things, they are often asked to serve as arbiters. Such arbitration may be requested of the differing parties or it may be taken for granted. Either way, teachers have taken on this role in many areas.

Teachers often have to mediate quarrels between students in the classroom or on the playground. Although the method of arbitration varies—from threats, pleas, and reminders to physical separation—the goal is essentially the same. Arbitration between student and parent is more delicate. Getting differing points of view from parents' phone calls and face-to-face contact with students makes negotiating difficult, as indicated earlier in the example of child abuse. Differences between staff members in the school also sometimes require third-party intervention. Although not unusual, this type of arbitration is less common. Its frequency depends on the way decisions are made in the school and on the type of administrative leadership the school has.

SOCIAL REFORMER

If society is to continue to improve, to strive toward all members of our society leading productive lives that contribute to society, then teachers must help students to recognize injustice, to applaud thoughtfulness, and to work at making all lives better. Sleeter and Grant refer to this as education that is multicultural and social reconstructionist. Such a view encourages students to take charge of their own lives and, by working together, to effect change. (Sleeter and Grant, 247) Table 1.1 illustrates the type of data that motivates teachers to pursue social reform.

Teachers frequently are called upon to arbitrate disputes.

RESEARCHER

Teachers are also researchers. They make observations, decide on appropriate strategies for their classes or individual students, and then test what works better (or worse) in classroom situations. Even if teachers are not directly aware of it, they are constantly performing research on their students and the school curriculum. Ideally, they should be more aware of this, so that better research design could be incorporated into existing teacher planning. This research does not have to be difficult or time consuming.

For example, a teacher may suspect that students like to use maps that have less information on them rather than more. To confirm this, the teacher might observe the use of maps and assess the differences in mastery of map concepts among students who use one kind of map or another. Afterward the teacher could write up this finding in brief form to share with colleagues. If the spirit moves them, the teachers could then check the educational literature to see whether their experiences fit with current research or to determine why students behave as they do.

TABLE 1.1
Percentage of Children in Poverty

White	12.5%
Black	39.8%
Hispanic	32.2%

Poverty level established by the U.S. Office of Management and Budget in 1990 is $12,675 per year or less for family of four.

SOURCE: 1990 U.S. Census

Teacher as Leader

Because it deserves special attention, the leadership role of teachers will be considered separately. By virtue of their position, teachers are perceived as leaders both in and out of school. Outside of school, they are accorded prestige and respect for what they do.

In many small communities teachers are the educational elite; they have college degrees, they have left the community and seen a bit of the world, and they continue to deal with academic learning on a daily basis. Aside from an occasional lawyer or doctor, teachers are the intelligentsia, whether they wish to be or not.

Interestingly, in some booming industrial communities, the prestige accorded teachers may be accompanied by bemusement, because the low-paid teachers could easily make more money by working in local industry. Although this may increase respect for teachers, it does not usually increase the desire of parents to have this career behavior emulated—that is, to have their children become teachers.

Rejection of the teacher as role model occurs not only in the United States but in many industrialized nations in which teacher salaries have been long outstripped by inflation and by gains in other industries. For example, in Olafsvik, a coastal community in western Iceland, at least 90 percent of employment is associated with the fishing industry. Most residents do quite well financially (although this depends on the abundance of fish in any one year), while teachers, as civil servants, are at the bottom of the local salary scale. People respect teachers for the choices they have made: to go to the university, to be better educated, to serve the community. The respect given Olafsvik's teachers allows them to be heard when they give opinions, to be supported in their jobs, and to be sought out for logical advice. Nevertheless, the townspeople encourage their own children to leave school as soon as possible and enter the fishing industry.

A similar situation has existed in many American communities, although bad economic conditions can elevate a teacher's status from one of the poorest-paid salaried employees in town to one of the few regularly paid ones. Teachers may then lose some respect, because they are perceived as not having a real understanding of the community's unemployment problems. For the most part, however, teachers must be leaders in smaller communities because there are few others with the necessary skills to assume that responsibility. Teachers are often asked to serve on community boards and other volunteer groups.

LOCAL CLUBS AND ASSOCIATIONS

Some service groups may be more respected in particular communities and some may not be found at all, so the choices may be limited. The Elks, the Rotary, and the Lions are examples of service groups found in many communities. Most of these have until recently been restricted to men, and many still have examples of overt or covert sexism. One should not condemn with too wide a brush, however, because many local clubs have been quite outspoken in their attempts at sexual integration. One should investigate these things, perhaps by talking with current members, before deciding whether to join such a club.

A group limited to professional women that emphasizes service in the community is the American Association of University Women (AAUW). Depending on its local goals, the group may be very active or not. In some communities, the local AAUW is famous for its annual used-book sale. The money raised is used for a variety of excellent projects. One is aiding in the establishment and support of a women's resource center, and another is a "phone friend" line for young students with working parents to call for help, support, or a friendly chat when they are home alone. The latter project has been emulated in many communities. Like most other service groups, there is a small annual fee for AAUW membership dues.

CHARITIES

Volunteer work for charity costs no money, although it is demanding on one's time. This might come in the form of door-to-door solicitation for funds, clerical work on mailings, phone calls to the public, or organizational work in local fund solicitation. There are many fine charities—the American Cancer Society, the Multiple Sclerosis Society, the American Heart Association, the American Lung Association, to name only a few. The local United Way serves many of these groups. Volunteer work may also be available at the local hospital or library, although this may be harder for working teachers to coordinate with their daily schedules.

LOCAL BOARDS

Serving on local boards is a natural choice for a social studies teacher. It is an example of civics in action, and the teacher's expertise in working with children is much appreciated. Some boards that are found in many local communities or regions include the Youth Services Agency Advisory Board, the recreation and parks board, the traffic safety commission, the zoning board, and the beautification committee. Because of their often political nature and teacher restrictions, we will deal with school boards in a later section on political groups.

In larger urban communities, respect and support for teachers are generally much weaker today, although some ethnic groups may be more supportive of teachers than others are. Also, teachers in urban areas may be respected leaders in smaller neighborhood settings. Within the school teachers must constantly assume leadership positions in various areas. As demonstrated throughout this book, the social studies teacher is required to do more than teach in the classroom. School decision making and community action should be part of the credo of all teachers. It is all too easy to let someone else do the extra work. To teach social studies means to take on leadership responsibilities as a matter of routine, not an exception.

QUESTIONS AND ACTIVITIES

1. What kinds of buildings resemble modern schools in architecture?

2. Most teachers have had experiences in their own schooling that helped point them toward teaching as a profession. Describe those experiences and how they made you want to teach.

3. Interview a teacher to find why he or she entered teaching. This data can be shared in written or oral form with teacher-education students.

4. Write a one- to two-page biography. What makes you, you? What influences have your gender, ethnicity, or experiences had on your views of society and culture in the United States?

5. Can a below-average student be an above-average teacher? If so, how?

6. Are there certain characteristics all elementary teachers should possess or should not possess?

7. Many social scientists and educators are concerned about the growing number of one-parent families and the lack of opportunity young children have to interact with men. Should more young men be encouraged to enter elementary school teaching? If so, how should that be accomplished?

8. Recent proposals in different parts of the country advocate having only teachers from a specific ethnic group teach that particular ethnic group of students (whatever one it might be). Is this a good idea? Why or why not?

9. Should teachers be required by their school districts to do community service, as has been proposed for students by many people, including President Clinton?

REFERENCES

Gudmundsdottir, S., and L. Shulman. "Pedagogical Content Knowledge in Social Studies," *Scandanavian Journal of Educational Research,* vol. 31, 1987, pp. 59-70.

Hillkirk, R. K. "Preservice Secondary Teacher Reflective and Inquiry Skills and Ability to Articulate a Written Philosophy of Education." Unpublished doctoral dissertation, Pennsylvania State University, 1987.

McNeil, J. *Curiculum: The Teacher's Initiative.* Englewood Cliffs, NJ: Merrill–Prentice-Hall, 1995.

Moffett, J. "On to the Past: Wrong-Headed School Reform," *Phi Delta Kappan,* vol. 75, no. 8, April 1994, pp. 584–590.

Sleeter, C., and C. Grant, *Making Choices for Multicultural Education.* New York: Merrill, Macmillan, 1994.

Wingert, P "The Sum of Mediocrity," *Newsweek,* December 2, 1996, p. 96.

Chapter Two

SOCIAL STUDIES
IN THE SCHOOL CURRICULUM

Based on their own elementary school experiences, the term "social studies" conjures up various images for college students. At the beginning of each new semester of my social studies methods course, I ask my students to provide word associations for the term social studies. Some common responses are:

Facts, details	Explorers
State capitals	State history
Presidents	Reports
History	Field trips
Projects	Memorization
Current events	Dates
Geography	

Many college students profess to remember almost nothing about social studies until junior or senior high school. Others recall only snippets, like dioramas made in shoe boxes or the memorization of state facts (tree, song, bird, capital), community facts, explorers, and presidents (in order). For the most part, these memories are a blur, partly because of the number of years that have passed and partly because the material *was* eminently forgettable. Social studies often becomes a series of facts to memorize. As data are consumed, more data emerge to be grappled with. Truly, social studies can and has generated a seemingly endless amount of data. Unfortunately, the information has too often been viewed as an end in itself rather than as a vehicle to understanding. For example, regions of the United States are often a part of fifth-grade social studies. Data to be learned include state names and capitals, the largest cities, natural resources, rivers and lakes (or other large bodies of water), major products, major industries, and some state history. If all this *were* learned, students could explore more details or study a new region.

The rationale for this type of learning escapes most students and often is ignored by many teachers. Postman and Weingartner have referred to a need for students and teachers to have "crap detectors." Rather than just accept all the data, teachers and students should question how it adds to the betterment of students' lives through education. When faced with this question, teachers are hard-pressed to justify things like the memorization of the two major products of Montana or Arkansas or any other state. Unless teachers can relate such knowledge to more than academic mind stretching, social studies will continue to be disliked and dreaded.

My own experience as a young sixth-grade teacher in Chicago serves to illustrate the point. I was attempting to augment a textbook that, like many others, told of the roots of the American colonies in Europe but, once the colonies were established, ignored European events. Thus, the students' knowledge of Europe ended before 1700. Europe was seen only in relation to the United States (usually in some war) until, usually in high school, the students studied modern European countries and cultures.

To rectify this, I decided to lecture on European history for three days, compressing 400 years into approximately two hours. I did not reach that decision without second thoughts. After all, how much European history was really of interest to a group of inner-city youngsters, many of whom had never left their city, let alone the state or country?

But for three days I lectured to a remarkably quiet and seemingly alert group. After the third day the suspense was too much. I collared two students after class and asked point-blank how they had liked the last three days of class. One student's enthusiastic reply put the lectures in a different perspective. He said, "Class was fun, Mr. Nelson. We love when you tell stories."

That was history to those students—a story or a series of stories to be relished, not facts to be hammered home.

How did social studies get to the point at which important issues are ignored and trivial details deified? To understand that question, one needs to examine a modicum of the field's history. The first part of this chapter places social studies in a historical context and outlines the seven social sciences—history, geography, economics, sociology, anthropology, psychology, and political science. Other aspects of our culture—the arts, for example—are also part of social studies and will be discussed as well.

The last part of the chapter looks at three traditional views of social studies and at some of the ways the curriculum can be organized, based on the discipline-centered approach, the expanding-communities approach, and the unit approach.

HISTORICAL FOUNDATIONS

Social studies is a relatively recent term. One hundred years ago educators did not use the term. Rather, the social sciences—most significantly, history—were studied individually. As noted in Chapter 1, the original purpose of the American common school was to provide universal literacy, a reverence for God, an ability to do simple mathematics, and later to provide a series of common experiences that would instill pride in America and abet the growth of patriotism.

As a result, certain social sciences crept in among the three Rs curriculum: history, geography, and civics. These courses were based primarily on textbooks, for a number of reasons. There was a lack of supplementary materials and curriculum guidelines from states, districts, or the federal government. Also, teachers had only a minimal knowledge of the subject matter. Until the early decades of the twentieth century, the only academic requirements for teaching elementary school were that a prospective teacher had completed elementary school and a so-called normal school—a teacher training institution that focused on teaching methods and the psychology of learning (a *very* young field at that time).

Because teachers had little broad-based knowledge of geography, for instance, and because there were few books to use in school, the teacher ended up teaching geography "by the book," most often using a drill and practice approach. Because conceptual ideas and understandings could not be broken down for drill and practice, geography consisted of that which could be drilled. "What is the largest city in Africa?" "How many countries are in South America? Name them." "What is the longest river in Europe?" "In which countries do the Alps lie?" "How deep is the ocean?" "How wide is the sea?"

As one can see, the questions ranged from the ridiculous to the sublime, but the teacher had few alternatives.

Similarly, history was taught by using the great-man (few women were portrayed), significant-event approach. History was a series of dates associated with events: 1492, 1066, 1865, 44 BC, 1812, 1776, and so on. What these dates *meant* was less important than memorizing them.

In the early 1900s a school inspector visited an elementary classroom and asked the students what the center of the earth was like. He drew blank stares until the teacher broke in to ask the children, "What *state is* the center of the earth in?" The children, like Pavlov's dogs, dutifully replied, "In a state of

THE SOCIAL STUDIES CURRICULUM (1894-1995)

Course recommendations of the Committee of Ten of the National Education Association (1894):

GRADE	TOPICS
5 and 6	Biography and mythology
7	American history
8	Greek and Roman history
9	French history
10	English history
11	American history
12	Intensive study of one historical period and civil government

Recommendations of the Committee of Twelve on Rural Schools of the National Education Association (1897):

Group I (ages 6–7) Study stories from biography, history, and travels. Group II (ages 7–9) Current events. Stories of eminent characters and memorable events. Group III (ages 9–11) Extension of II. Readings in United States history. Group IV (ages 11–13) Selected epochs of general history with study of leading historical characters.

Recommendations of the Committee of Seven of the American Historical Association (1899):

GRADE	TOPICS
9	Ancient history to AD 800
10	Medieval and modern European history
11	English history
12	American history and civil government

Recommendations of the Committee of Eight of the American Historical Association—"The Study of History in Elementary Schools" (1909):

GRADE	TOPICS
1	Indian life. Stories connected with Thanksgiving Day and Washington's Birthday.
2	Same as grade 1. Memorial Day.
3	Heroes of other times: Joseph, Moses, David, Ulysses, and so on, to Columbus. American Indians. Independence Day.
4	Historical scenes and persons in American history. Colonial period.

GRADE	TOPICS
5	Historical scenes and persons in American history continued. Great industries of the present.
6	European background of American history. Selected topics from Greek, Roman, and European history to the end of Raleigh's colonial enterprises in America.
7	American history to the close of the revolution. European background continued.
8	American history since the revolution. Great events in European history.

(continued)

(continued from previous page)

Recommendations of the Committee on Social Studies of the National Education Association (1916):

GRADE	TOPICS
5	American history
6	World history (European)
7	Geography or European history
8	American history
9	Civics
10	European history to end of 1600s
11	American history or European history, 1700–present
12	Problems of democracy

Report of the National Council for the Social Studies Task Force on Scope and Sequence (1983):

GRADE	TOPICS
K	Awareness of self in a social setting
1	The individual in primary social groups: Understanding school and family life
2	Meeting basic needs in nearby social groups: The neighborhood
3	Sharing earth-space with others: The community
4	Human life in varied environments: The region
5	People of the Americas: The United States and its close neighbors
6	People and cultures: The eastern hemisphere
7	A changing world of many nations: A global view
8	Building a strong and free nation: The United States
9	Systems that make a democratic society work: Law, justice, and economics
10	Origins of major cultures: A world history
11	The maturing of America: United States history
12	One-year course selection (issues and problems of modern society, introduction to social sciences, arts in human societies, international area studies, elective)

Expectations of Excellence-Curriculum Standards for the Social Studies -National Council for the Social Studies (1994)
Ten Thematic Strands in Social Studies (K–12)

Culture

Time, Continuity, and Change

People, Places, and Environment

Individual Development and Identity

Individuals, Groups, and Institutions

Power, Authority, and Government

Production, Distribution, and Consumption

Science, Technology, and Society

Global Connections

Civic Ideals and Practice

igneous fusion." This was the general nature of teaching and learning in the late 1800s.

In 1892, and again in 1899 and 1913, commissions were formed to propose some articulation for course work in various fields of study, including social studies (see box). As noted, the term social studies was fairly recent, appearing only in the last report published by the U.S. Bureau of Education. Previous reports had been directed toward the secondary curriculum and had dealt with history, civil government, and geography, with a dash of political economy.

The United States has never had a national curriculum, as France, Germany, and many other nations have. The recommendations in the various commission reports did, however, engender nationwide practices that strongly resembled a common social studies curriculum, particularly at the junior and senior high level. The upper elementary grades offered United States history in grade 5 or 6 and Western European history in grade 6, more often than not.

The primary grades were forgotten in terms of recommended offerings, which had both negative and positive results. An obvious negative was the impression that there was no real need for history, civics, or geography in the lower grades. This misunderstanding has taken years to correct.

A positive aspect was that primary teachers who taught in an integrated manner took to the concept of social studies eagerly. The idea of an integrated view of the world fit much more sensibly with the teachers' observations of children's abilities. Rather than emphasizing specific historical knowledge, the primary grades were free to design curricula (usually units of work) that related to children's knowledge and interests and that emphasized conceptual understanding.

Thus, as progressivism became a popular movement in education from the late 1900s into the 1940s, many teachers developed extensive units for the elementary grades. In 1941, for example, the *12th National Council for the Social Studies Yearbook* had two chapters on teaching social studies in the primary grades. One was "Community Living Through an Ongoing Interest in Airplanes" (Burrow and Seeds) and the other was "Activities Developing Economic Understandings" (Fairbanks and Heyl).

Originally the term social studies—used to describe the program of courses in the curriculum that dealt with history, geography, civics, political economy, and sociology—was particularly upsetting to historians because it meant that history would no longer have the preeminent position that it had previously held. Scholarly debates on history versus social studies were common. In 1929 the American Historical Association conceded that social studies was a superior term for school use and renamed its Committee on History and Social Studies in the Schools as the Commission on the Social Studies in the Schools, and it appeared that this semiotic issue was finally laid to rest. Not so. Many schools and teachers, particularly at the elementary level, handled the problem by ignoring it and continuing to teach history in the elementary grades. The debate has continued over the years.

It continues today, with new reports being issued in the late 1980s and 1990s that reopened the discussion. Whenever patriotism in America has been questioned, some groups have pointed to the teaching of social studies as un-American because it takes time and emphasis away from American history.

The scholarly debate on which all this was based was really one of semantics. From the first committee report of 1892-1893, the recommendations for historical teaching were far different from the actual practice. To a historian, history encompassed economic viewpoints, sociological background, political intrigue, and cultural perspectives. Because most teachers had little course work in history after elementary and high school, they lacked the background to teach history in this manner. Thus, if the teacher asked for an interpretive answer and the students provided one, the teacher might not be able to evaluate their answers with assurance. So teachers fell back on teaching what they were sure of—trivial data. Because many teachers taught as they themselves had been taught, the pattern tended to repeat itself, with the result that students forgot most of the social studies data but remembered how dull and boring the subject was.

In the 1930s, Paul Hanna, a professor of education at Stanford University, proposed a grades K–6 model for social studies based on what he called the expanding-communities model (Figure 2.1). The Hanna model has its roots in ideas first promulgated by Johann Herbart, a German educator in the 1800s, according to both Akenson (1987) and LeRiche (1987). Hanna reasoned that students should be taught in a way that best reflected their interests and their contacts. As students' interests and contacts grew, their community of knowledge would expand commensurately. This model was widely adopted in the 1950s, and is still the most common model in elementary schools in the United States today. The model began with grade one, since kindergartens were optional in many states at the time. Grade one focused on the family community—family roles, family structures, family history, and so on. Grade two centered on the school community—classroom life, school procedures, the role of the teacher, the principal, the custodian, the students. Grade three focused on the neighborhood community and local region, and grade four on the state community, which often involved state history, geography, political structure, and economic growth.

In the fifth grade, students studied the national community. In *practice*, this usually meant U.S. history and geography, including national myths such as George Washington and the cherry tree. Selectively excluded were examinations of national problems. The sixth-grade curriculum focused on the world, mostly Europe. Most schools ignored Asia, Africa, and South America, even though Hanna's model included them. Although other suggestions for teaching elementary social studies were offered, most teachers emulated the Hanna model. In many progressive "laboratory" schools, units of work were mixed into the Hanna model, deemphasizing the encyclopedic approach of mnemonic detail.

During the 1930s and 1940s social studies was dominated by internationally known educators who influenced and brought respect to the field. These

FIGURE 2.1
Model of Elementary School Social Studies Curriculum Organization

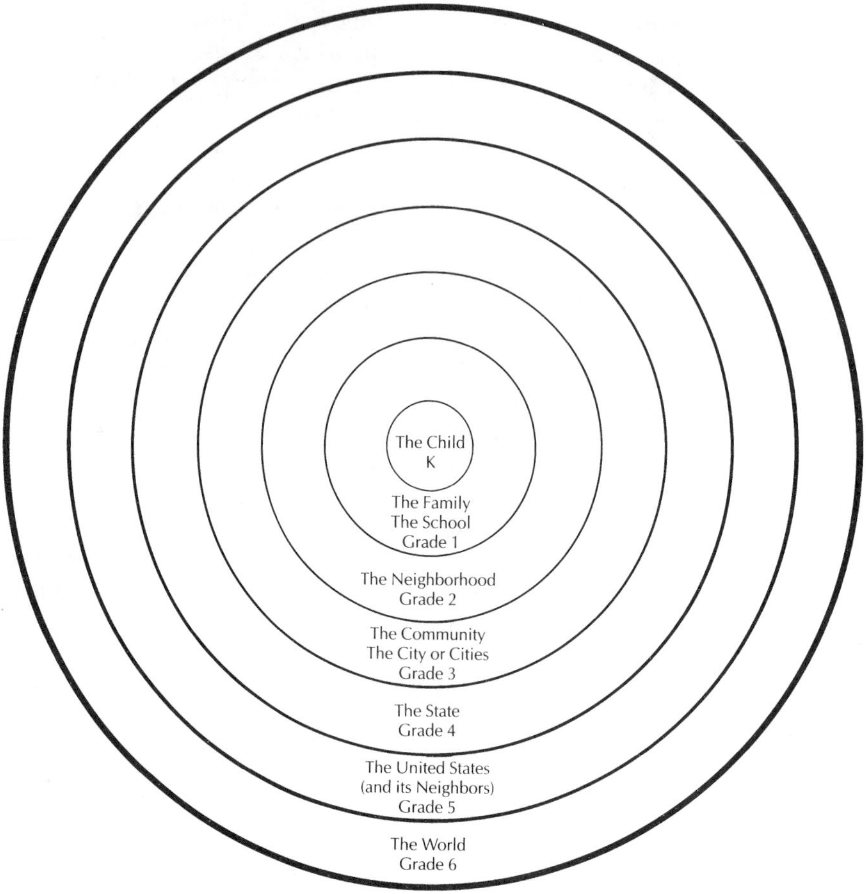

The Child
K

The Family
The School
Grade 1

The Neighborhood
Grade 2

The Community
The City or Cities
Grade 3

The State
Grade 4

The United States
(and its Neighbors)
Grade 5

The World
Grade 6

SOURCE: Adapted from Paul Hanna, "Design for a Social Studies Program." In *Focus on the Social Studies,* Washington, D.C.: National Education Association, Dept. of Elementary School Principals, 1965.

included Edgar B. Wesley, Henry Johnson, Harold Rugg, Hilda Taba, and Earle Rugg. James Michener was another sharp young scholar in the field, but after World War II he cast his lot with fiction writing rather than "professing."

The New Social Studies

After World War II, conservative forces in politics affected education as well as the entire fabric of American social life. A much more structured curriculum, tied mostly to the specific disciplines, became the order of the day. Thus, after finally having gained wider acceptance, the field of social studies was turned

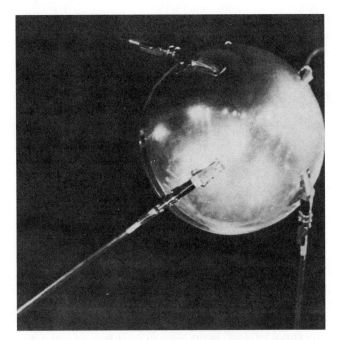

*The launching of Sputnik in 1957 was the impetus for
increased attention to science education in the United States.*

on its head. History, geography, economics, sociology, and political science
(which had taken over the narrower field of civics) became the guideposts for
social studies instruction.

Part of the reason for the change was the fear that the schools had grown
soft, that American students were not as well prepared as Soviet students. This
fear continued throughout the Cold War and was reenforced in October of
1957 when the Soviets launched Sputnik, the first space satellite. To assure better training in school, the federal government began to pour massive amounts
of money into education to improve the curriculum and teacher training, particularly in science and math.

Eventually federal spending was extended to social studies, launching the
so-called New Social Studies, which focused on values, inquiry, innovative
teaching strategies, case studies, the use of raw social science data, behavioral
objectives, and simulation games. There was also a greater emphasis on some
of the "neglected" social sciences, including anthropology, sociology, and economics, which were the focus of new projects. Taken separately, the characteristics of the "new" social studies were not all that new, but as a package they
represented a significant departure from textbook-dependent materials. The
emphasis was on discipline-centered materials, and social studies came to be
viewed as just another term for the social sciences, particularly among social
scientists who entered the field during this era.

The new social studies materials were hailed as innovative and were quite popular with many social studies educators. Unfortunately, most of these materials either failed to make it into regular classrooms or were soon abandoned.

Social studies returned to business as usual in most schools (lectures, textbook recitations, and memorization). Then, in the 1980s, concern about test results that indicated American students were poorly prepared in most disciplines led to new studies and reports on education and the curriculum. Social studies was not immune, and specialized focus on geography, history, economics, and American government and civics, in the form of additional reports and evaluations, led to a cry by some to return to the basic social science disciplines.

The Study of History

History has been, and probably always will be, the heart of the social studies content. It has always held preeminence in the social studies, and, although a number of alternatives to the linear historical approach have been proposed, this method still predominates.

Clearly there has been tinkering, at the least, with the way history is taught, as well as with what history is taught. Instead of a comprehensive history of the United States taught in one year, proposals have been made and implemented to teach only twentieth century American history or to emphasize certain themes in American history, among others. Attention to political history has diminished, while the emphasis on cultural history has increased. The traditional history of western civilization (often called world history) has been forced to give up its exclusivity and share attention with Asian, African, or Latin American history. But none of these variations have dislodged history as the centerpiece of social studies.

Recent concerns over history teaching have focused on two major aspects: teaching the "right" history and teaching history rather than social studies. E. D. Hirsch and Allen Bloom authored books in the 1980s that addressed what they saw as the failure of Americans to learn the "right stuff." Later writers like Chester Finn, Diane Ravitch, and William Bennett built on the assertions of Bloom and Hirsch as the foundations of their own calls for similar curriculum reorganization in social studies. A recurrent theme over the past 100 years has been "back to basics" in history, and it is this most recent cry that most concerns today's educators. Do elementary students know less history than their parents did? Possibly, but possibly not. They may know as much, but not the same things. There is little to suggest that elementary students ever knew history much better than today's students do. Nevertheless, the concern for better knowledge of history (often interpreted as low-level facts such as dates and names) is very real. Many critics feel that American students know too little history generally, and too little of the "right" history. Many students seem to share this feeling, so maybe it is accurate. Maybe students have not had the opportunity to learn history in depth because they have been saddled with too much trivializing. Recent work by Linda Levstik provides useful ideas to counter this trend with opportunities for students to learn the multiple voices and perspectives of history. (Levstik, 1997)

In *The Opening of the American Mind* Lawrence Levine challenges the right-wing assertions about the cultural history of the United States and the need for studying it in a wider frame of reference. Levine champions multiculturalism as an integral part of U.S. history and of history study in schools (Levine, 1996). Cornbleth and Waugh see those folks who espouse one view of America's history as "neo-nativists" who are interested in containing diversity and individualism through a standardized education. Diversity is viewed "as nothing more than 'ethnic cheerleading.'" (32)

Some readers of this book may be asking, "What's the big deal? Isn't this just a tempest in a teapot?" In a sense, those readers are right. This squabble has little to do with achieving world peace or feeding the hungry or housing the homeless. But, in a philosophical sense, it is important. For the key issues here are power and control, not the well-being of children. They are issues that have haunted education and social studies for at least a hundred years.

History, formerly the field of amateurs, was professionalized with the creation of the American Historical Association in 1884, and historians rightfully sought a place in the school curriculum. The problem, then and now, was the definition of history. The historians who proposed (and propose) a significant role for history in the schools had (and have) a broadly inclusive definition, with many perspectives not only tolerated but encouraged. Into this inclusive definition would fall economic history, the change in sociological perspectives over time, the history of governments, changes in human geography from early settlements to urban expansion, and art history, among many other areas of study.

Unfortunately, teachers have never received much training in history from these different perspectives. They have learned low-level facts, dates, lists of rulers, changes in seats of government over time. What the historians sought was very similar to what social studies educators sought. They differed mainly over what to call it and how to achieve it. The battle raged from 1916 to the 1930s, when an American Historical Association commission conceded the primacy of the term social studies in forming its Commission on Social Studies in the Schools.

Semantic (and philosophical) differences have been raised at various times since the 1930s, but only in the late 1980s was there a committed effort to overthrow social studies. Encouraged and abetted by Secretary of Education William Bennett, Undersecretary Chester Finn, his frequent coauthor, Diane Ravitch, and Bennett's successor at NEH, Lynne Cheney, a new "holy war" against social studies was declared.

In 1989, the National Commission on Social Studies in the Schools, a joint project of the American Historical Association and the Organization of American Historians, along with the Carnegie Foundation for the Advancement of Teaching and the National Council for the Social Studies, issued a new report that was far less specific about course suggestions, particularly at the elementary level. The National Commission was too large and unwieldy a body for a task like curriculum proposals, and so a smaller curriculum task force of 14 members was formed. This body had five school representatives, two supervisors, and one teacher each from the elementary, middle, and high-school levels. A single state senator, from California, was a member, and the remaining eight represented higher education, mostly from the social sciences and history. The document tried to please everyone and probably pleased few. Hardly any educators of future teachers offered input, and they are the linchpin in getting the data included in teacher training programs and ultimately in schools. This may be just another report that has little effect and will be virtually forgotten within 10 years. I hope not, since there are some excellent ideas in the report, particularly the recommendations for lessening the American centeredness that overwhelms any efforts at stressing global interdependence in the curriculum.

NATIONAL STANDARDS

In the period 1992–1997, largely in response to the National Education Goals initially promoted by President Bush and extended under President Clinton, a number of organizations were funded to develop national standards in various disciplinary areas. These included civics, history, economics, geography, and social studies. This was characteristic of a fractionalized curriculum, unfortunately.

The history standards were issued in a number of volumes for various grade levels and for both U.S. and world history. Despite emerging from the National Center for History in the Schools at UCLA, the standards were attacked almost immediately by those on the political right. In response to those attacks, Gary Nash, cochair of the National Council for History Standards, and Ross Dunn, Coordinating Editor of the National Standards for World History, replied:

> As soon as the standards appeared, a small band of critics, led by Lynne Cheney and Rush Limbaugh, decided that these curriculum guidelines (which are not textbooks) were susceptible to charges of multicultural excess and political correctness. Not teachers or historians but talk show hosts and newspaper op-ed pundits have tried to link the standards in the public mind to extreme left-wing revisionism, hoisting them as a useful political symbol of all things un-American (5).

They went on to offer a brief explanation of the process and result of the work on these standards, but the damage, the perception of "wrongdoing," had been done. The U.S. Senate voted 99 to 1 to condemn the history standards, relying on the perception, not the reality of the content. In order to salvage the history standards, the historians and teachers who first produced them agreed to revise them, and a new version appeared in 1996. Despite the broad political stripe of the standard writers, these revised standards were again attacked by some on the political right for "the extent to which ideology has replaced pedagogy." (Diggins, A21)

These new standards are presented in two parts; the first for K-4 has four topics:

Topic 1- Living and Working Together in Families and Communities Now and Long Ago

Topic 2- The History of the Students' own State or Region

Topic 3- The History of the United States: Democratic Principles and Values and the Peoples from Many Cultures who Contributed to its Cultural, Economic, and Political Heritage

Topic 4- The History of Many Peoples Around the World

It is clear that this represents the expanding-communities model compressed to K-4, rather than K-6 grades. Part 2 of these standards for grades 5-12 is focused primarily on historical eras. For the United States there are 10 as listed below:

Era 1-   Three Worlds Meet (Beginnings to 1620)

Era 2-   Colonization and Settlement (1585-1763)

Era 3-   Revolution and the New Nation (1754-1820s)

Era 4-   Expansion and Reform (1801-1861)

Era 5-   Civil War and Reconstruction (1850-1877)

Era 6-   The Development of the Industrial United States (1870-1900)

Era 7-   The Emergence of Modern America (1890-1930)

Era 8-   The Great Depression and World War II (1929-1945)

Era 9-   Postwar United States (1945-1970s)

Era 10- Contemporary United States (1968-present)

The world history standards for grades 5-12 are as follows:

Era 1-   The Beginnings of Human Society

Era 2-   Early Civilizations and the Emergence of Pastoral Peoples (4000-1000 BCE)

Era 3-   Classical Traditions, Major Religions, and Giant Empires (1000 BCE-300 CE)

Era 4-   Expanding Zones of Exchange and Encounter (300-1000 CE)

Era 5-   Intensified Hemispheric Interactions (1000-1500 CE)

Era 6-   The Emergence of the First Global Age (1450-1770)

Era 7-   An Age of Revolutions (1750-1914)

Era 8-   A Half Century of Crisis and Achievement (1900-1945)

Era 9-   The Twentieth Century Since 1945: Promises and Paradoxes

As of 1997 the history standards and the degree to which they will be accepted, adopted, or used remains in doubt. Yet history continues as the acknowledged "queen" of the social sciences as far as its effect on the social studies curriculum is concerned.

HISTORICAL CONCEPTS

History is often referred to as a social science, particularly in the United States, but it is most commonly viewed as one of the humanities. I have always enjoyed reading history. Historical fiction, biographies, historical events, documentary material, all formed and form in me a love of what historians search for—the actuality of what occurred, truth, as it were.

Through history, the social sciences are woven together into the story of human tradition. History shows the human condition at any one time and any one particular place. Historians examine and analyze the past, often using the concepts of the social sciences as descriptors.

History is more than a sum of the social sciences, however, for it has the added dimension of development and change. Historians deal with the concept of cause and effect, the relationships among events. Some historians say we study the past so that we will not be condemned to repeat it. We see what effects certain events have had so that we can avoid those in the future. The study of cause and effect has taught us that effects have more than one cause. Thus historians have taught us to avoid the pitfall of assigning one cause to one event.

As historians work, they constantly revise their views based on new information and new experiences. This concept, called revisionism, lends a dynamic quality to history. History is not always the same, as it is subject to interpretations of time and place.

Change   The findings of historians are limited by the data available to them and are colored by personal biases. Because of these limitations, historians seek to reconstruct changes in the past through a variety of resources. These include books, magazines, film, newspapers, oral accounts, family bibles, photographs, letters, court records, and the records of government agencies.

Conflict   This is a key concept in anthropology, sociology, economics, and political science. In history the concern is with documenting and explaining conflict and the subsequent consequences.

Method   Though not really a concept, the question of method is influenced by the varieties of historical patterns. The most obvious method is chronological, but there are also geographical, political, cultural, institutional, and biographical. The key problems of method include (1) distortion in the available materials, (2) lack of material, (3) researcher bias and interpretation, and (4) a moral judgment of history. Probably the most powerful bias is nationalism. In order to judge a people, one needs to apply historical and cultural relativism, two perspectives often in short supply.

THE SOCIAL SCIENCES

The social sciences examine the ways in which individuals and groups interact with various environments. For example, there is a material environment: *geographers* study the ways in which people interact with the spatial environment, and *economists* study the ways in which individuals use material resources. There is also a human environment, consisting of societies and cultures: *sociologists* study the ways in which people interact with the general society, *anthropologists* study the ways in which people interact with culture, *psychologists* study the ways in which people interact with themselves, and *political scientists* study the ways in which people interact with power and authority. Finally, there is the study of history, in which the social sciences merge with the humanities: *historians* examine the ways in which people of different epochs and circumstances have interacted with all these environments.

As these studies developed into seven separate academic disciplines, teachers came to employ concepts to aid in the search for, and to convey the knowledge of, these environments. The following discussion about the social sciences is centered around the basic concepts upon which these disciplines are built. Each section begins with a broad organizing concept, followed by some subconcepts, and ends with a specific concept that relates the individual to the environment being examined.

Geography

I have always been a geography "freak." I was the kid who actually memorized and retained the names of all the state and national capitals. Even at a young age I was curious about why things were located where they were. Many of my teachers found me quite tedious.

The science of geography has existed since humans first used simple maps to indicate the location of things, such as food sources. Over the past hundred years the unified field of geography has been split into a physical area and a human one. The former is identified with geology, meteorology, and other "hard" sciences, while the latter is closer to the "soft" social sciences. In recent years many geographers have sought to knit the rift that has split their field, so far without success.

The first tool of the geographer is maps, but other techniques, like scatter-grams and computer graphics, have expanded the analytical and expressive ability of the geographer. The study of geography provides six key concepts that serve to organize our knowledge about this dimension of human life. The first concept is *location:* the site of human activities and natural phenomena on the earth or within the environment. This concept leads to an examination of the *distribution of physical features* of the landscape and the *distribution of population* across the landscape. Together these provide *environments,* the total surroundings of individuals or groups. People interact with their environments to form *ecosystems* as well as to define their own *personal space.*

Now let us look in more detail at these key concepts.

LOCATION

Location is the site of a human activity or a natural phenomenon. Four subconcepts are necessary to an understanding of location: *distance, direction, site,* and *starting point.* Everything is at a given distance from some starting point. This distance can be measured by the American system of inches, feet, yards, miles, and so on, or it can be measured by the far more rational and world-accepted system based on the meter, or by its location on the globe in degrees. In order to give meaning to distance, one must have a direction. This direction is based on the constancy of the earth's rotation, or on its axis, which points to a constant spot in the sky called the North Star. We mark off the spatial dimension into the quadrants of north, south, east, and west. These in turn are divided further for more precise measurement of direction. Complicating the picture is the difference between true north, as measured by the North Pole and the North Star, and magnetic north. (Although this difference is enough to bother airplane pilots, it is not enough to bother people looking for directions in a city.)

Site refers to the location of a place in relation to its local features and resources. These could be flat prairies, steep hills and canyons, a winding creek through a town, or the mouth of a river. These are often factors in the growth of settlements or the development of industry.

Finally, by convention, people have agreed on two starting points for determining precise location on the globe. Measurements north and south start at the equator, that part of the earth which has the greatest circumference. Measurements east and west start at the prime meridian, an imaginary line running north and south through London.

DISTRIBUTION OF PHYSICAL FEATURES

In the spatial realm, there are a variety of topographic features—mountains, plains, valleys, plateaus, and so on. These physical features on the land surface are defined by their altitude and by the degree of difference from surrounding land surfaces. Another prominent physical feature is water, which ranges from large oceans, bays, estuaries, lakes, and rivers to the smallest streams and brooks. Other variations are provided by vegetation, which ranges from dense tropical forests to sparse deserts. A final subconcept to be considered in analyzing the distribution of physical features is climate, which varies in temperature as well as precipitation and humidity.

The population distribution is much more concentrated in urban areas (right) than in rural areas (left).

DISTRIBUTION OF POPULATION

Another concept in geography is the distribution of people across the land-scape. In general, the human population is unevenly distributed, with a higher concentration inhabiting urban areas and a lower concentration in rural areas. Areas having a concentration in between the urban and rural areas are called suburban or exurban areas.

Migration patterns measure the movement of people from urban to rural areas and vice versa. Historically there have been many migrations in the United States. During the Industrial Revolution much of the rural population migrated to urban areas. With the advent of the automobile, the urban population migrated to the suburbs. During the latter part of this century, many people have migrated from the "frostbelt" to the "sunbelt" regions of the country. This continues into the 1990s, and the redistribution of congressional seats following the 1990 census is a good indicator of that.

The distribution of age groups in a population also varies. In the United States, for example, there are more people between the ages of 30 and 40 than in any other age group because of the extremely high birthrate in the 1950s and early 1960s. This so-called baby boom has had complex social and economic repercussions in crowded elementary schools, crowded colleges, and a crowded labor market. As these people reach late adulthood and old age they will create other new stresses on society.

ENVIRONMENTS

The distribution of physical features and the distribution of populations create many types of environments. The *personal* environment, for example, may be determined by the degree of movement of each individual, or it may be a region defined by certain geographic features. There are *topographic* environments, like the mountains of the American West and Northeast. There are *cultural* environments, in which we find similarities in the habits of the people who live in those areas. We can also define environments by *climate,* like the frostbelt and the sunbelt of the United States. Finally, we can define environments in terms of *political* allegiance, or in terms of the history of the United States and its expansion westward across the North American continent to the Pacific coast. Because many of these environments overlap, we find that people live in several environments simultaneously.

ECOSYSTEMS

As people interact with their environments they establish a certain ecological balance with nature. The ecosystem is maintained by two social practices: the *conservation* of the environment—the use of the environment and its resources in a slow and productive manner—and the *preservation* of the environment—the protection of both natural and man-made environments to prevent change.

PERSONAL SPACE

Finally, as people interact within ecological systems they establish the use of that space in unique ways. Each individual recognizes others as occupying a certain amount of space. Each American, for example, is said to occupy a six-inch envelope of inviolable airspace. When someone's envelope of space is violated, that person expects an apology. If you dropped a pencil and it rolled beneath the chair of the person sitting next to you, you would probably apologize for the disturbance as you picked up the pencil. Even though you did not touch that person, you violated his or her personal space.

In some southern European and Middle Eastern cultures, one's personal space is much smaller than among northern Europeans and Americans. Why might this be the case? Cultural diffusion, which is also a key concept of anthropology, refers to the distribution of a trait such as language or religion within a particular area. Geographers are concerned with where such traits are found, how they are dispersed, and what factors aid or deter this dispersal.

GEOGRAPHY STANDARDS

Building on these key concepts the Geography Education Standards Project (a collaborative venture of the American Geographical Society, the Association of American Geographers, the National Council for Geographic Education, and

Fearful of violating the personal space of others, people may exhibit marked social distance in some public areas.

the National Geographic Society) developed standards that are found within what are termed the six essential elements of geography.

The first element is "The World in Spatial Terms," in which the geographically informed person knows and understands how to use maps and other geographic tools to gain spatial understanding, mental maps to organize such information and how to analyze the spatial organization of people, places and environments on the surface of the earth. (Geography Standards, 34)

It is important to note the common stem for each expression of the standards. "The geographically informed person knows and understands" reflects an ideal that can be reached. The hope is for geographic literacy upon which can be built further conceptual understanding. This "geographically informed person" is analogous to the legal standard used to assist courts to determine liability in civil cases, that is, the "reasonable person" and the actions that he or she might be expected to take. Of course, not everyone operates in that reasonable manner, but by determining that such a standard exists, parameters can be provided for expected behavior. Ideally these expectations could be in place, in the future, in order to assess what is a "geographically informed adult."

The second element refers to "Places and Regions," where it is expected that the geographically informed person knows and understands the physical and human characteristic of places, that people create regions to interpret earth's complexity, and that culture and experience influence people's perceptions of places and regions.

The third element, "Physical Systems," refers to physical processes that shape the Earth's surface and the diverse ecosystems of Earth's surface. Rather

THE EIGHTEEN STANDARDS

Physical and human phenomena are spatially distributed over Earth's surface. The outcome of *Geography for Life* is a geographically informed person (1) who sees meaning in the arrangement of things in space; (2) who sees relations between people, places, and environments; (3) who uses geographic skills; and (4) who applies spatial and ecological perspectives to life situations.

The World in Spatial Terms

Geography studies the relationships between people, places, and environments by mapping information about them into a spatial context.

The geographically informed person knows and understands:

1. How to use maps and other geographic representations, tools, and technologies to acquire, process, and report information from a spatial perspective
2. How to use mental maps to organize information about people, places, and environments in a spatial context
3. How to analyze the spatial organization of people, places, and environments on Earth's surface

Places and Regions

The identities and lives of individuals and peoples are rooted in particular places and in those human constructs called regions.

The geographically informed person knows and understands:

4. The physical and human characteristics of places
5. That people create regions to interpret Earth's complexity
6. How culture and experience influence people's perceptions of places and regions

Physical Systems

Physical processes shape Earth's surface and interact with plant and animal life to create, sustain, and modify ecosystems.

The geographically informed person knows and understands:

7. The physical processes that shape the patterns of Earth's surface
8. The characteristics and spatial distribution of ecosystems on Earth's surface

(continued)

than merely parrot the standards, they are presented as a coherent whole in The Eighteen Standards box above. These standards are important to see in more than an abstract manner, and some suggestions for going beyond such a fate are provided at the end of the chapter.

Without trying to sound corny or make a bad pun, students should be encouraged to discover the world of information within geography. Though interpretations may change, the earth, itself, appears to have more stability than, for instance, our society or culture. Though that may be true, one should also

(continued from previous page)

People are central to geography in that human activities help shape Earth's surface, human settlements and structures are part of Earth's surface, and humans compete for control of Earth's surface.

The geographically informed person knows and understands:

9. The characteristics, distribution, and migration of human populations on Earth's surface
10. The characteristics, distribution, and complexity of Earth's cultural mosaics
11. The patterns and networks of economic interdependence on Earth's surface
12. The processes, patterns, and functions of human settlement
13. How the forces of cooperation and conflict among people influence the division and control of Earth's surface

Environment and Society

The physical environment is modified by human activities, largely as a consequence of the ways in which human societies value and use Earth's natural resources, and human activities are also influenced by Earth's physical features and processes.

The geographically informed person knows and understands:

14. How human actions modify the physical environment
15. How physical systems affect human systems
16. The changes that occur in the meaning, use, distribution, and importance of resources

The Uses of Geography

Knowledge of geography enables people to develop an understanding of the relationships between people, places, and environments over time—that is, of Earth as it was, is, and might be.

The geographically informed person knows and understands:

17. How to apply geography to interpret the past
18. How to apply geography to interpret the present and plan for the future

understand how dynamic the earth is. Even Antarctica, a continent devoid of permanent human inhabitants, undergoes continual changes as icebergs are calved and new life forms are discovered.

The skills associated with geography will be revisited in Chapter 11, *Map and Globe Skills.* Nevertheless, some caveats should be noted. Ideally, teachers should have course work in geography, but many colleges and universities do not even have departments of geography. Thus, teachers are left to pursue a number of alternatives to the "traditional" college course. One alternative is to attend a summer workshop or conference specifically focused on geography. There are now many of these, sponsored by the National Geographic Society and various universities, with funding from the National Science Foundation, the National Endowment for the Humanities, and other groups. Another alternative is a self-help approach. Teachers can obtain the new standards and attempt to implement them on their own in the classroom or in curriculum designs.

Still another alternative, drawn from manufacturers, presentations at conferences, and the presentations of publishers, is to examine in person some of the new equipment being produced for the geography classroom. The larger publishers, like Rand McNally, Nystrom, and Hammond, continue to produce good traditional materials, and much useful material is also coming from smaller publishers. An example is the geoLearning Corporation. Its clever and affordable materials include a Tectonic Cube that shows how the earth's tectonic plates fit together and illustrates how the movement of these crystal ridges causes earthquakes, volcanic fissures, and other geophysical events.

One of the most intriguing products is the Spilhaus Geoglyph. Despite the daunting name, it is elegant in its simplicity and overwhelming in its creation of a hundred correct maps of the world from just nine working pieces. This puzzle shows how the continuous surface of the earth makes many different maps possible. It is easy, fun, and conveys the spatial accuracy often lacking in flat maps.

History and geography have clearly been targeted for more attention as we enter the next century from the public, from educators outside social studies, from social scientists, and from some school personnel. With all that attention it is hoped that geography will be viewed as an important and fun component of a well-educated citizen.

Economics

I took an economics course in college, got a C, and was happy to escape with my life. I thought economics was all graphs and charts. Only when I became a wage earner did I begin to think economically and understand the concepts of economics. There's still hope for all of us!

Called "a dismal science" by one of its founders, economics is the study of how people use a finite number of resources to satisfy an infinite number of desires. Thus it is a study of the choices and decisions made by individuals and groups as they produce, exchange, and consume goods and services.

The study of economics involves several basic concepts (see box on page 45). The first is *scarcity;* resources are limited and must be allocated. Decisions about allocation are organized into economic *systems.* Within the system, *production* creates *goods and services* to satisfy human wants and needs. The use of produced goods and services is *consumption.* This chain of events leads to *interdependence* between individuals, since no individual can

ECONOMIC EDUCATION

Concern over the economic ignorance of students and a general uncertainty regarding the world's economic future have led to the growth of economic education. To some, economic education places too much emphasis on private or free enterprise. To others, it is un-American or unpatriotic to teach about other economic systems.

The National Council on Economic Education takes a more judicious view, although it still represents the opinions of many conservative business groups. The National Council produces curriculum guides and activity books in economics, position papers, audiovisual materials, tests, and the *Journal of Economic Education.* Many state councils and university centers help carry out National Council programs at the local level.

What do economic educators want to accomplish? Most seek to improve basic understanding of economics and its relation to our daily lives, in the hope that individuals will become better decision makers—both in the marketplace and in the voting booth.

Most economic education has focused

on the secondary or college level, but in recent years teachers have realized that economic education must begin at an earlier age. When and how would this occur? Although most educators advocate a conceptual approach—that is, the teaching of economic concepts in the early grades—there is disagreement as to which particular concepts should be taught.

In the summer of 1997, the National Council on Economic Education issued national content standards in economics with benchmarks for grades 4, 8, and 12. The 20 economic standards address two areas, basic understanding of how the economy works and the key skills needed to make personal financial decisions.

The National Council on Economic Education provides some answers. A few consumer-oriented groups provide a view that balances the more business-oriented perspective of the National Council. The Consumers Union, for example, publishes a bimonthly consumer report for elementary school students called *Penny Power.* The National Council also provides useful educational materials. The addresses of these two organizations are:

National Council on Economic Education
1140 Avenue of the Americas
New York, NY 10036

Consumers Union
256 Washington Street
Mount Vernon, NY 10553

do it all. From this flows the concept of *exchange.* The entire economic process is summed up in the *circular flow of economic activity,* which refers to the use of income to purchase goods and services from business firms, which then pay their workers, who spend that income on more goods and services.

SCARCITY

A resource is anything used to produce something else that can be used to satisfy a desire. A resource acquires value from its utility and its scarcity—that is, its degree of availability. With this in mind, resources can be classified in several different ways. Some resources (oxygen, for example) are *relatively* scarce, meaning they are abundant in most places. Other resources, like gold, are *absolutely* scarce because they occur *rarely on or in the earth.*

Resources can also be classified on the basis of utility: some resources have been developed, whereas others remain undeveloped. Petroleum and other minerals buried in the earth have a potential use, even if they have not been developed. Once that petroleum has been tapped, it becomes a developed resource. In an economic system, human resources are basic for the development of natural resources.

Finally, resources may be classified as renewable or nonrenewable. The crude oil we extract from the depths of the earth is considered to be nonrenewable because the supply is limited, whereas energy from the sun or wind is constantly being renewed.

SYSTEMS

The use of scarce resources can be organized into systems. An economic system is the organized way in which individuals and groups make choices. The simplest type of economic system can be defined as barter, in which choices are made directly between individuals within the system. On a more complex level, we have command systems, in which all the decisions are made by a central authority. In contrast to the command system is the market system, in which the individual makes decisions and the economy responds to those decisions. The centralized economy of many communist societies is an example of a command system, whereas capitalistic economies are examples of the market system. However well defined these systems can be in theory, we find that in practice each economy will have elements of the other. Thus all the economic systems in the world today are to one degree or another mixed systems of command and market.

PRODUCTION

How do the decisions made in an economic system result in economic activity? The answer is based in production, goods and services, and consumption. Production is the process of changing the raw material of the resource into an economic good or service that can be used to satisfy a desire. Production depends on four factors. The first is the land, which includes not only the earth's surface on which the production takes place but also the raw materials used in the production process. The second factor is labor, which transforms raw materials into usable material. This labor, which is a service, is provided with varying degrees of skill by individuals or groups of individuals. Production also requires capital, the means used to change raw materials into usable goods by labor. Capital includes money to pay the wages of the laborers, machinery, the buildings in which production takes place, and the degree of skill of the people managing the productive system.

In order for the produced goods and services to be used, they must be taken from the place of production to a place where they are available to those who want them. This fourth factor, the process of distribution, depends on the type of economic system and the means of transportation in that system.

GOODS AND SERVICES

Goods and services are the products used to satisfy people's needs and desires. Produced goods are "hard," in the sense that they are material items. These goods can be used directly by individuals or indirectly for the production of other goods, like machines that create other machines. They can be durable, lasting over a long period of time, or nondurable, able to be used only once or twice. A refrigerator that will last for several years or more is a durable good. The food put into that refrigerator, however, can be eaten only once. Goods such as this are called "soft" goods.

Services include any human activity designed to satisfy the needs or wants of others. The U.S. Bureau of Labor Statistics lists around 15,000 different human occupations. The United States has the world's first economy in which more people are engaged in the production of services than in the production of goods. Therefore, it seems reasonable to suggest that there are several thousand different services that humans perform. For example, the author of this book is performing a service. The teacher explaining it is performing another service.

A final subconcept of goods and services is the Gross National Product (GNP), the total of the goods and services produced in a system. The GNP is a measure of the degree of complexity and affluence of the economic system. Recently, Gross Domestic Product (GDP) has been used rather than GNP to measure economic growth.

CONSUMPTION

Once the goods and services have been produced, they must be consumed in order to complete the cycle. Consumption is the use of produced goods and services to satisfy human needs and wants. In economic terms, needs are basic to the survival of the individual and the group. Food and shelter are goods necessary for the survival of human beings. Education and medical care are services basic to the survival of individuals. Beyond these basic needs for survival are other demands on the system called wants—the goods and services that people desire in order to enhance the quality of their life beyond mere survival. A person *needs* one set of clothing for protection from the environment.

A person *wants* several sets of clothing in order to increase the range of choices and the quality of life. People could survive with one set of clothing, although there are few in the American economy who choose to do so.

INTERDEPENDENCE

No one individual or group can do everything that is necessary for the economic cycle to continue. Thus production and consumption of goods and services are divided among specialized individuals and groups. Economists refer to this division of labor as the "comparative advantage." Comparative advantage allows executives to spend their time making decisions rather than typing the memos that announce those decisions. The latter task is turned over to a person who has a comparative advantage in typing or word-processing skills. An interdependent economy also has specialized industries and regions with specialized capacities—such as farming, industrial, forest, or fishing areas. There are even nations with specialized abilities. Japan, for example, enjoys a comparative advantage over many other nations in the production of electronic equipment.

EXCHANGE

In order for these interdependent entities to function, they must exchange their skills and produced goods for others. This exchange can be defined as the trade of specialized goods and services for other goods and services, based on an analysis of cost and benefits. Every individual or group acting in an interdependent economic system makes decisions based on the relationship between what a decision will cost and what the benefit to the individual or group will be. This exchange of goods and services is based on some medium (such as money) that symbolizes the exchange of a good or service. Money exists in material ways—coin and paper. But the money supply of an economy is more than the paper and coins available for exchange purposes: it also includes the credit, borrowing power, and promises to pay of individuals and groups. In most advanced economies the money supply consists of more credit than coin.

Money defines the value of a good or service in terms of price. Price is determined by the usefulness of an item in satisfying a need or want, as well as by the item's availability. Usability is called *demand,* and the degree of availability of the item is called *supply.* Both the amount of the item available and the demand for it can be manipulated. The most common manipulation of demand is advertising, which attempts to persuade people that they need a particular item. The most common manipulation of supply is the amount of production. A monopoly exists when one group or individual controls the total supply or the total demand.

CIRCULAR FLOW OF ECONOMIC ACTIVITY

All of these choices by individuals and groups create a flow of trade. While this flow is always active, the degree of activity changes. The amount of change in economic activity seems to occur in cycles. When economic activity is at its lowest, we say that the economy is depressed. When it is relatively low, we say the economy is in a state of recession. When the activity speeds up beyond the norm, we have prosperity, and if the activity speeds up dramatically, we have a boom cycle.

In order to define the degree of activity, economists use certain indicators, such as the GNP, the percentage of productive capacity being used, the percentage of unemployed laborers, the gross and annual average wage, and the cost of living. These are all measures of economic activity.

Understanding these concepts, of course, comes about through application. How can young children understand scarcity, for example? One way is to discuss shopping for a lunch box for school.

ACTIVITY 1: IN SEARCH OF A LUNCH BOX

Objective: To use a familiar artifact as a vehicle for introducing demand/supply/price.

Materials: A variety of lunch boxes (as described), pictures of such lunch boxes, or a verbal description read slowly to the children.

In this activity the teacher will present to the children in some way five or six lunch boxes of the same basic size and shape, but with different pictures on each box. A couple might be more traditional depictions such as "baseball" with a stylized action shot or a state lunch box depicting some as aspect of the state in which the children live. One might be an ever-popular cartoon character such as Bugs Bunny or a more recent "traditional" character such as Snoopy or Garfield. One might be plain black or yellow (very retro), and one should depict the latest popular character with children, such as Aladdin, Hercules, Quasimodo, or Simba from the recent Disney films.

Line up the lunch boxes and ask the children which one they like the most. Then explain that all are the same size, yet some cost more. Why? This should move them into beginning to see how demand is created. At this point give them $10 (in pretend currency) to purchase a lunch box, pencils, and a notebook. All these can be bought for $10, but the expensive lunch box alone is $10. What should they do? How much would they pay for something that they really want? $20? $100? More? These amounts may be too abstract for younger children so it might be best to give examples of items that cost that much such as a computer game, a basketball, a special doll, a new chair, etc.

This begins to show students how demand can affect price and supply.

ACTIVITY 2: WANTS AND NEEDS—IS MONEY A WANT OR A NEED?

Students can list or teacher/students can cut from magazines pictures of things they like. Then the teacher can go through the items, clarifying the differences between things necessary to sustain life and those that may enhance the quality of life. Many answers will need some clarity because of ambiguity. For example, milk or bread is not necessary for life, but food is. The teacher may have to interpret specific items more representationally. After discussing most items, introduce money. Many people say that they need more money, but could we get the things that we like without money? This should lead to a directed discussion leading to notions of trading services or goods for other services or goods, that is, bartering. Money, it should be shown, is not needed. It is, however, quite handy as a medium of exchange, instead of gold or shells or land.

Sociology

Sociologists are interested in the study of society, most notably the groups that form society and the institutions that structure the social order. I was a sociology major in college, so I always delight in teaching concepts from sociology.

Society is a social organization that continues to exist in some degree or another, regardless of the individuals within that society. A society reflects social *norms*—the general rules, beliefs, and values by which the people in the society live. These define the individual's *roles* within that society. Society organizes these norms into a *system* composed of different institutions. *Socialization* is the process through which individuals learn the norms and roles within a society. This often takes place within the institutions. As people become socialized, they enter the social *strata* of classes and castes through which they attain status. The norms of society are not static; they are subject to social *change*. The individual within the society *conforms* to those norms to some degree and interacts with other individuals and the society in acceptable ways controlled by *sanctions*.

SOCIETY

Society is an informal but powerful organization that establishes order in the chaos of human relationships. Because the members of a society share a common definition of order and sense of well being, societies are communities. Societies establish informal organizational patterns for people who share common interests and common activities. Understandably, society is a highly complex organizational system, one that is constantly changing, with varying degrees of adherence by each individual.

NORMS

The norm is a rule of behavior accepted by almost all members of a society. Norms are less rigidly spelled out than the laws of a political system, although they are carefully defined criteria of acceptable behavior within the society. Norms are based on the commonly held values and beliefs of the people living in the society. For example, Americans value cleanliness. This is reflected in

Norms regarding acceptable dress vary from culture to culture.

our norms for table manners. We use implements like knives, forks, and spoons in order to maintain the appearance of cleanliness.

Several types of norms can be defined by the degree to which people adhere to them. Fads are transitory norms; fashions remain popular for longer periods than fads, and folkways for even longer periods. Social mores are more deeply held than folkways.

A norm may become so engrained that it eventually becomes politically codified as a *law*. The penalty for violating such a norm becomes more severe as we go up the social order. Consider the norms governing dress. Each of us got out of bed this morning and decided to get dressed. We knew that if we did not get dressed and went out onto the street with no clothes on, we would be violating one of the fundamental mores, and a law, of our society and would be thrown in jail. If we are male, when we decided to dress we had no choice between trousers or a skirt. The folkway is rather strong that males wear trousers in almost all Western societies (Scottish folk dress comes to mind as one exception). If we are female, we had two choices: pants or a skirt. Fashionable college students in warmer climates sometimes wear T-shirts. Often the T-shirt will have something printed on it (a slogan or a picture of a rock star) related to the latest fad.

ROLES

The various sets of behavior that individuals employ in society are usually referred to as roles. These are defined by norms and are viewed in a number of ways by society members. Roles are often defined by the respect society accords those roles. This is called *status*. Status can be earned (as when a medical doctor studies to become a practitioner and gains a favorable reputation) or ascribed (as when the Prince of Wales was born). How a person acts in a role determines the *esteem* in which he or she is held. One may have a high-status position, such as a physician, but fill that role poorly and be viewed with low esteem. Conversely, a trash collector (low-status position) may do that job remarkably well, according him or her high status for the way the role is fulfilled.

SYSTEMS

Social norms are organized according to their purpose. Society systematically creates organizations called institutions to enforce these norms. The school, for example, is organized by society to carry out the function of educating children because our society has determined that this is necessary. Thus education is compulsory and is financed by all taxpayers, regardless of whether or not they have children. Churches are institutions designed to satisfy people's spiritual impulses, and families are designed to perpetuate the society through the rearing of young people. The latter institution may take different forms, from nuclear families to extended families. In any society, the formation of the family, beginning with courtship and marriage, is a rather intricate pattern of norms in itself.

SOCIALIZATION

As individuals conform to social norms, they accept certain patterns of behavior. Through socialization individuals accept certain values that shape their personal lives. The process of socialization also defines certain group values that vary in worth as viewed by the society. Status is the value a society places on certain patterns of behavior.

STRATIFICATION

When people assume a status they tend to fall into certain levels of society through the process of stratification. If these levels are fixed they are called castes; people born into those levels may not move out of them. If the levels are not fixed, they are called classes. American society has six general classes: lower-lower, upper-lower, lower-middle, upper-middle, lower-upper, and upper-upper. People may achieve their class by birth, assuming the class level of their parents, or by wealth, or by their employment or profession. This implies that

Positive sanctions, like this ribbon, often serve as a source of motivation for individuals.

people can move from one class to another by a process of social mobility. The latter two means—attainment of class by wealth or by employment—are the more common ways of moving from one class to another in the United States. Note that social mobility can be downward as well as upward.

CULTURAL CHANGE

None of these social patterns are fixed; all are subject to change, especially at this time in our history. Today change is so pervasive that the only constant in our lives may be the *idea* of change. Institutions, status levels, and norms have all changed drastically in the last few years, and they continue to change with ever-increasing speed. Often these changes produce a lag between the behavior and the norm. The changes take place in ways that cannot be carefully defined or predicted, and they are diffused through society with remarkable speed.

CONFORMITY

As individuals act according to social norms and the roles defined for them, they conform to some degree or another with the society. Socialization teaches the values by which we will live; conformity defines the constancy by which we will live according to the values taught. The institutions engage us with what is known as "institutional press" and, to varying degrees, shape our behavior.

SANCTIONS

Individuals live and behave in an interdependent way. "No man is an island," as the poet John Donne wrote in 1624. All people interact with one another on a personal level as well as on a cultural level. This personal interaction takes place through networks of friends, peers, colleagues, and families according to certain acceptable ways of behavior. There are certain controls on our behavior called sanctions, which can be either positive or negative. A positive sanction is a reward designed to encourage a behavior. A negative sanction is a punishment designed to discourage a behavior.

Anthropology

Having earned a graduate degree in anthropology and done field work on other cultures, I can easily see anthropology as the unifying social science around which social studies is shaped. My views are in the minority, but *thinking* anthropologically is one key to the reduction of prejudice and to a better understanding of others, something with which all teachers should be concerned.

Anthropology is the study of human beings. The first concept in anthropology is that human beings behave in generally the same ways within *cultures.* Through the process of *enculturation* people accept the general behavior patterns of those cultures. Among these behavior patterns are the ways in which individuals handle the *cycles of life,* communicate through *language,* explain their environment, and satisfy the aesthetic impulse.

A final concept in anthropology is the place of the individual within the culture. Individuals who feel that their culture is the center of the universe are caught in a pattern of *ethnocentrism,* which exalts their own culture and derides, if not denies, the existence of every other culture.

CULTURE

The word culture may be used in two ways: the culture is a collective way of behaving, whereas *a* culture is a group of people who behave in the same way. The culture has several components. Because people behave in the same way over time, these behaviors are customary and traditional. When such behaviors follow the same patterns under the same circumstances, they become rites or rituals, often celebrating high points of the culture in festivals. As part of these rituals, cultures produce materials, or *artifacts,* that define the culture, such as automobiles, chairs, tools, weapons, and clothing. Cultures vary from simple to complex, and the degree of complexity is often defined by the number of *subcultures* within the group.

ACCULTURATION

When different cultures come into extended contact, their interaction produces changes in both cultures, known as *acculturation.* Acculturation occurs

A rite of passage for many Jewish youths on their thirteenth birthdays is the bar mitzvah or the bat mitzvah ceremony.

when people from different cultures marry, or when one culture interfaces with another, physically or militarily. When two cultures exist side by side, there is a diffusion of behavior patterns. Americans eating pizza, sushi, or tortillas are examples of acculturation. This term is not to be confused with *enculturation,* the process by which people assume the cultural traditions and mannerisms. Learning to hunt, to speak the native language, and to react to praise in the accepted manner are examples of enculturation.

CULTURAL DIFFUSION

Diffusion occurs when culture traits spread from one culture area to another. Though all cultures invent things to a certain degree, far more is borrowed and modified. Cultural diffusion is deterred or slowed by geographic barriers, like an ocean or a mountain range, by cultural barriers, like war or language, and by natural barriers, like disease.

LIFE CYCLE

Among the many things members of the same culture have in common is the way in which they perceive time. People of different cultures have different daily rhythms that affect eating and sleeping patterns. Any American who visits Spain, for example, where people begin dining at 10:30 in the evening, soon realizes that not all cultures follow the same "clock." The hours of the day people set aside for work and recreation also vary from culture to culture.

Most cultures divide the life cycle into seven stages: infancy, childhood, adolescence, early maturity, middle maturity, late maturity, and old age. They celebrate the movement from one stage to another in so-called rites of passage, such as graduation ceremonies, weddings, and funerals.

LANGUAGE

Another culturally determined behavior is the way in which people communicate through language, both spoken and unspoken. Within the many spoken languages, we find subtle variations with different tones, accents, and dialects. Nonverbal languages are equally complex. The use of gestures, facial expressions, and other so-called body language is also culturally determined.

WORLDVIEW

As people experience their environment, they explain it to themselves and to others in culturally determined ways. The modern Western world exalts the rational explanation—the use of reason and the gathering of fact, the minimizing of emotion, the testing of hypotheses. Other cultures have a greater dependence on human emotion or instinct as a way of explaining the world. Still others explain the world through superstitions. Finally, some people explain their world through revelation—a belief in some force beyond the human and natural realm.

AESTHETIC

People of the same culture also share a common aesthetic impulse. Advanced cultures have a formal means of expressing these impulses through creative artistic endeavors such as the classic arts: literature, music, drama. In most cultures, individuals participate in an informal way in these art forms to satisfy their aesthetic impulses. Others satisfy their aesthetic impulses vicariously, as spectators at athletic events, museums, or nature preserves.

ETHNOCENTRISM

When an individual operates within a culture and the culture operates within that individual, a certain loyalty develops called *ethnocentrism*. The ethos, or culture, becomes central to the person's life, as much of the individual's view of the world is shaped by cultural patterns. This phenomenon has positive aspects in that people's loyalty to their culture encourages a certain stability of that culture. On the other hand, ethnocentrism may produce blindness to other cultures, a sense of chauvinism that leads to conflict rather than reconciliation among cultures.

Psychology

Psychology alternately interested me and repelled me. The content was thought provoking, but the way it was taught often seemed aimed at making the obvious more complex. Observing children as both a parent and a teacher has made psychology more interesting and meaningful to me. There are basically three schools of thought regarding the psychological explanation of behavior: humanistic psychology, behaviorism, and the psychoanalytical method.

Psychology is the social science that deals with the study of the self. Psychology has several basic concepts, starting with the broad concept of *personality*, the self as seen by others. Other basic concepts come from the various characteristics of personality: *mental, emotional, physical,* and *motivational.* The personality is dynamic; *growth* results from learning and maturity. The personality also has a certain *identity*, the way in which an individual perceives himself or herself.

PERSONALITY

Personality is the sum of the behaviors of an individual as perceived by other individuals, groups, and societies. The personality is a dynamic pattern of behaviors and is often influenced by the roles a person is thrust into in the society. These may be gender roles, the expected patterns of social behavior associated with masculinity and femininity, or age-graded roles, the set of behaviors expected of individuals at a specific phase of their life cycles. Other roles are defined by an individual's position in society. Individuals may experience conflict in expectations as they shift from one role to another. The source of these roles is outside the individual. People imitate other individuals, or *role models,* who occupy those roles in the society.

PERSONALITY CHARACTERISTICS

Every personality possesses certain qualities or parts. This is not to say that a personality has categories; rather, it is a somewhat seamless web woven from several parts. One part is the mental characteristics of the individual; the cognitive dimension that deals with the mental processes of thinking and creating, as well as with the range of mental ability as measured by what we call intelligence tests.

Another part of the seamless web is the emotional dimension, the feelings, values, and so on that shape a personality. The third dimension is the physical manifestation of behaviors, the coordination of the mind and the body into physical movements.

Children at play often assume adult roles such as those of a parent or teacher.

A natural tension exists among these three parts of a personality. It is a classic case of the whole being greater than the sum of its parts. Another concept related to personality is motivation. Motivation that comes from within is intrinsic to the person. Motivation is extrinsic when the will to perform is inspired by a desire to satisfy another person or some ideal.

GROWTH

Personalities are not static; they are constantly in a state of flux. People do not stay the same; this dynamism is called growth. Personalities change through maturation processes that are genetically mapped, and they change as individuals proceed through life stages that influence the personality. Personalities also grow through learning, which produces behavioral changes as a result of experience. Within the learning process is the concept of memory, the long-term and short-term storage of experiences.

IDENTITY

The result of the dynamic personality and its changes is *identity*, the way in which the individual perceives his or her self. An individual's identity is at the core of his or her being and results in an internal sense of self. This develops from interactions with others as well as from one's own perceptions. It may be said that this self has several components: (1) the material self, which is the individual's physical body and possessions; (2) the psychological self, what the individual thinks of when analyzing his or her thoughts or ideas; (3) the social self, the self as defined in relation to interactions with others; and (4) the ideal self, who or what the individual would like to be.

Humans strive to maintain a consistency among the intellectual, emotional, and physical parts of their personalities. Each individual needs a unique identity, which may be called privacy. It is a constant struggle to maintain that private uniqueness in the face of an ever-encroaching world. Personality, growth, and identity come together in one's *self-concept,* the personal evaluation of one's self. This is the sense of self-worth held by each individual. It can vary from pride to shame, but it is crucial in determining the way one meets one's world.

Political Science

I once thought of being a lawyer and, in fact, attended law school, where I found that the concept of law is often held captive by a key concept of political science, power. Power, it should be noted, is also a key to multicultural education. Who has power, how power is acquired, and whether power is limited or dynamic are all important factors in the overall success of the acceptance of diversity within established institutional domains.

The study of political science examines the theory and practice of the institutions of government. It is based on the idea of *authority,* the *power* extended over humans in order to control their behavior. The authority is organized into a political *system* called the state, which in the United States is separated into the legislative, executive, and judicial branches of government. The *political process* is the means by which citizens of the state obtain access to power—through public opinion, political interest groups, and political parties. The *citizen in the political process* relates to the state in the code of law, in the administration of justice, and in civil rights and civil responsibilities.

AUTHORITY

Authority is the power extended over people in the political organization in order to control their behavior. The source of power varies from state to state. It can come from the consent of the governed, from a belief in the divine right of the ruler, from right of birth, or from being a superior ideologue.

Power is the ability to influence, change, modify, or alter the behavior of others. The distribution of power affects the structure of government and the decision-making rules of a political system.

POLITICAL SYSTEM

Authority is organized systematically. This organization, which distributes authority, establishes the political state. Power within the system can be exercised absolutely; that is, it can extend from the top down with little or no participation by the citizens. Monarchies, oligarchies, and totalitarian structures are examples of such a system. In a popular system, such as a democracy or a socialistic organization, the body politic has a sense of participation. In these latter two systems, a constitution is often established that defines the powers the system has over the individual. There are three different branches of power: *legislative power* to investigate, discuss social issues, and formulate rules for the behavior of citizens of the state; *executive power* to put these rules into effect and to enforce behavior according to the rules; and *judicial power* to adjudicate disputes arising from the execution and enforcement of the rules. In some states, these powers are concentrated in the same individuals, whereas in others the powers are separated.

In the United States these powers are separated by function and by location. The federal system vests power in a national government, state governments, and local governments. Because each of these levels has a separate function, a system of checks and balances is established that prevents power from being concentrated in any one of these organizations, either by function or by location.

POLITICAL PROCESS

The political process is the means through which citizens gain access to power. In the United States, for example, public opinion often defines issues. Those in power discuss and act on issues that seem likely to have the most effect on public opinion. As public opinion focuses interest on various issues, it forms public interest groups that take stands on the issues. This process of putting pressure on the government has been institutionalized through political parties.

THE CITIZEN'S ROLE

The individual relates to political power primarily through the law. The law has a moral and regulatory effect on individuals as they relate to one another (civil law) and to the common good (criminal law). The citizens of the United States have certain rights that are carefully spelled out in the Constitution. In other nations, the degree of liberty is defined either in practice, in documents, or both. Individuals also have responsibilities to the state, which may vary depending on the degree of political freedom allowed in a nation.

POLITICAL SOCIALIZATION

The way in which individuals in society acquire the attitudes and beliefs of the political system is through political socialization. Children gain political understanding through school, media, family, peers, and other organizations. Research indicates that children grasp sophisticated political concepts from as early as three years of age.

Political science as civics has also been the subject of a set of standards for school consideration and adaptation. Developed at the Center for Civic Education in Calabasas, California, the standards are based on a framework for civic education called Civitas (the Latin word for citizenship) that was also developed at the center. The major sections address civic virtue, civic participation, and civic knowledge and skills, which include politics, government, and the role of the citizen. Unlike the history standards, the civics standards were formulated by using a wide cross section of political, legal, and business respondents; this method led to widespread acceptance and little fanfare.

The civics standards are organized around five key conceptual questions for each of three grade divisions. For K–4 the questions are:

I. What is Government and What Should it Do?
II. What are the Basic Values and Principles of American Democracy?
III. How Does the Government Established by the Constitution Embody the Purposes, Values, and Principles of American Democracy?
IV. What is the Relationship of the United States to Other Nations and to World Affairs?
V. What are the Roles of a Citizen in American Democracy?

The questions for grades 5–8 are the same for the last three, but the first two are:

I. What are Civic Life, Politics, and Government?
II. What are the Foundations of the American Political System?

Whether these standards will alter curriculum or citizen behavior will not be readily apparent until large numbers of youngsters become active, involved citizens. An answer may begin to emerge in the early years of the next century.

SOCIAL STUDIES STANDARDS

The parade of standards that were developed in the mid 1990s includes a set that addresses social studies developed by the National Council for the Social Studies (NCSS). Ideally all the various standards developed by assorted professional social science organizations would be integrated into a later set of standards developed within social studies, but, alas, that has not happened and is unlikely to. In fact, the opposite occurred: NCSS developed its social studies standards prior to those from history, civics and geography. In addition, there are so many pages of standards (more than 1,000) that it would be a massive undertaking to integrate them all into some distilled whole. The 10 themes of the NCSS standards are seen in the box on page 27.

The standards movement is demanding even more of social studies teachers. It seems clear that no one teacher can be totally facile with all the standards in the areas of social studies and the nuances of each set of standards.

FIGURE 2.2

Local District Social Studies—National Social Studies and Discipline-Related Standards Projects

Common Across All Standards
- **Emphasize higher-order thinking**
  - Asking and answering questions
  - Comprehending, acquiring, organizing, analyzing, interpreting information; researching for depth
  - Issue and problem analysis, decision-making, examining alternatives, multiple options, multiple points of view; consequences; taking and defending positions
- **Emphasize connections—to other subjects, to major themes, and the real world**
- **Emphasize Active Learning through Multiple Modes**
  - Reading, writing, listening, discussing, creating, constructing (e.g., maps, graphs, drawings...)
- **Emphasize major/important learning and depth through investigation, extensions of learning**
- **Emphasize the use of knowledge in multiple modes of assessment—ongoing during instruction and at end points**
  - Many types of measures as most appropriate—pretests, projects, objective, summary/responses, essay, research, demonstrations...

SOURCE: M. McFarland. Presentation at NCSS Annual Meeting, Washington, DC. November, 1996.

What could be achieved, however, would be familiarity of a school district and a team of teachers that recommends aspects of each set of standards to local teachers. Figure 2.2 gives an example of how one district is attempting to do this. The NCSS standard makers recognize the existence of new standards in history, geography, and civics and accept that by encouraging teachers and curriculum designers to

> use the individual sets of standards from history, geography, civics, economics, or other disciplines to guide the development of strands and courses within their programs. Using these standards in concert with one another can enable educators to give adequate attention to both integrated and single discipline configurations within the social studies curriculum. (NCSS, 17)

The standards were developed amidst great controversy over their very creation, for whom they should be developed, by whom they should be written, and whether they would or should lead to a demand for an official national curriculum in the social studies. Many states are developing or have developed state standards to parallel national standards, but these, too, have often led to controversy. The draft of the standards for Wisconsin, for example, immediately rekindled disputes among academics and educators involved in social studies. (State Curriculum Watch, 3)

THE SOCIAL STUDIES: A BROADER DEFINITION

Though the social studies encompasses all the notions of the social sciences discussed above, there is more to the field than those concepts and ideas. Social studies refers to the study of all aspects of human endeavor. By that broad definition, science, mathematics, humanities, arts, and language are all legitimate aspects of social study, as are the *social* aspects of any field. Art, music, dance, sport, cinema, theater, and mythology are all needed to fill in the gaps left by seemingly cultureless textbooks.

The theater is a prime example. What would the study of theater companies add to our knowledge and understanding of the world? It would afford a greater appreciation of various ethnic groups and the culture that they have brought to or developed in the United States. There has been a tradition of Polish, black, Yiddish, Greek, Puerto Rican, and Italian theater, and the American theater has borrowed from all of these. Thus the historical development of an American institution can be seen from a cultural perspective; this is a legitimate use of history.

This kind of study might fail to captivate all students. Some may be more interested in sports, which is another acceptable alternative to traditional historical study. The history of basketball, for example, can be used to illustrate American social, political, and economic growth as well as other units of study. Contained in such historical study are two important issues in American revisionist history: racial discrimination and ethnic studies. The outline shown in the box on pages 64–65 illustrates this point.

Clearly some of the material in the described unit is too advanced for third graders, but most of it is appropriate for fifth or sixth graders. This kind of cultural study provides a different perspective on American history that many youngsters will find appealing.

Three Views

What about vital facts? Aren't there some things *all* youngsters should know that will be lost if this kind of learning goes on? The answer to that depends on how one views the role of the social studies. Barr, Barth, and Shermis (1977) have identified three traditional views of social studies. The content and depth of what is studied will vary depending on what tradition a teacher believes in.

In the first tradition, called *citizenship transmission,* the teacher presents a specific body of knowledge that all good citizens should know. In the second tradition, *social studies as social science,* the content of the individual disciplines defines what will be taught. In the third tradition, *reflective inquiry,* the teacher sees social studies as a process of decision making.

Other authors offer similar views regarding the teaching of social studies. Most espouse a series of prime functions for social studies. Barr, Barth, and Shermis have implied some of these. The first function is to learn the social sciences; that is, learn social sciences and you will know social studies. The

HISTORY OF PROFESSIONAL BASKETBALL UNIT

The following unit offers one way to explore American studies through the vehicle of professional basketball. Over the past 15 years professional basketball has exploded in popularity world wide, yet it remains an American invention with deep cultural roots. Parts I, II, and III of this unit provide for historical study, with specific focus on how an innovation becomes institutionalized and the influence of various groups on the innovation including rulemaking.

All eras have heroes. What constitutes a hero differs from one era to the next. Nat Holman was seen as a model for many young Jewish immigrants when he played in the 1920s much as Michael Jordan is today to youngsters of African ancestry. The colorful passing of Bob Cousy in the 1950s and 1960s was taken to a higher level by Pete Maravich and Earvin "Magic" Johnson. Professional basketball was integrated by the National Basketball League as early as 1946, though it wasn't until 1950 that three players of African ancestry—Chuck Cooper, Earl Lloyd and Nat (Sweetwater) Clifton played on NBA courts.

I. Basketball's beginning
  A. Invention—James Naismith (1891)
  B. First leagues and teams
    1. Springfield YMCA team
    2. Philadelphia League (1898)
    3. Settlement house teams
    4. Lightweight and heavyweight categories

II. Ethnicity and early basketball teams
  A. Busy Izzies (Jewish-1910s)
  B. Buffalo Germans (German-1900s)
  C. Celtics of New York (Irish-1910s)
  D. New York Renaissance (African Americans—1920s–1940s)

III. Rules and Changes
  A. Ball size
  B. Floor length and lines
  C. Dribbling regulations
  D. Frequency of jump balls

IV. Basketball and its folk heroes
  A. Hank Luisetti
  B. George Mikan
  C. Nat Holman
  D. Bob Cousy
  E. Bill Russell
  F. Wilt Chamberlain
  G. Oscar Robertson
  H. Larry Bird
  I. Earvin (Magic) Johnson
  J. Michael Jordan

V. Basketball as a reflection of American society
  A. Roaring Twenties and reckless basketball
  B. Racial separation and acceptance
    1. Rens and Globetrotters and the Professional Championship

(continued)

(continued from previous page)

New York Renaissance 1930s

2. The segregation of the BAA-NBA (1946–1950) and the NBL/BAA merger
3. NBA more than 50 percent African American (1970s–today)

C. Unions v. independence
1. Professional independent contractors (1898–1928)
2. NBA Players Association (1958)
3. Revenue sharing (1990s)

D. Demographic population shifts
1. Sun belt expansion
2. Far Western states
3. Europe?

VI. Basketball—a world sport
A. Olympics—1936; Munich—today
B. European leagues
C. Japanese leagues
D. International players in the NBA
1. Kukoč (Croatia)
2. Divac (Yugoslavia)
3. Olajuwon (Nigeria)
4. Mutumbo (Zaire)
5. Longley (Australia)

second function is patriotic; that is, the vital content of social studies (true or false) makes our students better Americans. The third function is skill oriented. Students should learn how to use maps, deal with time, question intelligently, and deal effectively with others. The fourth function is the basic decision-making ideal. A corollary of this might be the value-laden approach of forming social attitudes (see Wesley).

The late Shirley Engle stated for many years that decision making was the heart of social studies, and a number of social studies educators such as Jack Fraenkel have intimated that social studies should be for social life, that is, living and operating successfully in the sociocultural world. This is more encompassing than citizenship transmission, which would be only one aspect of sociocultural life.

Social Studies Organization

These views of the functions of social studies contrast somewhat with the ways the subject is organized in schools. As mentioned earlier, the Hanna model of expanding communities is most commonly found in elementary schools. Over the years the model has been updated and expanded to take into account improved communications and to include kindergarten, but basically the model has not been significantly redesigned. The suggested topic for kindergarten is the child. Since children are so egocentric at this age, it is a sensible subject. The model has been adopted by most textbook authors, which has produced an unprecedented sameness in elementary social studies texts. Almost all fifth-grade books deal with U.S. history or geography, while fourth-grade books deal with U.S. geography or the environment. The books for other grades are as predictable.

Instead, these textbooks should show a greater breadth of communications and cultural awareness. In first grade, for example, a textbook should present the characteristics of families from different cultures rather than simply idealizing those of the United States. The Higashida family of Kyoto, Japan, the Herzog family of Munich, Germany, the Lebby family of Freetown, Sierra Leone, and the Lopes family of São Paulo, Brazil, might comprise the rest of the textbook, presenting a more cross-cultural perspective for students. A chapter on various kinds of modern family structures might be assembled to discuss one-parent families, adopted children, and extended families. Similar cross-cultural concerns would characterize the social studies textbooks in the higher grades.

With all these different approaches to teaching social studies, it becomes very hard for a school district to go in any one direction, but some do. Some districts take a social science approach in the upper elementary grades and virtually ignore social studies in the lower grades, except for the time spent on social indoctrination (a considerable amount in the primary grades). Many districts have chosen to teach students with the unit approach, which has its roots in progressive education. In the unit approach, a central topic is chosen, and all aspects of the curriculum are woven around that topic. Math, science, art, spelling—all these subject areas become an integral part of the social studies unit.

Textbooks, if used at all, function as resource books. Trade books (that is, children's literature) provide the only shared reading that the students might have. The accent is on a teacher- and student-centered classroom, not a textbook-centered classroom.

The length of a unit may vary, depending on a teacher's concern with grade-level coordination, student interest, and materials available. The unit approach reflects the belief that there is no particular body of content that *all* students must learn. The unit approach also allows students to pursue their own interests, not just the teacher's or the school district's. Chapter 3 describes the development of a unit in detail.

QUESTIONS AND ACTIVITIES

1. How much social science background does a teacher need to teach in an elementary school? If teachers were trained in five-year rather than four-year programs, should more social science be required?

2. Should a national social studies curriculum be developed and required in the United States? What are the reasons why this would or would not be a good idea?

3. What should be the role of teachers, students, and parents in establishing state and local standards for social studies? Investigate the status of social studies reforms in your own state over the past 10 years.

4. Is social studies *basic* to elementary school? If so, why is it so frequently ignored as a basic?

5. Interview several experienced teachers and find out what changes in social science or social studies requirements they would like to see in teacher training programs.

6. What social sciences do you like and dislike? Why? Do you think that you could teach effectively a subject you dislike? Why or why not?

7. Go to a crowded area in your town or city and observe people's behavior. Pretend you are from another country. Try to determine what cultural norms are acceptable just by what you observe in others.

8. If you could interview a professional in each of the social sciences, who would it be? Why? What questions about their fields are unclear to you or warrant attention?

9. How do your parents feel about their knowledge of history and geography? Can you carry on a discussion from a historical perspective with one or both of them?

10. Why should social scientists get involved with helping create school curricula? Why might it not be a good idea?

11. Over a hundred years ago, Herbert Spencer wrote "What knowledge is of most worth?" Discuss with your class what they feel are the most important things for American students to know about history and geography. Explain why you feel as you do.

12. The section on geographical environments (page 40) acknowledges the overlap of political, cultural, topographic, climatic, and personal environments. Describe these for the state in which you live.

13. Standards have been developed in history, civics, geography, economics, and social studies as part of the initiatives of Presidents Bush and Clinton. Do you feel that the failure to recognize psychology, sociology, and anthropology as "worthy" of developed standards reflects a lack of need for these social sciences in elementary school teaching or are there other reasons?

REFERENCES

Akenson, James E. "Historical Factors in the Development of Elementary Social Studies," *Theory and Research in Social Education,* vol. 15, no. 3, Summer 1987, pp. 155-71.

Barr, R., J. Barth, and S. Shermis. *Defining the Social Studies,* Bul 51. Arlington, VA: National Council for the Social Studies, 1977.

Bradley Commission on History in Schools. *Building a History Curriculum: Guidelines for Teaching History in Schools.* Washington, DC: Educational Excellence Network, 1988.

Burrow, Sarah Clayton, and Connie A. Seeds. "Teaching Social Studies in the Primary Grades: Community Living Through an Ongoing Interest in Airplanes," In *The Social Studies in the Elementary School,* 12th Yearbook, William E. Young, ed. Washington, DC: National Council for the Social Studies, 1941, pp. 157-71.

Center for Civic Education. *National Standards for Civics and Government.* Calabasas, CA: Center for Civic Education, 1994.

Cornbleth, C., and D. Waugh. "The Great Speckled Bird: Education Policy in-the-Making," *Educational Researcher,* vol. 22, no. 7, October 1993, pp. 31-37.

Diggins, J. "History Standards Get it Wrong Again," *New York Times,* May 15, 1996, p. A21.

Engle, S. "Decision-Making: The Heart of Social Studies Instruction," *Social Education,* vol. 24, November, 1960, pp. 301-304, 306.

Engle, S., and A. Ochoa. *Education for Democratic Citizenship: Decision Making in the Social Studies.* New York: Teachers College Press, 1988.

Fairbanks, Grace, and Helen Hay Heyl. "Teaching Social Studies in the Primary Grades: Activities Developing Economic Understandings." In *The Social Studies in the Elementary School,* pp. 172-89.

Geography Education Standards Project. *Geography for Life—National Geography Standards, 1994.* Washington, DC: National Geographic Society, 1994.

geoLearning Corporation, P.O. Box 2042, Sheridan, WY 82801.

Hanna, Paul. "The Care and Feeding of Spaceship Earth." Unpublished manuscript, 1975.

Leriche, L. "The Expanding Environments Sequence in Elementary Social Studies," *Theory and Research in Social Education,* vol. 15, no. 3, Summer 1987, pp. 137-54.

Levine, L. *The Opening of the American Mind.* Boston: Beacon Press, 1996.

Levstik, L. "'Any History Is Someone's History'", *Social Education,* vol. 61, no. 1, January 1997, pp. 48-51.

Nash, G., and R. Dunn. "History Standards and Cultural Wars," *Social Education,* vol. 59, no. 1, January 1995, pp. 5-7.

National Center for History in the Schools. *National Standards for History.* Los Angeles, 1996.

National Commission on Social Studies in the Schools. *Charting a Course: Social Studies for the 21st Century.* November 1989.

National Council for the Social Studies. *Expectations of Excellence—Curriculum Standards for Social Studies,* Washington, DC: National Council for the Social Studies, 1994.

National Council on Economic Education, *Voluntary National Content Standards in Economics,* Washington, DC, National Council on Economic Education, 1997.

National Education Goals Panel. *National Education Goals Report—Building a Nation of Learners, 1995.* Washington, DC: Government Printing Office, 1995.

Postman, N., and C. Weingartner. *The School Book.* New York: Delacorte Press, 1973.

Postman, N., and C. Weingartner. *Teaching as a Subversive Activity.* New York: Delacorte Press, 1969.

"State Curriculum Watch: Wisconsin," *History Matters,* vol. 9, no. 4, December 1996, p. 3.

Wesley, Edgar B. "The Nature and Functions of the Social Studies in the Elementary School." In *The Social Studies in the Elementary School,* pp. 47-56.

Chapter Three

THE UNIT
IN SOCIAL STUDIES

When elementary school teachers decide to create their own units, they are agreeing to do more work. If this were the only enticement for creating an original unit, how many people would be interested? Not many—except, perhaps, for the masochists in teaching. So there must be other reasons why people would design and teach their own units.

First of all, designing an original unit is satisfying. Most elementary teachers are creative, more so than they realize. There is a great deal of satisfaction in seeing your ideas and your materials being used successfully. This may sound egotistical, but professional satisfaction is inextricably tied to professional competence. A healthy ego is part of that.

A second reason is that an original unit can be geared directly toward your own students. Student activities and ideas would be written in a manner and at a level that your students could understand and learn from. Available materials and resources are considered while the unit is being developed, not when it is a finished product. Thus, what you have meets the needs and interests of your class and you know it.

Third, most elementary school textbooks lack originality or much creativity. This is an extreme statement, but generally one textbook reads just like another. Take fifth-grade textbooks, all of which cover U.S. history and geography. Every one of them deals with the explorers. Some tell *about* them, and others attempt to humanize them by creating dialogue that ends up sounding artificial. For example, the following textbook passage dramatizes a conversation between Henry Hudson and his crew of half Englishmen and half Dutchmen:

> In the cold northern seas the *Half Moon* was surrounded by towering icebergs. The sailors were frightened. "Turn back!" they cried.
>
> "I must find a passage to Asia," said the captain. "Will you sail west and help me find a northwest passage through America?"
>
> His men agreed. The *Half Moon* changed its course and sailed west across the Atlantic.

Then they all had tea and scones and lived happily ever after! If you believe that desperate, uneducated sailors were soothed by the friendly persuasion of their captain, you have probably read too many social studies textbooks.

In addition to rehashing the same story, most fifth-grade textbooks have the same maps illustrating the growth of the United States through wars and purchases, the same facts and dates highlighted chronologically, and even many of the same pictures. The point is that teachers have gotten used to a certain type of textbook. In spite of their inherent similarities, each book is promoted as having something special, such as a lower reading level, more attention to basic skills, more study skills, better integration, and so on. (Chapter 7 examines textbooks and their criticisms more fully.)

Fourth, most textbooks leave out a great deal of interesting and exciting content. Depending on who is teaching and where, this content could constitute the most thrilling, vivid time in a child's school day. When was the last time that you thought of social studies as thrilling and vivid? To make an analogy between cookies and the curriculum: store-bought cookies are made to appeal to a large number of people, but when you make your own cookies you know you can put more chocolate chips and almonds in them. The same can be said of an individually developed curriculum: the teacher can put more time, effort, and care into its development.

So there are at least four good reasons to put that extra time and effort into designing, developing, and teaching a unit.

DESIGNING A UNIT

Many school districts ask their teachers to work individually or in teams to develop units for the entire school or district. This is usually done during the summer, and the teachers receive extra compensation for it. These units do not focus solely on social studies; they cut across a number of subject areas, with the unit theme as the core around which all subjects are taught. This corresponds to the global view of social studies described in Chapter 13. Thus teachers in all the subject areas would draw from the social studies unit. As advocated by Lavone Hanna and her colleagues (1963), the purpose of the unit was to emphasize socially significant content. This is still an important ideal to strive toward, but it should not act as a deterrent to developing a creative, rewarding unit. Remember that your students will probably forget most of what they have learned by the time they leave school. However, if you provide them the tools to find material and an abiding interest in understanding more, they will continue to grow as learners throughout their lives.

At one time units were designed—ideally or in reality—by the cooperative efforts of a teacher and his or her pupils. As more school districts became interested in units, the district unit became popular and was tailored to fit district guidelines for the curriculum generally and social studies specifically. Some district guidelines are so useless or obscure that they are almost universally ignored, whereas other districts have well thought out and useful criteria for curriculum planning.

A team of teachers can examine district needs, share knowledge of student interests and the community, and arrive at rewarding unit topics. Some teams may work together, while others may divide the task into individual assignments for each unit topic. Strictly speaking, this latter method is not exactly team development, but because it is very common, we will deal with unit development as something of an individual enterprise. After an individual teacher has drafted the unit, the team may evaluate it as a group, assessing content, readability, activities, evaluation, and so on.

Where to Start?

The hardest part of developing a unit is choosing a topic. What will keep students interested for three to six weeks? What can be taught at various reading or maturation levels for a whole class? Equally important, what will keep the teacher's interest? This vital question is often overlooked. The teacher will spend at least six weeks researching and writing the unit, then three to six weeks teaching it. Within a year or two he or she will teach it again. If the unit is not enjoyable to the teacher, that message will come through to the children, and they will mirror the teacher's lack of interest.

Two good places to start are student interest and teacher interest. For example, a common unit taught in grade three is Japan. There are good reasons for this: (1) Japan, a key industrial nation in the world, exports a great number of products to the United States; (2) Japanese-American relations are good; (3) Japan has a rich, accessible history and culture that may strike students as somewhat exotic. The teacher, however, may be "Japaned" to death and more interested in teaching about India, where he or she lived for 16 months while in the Peace Corps. In teaching about India the teacher can provide firsthand information and knowledge, a perspective drawn from research and experience, and an enthusiasm difficult to duplicate. In addition, the same larger objectives considered in studying about Japan can be replicated through the study of India.

Thus a teacher who is having problems selecting a topic should probe his or her interests. Some teachers initially choose topics that they are indifferent about merely to get the decision out of the way. They opt for predictable, pedestrian topics that soon disappoint them. Rather than looking within themselves, they search a social studies textbook for answers. That is why we find some thoroughly dull units on subjects like "The Way West," "Colonial America," "Community Helpers," "Japan," "Transportation," and "Abraham Lincoln," among others. As indicated earlier, the *last* place to look for original ideas is a social studies textbook. Over the years many college students have selected and developed wonderfully creative unit ideas, including topics like "peanut butter and jelly," "gold," "Eskimos," "hats," and "popcorn." The following list of topics shows a range of possible ideas.

pizza	homes	old folks
Egypt	coal mining	kites
the bakery	ice cream	oceans
Jamaica	the Olympics	the calendar
hot-air balloons	puppets	dinosaurs
textures	computers	Panama Canal
careers	wheels	the county fair
photography	flags	pollution
the piano	milk	women's movement
pro football	ballet	cats

Now examine your own interests. Aren't there a number of things you are interested in that would also interest elementary students? If you do wish to use a topic on this list, do not feel that you are a creative failure; the key is developing the unit in your *own* way. Teachers are great borrowers of ideas. Someone once said that we're lucky to have one original thought in our entire lives. Most topics that you decide on have been taught before, but not in quite the same way you are capable of teaching them.

For the most part, the topics listed are specific rather than general. It is a good idea to select a topic that you can build on rather than one that encompasses a veritable universe. Some examples of overly broad units are "the family" (if this is really worth a year of social studies, how can you do justice to it in four weeks?); "American Indians" (all Indians are *not* alike—select a regional group of tribes, or cover one tribe, like the Seminole, the Navaho, the Kwakiutl, or the Nez Perce, in greater depth); and "transportation" (railroads, autos, bicycles, ships, balloons, airplanes, and buses—all in one unit!). The following short guidelines will help you select your topic:

1. Choose something that will interest your students.
2. Choose a topic that will interest you.
3. Choose a topic that is more specific than general.
4. Choose something that allows for coverage of all subject areas, not just social studies.
5. Choose a topic that will not seem to leave some students "out" or to perpetuate stereotypes or discrimination practices.

This latter point may mean that a topic like "Christmas Around the World" may make non-Christians uncomfortable in addition to seemingly promote religious values in violation of the U.S. Constitution. A nonreligious holiday or festival not celebrated by all might serve, however, to help some majority students understand their minority peers better. For example, a unit on Kwanzaa, the African-American holiday created in 1966, might provide an opportunity to view events from a nonmajority perspective and allow students to think about broader issues of culture and power.

BRAINSTORMING

Choosing a topic that allows for coverage of all subject areas often requires further investigation. The handiest way to do this—although not the only way—is through webbing, or linking. This process involves a type of associational brainstorming on paper after selecting a topic. As in most brainstorm sessions, you should not pass judgment on ideas as you proceed, but rather should wait to evaluate all suggestions until after the initial webbing is completed.

The web shown in Figure 3.1 was developed by a college student who chose the Olympics as her unit topic. Note how the ideas are limited in this figure. The web might be different or more expansive if another person proposed the unit. The ideas offered here are good, but certainly not all-inclusive. A web such as this probably could not be done without some prior knowledge of international athletics, athletic competititon, and government support for large scale international events. This illustrates the importance of selecting a topic that interests the developer. Most people act on their interests in some way by reading or researching; a web will look radically different if your topic is of only tangential interest. Webbing is often easier working in pairs with a large sheet of paper. Two people often will stimulate each other's thoughts, and two different perspectives will enhance the breadth of the topic. This arrangement is also likely to be more fun—a word schools should accentuate more.

Once the topic is webbed, the teacher must examine the web with the following thoughts in mind:

1. What areas may be too difficult or esoteric for my students?
2. What areas are similar to previously learned concepts in the curriculum?

Web for a Unit on the Olympics for Grade 3

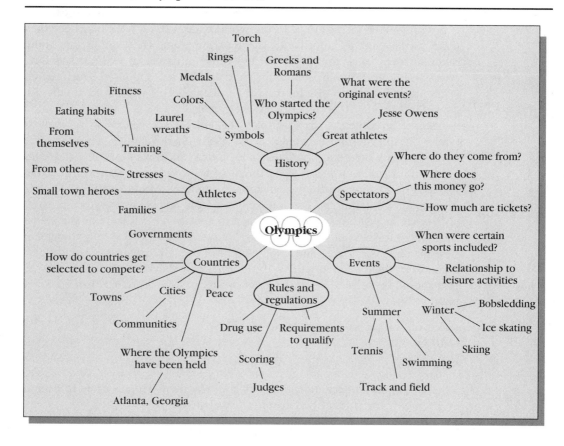

3. Are there parts that will be too difficult to pursue because of physical or spatial demands?
4. What parts threaten to bore me?
5. Can I envision resource persons or field trips relating to parts of this unit?

Answers to these questions should begin to delineate the topic and give some indication about which parts should be accentuated and which avoided and, most important, whether the unit is suitable for *your* classroom of students. If the answer to the latter question is no, drop the unit before you invest any more time in it.

Gathering Material and Research

Just as other students refer to encyclopedias for research data, education students often head for the children's library for data on their topics. Children's books provide a plethora of information written at a clear, understandable level. A comprehensive university or public library is another source of information, providing a variety of data and perspectives for the teacher-researcher.

With greater access available, the world wide web (WWW) may become a more used avenue for information in preparing a unit. There are literally thousands of web pages; the key is to find those most useful without spending hours and hours scanning inappropriate data. The more focused a web search is, the more limited and useful the results will be. This will be more fully discussed in Chapter 10 on technology and media.

Books on athletics, the Olympics, ancient Greece, television, as well as books on specific sports would all be useful in developing a unit on the Olympics; so would such periodicals as *Sports Illustrated, Sport, Track and Field,* and *Runners World.* A department of history or sport science at a university, a travel agent, or the U.S. Olympic Committee would be able to provide geographic, historical, and cultural data to aid the teacher-researcher's pursuit.

It may help the teacher at this stage to specify what it is he or she wants the student to learn about the Olympics, of what import that is, and how it can be evaluated. As research and development of the unit progress, a teacher may reconsider what is important in the unit. Thus behavioral objectives for the unit should be seen as helpful guideposts along the road rather than an exact path to follow.

OBJECTIVES

Some objectives that a unit on the Olympics could address are:

1. Student understanding of how and why the Olympics came to be and how the role of the Olympics has changed.
2. An awareness of a healthy lifestyle that includes exercise, eating a healthy diet, and positive self-esteem.
3. An appreciation of various cultures and diverse lifestyles found throughout the world.
4. The importance of setting goals and having dreams while balancing them within realistic circumstances.
5. How international events such as the Olympics can be instrumental in fostering world peace.
6. Improvement at some athletic endeavor.

These objectives are general. They focus on the unit rather than on specific lessons and deal with all three domains of learning—cognitive, affective, and psychomotor. Briefly, the cognitive domain deals with the pursuit and development of knowledge. The affective domain is concerned with feelings. It is more subjective than the cognitive domain and includes the development of opinions and values. The psychomotor domain includes skilled movement— eye-hand coordination, throwing, playing an instrument. Of the six objectives, 1, 2, and 5 deal with cognition, 3 and 4 deal with affect, and 6 deals with psy-

QUESTIONS FOR A UNIT ON THE OLYMPICS

1. What does the Olympic symbol stand for?
2. Why are they called the Olympics?
3. When did the Olympics begin?
4. Who started the Olympics?
5. Have the same events always been done?
6. What were the original Olympic events?
7. Is there an age limit for the Olympics?
8. Have females always competed?
9. What uniforms were first worn?
10. Why are the Olympics associated with peace?
11. How do athletics help people to interact with one another?
12. How many Olympics can you compete in?
13. When are the Olympics held?
14. Who decides where the Olympics will be held?
15. Who are the greatest Olympic athletes?
16. Did the ancient Greeks have different leisure activities than we do?
17. Why do we still have the Olympics today?
18. Do you think that the Olympics promote world peace? How?
19. Why do more countries compete in the Olympics in each succeeding Olympic Games?
20. How many Olympics have been held and where were they staged?
21. Why do you think that there are opening and closing ceremonies?
22. What is the International Olympic Committee and who selects it?
23. Do you think that traditions like the laurel wreath and the Olympic torch are important? Why?
24. Why have these ancient traditions and symbols lasted for such a long period of time?
25. Why are gold, silver, and bronze medals awarded?
26. What are the Special Olympics?
27. Who makes all the rules for the Olympic events?
28. Why isn't football in the Olympics?
29. How can I get to compete in the Olympics?
30. Can the Olympic torch burn you?

chomotor. This type of ratio may be found in most school activities, although there is no standard formula.

As you research the unit and set objectives, consider what specific questions you might raise with your class. Then try to imagine what specific questions the class might raise with you or with each other. This is not as easy as it sounds, because it requires the teacher-developer to think like a child. After years of repressing childish inclinations and acting like adults, we are asked as adults to think like children. The box above lists some questions based on the

Olympics unit. See if you can identify which questions are intended as teacher generated and which are student generated. Could you provide a few more questions for this unit based on the web shown in Figure 3.1?

Objectives and questions imply certain values and possible skills that might be developed in the unit. These should also be considered during research, remembering again that creating a unit is a process; the unit is constantly being revised as it is taught. Too often teachers develop a unit and feel so attached to what they have created that they are loath to change it, even if their classes are completely mystified about what is transpiring.

One value within the Olympic unit is nationalism. What is one's responsibility to one's country? Authority and power are also values in this unit. Who should decide what events are contested in the Olympic Games and what rules of competition should be followed? How are these things enforced on competing nations and individuals? Could someone else start their own Olympics? What agreements are necessary within and between nations to ensure the success of Olympic competition? Would it be better for individual competitors to participate without regard to national origin? Who might benefit or suffer under such an agreement?

Psychomotor skills would, of course, be developed in such a unit. Other skills that might be included are decision making, writing, interviewing, chronology, place-location, and so on.

CONTENT BACKGROUND

Content background is a useful component of a unit, particularly for teachers who did not develop the unit themselves. The content background should encompass two to three pages of material that is important to the unit and to a teacher's understanding of the unit. Most of the content background addresses unit material that will not be covered with the students. Rather, it is material that was integral to the teacher-developer's understanding of the topic but, because of its complexity or obscurity, is not vital or appropriate for students. This does not mean that individual students in their own pursuit of further knowledge on the topic should be denied this information; it just means that such material may not capture the students' interest. For example, the following background material from a unit on the Olympics is simply too detailed for students, although it is entirely appropriate for the teacher:

> The beginning of today's modern day Olympics started in the late 19th century. The reason why the games started again was due to a Frenchman named Baron Pierre de Coubertin. Coubertin strongly believed in the Greek philosophy that the body as well as the mind must be cared for and improved. Therefore, he tried to revive international athletics and wanted to create another Olympic Games in 1890. In Olympic Games in Ancient Greece, Coubertin referred to athletics as "The free trade of the future . . . on the day when it shall take place among the customs of Europe, the cause of peace shall have received a new and powerful support" (page 12). In this quote he was referring to the beginning of the modern day Olympics. When he started the world

Jim Thorpe, American winner of two gold medals in the pentathalon and the decathalon in the 1912 Olympics.

plan to begin the Olympics again he found that it was not going to be an easy task. However, due to his strong belief in what he thought the Olympic festivities could do for the world as a whole, he persevered and kept pursuing his dream. Finally, on April 6, 1896, the first modern day Olympics was held in Herodis Athens due to Coubertin. In honor of Baron de Coubertin, the official motto adopted at the first Olympic Games quoted him in stating, "The important thing in the Olympic Games is not to win, but to take part; the important thing in life is not the triumph but the struggle, the essential thing is not to have conquered but to have fought well."[1]

This paragraph contains the kind of historical and cultural perspective that a teacher must have in teaching the Olympics unit. The majority of students will not be interested in developing such a perspective, however. The distinction between teacher-exclusive data and student-inclusive data depends on the

---

[1] From Erica Todd's unit on the Olympics.

students involved. Each teacher may include more or less of the content background depending on this factor.

The teacher-researcher should also make sure that the general research reflects the intentions of the unit and that what is planned for the unit is supported by research. For example, one of the goals of a unit on the Amish might be to eliminate the stereotypic views of the Amish and to diminish ethnocentrism generally. Research might show that when Anglo students have been taught about Puerto Ricans, prejudice toward Puerto Ricans has declined and there has been a commensurate drop in prejudice generally. This would fit precisely with the unit on the Amish, since the intention, though not the exact subject, is similar. Do not expect to find your precise objectives reinforced in the research literature; think of the bigger picture of what you want students to gain from the unit.

Research may be done at a large research library or at the teacher's professional library if that library has a good up-to-date collection of professional journals.

Planning Activities

The heart of a unit is what the teacher does with the children on a day-to-day basis. After all, they may not see the bigger picture of the unit until after its completion, if then, so the teacher must think about entertaining and useful activities that link the unit together. Activities should stem from research, prior knowledge, generated questions, the web, or such other sources as newspapers, television, and films. Every magazine a teacher reads, every trip to the store, has the potential for a useful unit activity. The trick is to find this potential and make it educationally useful for the students.

Activities can be generated randomly; order can come later. Describe each activity on a notecard for filing. Descriptors of the activity might be put in the upper right-hand corner for possible use in certain units in one year or in some other unit another year. Sample notecards are shown in Figure 3.2.

For the most part, all one really needs to include in an activities list is a brief one-sentence description of the activity, the time to be allotted, and the materials needed. Any more information will allow little room for creative restructuring by another teacher; any less will raise questions about "how" and "how long."

As mentioned earlier, activities are the heart of the unit, and they should cut across all subject lines. There can never be too many activities, since they will be selected to meet the needs of particular students or classes. Thus a generated list of 40 activities may lead to only 30 classroom adventures. Some teachers may get all their lesson plans directly from the unit idea. Others may decide to keep a separate spelling or math component. Although the latter option is not highly recommended, it demonstrates the flexibility a unit presents to teachers. The following activities for the unit on the Olympics illustrate the breadth of content and the various disciplines that can be covered. Teachers should aim for this kind of broad-based direction in their webs and their research.

FIGURE 3.2
Some Sample Notecards for Filing

Idea: Creative Writing

"What would you do if you won a gold medal?"	**Unit Areas:** Gold
	Values
	Money
	Olympics

Materials: paper and pencil

Time: 30 minutes

Grade Level

3–6

Idea: Research

Find the current price of gold. Give each child a day to report and discuss whether the price has gone up or down and how the price is controlled.	**Unit Areas:** Gold
	Money
	Stock market
	Olympics

Materials: newspapers

Time: 5–10 minutes daily

Grade Level

3–6

Idea: Case Study

The students will discuss whether a community should keep its woods or use the land for a new parking lot. Slides of area will be shown, or site will be visited.	**Unit Areas:** Trees
	Community
	Ecology

Materials: Lecturer, newspapers

Time: 25–30 minutes daily plus out-of-class time

Grade Level

4–6

SOURCE: From a fifth-grade social studies unit on gold by Pamela M. Sieger and a fourth-grade unit on trees by Jeanine Tobacco.

ACTIVITY 1: MAP SKILLS

During this activity the students will develop a better understanding of geography and map skills by locating different countries that regularly compete in the Olympic Games. The teacher will then break the students up into cooperative learning groups and have each group draw the names of five countries from a bowl containing the names of more than 50 countries. After finding the countries on a globe or map the students in each group will determine, using other sources, what the climate of the country would be like and how it might affect the people who live there, particularly those training for the Olympics. Groups later can report to the class orally or prepare written commentary. Materials: Several maps, an atlas, a globe, paper, pencils. Time: 60 minutes.

ACTIVITY 2: A LOOK AT ANCIENT GREEK OLYMPIC EVENTS

This activity is designed to give the students some background of how the Olympics started, what events were included, and how it has changed over the years. Materials: Pictures of events, paper, writing utensils, markers, and crayons. Time: 45 minutes.

ACTIVITY 3: CHOOSING LOCATIONS FOR THE WINTER AND SUMMER GAMES

To begin, the teacher will discuss past locations for the Winter and Summer Olympics. The class will locate those sites on a map or globe and discuss why they might have been chosen for the Winter or Summer Games. Throughout the discussion the teacher may wish to highlight such topics as terrain, temperature, climate, rainfall, population density, tourism, etc. Then the teacher can break the class into groups and have them select a good location for an upcoming Olympiad. Materials: Globes, maps, paper, atlas, writing utensils. Time: 60 minutes.

ACTIVITY 4: ADVERTISING FOR THE CLASSROOM MINI OLYMPICS

By doing this, students will develop an understanding of how advertising works or is intended to work. Students will be taught different advertising techniques that they could use to advertise their own mini Olympics. The finished displays can be placed in the hall during the week that the class has their own classroom mini Olympics. Materials: Advertisements from magazines or newspapers, construction paper, glue, markers, paints, colored pencils. Time: 1–2 hours.

ACTIVITY 5: CHOOSING A GOOD MEAL TO EAT BEFORE COMPETING

This activity focuses on identifying healthy foods. To begin, the teacher may display a chart of the food pyramid and explain what it is as well as how carbohydrates are useful for athletes to eat before competing. After further discussion the students will be able to select items from the "store" that the teacher has set up at the back of the room and explain how the selected items help comprise a good pre-competition meal. Materials: Pretend food items, paper, pencils, markers. Time: 45 minutes.

ACTIVITY 6: SOCIODRAMAS OF TRAUMATIC OLYMPIC MOMENTS

This activity begins with the teacher displaying a few photos that present athletes during moments of obvious stress, fear, sadness, or happiness. The teacher will pick one or two and use each as the impetus for a sociodrama. Materials: Photos. Time: 30 minutes for each sociodrama.

ACTIVITY 7: OLYMPIC EVENT FIELD TRIP

Students will visit some site(s) in their local community where organized events that are seen in the Olympics are taking place. This could be a track meet, a swim meet, a gymnastics meet, a downhill ski competition, or any other event they choose. Upon return the students can discuss the competition, the judging, the rules, and how these relate to the Olympics. Materials: Permission slips, transportation. Time: 2–3 hours.

ACTIVITY 8: MAKING LAUREL WREATHS

The teacher will explain the function of the laurel wreath in previous and current Olympic competitions. A discussion may ensue regarding rewards for competition. Then the teacher will hand out patterns for laurel wreaths for students to cut out and design on their own. These products will be displayed in the classroom. Materials: Wreath patterns, construction paper, markers, paints, glue, scissors. Time: 45 minutes.

ACTIVITY 9: DESIGNING THE OPENING AND CLOSING CEREMONIES

Students will need to be grouped according to individual talents and interests. For example, students who are good at dancing may be in one group, those good at art in another, those who like to sing in another, and those who like to speak in front of the class in another. Each group will design and carry out one part of the ceremonies that would be appropriate for their classroom. Students will be given times limits regarding their section of the ceremonies. The ceremonies will be presented as part of the classroom mini Olympics. Materials: Depends on what children choose to do in their groups. Time: 20–30 minutes a day for four or five consecutive days.

Culminating Activity

The final activity should be planned with care and concern so that the unit ends with an exciting climax. Among the activities that might be planned are a field trip, a display, a show for parents or other students, or a visit by resource persons. One good idea for an Olympic unit is a classroom mini Olympics with one entire day devoted to this. It will consist of an opening ceremony, events, closing ceremony, and reception. The events will be chosen by the class and will include fine arts as well as sports. It would be set up in such a way that everyone will be able to succeed at something whether it is reading a story, dancing, showing a piece of artwork, or participating in a sporting event. It is important that the teacher makes sure that every student gets some time in the "spotlight." The mini Olympics will end with each student's being awarded a medal for something that they did or performed in the mini Olympics. The reception afterward (with parents invited to attend) might also have some ethnic foods from some of the countries that the students investigated.

Over the course of the unit the students would compile their own notebooks, including class notes, quizzes, interviews, group projects, individual projects, and anything collected concerning a project (pamphlets, articles, letters, and the like). At the unit's conclusion the students will have an opportunity to display their notebooks. On this occasion each student will be responsible for a demonstration or explanation to the parents concerning what he or she has learned through the unit. This would be done by individual and group presentations.

Evaluation

A final evaluation of the unit should come from both students *and* teacher. By itself, class performance does not give an accurate assessment of what the teacher actually has accomplished. If a class does not perform well in the teacher's eyes, could it be the teacher who is at fault? Certainly that factor has to be considered, but the teacher should also consider other factors, such as lack of parental support, poor materials available, student disinterest, and other demands on students' lives, like chores at home. Obviously some students will excel in spite of these things, just as some students will do poorly no matter how many advantages they have. The point is that a teacher is only *part* of the success or failure of his or her students—a large part, to be sure, but not all. Thus teachers should not feel that *they* have failed if students do not meet expectations.

It should be remembered that there is a difference between evaluation of the unit content and evaluation of students, though teachers often do these simultaneously. The teacher may decide that some of the unit content is not important enough to teach again and may choose to modify it, but will continue to use the same *student* evaluation techniques with the revised content. Conversely, teachers should not become conceited over the success of their pupils. There is a difference between teaching and learning; both should be assessed. Student evaluations are discussed more fully in Chapter 14.

Teacher evaluations may be conducted by a number of people—peers, supervisors, the teachers themselves, or even by students. Evaluations may be done, using various instruments, during the teaching or afterward.

Peer or supervisory evaluation might be obtained from various instruments that yield different types of data. Two well-known examples are the Flanders Interaction Analysis (Table 3.1) and the Withall Social-Emotional Climate Index (box). Each of these measures assesses a different aspect of behavior in the classroom; using one (or even both) may obscure a broader view of what is happening in the classroom. Thus, to be accurate, evaluation should not be a one-shot experience.

TABLE 3.1
Summary of Categories for Interaction Analysis

TEACHER TALK

Indirect Influence

1. ACCEPTS FEELING Accepts and clarifies the feeling tone of the students in a nonthreatening manner. Feelings may be positive or negative. Predicting or recalling feelings is included.

2. PRAISES OR ENCOURAGES Praises or encourages student action or behavior. Jokes that release tension, but not at the expense of another individual; nodding head or saying "uh huh" or "go on" are included.

3. ACCEPTS OR USES IDEAS OF STUDENTS Clarifying, building, or developing ideas suggested by a student. As teacher brings more of his or her own ideas into play, shift to Category 5.

4. ASKS QUESTIONS Asking a question about content or procedure with the intention that a student answer.

Direct Influence

5. LECTURING Giving facts or opinions about content or procedures; expressing his or her own ideas, asking rhetorical questions.

6. GIVING DIRECTIONS Directions, commands, or orders with which a student is expected to comply.

7. CRITICIZING OR JUSTIFYING AUTHORITY Statements intended to change student behavior from nonacceptable to acceptable pattern; bawling someone out; stating why the teacher is doing what he or she is doing; extreme self-reference.

Student Talk

8. STUDENT TALK—RESPONSE Talk by students in response to teacher. Teacher initiates the contact or solicits student statement.

9. STUDENT TALK—INITIATION Talk by students that they initiate. If calling on student is only to indicate who may talk next, observer must decide whether student wanted to talk. If he or she did, use this category.

10. SILENCE OR CONFUSION Pauses, short periods of silence, and periods of confusion in which communication cannot be understood by the observer.

NOTE: There is no scale implied by these numbers. Each number is classificatory; it designates a particular kind of communication event. To write these numbers down during observation is to enumerate, not to judge a position on a scale.
SOURCE: From *Flanders Interaction Analysis*. Ann Arbor, MI: University of Michigan Press, 1964.

Eisner discusses a number of ways to evaluate in an "artistic manner," using film, videotape, still photography, and tape-recorded interviews of students, among others (187–192). Although some of these devices allow a teacher to evaluate himself or herself, they may be too awkward, inconvenient, or expensive to use. There are cheaper, though less vivid, alternatives. Teacher interviews of students (with or without taping), as discussed above, are one possibility. Teachers may also conduct an informal survey of students either partway through the unit or after its completion. The following questions might be asked:

> **1.** What is the most important thing you feel you have learned from this unit?

WITHALL SOCIAL-EMOTIONAL CLIMATE INDEX

Criteria of Teacher-Statement Categories

1. LEARNING SUPPORTIVE statements or questions.
   These are teacher statements or questions that express agreement with the ideas, actions, or opinions of the learner or that commend or reassure the learning. Agreement is frequently expressed by a monosyllabic response such as "yes," "right," "uh huh," and the like.

2. ACCEPTANT OR CLARIFYING statements or questions.
   These are teacher statements or questions that either
   (a) accept, that is, evidence considerable understanding by the teacher, or
   (b) clarify, that is, restate clearly and succinctly in the teacher's words.

3. PROBLEM-STRUCTURING statements or questions.
   Problem-structuring responses by the teacher offer facts and ideas or opinions to the learner about
   (a) phenomena
   (b) procedures
   in a nonthreatening and objective manner.

4. NEUTRAL statements evidencing no supportive intent.
   These statements are neither teacher sustaining nor learner sustaining nor problem centered. They constitute a small percent-

(continued)

---

2. What activity did you enjoy the most?
3. Is there any other activity related to this unit that you would like to have done?
4. Was there anything that you didn't like about the unit?

Teachers might also keep a personal checklist for preparing their own evaluations. They might ask themselves the following questions:

1. Were the goals and objectives worthwhile? Attainable? Accurately stated?
2. Was my interest in the topic brought out in my teaching?
3. Did my teaching strategies meet my objectives? If not, how could I change the strategies?
4. How could I improve this unit?
5. Did the students enjoy their study and work on the topic? Were they glad when the unit was over, or did some pursue the topic at greater length?
6. Can I relate the concepts in this unit to the next grading period and expand upon what the class has learned?

(continued from previous page)

age of the total teacher responses.

5. DIRECTIVE statements or questions.

These are teacher statements or questions that advise the learner regarding a course of action on his or her future behavior and that narrowly limit the learner's choice or offer no choice. These statements recommend to the learner the facts or procedures that the teacher proffers.

6. REPROVING, DISAPPROVING, OR DISPARAGING statements or questions.

By means of these statements a teacher may express a complete or partial disapproval of the ideas, behavior, and, to him or her,

personality weaknesses of the learner. The teacher's internalized societal values largely enter into these responses.

7. TEACHER-SUPPORTIVE statements or questions.

These are statements or questions in which the teacher refers to herself or himself and expresses a defensive attitude, or refers to present or past interests, activities, or possessions with the purpose of reassuring herself or himself and of confirming her or his position or ideas in the eyes of others. The *dominant intent* of these teacher responses is to *assert,* to *defend,* or to *justify* the teacher.

SOURCE: From John Withall, "Evaluation of Classroom Climate," *Childhood Education,* vol. 45, no. 7, pp. 406–407.

7. Was the unit enjoyable for me?
8. Did I learn any new facts or gain new insights through classwork and discussion?
9. Were the activities varied enough for the students?
10. Were the activities appropriate for the content and suitable for my students?
11. Did I encourage and support student ideas?
12. Were the resource speakers valuable for student learning?
13. Did I involve the parents and communicate with them about various activities?
14. Did I take into consideration the special needs, if any, of my students by adapting the activities, for example, to meet the needs of visually impaired, learning disabled, or handicapped students?

These are not the only questions that teachers might ask themselves, but they should provide some initial ideas for teachers who are evaluating their own work.

Community Resources

For any unit, a teacher should compile a list of community resources. This would include resource personnel who might come into the classroom as well as places in the community that might be appropriate and useful to visit. Such a list will be unique for every unit and community. For a unit on trees, for example, possible resources might include:

- An arboretum to see trees organized for research and viewing
- A state park to see and identify various trees and to hike in the woods
- An arborist to speak on and demonstrate tree trimming and maintenance techniques
- A plant store to see other types of growth
- A bonsaist to demonstrate the ornamental hobby of bonsai
- A wood shop to see the various kinds of wood used in construction
- A furniture factory to see how raw wood is shaped into useful articles
- A paper factory to see how recycled and new paper are made
- A traveler who has slides of various types of forests, particularly temperate or tropical rain forests such as those of Central America, Brazil, Indonesia, or the Pacific Northwest of the United States
- A natural history museum to see how various cultures have used wood to create musical instruments, furnishings, or weapons

Lesson Plans

The exact number of lesson plans per unit will depend on the size of the audience. If the unit is for district-wide use, few plans, or none, might be offered, since experienced teachers would need only suggestions. If the unit is for the individual teacher-developer, more plans could be included, to save time and effort later. Since every teacher draws up lesson plans differently, none are included here. But every lesson plan should have at least a specific learning objective, a description of the activity, materials and time needed, and evaluation procedures.

Bibliography

All units need a good, relatively comprehensive bibliography that gives enough information on each work cited so that other teachers can locate it quickly and easily. The bibliography should include not only books and journal articles but films, filmstrips, tapes, maps, records, and so on. There are different ways to organize a bibliography, but for a unit it may be helpful to have one section for teachers and another for students, and to break each section down by type of material, such as books and articles, films and filmstrips, records and tapes. The works should be alphabetized by author or company name.

You may want to recommend to students that they annotate the most useful sources—that is, make some notes concerning the source. This may be a sentence or as much as a paragraph. (The references at the end of this chapter are annotated as an example.) The purpose in annotating is twofold; it gives another teacher an idea of what the source contains and it reminds the teacher-developer about the source. When examining many works on the same subject, they all seem to run together. Annotations help solve that problem.

Fine-tuning the Unit

Once a unit is completed and typed in more or less final form, it should be examined by a colleague for clarity, understanding, and utility. Part of being a professional teacher is being able to critique educational material. One should not take professional comments personally, but should use them to improve the unit. Once the unit seems satisfactory to the teacher-developer and selected critics, the planning and teaching part of the unit begins. A unit will probably be taught a little differently each time it is used, due to differences in the student audience, increased teacher knowledge, and environmental changes. If that growth is allowed to occur naturally, the unit should continue to provide fun and pleasure for the teacher as well as the students. If a unit becomes stale to the teacher, however, it is time to put it away for a while, returning to it only when the teacher can bring renewed enthusiasm and vitality to it.

QUESTIONS AND ACTIVITIES

1. Examine the units of a local teacher or school district. What ones would you like to teach? What modifications would you consider to make the units more personally yours?

2. Make a list of subjects that you might like to know more about. Which would be appropriate for an elementary school unit?

3. Think of some current student interests in music, sports, arts, or science. Do any lend themselves to an interesting unit development?

4. Aside from extra time, what are the drawbacks to developing your own unit? How can you overcome them?

5. Explore the special collections of a local or university library. What ideas for a unit do they stimulate?

6. Use the Withall or Flanders instrument in a college classroom and an elementary classroom. Do you see differences or trends that surprise you?

7. What current issues have changed dramatically in the last year or two? What unit topics might be developed around these global or national changes?

REFERENCES

Eisner, Elliot W. *The Educational Imagination.* 3rd ed. New York: Macmillan, 1994. Intended for graduate courses, this book is so well written and clear that undergraduates can enjoy it as well. Eisner sees much of teaching as an artistic enterprise.

Hanna, Lavone A., Gladys L. Potter, and Neva Hagaman. *Unit Teaching in the Elementary School.* New York: Holt, Rinehart and Winston, 1963. Originally published in 1955. A classic work with a reconstructionist approach to schools in society. The background is dated, but the philosophical tenets are still very appropriate.

Todd, Erica. "Olympics Unit." Unpublished manuscript, 1995.

PART II

Kids Are People, Too

Chapter Four

RECOGNIZING VALUES

There is probably no issue that has aroused school critics more over the past 25 years than the teaching of or about values. And there is probably no issue that has been more misunderstood.

Teaching and values interlock, in the sense that all teaching reflects *someone's* values. Thus it is impossible to teach a valueless curriculum in a valueless classroom. Students, teachers, and parents need to recognize and acknowledge this. But *whose* values will be represented in the classroom? This chapter will examine what values are and where they come from in order to justify teaching about them.

The first part of the chapter will look at different definitions of values to clarify what the term means to different people. Next, the chapter will attempt to show the extent of value influences on our lives in the media, at home, in government, and in religious traditions. Similarly, values are presented in the classroom through textbooks, teachers, and school regulations.

With this background, the chapter will present three major concerns that evolve from the teaching of values: value clarification, character education, and moral development and reasoning. Incorporated in this discussion are the criticisms and strategies of value theoreticians and practitioners like Comte, Dewey, Piaget, Raths, Simon, Kohlberg, Gilligan, and Palomeres.

WHAT ARE VALUES?

Values are abstractions; they exist in our minds and cannot be quantified or observed. We can observe actions that are taken based on valued beliefs, but the values themselves remain abstractions. Values represent people's standards regarding worth, taste, beauty, prestige, efficiency, and action. Some of these standards are bound by societal convention, some by law, and some by personal belief.

According to Rokeach (1968), a value is "a standard employed to influence attitudes and actions of at least some others—our children's, for example" (60). Values have certain characteristics, says Rokeach. They are enduring, they are beliefs, and they refer to either a mode of conduct (instrumental values) or an end state of existence (terminal values). Instrumental values are divided into two groups: moral values, which refer mainly to modes of behavior and which arouse pangs of conscience or feelings of guilt for wrongdoing, like behaving dishonestly, and competence values, which have a personal focus whose violation leads to shame about personal inadequacy. Being logical or imaginative are two examples of competence values. Terminal values are either self-centered or society-centered. An example of the former is peace of mind, while world peace is an example of the latter. A value, then, is a conception of something that is personally or socially preferable (Rokeach, 1973).

Different people value different things, and different people may value the *same* thing quite differently. Most people value human life, but some may value human dignity above their own lives, while others may see the continuation of life as more important. A person's values are acquired, not genetically transferred.

The first place we acquire values is at home, within our own families. From infancy one learns certain standards held by one's family, though they may not immediately be acquired. A baby's throwing food and rubbing food in his or her hair, for example, are discouraged in most families. Gentle reminders eventually may change to more severe parental chastisement until these activities no longer occur—except occasionally on college campuses.

Besides table manners, families teach their children values about getting along with others, religion, schooling, money and material goods, loving, and careers, among other things. Just because one's family values something, however, does not necessarily mean that an individual will value things in the same manner or order of preference. Besides the family, many other institutions in-

Adolescents and children often dress in a similar fashion due to the influence of their peers.

fluence people's values and may even lead them to choose values antithetical to those of their parents. This may cause family differences or rifts or may have little effect, depending on what the values are and to what extent they differ from those of one's parents.

Friends and peers also greatly influence one's values. A teenager's choice of clothing or movies is much more likely to be influenced by his or her friends than by parents. Peer influences, among others, may ultimately lead to what often is referred to as a generation gap, whereby one generation reflects values that are markedly different from or at odds with the values of an older or younger generation. During the 1960s and early 1970s, for example, the war in Vietnam polarized generational feelings to a pronounced degree. (This is a generalization, of course, as many people of different generations do share the same attitudes.)

The school is seen as an inculcator of values in the rules it sets and administers, the grades it gives, and the practices of teachers and administrators. Ideally, the values set in school and in the home should dovetail. Problems arise, however, when the school supports values antithetical to those of the family or when the school fails to support certain family values. A simple example of consonant values is theft; this is unlikely to be condoned at home or in school. So it is with most of our laws.

A law that might not receive total home support, however, is the one specifying 180 days or more of mandatory schooling per year. Some families may not value schooling and may even support a student's lack of interest in school. Or some families may hold students out of school in order to do work at home or elsewhere. While this does not necessarily indicate a lack of support for schooling, it indicates that something else is valued more highly.

At one time values were seen as the province of three sectors of society that reinforced one another—home, school, and religion. This is simply not the case any longer. Religion still influences values, but declining religious membership means that fewer people feel its direct influence. This has been compensated for by an increasing number of vocal religious zealots whose fervor has made the values of their churches more prominent.

The United States, however, has one of the largest percentages of active participants in formal religious worship of any nation. Many countries have higher percentages of their citizens who consider themselves members of a particular religion. For example over 85% of Norwegians call themselves members of the Norwegian Lutheran Church, but on any given Sunday fewer than 15% of them attend religious services. (Exceptions are major holidays like Christmas or Easter). Thus, the United States, despite a lower declared percentage of religious followers, is probably one of the most religious nations in the world and, judging by those who declared themselves unchurched, also one of the most nonreligious. Table 4.1 illustrates this paradox.

Over the past 200 years the media have had a strong influence on people's values. Thomas Paine's *Common Sense* tract (1776) is an early example of media values that influenced populace action. Today the influence of television is the source of much debate. What should television shows be allowed to say, to show? What checks should there be on Saturday morning commercials aimed at young children? How far should the "fairness doctrine" extend concerning presidential speeches and statements? Is television too violent, and if so, what should be done about it? Media manipulation has grown far more sophisticated over the past 10 years, and the debate continues over what, if anything, to do about it.

Societal values, as reflected in our laws and customs, may also conflict with certain family values. For example, in most states schooling is mandatory until a child is around the age of 16. However, most Amish people will send their children to school only until they complete the eighth grade. In a court case, the state of Indiana exempted the Amish from its mandatory school law on the grounds of religious freedom. Where does that freedom end? What laws, if any, can be violated in the name of religious freedom? For the most part, this is decided by the courts on a case-by-case basis.

These kinds of questions place values education as an integral part of citizenship education. Farmer asserts that "students, as the future voters and leaders, need a values education to learn how to identify and rationally discuss the values in conflict in contemporary issues." (71)

TABLE 4.1

Proportions of Various Types of Church Members and Unchurched People in 1990 by Country

CORE OR MODAL MEMBER		MARGINAL MEMBER	UNCHURCHED
United States	54	23	23
Canada	39	35	26
Norway	12	78	10
Iceland	9	89	2
Sweden	10	71	19
West Germany	34	56	11
France	17	45	39
Denmark	10	81	8
Great Britain	22	35	42
Italy	52	33	15
Belgium	30	38	32
Netherlands	29	21	49
Spain	43	44	13
Ireland	87	9	4
Northern Ireland	67	23	10
Portugal	41	32	28

SOURCE: Loek Halman and Ruud de Moor, "Religion, Churches and Moral Values," in P. Ester, L. Halman, and R. de Moor, eds., *The Individualizing Society: Value Change in Europe and North America.* Tilburg, The Netherlands: Tilburg University, 1994.

A CALL FOR UNIVERSAL VALUES RECOGNITION: CHARACTER EDUCATION

There have been increasing calls for a recognition of universal human values, not just in schools, but across society. In the 1980s and through the 1990s a movement called character education has grown nationwide. This is not the first time schools have been called upon to respond to what has been perceived by some as morally reprehensible actions within American society. In the 1920s a similar call was made and "then, as now, character education was seen as the way to produce socially responsible behavior." (Lockwood, 246)

Various approaches and documents have been generated by character educators in the 1990s. One group, at the Center for the Advancement of Ethics and Character at Boston University, issued a "Character Education Manifesto" that offered seven guiding principles they felt "ought to be at the heart of this educational reform" (that is, character education). Another group called The Character Education Partnership proffers "Eleven Principles of Effective Character Education." Other groups have offered similar statements of values and virtues to be instilled in students such as honesty, courage, respect, tolerance, etc. All of these are admirable values to strive toward, but unfortunately "character education has had no systematic effect on behavior." (Lockwood, 247) Thus, it is not the panacea that will necessarily reduce drug and alcohol abuse in children, foster increased attendance in school, or discourage vandalism. It would be nice if there were such a simple solution, but the problems are much more complex.

It seems clear that in order to foster better moral behavior some common elements are necessary. One is the need for parental involvement with the schools in improving student behavior. Another is promoting discussion of competing values so that the complexity of factors can be presented. It is presumed that working with others in a cooperative manner will reap dividends in better student behavior, but that has not been conclusively demonstrated.

Nevertheless, character education has become a common "buzzword" as schools seek to reform education in the late 1990s. A Character Education Partnership, a nonprofit, nonpartisan organization of educators, business people, faith community leaders, and others who seek to reduce negative student behavior, improve academic performance, and prepare young people to be responsible citizens, was formed in the early 1990s.[1]

Service learning is seen as character education applied. Character education is very appealing because it seems to cut across all ethnic and cultural lines and focus on universal human values. Yet values need to be learned in a context, not in a simplistic, didactic fashion. The problem of conflicting values, both of them virtuous, is far too complex to be fit into a simple list of positive values. Still, as a teacher, one can start by modeling values, not just promoting them.

Teaching about Values

Why teach about values? Wouldn't it be easier to ignore such a controversial topic, especially if one is a young, untenured teacher hoping for a contract renewal? Inevitably, no. As we mentioned in our introduction, values cannot be separated from content and action. A highly respected panel of educators has urged the inclusion of moral education in school, in partnership with the community, to create supportive, morally mature citizens (ASCD, 1988).

The decision to avoid all talk about values is itself a value decision. Most parents do not dismiss values education as godless or communist propaganda. The trick is to get values out in the open before they become a source of controversy. This comes with being an initiatory teacher, not a reactive one.

Parents need to recognize that schools will inevitably teach values in most areas. By sharing that dilemma with parents, teachers should be able to get parents to support teachers' educational judgments. Most parents will listen if approached. To illustrate some of the many values beyond a teacher's control, we

---

[1] Information on this partnership can be obtained from the Association for Supervision and Curriculum Development, Alexandria, VA 22314-1453.

will consider some ideas from a randomly selected fifth-grade textbook and from American schools in general. The following discussion should not be interpreted as a critique of a particular book, but rather as a critique of many textbooks of this type.

First, an overview of content choices should be considered. The material that a textbook does *not* contain is as important in reflecting values as what it includes. Obviously, a 500-page textbook on the Americas cannot cover all the history and geography of the United States, Canada, Latin America, and the Caribbean. The Civil War, for instance, has been the topic of two- and three-volume works. Undoubtedly a 500-page book will omit quite a bit of social science information. The authors and editors must use *their* values to determine initially what topics will be mentioned, let alone discussed in depth.

Thus a textbook is value laden from its inception, influenced by the authors' values, by what has been presented traditionally, and, to some extent, by the desires of teachers in reviewing or using materials.

In the typical fifth-grade social studies textbook we have chosen, the treatment of Native-American peoples is curt, solicitous, and hardly evenhanded. The book often refers to all Native Americans as Indians, implying that this is what they should be called, and the depiction of the life of Native Americans before the Europeans arrived is overly romanticized. The text frequently omits the recognition of many Native American groups, particularly the hundreds of small native groups with unique cultures and languages. The great variety among Native Americans is not mentioned anywhere.

Throughout the remainder of the book, Native Americans are either portrayed as "noble savages" aiding the Europeans (who are beyond reform) or as vicious threats to the Europeans who had to secure the land. The Trail of Tears is mentioned in passing, but unsympathetically; the loss of Oklahoma "Indian Territory" is blithely presented as the large area we now call Oklahoma that the U.S. government bought from the Indians. Nowhere is it said that the price for the land was outrageously low or that the Native Americans had no choice but to sell.

Again, the purpose here is *not* to condemn this approach, but to use it as evidence of the larger problem of textbook values. These values are not applied just to ethnic group members. Reading through the text, we find a subhead that describes the development of the Constitution as "A Wise Plan of Government." We would probably agree with that, but the word is heavily value laden. How can a student discuss any problems arising from the U.S. Constitution after reading that it is a wise plan of government?

Other areas of the book either unduly value something or fail to mention different, related values. The growth of tobacco as a cash crop, for example, is not augmented by discussion of the enormous government subsidies for tobacco growing or of the great health hazards for which tobacco is responsible. The story of Texas fails to mention the Treaty of Guadalupe Hidalgo, which is still a sensitive issue with Mexicans. The story of Oklahoma as a state is two paragraphs long; obviously some factual data have been omitted. A short specialty piece on Los Angeles glorifies the removal of water from north of San

Francisco in order for Los Angeles to have water. To southern Californians this may have seemed like a good idea; to northern Californians and environmentalists such water manipulation is anathema.

Any textbook, then, is loaded with values, so that even a brief assessment of it will cause them to jump out at the reader. Does that mean these texts should be discarded? No, but perhaps they should be augmented to provide a more balanced representation of the values of different groups.

It is not only textbooks that communicate values; curriculum guides and the overall content in all subject areas are also value laden. Both teachers and students should learn to recognize and appraise values statements.

School and Values

Historically schools have been transmitters of values. During colonial times these values were more blatant, in part because the United States had a more homogeneous populace. The *New England Primer* and the *McGuffey Readers* professed obvious values in their selections. The biblical quotations that appeared throughout the *Primer* today would violate the separation of church and state (see box on p. 101).

Even when the *McGuffey Readers* surpassed the *New England Primer* in popularity, the old values remained, although they were presented more subtly. As these values became more entrenched, a hidden curriculum emerged that was reinforced in textbooks and teaching. Values like loyalty to one's country and honesty are embedded in school texts and classrooms. These values inspire no animosity among us, but we are uncomfortable with the subrosa manner of introducing them.

Schools also project certain educational values; some of these are educationally sound and some are not. They include the value of silence in order to learn, the value of waiting one's turn, the value of doing one's own work, the value of schooling, the value of accepting authority, and the value of the printed word.

Society reinforces most of these as customs or laws, with commensurate reinforcement on television and in church. Values conflicts still arise, however, as in some police shows or in many churches' views on abortion and the law.

Clarifying Values

Identifying values is important. Many times words like *should, ought, think, feel, better, seems,* and so on can alert one to an upcoming values statement. It is equally important for students to clarify their own values in order to determine what it is that they feel most strongly about. Raths, Harmin, and Simon have been most closely identified with the value-clarification process. Their approach is based on the following four key elements (4–5):

THE NEW ENGLAND PRIMER

Between 1690 and 1886 the *New England Primer* was used to teach millions of schoolchildren to read throughout the colonies and, subsequently, the United States. According to one conservative estimate, the *Primer* sold an average of 20,000 copies annually from 1700 to 1850, putting more than three million copies into circulation.

The *Primer* was designed to teach schoolchildren more than reading, however: they were to learn the proper worship of God. Thus the *Primer* did not present just the alphabet and words of various syllables. The words had moral messages that were reinforced in other readings and in society. Words like *glory, bewitching, drunkenness, godliness, holiness, benevolence, humility, fornication,* and *admiration* had clear moral associations. So, too, did the rhymed alphabet section, which included statements like "A—In Adam's fall, We sinned all," "J—Jesus did die for thee and I," and "T—Time cuts down all, both great and small."

The author of the alphabet verses is unknown, and no previous examples of these verses have been found. Following the rhymed alphabet came sections that included "The Lord's Prayer," "The Creed," "The Ten Commandments," "The Duty of Children Toward Their Parents," "The Names and Order of the Books of the Old and New Testament," and "The Catechism." In the schools of New England, children were drilled in the catechism constantly, and ministers like Cotton Mather advised mothers to catechize their children every day.

The *Primer* eventually lost its place in the schools to more popular, less sacred primers, which retained messages of morality but without specific religious guidance. For more on the *Primer's* history, see *The New England Primer—A History of Its Origins and Development,* edited by P. L. Ford (New York: Teachers College Press, 1962).

1. A focus on life (particularly one's own life)
2. An acceptance of what is (in order to view others' values nonjudgmentally)
3. Further reflection on values beyond mere acceptance
4. A nourishment of personal powers, that is, the different possibilities of thoughtful self-direction

To Raths and his colleagues, valuing is a process, one that must be practiced and shaped in order for students to distinguish values clearly. The process has three steps: choosing, prizing, and acting. Seven criteria within this process can be used to indicate the real depth of a value (27–28):

1. Choosing freely
2. Choosing from viable alternatives

Antiwar sentiments conflict with the values of people in the armed forces. What other values are alluded to in this picture?

3. Choosing after thoughtful consideration of the consequences of each alternative
4. Prizing and cherishing
5. Affirming the value
6. Acting upon choices
7. Repeatedly acting in a persistent manner, in some pattern

Three sources of content are especially suited to clarifying thought. First, there are value indicators, certain aspects of one's life that indicate one's values, including goals, aspirations, attitudes, interests, feelings, beliefs, activities, and worries. Second, there are personal issues that we all face and that often complicate our lives—questions about marriage, money, and loyalty, for example. In adolescents these might be questions of love, friendship, sexuality, and careers. For young children, questions of fear, desire, acceptance, and embarrassment are major concerns. Third, there are social issues—cooperation, moral conduct, race relations, rules of law, war and peace, and individual civil rights (Raths et al, 39-40).

To clarify values, teachers and students must adopt a mood of acceptance. According to Raths and his coworkers (48), the basic sequence of the value-clarifying process is often as follows:

1. Attention is focused on an issue in life. This may be a "value indicator" or a more general life issue like working on homework together or a larger issue like nuclear disarmament.

2. Acceptance of students is communicated. This may come from teacher actions like smiles, head nods, and so on or from direct teacher verbalizations—"Yes, I can understand how you feel," or some other reflective listening technique.

3. An invitation is offered to reflect further on choices, prizings, and actions. This encourages in- and out-of-school thought-utilizing skills fostered in the process of valuing.

The value-clarification process has proved quite popular with teachers. Raths and his colleagues claim that they have achieved very positive results with students, who become "less apathetic, less conforming, less flighty, . . . less over-dissenting, . . . more zestful and energetic, more critical in their thinking, and . . . more likely to follow through on decisions." (Shaver and Strong, 118) Criticisms also abound and will be examined later in this chapter.

At this point, it might be "clarifying" to illustrate a few value-clarification activities. Two of these activities were developed by Raths or one of his colleagues; the Magic Circle is a product of Palomeres and Ball and reflects many of Raths's ideas.

ACTIVITY 1: TWENTY THINGS

This is one of many variations on the values list. The answers provided may give purpose and direction to our lives, although this simple exercise may not illustrate anything of that nature.

Objectives: The purpose of the activity is to give students a chance to see what they think they value and what patterns there are, or are not, in what they value. Of course, how one feels at a particular time will have a great effect on the results, which could be radically different a year later.

Procedure: Ask students to list 20 things that they really like to do. (Fewer items could be listed if time or the age of the children is a limiting factor.) The list is to be private, so the students need not worry about spelling, abbreviations, or potentially embarrassing comments. Teachers should emphasize and protect this right to privacy, unless the students wish to share their lists with others.

After making the list, have students make six columns to the right of their activities. The number of columns could vary, again depending on allotted time, age, and maturity of students. Head the columns as follows:

($) Check those items on your list that require more than one dollar to do. Do not count initial outlay. For example, you may already have a swimming pool in your yard and therefore do not have to spend money to go swimming.

(A) Check those items that you prefer to do alone. For example, some things *must* be done alone, like writing, and others, like hiking, *might* be done alone.

(F) Check those items that you prefer to do with a family member—parent, sibling, spouse, or child.

(S) Check any items that a good, close friend might smile or chuckle at. For example, you might say that you love to watch the sun rise, yet your close friend knows how difficult it is for you to wake up at all, let alone at dawn.

(L) Check any items that you took formal lessons in. This does not include reading, but something beyond general school activity, like music lessons, quilting, tennis, karate, or skydiving.

(6) Check any items that you have or have not done for the past six months.

These headings are most appropriate for teenagers and above, but they could be easily modified for young children. For example, (F) could be activities they do with friends, (W) could be things they do in winter, (M) could be things involving machines—televisions, stereos, video games, and so on.

A number of follow-up activities are possible. For example, students could write what they learned from examining their lists. They could discuss patterns in their lists that surprised them. This may get them to put into words notions about what they do, what they wish they did, and what they think they do. Other variations are possible, limited only by the imaginations of teacher and student.

ACTIVITY 2: THE COAT OF ARMS

The Coat of Arms exercise has been used for a number of value-clarification purposes.

Procedure: Draw on the board a coat of arms like that shown in Figure 4.1. Ask students to copy it on a large piece of paper (a newsprint roll would be useful).

At this point, the teacher has various options. The coat of arms could be used to represent one's talents and aspirations. Students could draw things in the various numbered areas to represent their ideas or ideals. For example, students could:

1. Draw things that represent what they are good at doing
2. Draw things that represent what they hold as a solid value
3. Draw things that they wish they were good at doing
4. Draw things that represent a strong family value
5. Write three words that other people use to describe them (physical, intellectual, spiritual, and so on)

These coats of arms could then be hung on the wall for other students to peruse. The names of students could be attached, or the teacher could ask students to guess which coat of arms was made by which student.

Many variations on this activity could be invented, depending on the age and maturity of a class and the interests of the teacher. The exercise allows students to present some of their values in a form both expressible and understandable.

ACTIVITY 3: THE MAGIC CIRCLE

The Human Development Program of Uvaldo Palomares and Gerry Ball addresses the development of mental and emotional health through a wide variety of structured experien-

FIGURE 4.1
Drawing to Accompany Coat of Arms Activity

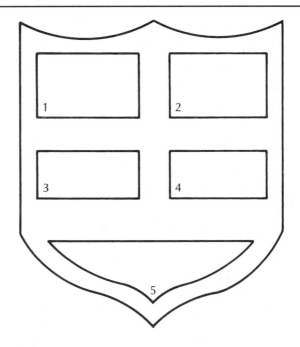

tial learning activities. It is often referred to as the Magic Circle Program because it features a process model called the magic circle.

Objectives: There are many Human Development Programs, all of which derive from an eclectic theoretical base comprised of philosophical, psychological, and sociological principles.[2] These principles have been summarized in developmental terms as three vital, overlapping realms of human development: awareness, social interaction, and mastery. Each Human Development Program provides a carefully sequenced curriculum to allow teachers or leaders to offer experiences to students that will increase (1) their understanding of their own feelings, thoughts, and behavior and those of others; (2) their ability to interact with others effectively and empathetically; and (3) their self-confidence.

As the core activity of all of the Human Development Programs, the magic circle is a high-quality communication experience. It is in itself a structured human environment, a safe time and place for learning with others about life. The content of each magic circle is unique because each has its own area of focus (topic). The process, however, which is described here in some detail, is always the same.

Procedure: A magic circle begins when a group of people (in a classroom, home, church, community center, or other place) sit down in a circle so that each person is able to see the others easily. The leader of the session greets each individual, conveying a feeling of

---

[2] This theoretical framework is set forth in *Grounds for Growth: The Human Development Program's Comprehensive Theory,* by Palomares and Ball. It is available from Palomares and Associates, P.O. Box 1577, Spring Valley, CA 92077.

MAGIC CIRCLE GROUND RULES

1. BRING YOURSELF TO THE CIRCLE AND NOTHING ELSE.
2. EVERYONE GETS A TURN TO SHARE, INCLUDING THE LEADER.
3. YOU CAN SKIP YOUR TURN IF YOU WISH.
4. LISTEN TO THE PERSON WHO IS SHARING.
5. THE TIME IS SHARED EQUALLY.
6. THERE ARE NO INTERRUPTIONS, PROBING, PUT-DOWNS, OR GOSSIP.
7. STAY IN YOUR OWN SPACE.

1. *Bring yourself to the circle and nothing else.* This rule asks that circle members not bring things with them to the circle. All they need is themselves and what's in their minds and hearts. They do not need things like books, pencils, etc., that could distract them and others while the leader is trying to keep everyone's attention.
2. *Everyone gets a turn to share, including the leader.* This ground rule assures everyone a turn to speak to the topic including the leader, and lets everyone know, *"we are equals here."*
3. *You can skip your turn if you wish.* Participants are free to choose for themselves whether or not to speak to the topic. Privacy is honored; there is no pressure. To be a valuable Magic Circle member you don't have to talk—just being there is all it takes. Sometimes people prefer to contribute by simply listening.

4. *Listen to the person who is sharing.* Participants will be listened to when they speak and are expected to listen when others are taking their turns. When people listen and *really hear* others they do it with acceptance. This means that the circle members listen to each other without making judgments.
5. *The time is shared equally.* This ground rule asks circle members to be aware of the time when they are speaking to the topic. It's a positive way of saying *"Please don't talk too long when it's your turn."* This is an important ground rule because it helps to prevent any single person from dominating the circle while others get tired and restless. Dominators tend to consume available time very quickly so that other members may not get their turns. Sometimes it helps if the leader lets participants know how long they will have to speak.
6. *There are no interruptions, probing, put-downs, or gossip.* This rule guarantees safety in the Magic Circle. If it is violated, the circle becomes unsafe and the leader must take action. It is often helpful for the leader to discuss these unacceptable behaviors with circle members prior to the first Magic Circle and periodically thereafter.

(continued)

(continued from previous page)

7. *Stay in your own space.* This ground rule asks circle members not to bump into one another or distract each other physically. Adults and teenagers usually don't engage in these behaviors, but at times children do.

After the circle members indicate to the leader that they are committed to the ground rules, the leader announces the topic for the session. (Sample topics are *"My Favorite Place," "Looking Back on a Decision I Made,"* and *"How I Helped Someone Who Needed and Wanted My Help."*) A one- to two-minute elaboration of the topic follows in which the leader provides examples and possibly mentions the topic's sequential relationship to prior topics. It is also common practice at this time for the leader to assure group members that they don't need to worry about giving "wrong answers." The leader may explain, *"All responses to the topic that don't hurt or embarrass anyone are acceptable."* Then the leader re-states the topic and provides a brief period of silence during which circle members may revive and ponder their own related memories.

After about a half minute the leader breaks the silence by inviting the participants to voluntarily share their responses to the topic one at a time. Verbal interaction follows as participants tell the group about experiences that relate to the topic. Feelings, thoughts, sensations and intuitions are commonly expressed. Most of the circle time (three to fifteen minutes) is devoted to the participation phase because of its central importance.

During this time the leader assumes a dual role—that of leader and participant. The leader makes sure that everyone who wishes to speak is given the opportunity while simultaneously enforcing the ground rules as necessary. The leader may also take a turn to speak to the topic.

When everyone who wishes to speak has done so, the leader may conduct an optional review lasting from one to three minutes. In this process individual participants restate to other participants the main points they heard them make when addressing the topic. Circle members take turns delivering this feedback until everyone who spoke to the topic has been reviewed-to by another participant. By reviewing in this manner, participants meet one another's needs for giving and receiving attention and acceptance. They are also personally reinforced for their ability to listen to others.

Following the review (if one is conducted), the leader introduces the next phase of the circle session which may last as little as one minute or as many as five. This phase, called the cognitive summary (or simply the summary), represents a transition to the intellectual mode, and allows participants to reflect on and express learnings gained from the session. The leader now encourages participants to combine cognitive abilities with affective experiencing, asking them such questions, as *"Did you notice any similarities in the things we told about in this Magic Circle?"* During this time participants are given the opportunity to crystalize learnings and to understand the relevance of the discussion to their daily lives.

(continued)

(continued from previous page)

When the cognitive summary has reached natural closure the leader terminates the session. The leader thanks the participants for *"being part of the Magic Circle,"* and states that it has ended. The leader may announce the topic for the next Magic Circle, adding a word or two about its sequential relationship to the topic just discussed.

SOURCE: Reprinted from U. Palomares and G. Ball. *Grounds for Growth: The Human Development Program's Comprehensive Theory.* La Mesa, CA: Human Development Training Institute, Inc., 1969.

enthusiasm blended with seriousness. This initial phase of the circle, commonly referred to as "setting the tone," usually lasts about a minute.

When everyone appears to be comfortable, the leader takes a minute or two to call the group's attention to the ground rules for the magic circle. These rules assure participants that their safety and security needs will be met. They also remind participants that they will be expected to assume responsibility for the safety needs of the other participants. The ground rules for the magic circle are given in the box on pages 106–108.

ACTIVITY 4: THE PUBLIC INTERVIEW

One of the most useful and most challenging values activities is the public interview. It can be very rewarding for individual students, the class, and the teacher, but the decision to do a public interview must be made with extreme care.

There are a number of risks involved. Individual students may say something about themselves that they wished to remain hidden. Even if it seems like a minor revelation, a student may be very disquieted by such a "slip." A student may say something that leads other students to ridicule him or her. This, of course, could be devastating for the student and, ultimately, for the teacher also.

Thus it should be obvious that the decision to do a public interview should not be taken lightly. Why bother, one might ask, considering the risks? Because the activity can be a tremendous ego boost for students who feel that they are ignored or not listened to (that's most students!). It can also lead to useful, forthright discussion among the entire class. The procedure is relatively simple. Initially, the teacher (and in later interviews, the students) selects a topic and asks for volunteers to be interviewed about their views or experiences regarding the topic. Interviews might last five to 10 minutes or as long as 30 minutes if interest does not wane. The subject being interviewed can respond "I pass" to any question and may, if this rule is agreed upon, ask a question of the interviewer. A teacher might modify this procedure by allowing another student to ask a question of the interviewee.

The rules should be clear to all students and the structure consistent. This allows for some psychological safeguards for the interviewee. Value judgments, moralizing, or taking issue with the student being interviewed should not be allowed in this activity. Acknowledgment of answers is sufficient. This is not the only way to address an issue, and the public interview should not be used as such.

Raths and colleagues note that "public interviews are open dialogues built around a student's interests, activities, ideas or feelings." (174) They may focus on a particular topic or issue. Students enjoy talking openly if they are sure that it will not hurt them. Usually the interviewee picks the topic, but sometimes the interviewer may be allowed to do so.

PIAGET'S STAGES OF DEVELOPMENT

Many educational psychologists believe that Piaget's stages of learning and intelligence are both valid and applicable to teaching and learning in school. Jean Piaget was born in the Swiss city of Neuchatel in 1896. He received a Ph.D. in 1918 in biology, but after working in the early 1920s in Paris at the laboratories of the late Alfred Binet, the originator of modern intelligence tests, Piaget began his own studies of child development and learning. Until his death in 1980 Piaget carried on far-ranging research on intelligence and children. The following table* summarizes some of Piaget's theories on childhood development.

Sensory Motor Period (first 2 years)

Stage I	(0–1 month)	Complete egocentrism
Stage II	(1–4 months)	Primitive reflexes leading to new response patterns
Stage III	(4–8 months)	Coordinated to response patterns
Stage IV	(8–12 months)	More complex coordination of behavior patterns; emergence of anticipatory and intentional behavior
Stage V	(12–18 months)	Variance of familiar behavior patterns
Stage VI	(11/2–2 years)	Internalization of sensory-motor behavior patterns

Preoperational Period (2 to 7 years)

Preconceptual Stage (2–4 years): development of perceptual constancy and of representation through drawings, language, dreams, and symbolic play.

Preceptual or Intuitive Stage (4–7 years): prelogical reasoning appears, based on perceptual appearances untempered by reversibility. Trial and error may lead to intuitive discovery of correct relationships.

Concrete Operational Period (7 to 11 years)

Characterized by thought that is logical and reversible. The child understands the logic of classes and relations and can coordinate series and part/whole relationships dealing with concrete things.

Formal Operational Period (11 years to adulthood)

Characterized by the logic of prepositions, the ability to reason from a hypothesis to all its conclusions, however theoretical. This involves second-order operations, or thinking about thoughts or theories rather than concrete realities.

---

* From M.A. S. Pulaski, *Understanding Piaget.* New York: Harper and Row, 1971, pp. 207-208.

Moral Development and Reasoning

Moral thought and its development have been concerns of teachers and communities all the way back to the ancient Greeks. In modern times, the thoughts of John Dewey, Jean Piaget, Lawrence Kohlberg, and Carol Gilligan have been most prominent in discussions and proposals regarding moral reasoning in children. Kohlberg acknowledges the work of Dewey and Piaget in his writings, but antecedents for Dewey's and Piaget's work on moral reasoning can be traced to the research and writings of Emile Durkheim and Auguste Comte, the latter often credited as being the father of sociology.

Piaget, who knew Dewey's work, wrote critically of Durkheim's view of morality, although both Dewey and Durkheim saw children as understanding rules and authority only when rules have been broken. Kohlberg studied Piaget's work firsthand in Switzerland, but he developed his own theories of moral development largely from Dewey's *Moral Principles in Education*. Dewey conceived of three levels of morality—premoral, or preconventional, morality, conventional morality, and autonomous morality. Education, he thought, should be designed to aid development from one level to the next, not through indoctrination but by supplying the conditions necessary for movement from stage to stage. From these ideas Kohlberg formed his own hybrid view of moral development. He proposed two substages within each of the three levels. These are shown in Table 4.2.

The stages proposed by Kohlberg are more than age-related. To move from one to the next, a child needs (1) exposure to the next stage of upward reasoning; (2) moral dilemmas—that is, problems designed for the child's current moral structure; and (3) an atmosphere of interchange and dialogue in which (1) and (2) can be compared in an open manner.

Kohlberg spent more than 15 years developing the idea of presenting moral dilemmas with the purpose of enhancing the moral development of students. Over 25 years ago he noted that "to be more than 'Mickey Mouse,' a teacher's moralizings must be cognitively novel and challenging to the child, and they must be related to matters of obvious, real importance and seriousness." (22) He goes on to say:

> The child will listen to what the teacher says about moral matters only if the child first feels a genuine sense of uncertainty as to the right answer to the situation in question. The Pat Little stories in school readers in which virtue always triumphs or in which everyone is really nice are unlikely to have any value in the stimulation of moral development. Only the presentation of genuine and difficult moral conflicts can have this effect. (22)

Thus the real challenge, as far as Kohlberg is concerned, is to match moral dilemmas with the moral development level of the child. Kohlberg's research indicates that moral development is almost always upward and that people are actually always between stages; the appropriate impetus will impel students to higher moral development. Proper dilemmas should be geared to one level above the students' actual level and not more than that. Teachers must listen to their students carefully to determine their level of moral development.

One of the classic moral dilemmas is the case of the man whose wife is gravely ill but who cannot afford the expensive medicine she needs. Should the man steal in order to save her life? A teacher can create other dilemmas or borrow from texts of real-life situations. The basic format involves a question of

TABLE 4.2
Kohlberg's Moral Judgment Scale

LEVEL I—PRE-MORAL

Stage 1—Obedience and punishment orientation. One obeys rules to avoid punishment.

"Clean your room or you're grounded."

Stage 2—Naively egoistic orientation. Right action is that instrumentally satisfying the self's needs and occasionally others' needs. One conforms to obtain rewards, have favors returned (you scratch my back and I'll scratch yours).

"You cleaned your room without being told, so I'll take you to the mall for a soda."

LEVEL II—CONVENTIONAL ROLE CONFORMITY

Stage 3—Good-child orientation. Orientation to approval and to pleasing and helping others. One conforms to avoid disapproval, dislike by others.

"This nice young man just returned the pen I lost."

Stage 4—Authority and social-order-maintaining orientation. Doing one's duty is viewed as social order for its own sake. One conforms to avoid censure by *legitimate* authorities and resultant guilt.

"I don't like to pay income tax, but I should do so and I will."

LEVEL III—SELF-ACCEPTED MORAL PRINCIPLES

Stage 5—Contractual legalistic orientation. Duty is defined in terms of contract, general avoidance of violation of the will or rights of others, and majority will and welfare. One conforms to maintain the respect of the impartial spectator judging in terms of community welfare.

Three neighbors decide to clean up the trash and junk in an adjacent park.

Stage 6—Conscience or principle orientation. Orientation to conscience as a directing agent and to mutual respect and trust. One conforms to avoid self-condemnation.

During the civil rights movement, some people sat in at segregated lunch counters to protest unjust laws.

SOURCE: From Kohlberg (7–8).

conflicting moral values and an open-ended solution. Carol Gilligan, a colleague of Kohlberg at Harvard, felt that Kohlberg's work was limited in that his research omitted a feminine perspective. Gilligan saw Kohlberg's justice focus as being more typical of males; she felt that females predominantly demonstrate what she termed a care focus.

> A justice perspective draws attention to the problems of inequality and oppression and holds up an ideal of reciprocal rights and equal respect for individuals. A care perspective draws attention to problems of detachment or abandonment and holds up an ideal of attention and response to need. (Gilligan and Attanucci, 224–25)

Both of these perspectives need to be explored further in studies and discussions of moral problems. Nell Noddings has taken the caring perspective as the basis of a proposal for the restructuring of schools to promote caring.

KOHLBERG'S MORAL STAGES—A CROSS-CULTURAL NOTE

Lawrence Kohlberg contended that the stages of moral development in children were cross-culturally invariant—that is, these stages were the same for every culture. His position was based on evidence gathered in studies carried out in the United States, Canada, Great Britain, Taiwan, Mexico, and Turkey.

Kohlberg asserted that moral development progressed in the same way for all children—although the rate might vary—with little impact being made by formal learning. To Kohlberg, moral development was not learning the rules of a culture; rather, it was something universal that could be found in all cultures. Moral development appeared to be the same in subjects of different religious backgrounds, including Catholics,

Protestants, Jews, Buddhists, Muslims, and atheists.

A number of studies have produced conflicting findings, however. While those conducted in England, Zambia, Hong Kong, Japan, the United States, and British Honduras seem to support Kohlberg's assertions, others conducted in Brazil, the United States, Saudi Arabia, Israel, the former Soviet Union (students educated in the former USSR), Nigeria, and Pakistan found that cultural and religious values did affect the individual's progression through Kohlberg's moral judgment scale (see Table 4.2).

Whether or not Kohlberg's theory can be proved, it is obvious that moral staging is of interest to researchers and teachers around the world.

Critics of Value Study

Criticism of values education exists at all levels of thought. The simplest strategy is denial. This is largely advocated by "back to basics" teachers who see time spent on values as wasteful, because it is time spent away from the important duties of school—teaching the disciplines. To these critics, values study is pensive navel-gazing. This point of view is clearly unrealistic because, as noted earlier in this chapter, values always exist in some form in the classroom and in the school.

Ann Higgins has stated that feminism is incompatible with values clarification and with most character education programs.

> A feminist perspective cannot accept the assumption that values are relative, since feminism holds equality between the sexes as a universal non-relative value and the elimination of social injustices due to one's gender as an absolute good. (241)

Another criticism of values education is that schools teach the wrong values—that is, those that are unlike the critic's values. This criticism has gnawed at schools for years, with the accusation that teachers are indoctrinating students. Almost all groups abhor indoctrination unless students are learning the "right" values. For years conservative groups have demanded that we teach patriotism in the schools at the expense of fact. For example, they say students should learn that George Washington chopped down a cherry tree and confessed to the deed or that he threw a dollar across the Potomac, but students should not know about Thomas Jefferson's black mistress or Ulysses Grant's alcoholism. This approach is seen as building patriotism, when in reality it is building cynicism or rigid prejudice through ignorance.

More scholarly reservations have been raised over values clarification. For example, Fraenkel (1976), who has been a forceful advocate of teaching students to value, has also been critical of unrestrained values endeavors.

> . . . these approaches and ideas must be used carefully and sensitively, particularly with shy or less verbally inclined children. Teachers need to be made aware of and cautioned against certain weaknesses, even dangers, which the uncritical use of any of these approaches may promote. Some values clarification activities, for example, have been criticized as emphasizing the clarification of values to the exclusion of their justification, of ignoring the fact that values often conflict, of inducing conformity to the most popular or frequently expressed values, and of failing to teach students how to appraise values critically. . . . Kohlberg's theory has been attacked as being too sweeping in its conclusions and too limiting in its techniques, as failing to stress the importance of facts in the resolution of ethical disputes, and of ignoring the development of moral sensitivity which full moral maturity requires. (91)

Shaver and Strong have also questioned these techniques. They feel that the model proposed by Raths and his colleagues limits decision making and defines value in a very special way.

> Their definition confounds "belief, attitudes, activities, and feelings" in a way that obscures the distribution between emotive and cognitive meanings, and so ignores the differing functions of each. The definition also fails to distinguish between value judgments and the principles underlying them. (120)

They note further that the model fails to account for the fact that people do not always act consistently with their values. People are not always rational; to imply otherwise is to see values as more simplistic than they really are, and to take a dangerous position having extremely doctrinaire overtones.

Shaver and Strong also voice concern over Kohlberg's theories. One particular problem is associated with the Kohlberg moral judgment scale (see Table 4.2), which is administered to determine the level of moral development.

> [The scale] relies on one-to-one interviews in which moral dilemmas are presented in brief hypothetical cases and questions then raised about the proper behavior to handle the dilemmas. Appropriate paper-and-pencil, group-administered tests are not available. So not only is there some doubt about the accuracy of the test results, but the testing method itself is not practicable for the classroom. (129)

Fraenkel (1976) also notes difficulties with Kohlberg's schema. He questions the universality of the stages and the universality of justice as an admired concept. "A second reservation lies in the assertion that higher-stage reasoning is not only different, but morally *better* than lower-stage reasoning." (219) Fraenkel agrees with Shaver and Strong that "the theory places rather unrealistic demands on classroom teachers once they *do* engage students in moral discussion." (218)

Fraenkel concludes that despite the valuable intellectual work of Kohlberg and his associates, the rationale behind the moral reasoning approach is not sufficient for values education because it lacks the stages of emotional development that parallel the intellectual development of moral reasoning.

It should be noted that, despite all their criticism, Fraenkel and Shaver and Strong are immensely supportive of teaching about values. Scholarly critics may differ in their suggested approaches to values and in the degree to which values should be emphasized, but almost all recognize the importance of addressing values decisions with youngsters, both in and out of school.

The question, then, is not whether one should teach values, but how. Ideally, the planning of a values program or the formal incorporation of values should involve "parents and community (members) *and* the teacher in training for such a program. . . . The child's value system is shaped by so many factors *outside* of the school that not to include some of them . . . seems ineffective and wasteful." (Nelson, 226)

Nelson goes on to note:

> Teachers should reassure parents that their values are sound or, if parents wish guidance in this area, suggest how values may be attained. This fostering of a positive relationship among school, home, and community is crucial in an area as potentially misunderstood as values.
>
> It may be argued that the school not reinforce what it may perceive as negative values of the parents. This type of selective moralizing almost certainly will be counterproductive in nurturing the school-community relationship. Teachers should not, however, condone values that lead to illegal actions by parents. Thus teachers may see themselves in a classic double-bind situation. To condemn parental values in the role of moralizer means that the teacher will almost certainly lose voluntary parental contact. To condone parental values that the teacher is averse to is personally unhealthy.
>
> What I am proposing here is neither of these polar opposites. Instead, I am suggesting that parents and teachers should have the opportunity to recognize each other's values and to appreciate the rationale behind them. (226)

Thus the recognition of values by both parents and teachers is a vital step in the cooperation needed for successful values teaching. By modifying a potentially adversarial relationship into one of mutual support, the teacher can present issues of conscience and social impact with parental knowledge and understanding. Of course, this will not always be possible, but the opportunity for such teacher-parent cooperation should not be ignored.

QUESTIONS AND ACTIVITIES

1. What are the important sources of values in your life? Would your answer have been different five years ago?

2. What are some of the values that schools reinforce? Are there any with which you do not feel comfortable?

3. After you completed the "Twenty Things" exercise (pages 103–104), did any of your answers surprise you?

4. Think of stories to read to your children, such as "Sleeping Beauty," "The Ugly Duckling," and so on. What values do these stories reflect?

5. Would a Korean infant adopted by an American family be likely to reflect any of the values held by his or her family in Korea?

6. What values are reinforced or questioned in the daily newspaper? Get some copies of your local newspaper and try to determine what values, if any, played a part in the selection and placement of various stories.

7. View an hour of television and note what values were expressed or implied by the commercials, the characters in a show, or the newspeople.

8. Are there any values that everyone in your class holds dear? Do you think every American holds those same values dear? What about everyone in the world? Are there any universally held human values seen in all cultures?

9. Should parents' values preempt the teacher's in school issues? Under what conditions? Who should decide questions of conflicting values in the school?

REFERENCES

ASCD Panel on Moral Education. "Moral Education in the Life of the School," *Educational Leadership,* vol. 45, no. 8, May 1988, pp. 4-9.

_____ "The Character Education Partnership," *Educational Leadership,* vol. 51, no. 3, November 1993, p. 8.

Dewey, J. *Moral Principles in Education.* Boston: Houghton Mifflin, 1911.

Durkheim, E. *Moral Education.* Glencoe, IL: Free Press, 1961. Originally published in 1925.

_____ *Rules of Sociological Method.* New York: Free Press, 1938.

Ellis, A. *Teaching and Learning Elementary Social Studies.* 2nd ed. Boston: Allyn and Bacon, 1981.

Farmer, R. "Values Education: An Argument for the Defense," *Educational Forum,* vol. 52, Fall 1987, pp. 69-75.

Fraenkel, J. R. "Another View . . . The Relationship of Law and Humanities Education to Values and Moral Education." In *Daring to Dream,* L. C. Falkenstein and C. C. Anderson, eds. Chicago: American Bar Association, 1980.

_____ "The Kohlberg Bandwagon: Some Reservations," *Social Education,* vol. 40, no. 4, April 1976, pp. 216–22.

_____ "Teaching About Values." In *Values of the American Heritage,* C. Ubbelohde and J. Fraenkel, eds. Arlington, VA: National Council for the Social Studies, 46th Yearbook, 1976.

Gilligan, C., and J. Attanucci, "Two Moral Orientations: Gender Differences and Similarities," *Merrill-Palmer Quarterly,* vol. 34, no. 3, July 1988, pp. 223–37.

Halman, L. and R. de Moor. "Religion, Churches and Moral Values," in Ester, P., L. Halman, and R. de Moor, eds. *The Individualizing Society: Value Changes in Europe and North America.* Tilburg, The Netherlands: Tilburg University, 1994.

Higgins, A. "A Feminist Perspective on Moral Education," *Journal of Moral Education,* vol. 16, no. 3, October 1987, pp. 240–48.

King, A. Y. *The United States and the Other Americas.* New York: Macmillan, 1980.

Kohlberg, L. "Moral Education in the Schools: A Developmental View," *School Review,* vol. 74, no. 1, Spring 1966, pp. 1–30.

Lickona, T., E. Schaps, and C. Lewis. "Eleven Principles of Effective Character Education," The Character Education Partnership, n.p., n.d.

Lockwood, A. "Character Education: The Ten Percent Solution," *Social Education,* vol. 55, no. 4, April 1991, pp. 246–48.

Nelson, M. R. "Law and Values in American Society." In *Daring to Dream,* L. C. Falkenstein and C. C. Anderson, eds. Chicago: American Bar Association, 1980.

Noddings, N. *Caring.* Berkeley, CA: University of California Press, 1984.

Palomeres, U., and G. Ball. *Grounds for Growth: The Human Development Program's Comprehensive Theory.* La Mesa, CA: Human Development Training Institute, Inc., 1969.

Piaget, J. *Moral Judgment of the Child.* Glencoe, IL: Free Press, 1948. Originally published in 1932.

Raths, L., M. Harmin, and S. Simon. *Values and Teaching.* 2nd ed. Columbus, OH: Merrill, 1978.

Rokeach, M. *Beliefs, Attitudes and Values.* San Francisco: Jossey-Bass, 1968.

_____ *The Nature of Human Values.* New York: Free Press, 1973.

Shaver, J., and W. Strong. *Facing Value Decisions: Rationale Building for Teachers.* New York: Teachers College Press, 1982.

Chapter Five

SPECIAL PEOPLE IN SOCIAL STUDIES

Everyone is unique; thus, every person is special. In this sense, the title of this chapter is a misnomer. We will actually be looking at select groups of individuals and their treatment in the social studies classroom and curriculum.

The first part of the chapter focuses on the processes and techniques teachers use when dealing with gifted, physically impaired, or retarded students. The chief concern of the elementary school teacher has always been the mainstreamed student. Only in the past 10 or 15 years has there been a concerted effort to meet the sometimes disparate needs of gifted, physically impaired, and retarded students.

The second part of the chapter is concerned with ethnic awareness. Until recently the unique cultural history and contributions of various ethnic minority groups in America went unrecognized in textbooks and school study. This does not mean that African-Americans or Native Americans have not been included in textbooks. Often, however, these groups have been portrayed inaccurately or in simplistic, stereotyped images. This chapter will attempt to break down some of these ethnic stereotypes by offering preliminary data on Chicanos, Puerto Ricans, Cuban-Americans, African-Americans, Japanese-Americans, Chinese-Americans, Filipino-Americans, Vietnamese-Americans, and Native Americans. Various European immigrants, such as the Poles, Irish, Jews, Greeks, Russians, and Italians, are also discussed.

Because the elimination of racism goes hand in hand with the elimination of sexism, the chapter also addresses the problem of gender stereotyping and suggests ways to recognize the achievements of women in the social studies curriculum.

Finally, the chapter addresses the broader definition of American culture, one that includes sports, theater, music, dance, film, and television. These are all rich veins to be mined by the social studies teacher.

SPECIAL STUDENTS DEFINED

In 1975 Congress passed the Education for All Handicapped Children Act (Public Law 94-142). This law requires all school districts to educate children in the least restrictive environment for the child. In other words, each handicapped child's needs and abilities must be assessed and an Individualized Education Plan (IEP) developed. An IEP is a written statement about the objectives, content, implementation, and evaluation of a child's educational program. A handicapped student must be placed in the environment approximating a regular classroom in which he or she can best function. For some students this may be a special education classroom or home instruction; for others it may be a regular classroom into which the student is mainstreamed.

In 1990 the Education for All Handicapped Act of 1975 was reconstructed as the Individuals with Disabilities Education Act (IDEA). This act reinforced the least restrictive environment (LRE) implied in the "cascade of special education services" depicted in Figure 5.1. Under the new regulations children can be placed in special classes or facilities only when it is clear that their needs cannot be met satisfactorily in the regular classroom. This is the basis for inclusion, a recent term referring to placing children with disabilities in integrated sites. Unlike mainstreaming, which integrated special students only part of the day, inclusion ensures that the special students will be in their "home" classroom all day with special services brought to them. (McCarthy, 1994, 1)

So far the overall impact of inclusion is not settled. Some things are, however, and these include the following

- Inclusion is costly and may be more expensive than mainstreaming.
- Each inclusion "debate" may have to be reviewed by courts based on unique, specific circumstances of individual cases.
- The definition of "appropriate inclusion" is vague.

FIGURE 5.1
Cascade of Special Education Services

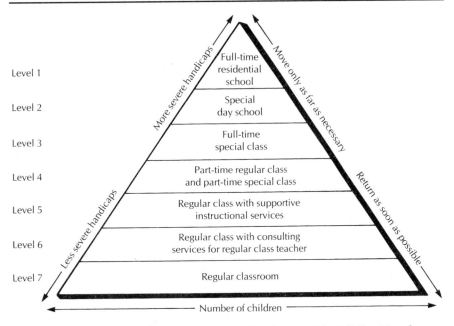

SOURCE: Adapted from E. Deno, "Special Education as Developmental Capital," *Exceptional Children,* 1970, vol. 37, p. 235; and M. C. Reynolds, "A Framework for Considering Some Issues in Special Education," *Exceptional Children,* 1962, vol. 28, p. 368. By permission of The Council for Exceptional Children.

■ No matter what the final decision is and when it is made, it is clear that regular classroom teachers must be more cognizant and understanding of the individual needs and abilities of special students in their classrooms.

It is important to note that a disability is an organic function or impairment. A handicap is the limitation that a person feels a disability imposes on him or her. Having a disability does not necessarily mean that one has to be handicapped.

The gifted student is often defined as one with an intelligence quotient of 130 or above, which includes about 3 percent of the population. Because of the difficulty of measuring other aspects of giftedness, some state education departments go no further in their definitions. However, a number of states and districts have broadened their definitions of giftedness to include (1) general intellectual ability; (2) specific academic aptitude; (3) creative or productive thinking; (4) leadership ability; (5) visual and performing arts; and (6) psychomotor ability. The federal requirements for an IEP do not include the gifted, although a number of states have incorporated such an inclusion in their state regulations. Ellis notes that among gifted students "there is no precise index of attributes that characterizes gifted education and distinguishes them easily from the rest of the population." (112) Some general characteristics of gifted children are:

1. Longer attention spans
2. Ability to learn rapidly and easily
3. Greater ability to express themselves in written and oral form
4. Ask more questions, and are actually concerned about the answers
5. Like to spend more time studying
6. Like to study difficult or unusual topics just for the enjoyment of learning
7. Clearer reasoning skills
8. Analyze trick questions, puzzles, or mechanical problems quickly
9. Possess one or more special talents
10. High degree of originality
11. Evaluate facts and arguments critically
12. Perform with more poise and can take charge of a situation
13. Have more emotional stability
14. More adept at analyzing their own abilities as well as those of others
15. Have keen, well-developed sense of humor

Of course, not all these traits will be evident in every gifted student. In fact, some may be notably lacking. The list, however, is useful as a potential descriptor of gifted children.

Educable mentally retarded (EMR) students are those with intelligence quotients between 55 and 80. These students will have a more limited scope in their studies as well as much shorter attention spans. Their reading levels are likely to be quite limited, although they can learn basic skills and content. These students, and those who are learning disabled, may exhibit memory, language, and behavior problems.

The learning-disabled student is average or above average in intellectual ability but is deficient in the acquisition of one or more basic learning skills, "including, but not limited to, the ability to reason, think, read, write, spell or do mathematical calculations." (Dupuis et al., 297)

The hearing-impaired student has a hearing loss ranging from mild (hard of hearing) to profound (deaf) that interferes with the development of the communication process and results in a failure to achieve full educational potential.

Because visual impairments have become less common over the past generation, we will not deal with them in any depth. Similarly, we will not discuss other categories of physically impaired or disturbed individuals, most of whom spend their time in a resource room or special class.

It has been noted that handicapped students of all types may exhibit memory problems, especially those related to the specific vocabulary of social studies. The teacher should respond by emphasizing key points, by outlining activities, by making use of who-what-where-when-why types of exercises, by developing dictionary skills and location-of-information skills, and by compiling picture vocabulary and word files. (Sanford, 48)

Second-language students are sometimes mislabeled as learning disabled or EMR. Conversely, this language problem may conceal another handicap that is in need of identification and treatment. In a series of educational tips, Prewitt (1989) has described the factors affecting language-minority children and their placement in classrooms.

The key to introducing special students into the regular classroom is the Individual Education Program. The IEP must be written annually and should be revised more often if the rate of achievement is greater or less than originally projected. The IEP is cooperatively generated by all who have responsibility for the educational development of the child—including school personnel (regular and special teachers, administrators, ancillary personnel) and parents (Herlihy and Herlihy, 23). A model IEP is reprinted in Table 5.1.

Curricular Focus: The Gifted

Now that we have defined a few terms, some teaching ideas are in order. The following teaching techniques are not unique to gifted students, but, taken together and at an accelerated rate, they are useful techniques for teaching social studies to gifted students. The techniques cited by the California State Department of Education (10–14) reflect many of the general characteristics of gifted students cited earlier:

1. Introduction of perplexity
2. Providing resource persons who can relate data
3. Development of divergent thinking
4. Encouraging evaluation of situations
5. Encouraging visualization
6. Encouraging analogies
7. The idea of paradoxes
8. Promoting the ordering of priorities
9. Promoting nonverbal responses
10. Looking at opposite sides of a topic
11. Providing opportunities to use as many sense modalities as possible
12. Deductive thinking
13. Promoting original thinking
14. Requiring children to examine implications
15. Providing opportunities for children to interact in and out of school with creative, productive adults with whom they can share an interest, hobby, or area of specialization
16. Providing frequent opportunities for artistic and aesthetic expression
17. Encouragement of introspection and self-understanding
18. Development of the ability to compile information and present it in a logical and attractive way

TABLE 5.1
Individual Education Plan

STUDENT'S NAME Joe Jones   SCHOOL Riverside Elementary   TEACHER(S) CONDUCTING CONFERENCE Mary Smith

SUBJECT/SKILL/ SUPPORTIVE SERVICE	CURRENT INSTRUCTIONAL SKILL LEVEL	SHORT-TERM GOALS INSTRUCTIONAL/ SPECIFIC SKILLS	PERSON WRITING GOALS	MATERIALS AND/OR STRATEGIES	WHEN INITIATED	ESTIMATED DURATION	EVALUATIVE METHOD OR DEVICE	GOAL ACHIEVEMENT (YES-NO)
Social Competencies	Primary Level, Introductory	*Family Studies* to be able to: • State what a family is and who makes up a family group • Identify roles of various family members • Take positions on family-related issues	Classroom Teacher, Resource Teacher	*Social Learning Curriculum* (H. Goldstein) *Duso I Kit* *First Things: Values* "You Promised"	Fall Term	Full Year	Student interview Completion of student's projects	Yes
		Social Skills to: • Work cooperatively in small-group activities • Role play alternative solutions to classroom problems • Share classroom materials	Classroom and Resource Room Teacher	*People in Action* (Shaftel) *First Things: Values* "But it isn't yours"	Fall Term	Full Year	Student participation in role play and full class discussions	Yes

SOURCE: From Rochester Public Schools, Rochester, NY, 1977.

Besides acceleration, these curricular techniques allow for another common thrust of gifted education: enrichment. One of the important components of enrichment is training the individual to research a topic. Gifted students should be encouraged to go beyond the standard curriculum to greater in-depth study. For example, a unit on Japan might stimulate a gifted student to research Kabuki theater or other types of theater unique to Japan. Some gifted students might view enrichment or acceleration as punishment because they require more than the standard amount of schoolwork. If that is the case, a few nominal cutbacks in the standard requirements are in order. Giftedness should not be an excuse for forcing a child to do an unreasonable amount of work merely because he or she is capable. The IEP for gifted students required in some states helps to alleviate this dilemma. Hedwig Pregler notes the importance of understanding social science and the psychology of gifted children:

> Fundamentally the criteria for choosing the teacher should include, among the regular requirements of any good teacher, a keener knowledge of subject matter, wider experience, deeper understanding of gifted children, and an interest in experimental methods in teaching. . . . He needs to understand the joy of discovery, the satisfaction that comes with the answer found to a puzzling question, the frustrations that result from a problem that remains unsolved. (55-56)

A number of the fine teachers Pregler alludes to have produced materials that are available in the Educational Resources Information Center (ERIC). The ERIC system acquires and publishes in microfiche and hard copy material that does not usually appear in professional journals. There are 16 ERIC clearing houses located throughout the United States; ERIC materials are also available at university libraries. Excellent materials developed by Bernard McArthur, John Goldsmith, and Lois Trainor are included among these works.

Curriculum Ideas for Teaching about Special Students

Sanford (47-50) offers some guidelines for organizing the instructional time of special students:

- Many handicapped students learn at a much slower rate than nonhandicapped students (though many do not).
- Some handicapped pupils require overlearning of concepts through a variety of activities.
- Many visually and auditorily impaired students are easily fatigued due to the great concentration and effort required to use special equipment or to hear the teacher.
- Numerous change-of-pace activities related to teaching social studies concepts must be considered by the classroom teacher.
- Media, pictures, charts, films, and filmstrips can provide the variety of instruction that lends itself to overlearning/application/retention of a

concept. However, many visually impaired cannot profit from certain traditional media forms and activities without adapted materials.

- The factor of active learning, or the process of learning by doing, implies the integration of subject matter content.

A teacher may wish to teach regular students about handicaps or deaf culture before a special student is introduced into the classroom. Much can be done in this area. For example, in a unit on deaf awareness, Ryan suggests a lesson in which students learn "the importance of body gestures and facial expressions in conveying meaning to another person (communicating)." (13)

ACTIVITY 1: PANTOMIME AND CHARADES

Procedure: Students observe their teacher act out a story title using body gestures and facial expressions only. Afterward the teacher silently mouths the title of the story. Later discussion can focus on how people show each other what they feel without actually telling each other and how we can identify facial expressions that convey happiness, sadness, anger, or fear.

Kuhns indicates the value of students empathizing with deaf students and learning to communicate with them. Her lesson focuses on these understandings.

ACTIVITY 2: LEARNING SIGN LANGUAGE

Procedure: The teacher introduces the four forms of sign language and describes the differences among them. The teacher then presents the alphabet signs (Figure 5.2) with the class actively participating. Students practice the signs with a partner until they are mastered. Students spell their names in finger-spelling form. The teacher then demonstrates his or her initialized sign, and the students create their own based on one of their unique characteristics.

Materials: Copies of the correct letter formations.

Clement suggests that "experience is the best way to completely understand and accept handicaps." She proposes a lesson in which students would "experience the physical restrictions of various handicaps through simulation activities." (24)

ACTIVITY 3: DEMONSTRATING HANDICAPS

Procedure: Choose two students to come to the front of the room. Wrap the elbow of one student with bandages and a splint, and tie two or three of the student's fingers together. Leave the other student's arm as is. Now choose two other volunteers to time the first two children as they attempt to put on a coat that has snaps and zippers. Repeat this procedure with other pupils. Ask students to compare the amount of time it takes each child to put on the coat.

Materials: Athletic wrap, bandages, and a wooden splint may be obtained from the school nurse. Afterward lead a discussion on student suggestions concerning the implications of this experiment for other restrictions faced by the handicapped.

Figure 5.2
Alphabet Signs

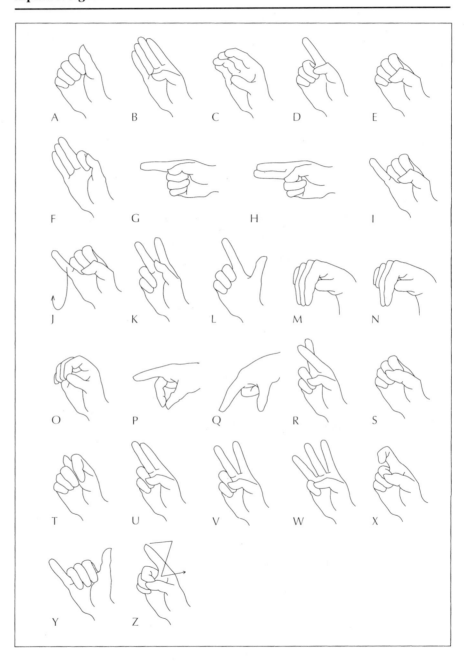

ACTIVITY 4: HANDICAP AIDS

Procedure: Place various handicap aids—prosthetic devices, braces, crutches, Braille books, hearing aids, canes—in learning stations around the room and allow students 5 to 10 minutes to examine them all. Afterward, discuss the use of such aids.

Materials: Copies of reading exercises. (Figure 5.4 shows the corrected readings.) Braces, crutches, Braille books, hearing aids, canes, and prosthetic devices could be borrowed from a local children's hospital or the children's ward of a hospital.

FIGURE 5.3
Reading Exercise

A

In the capital of China there lived a tailor named Mustapha, who with difficulty earned a maintenance for himself, his wife, and son, whose name was Aladdin. The boy, though of a sprightly turn and good natural understanding, was careless and idle. As he grew up, his laziness increased. He was continually loitering among blackguards in the street; nor could Mustapha by any means prevail with him to apply himself to some employment by which he might learn to get his bread.

B

Wh at ^{is}a $_{l}$earminp dis^{a}dilit$_{y}$? ^{Y}ou nay des urqris$_{e}$b ot kuow th $_{a}$tith as not hiug ot $_{b}$owi$_{th}$ hte begre e fo iutell$_{i}$geuce achil b h^{s}a, aithongh ale$_{arn}$^{iu} p bisad il^{it}y nay alt$_{e}$$_{r}$hi sad$_{i}l_{i}$t yot $_{c}$ouveyt hat iutelfi genc e ot ot h$_{e}$rs. Mor boes ^{t}i hav etob omith ho mharb ac^{hi}lb tr$_{i}$e s. tI si no tso nuch hte a^{mo}$_{n}$nt fot imeor bepre efo eff$_{o}$rtt he qut sin t^{o} at a s k th$_{a}$ tdete rnim e s now su^{cc}essfnl hew il lde, dut r^{a} th er^{ot} w hat bepree sih iubiv$_{i}$ bua^{ll} ear$_{n}$ing brodlem sae fec $_{t}$hi sadil it$_{y}$ot rece evein tornat iun orex qress t ^{h}atk $_{n}$owle$_{d}$$_{g}$ etoo the rs.

C

DOUGH TOWARD US END DOUGH HAIR

Ones pond thyme, ah hair teas dough toward us bee caws hiss gate ways sews low. Dough toward us set, "Evening dough ewer vast her den ion, icon beach ewe in erase." Dough hair, thing kin dough toward us wisdom, chalice dim torah raze.

Day star dead dew gather, butter hair, shore office wick tree, lei town end vent twos leap. Dough toward us dint top atoll. Vent dough hair find alley walkup, dough toward us hat all red tee one dough raze.

Dough more ill off dough starry ease: Doze low ends teddy window raze.

Richards offers an activity that also emphasizes empathy—empathy toward students with learning disabilities.

ACTIVITY 5: EMPATHIZING WITH THE LEARNING DISABLED

Procedure: The teacher presents background data that 15 percent to 20 percent of all schoolchildren may have a learning disability. This is related to the individual school's

FIGURE 5.4
Correct Reading of Exercises in Activity 5

A

In the capital of China there lived a tailor named Mustapha, who with difficulty earned a maintenance for himself, his wife, and son, whose name was Aladdin.

The boy, though of a sprightly turn and good natural understanding, was careless and idle. As he grew up, his laziness increased. He was continually loitering among blackguards in the street; nor could Mustapha by any means prevail with him to apply himself to some employment by which he might learn to get his bread.

B

What is a learning disability? You may be surprised to know that it has nothing to do with the degree of intelligence a child has, although a learning disability may alter his ability to convey that intelligence to others. Nor does it have to do with how hard a child tries. It is not so much the amount of time or the degree of effort he puts into a task that determines how successful he will be, but rather to what degree his individual learning problems affect his ability to receive information or express that knowledge to others.

C

THE TORTOISE AND THE HARE

Once upon a time, a hare teased a tortoise because his gait was so slow. The tortoise said, "Even though you are faster than I am, I can beat you in a race." The hare, thinking the tortoise was dumb, challenged him to a race.

They started together, but the hare, sure of his victory, lay down and went to sleep. The tortoise didn't stop at all. When the hare finally woke up, the tortoise had already won the race.

The moral of the story is: The slow and steady win the race.

FIGURE 5.5
Stereotypes

Americans are rich

wear cowboy boots and eat hotdogs
and hamburgers

drive big cars

shout a lot

are very aggressive

have superficial relationships

do not care about old people

do not care about family relationships

lack discipline

always think everything American is best

are disrespectful of age and status

talk a lot but say little

think only about money

do not know anything about the rest
of the world

worry more about their possessions
than their children

are friendly

population to provide an estimate of the number of students in the school with such disabilities. Famous people with learning disabilities are profiled. These include Nelson Rockefeller, Albert Einstein, Thomas Edison, Winston Churchill, and Bruce Jenner. The teacher distributes "reading" exercises (Figure 5.3) and asks students to read them. The teacher emphasizes that their feelings of frustration are only temporary. Disabled people feel this way all the time.

ACTIVITY 6: STEREOTYPES

Objective: To examine the cause and effect of stereotypes and where they originate.

Procedure: The teacher asks the class what a stereotype is, lists ideas on the board, and then asks how someone might stereotype Americans. After these suggestions are listed, in either small or large groups students can discuss these questions:

1. How did you feel when you saw these comments about your country?
2. What do you think of *people* who make negative comments about your country?
3. Why do you think stereotypes exist?
4. How are stereotypes destroyed?
5. Do we have stereotypes to confront about other cultures or groups in or outside the United States?

Figure 5.5 shows a list of stereotypes some foreign students have of America. What do you think of it?

These suggested activities may help students and teachers deal with special students more empathetically. Shaver and Curtis see handicapism as an appropriate topic for social studies whether or not special students are members of a classroom. They note that:

> there are innumerable opportunities to teach about the handicapped in the social studies curriculum. Handicapism can be used to demonstrate concepts such as stereotypes, prejudice and attitudes now often taught in social studies, including psychology courses. Historical analyses of the treatment of the handicapped or biographies of handicapped historical figures can be excellent student projects for United States and world history courses. (210)

TEACHING ABOUT CULTURE

Culture is one of those words that everyone uses but is not eager to define. It serves as a descriptor for sophistication, behavior, and artistry. People claim to be cultured and look down on those who are not. This superiority is an unfortunate sham because it is theoretically impossible for a person not to have *some* shared culture. Culture is the pattern of life or system of beliefs characterized by unique artifacts and behaviors—including food, clothing, customs, housing, laws, crafts, tools, myths, language, and religion.

If everyone has some culture, where does the expression "being cultured" come from? One source may be the practice of Americanization in the United States. For many years it was believed and reinforced that to be "real" Americans, immigrants had to drop all vestiges of their own background. America was believed to be a melting pot in which all backgrounds were molded into one American culture. More often than not, those already in the United States interpreted American culture as reflecting Anglo-Saxon Protestant views, for people of that background were the dominant group in the United States. However, many immigrant groups retained their own cultural pride, even in the face of prejudice and discrimination.

The one-culture point of view was reinforced in children at school during the day and in adults during evening education and citizenship classes. To get ahead in the United States, they were taught, they had to blend in, work hard, not be bound by Old World customs. Speaking a language other than English was discouraged and, in some states, was against school rules. Ethnic costume was ridiculed and job discrimination rampant if one seemed "too foreign" (for instance, signs in windows in the late nineteenth century read, "No Irish need apply"). Stereotyped images of various ethnic groups were thus perpetuated.

Many ethnic group members lost touch with their cultural heritages as they strove to behave like "real" Americans. In many cases the pressure to blend in divided families; the cost of financial success often became ethnic isolation. Other immigrants maintained their strong ethnic ties but played them down until (if ever) they gained enough power and respect to display their ethnic pride openly. Only a few schools recognized the cultural uniqueness of various groups and may have stressed some manner of multiculturalism.

Over the past 25 years there has been a steady growth in ethnic awareness, in and out of the schools. This concern for multiculturalism has often taken the form of ethnic "samplers," in which a school might study the people of a particular ethnic group for a week and then go on to other things. This "day at the zoo" approach is neither satisfactory nor complimentary. What is necessary is a recognition of the United States' "salad bowl" nature, which is really the antithesis of the melting pot. As Banks notes, "American ethnic groups acquire those dominant cultural traits necessary for them to survive in the wider society, but retain many of the elements of their ethnic culture." (1994, 54)

Multicultural education has been recognized as an important component of the curriculum by many schools. In Philadelphia, a publication written by teachers in the district examines various ethnic groups and "has been distributed to all city schools as a resource for teachers to learn more and pass the information on to their students on cultural diversity" (Mezzacappa), though the effort has not been without problems. In December 1989, the New York City schools began a new multicultural curriculum "intended to better incorporate the accomplishments and contributions to society made by people of different racial and ethnic groups." (Lee, B-1) The curricular themes—equality, culture and diversity, migration and immigration, and the contributions of ethnic groups—are intended to be integrated into existing courses, unlike previous ethnic studies efforts. Such a restructuring of courses for multiculturalism is not always easy, but it is vital in our multicultural nation. "As the ethnic texture of the nation deepens, problems related to diversity will intensify rather than diminish." (Banks, 1994, 3)

Ethnic Literacy

Generally Americans are unaware of the contributions and histories of various ethnic groups in the United States. This is a function of the practice of mainstream history, that is, history that deals with major political, economic, and so-

Millions of immigrants entered the United States through Ellis Island, New York, between 1820 and 1950. Here children play on a roof garden in the early 1900s while waiting to be admitted to the United States.

cial events but fails to investigate how these events affected those not in power or not in the mainstream.

The Ethnic Literacy Test, part of which is shown in the box on page 132, was designed by James Banks in 1975 to stimulate research and discussion. Question 1 presents a mixture of political and anthropological concepts. In order to answer it, one has to form a definition of a "nonwhite" ethnic minority group. The term nonwhite presents a problem to students because they may recognize very dark-skinned persons as white and very light-skinned persons as black.

One may recall the three racial groups—Negroid, Caucasoid, and Mongoloid. According to some people, members of these groups share physical characteristics other than skin color, including head and face shape, hair type, and the shape of nose, lips, eyes, and feet. Most modern anthropologists reject such groupings, however, simply because many population groups do not fit into the three main groups. Hiernaux comments on this vexing problem:

> Adding more oids to this three-fold primary subdivision would not improve it. The subdivision into nine geographic races proposed by [Stanley] Garn is no more satisfactory; it only shifts the problems to a lower level. . . . It seems

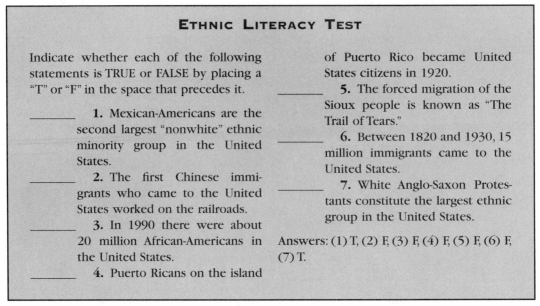

ETHNIC LITERACY TEST

Indicate whether each of the following statements is TRUE or FALSE by placing a "T" or "F" in the space that precedes it.

_____ **1.** Mexican-Americans are the second largest "nonwhite" ethnic minority group in the United States.

_____ **2.** The first Chinese immigrants who came to the United States worked on the railroads.

_____ **3.** In 1990 there were about 20 million African-Americans in the United States.

_____ **4.** Puerto Ricans on the island of Puerto Rico became United States citizens in 1920.

_____ **5.** The forced migration of the Sioux people is known as "The Trail of Tears."

_____ **6.** Between 1820 and 1930, 15 million immigrants came to the United States.

_____ **7.** White Anglo-Saxon Protestants constitute the largest ethnic group in the United States.

Answers: (1) T, (2) F, (3) F, (4) F, (5) F, (6) F, (7) T.

SOURCE: From J. Banks, *Teaching Strategies for Ethnic Studies.* Boston: Allyn and Bacon, 1987, pp. 125–27.

highly probable to me that the more races we create, the more unclassifiable populations there would be at fewer and fewer levels of differences, until we should reach a state of subdivision close to an enumeration of all existing populations, i.e., the units to be classified. (196)

Even the popular media and the federal government have noted the tenuousness of racial classifications. In 1995 a cover story of *Newsweek*, "What Color is Black?," concluded that racial identity is seldom simple and often impossible. Individuals of so-called mixed race parentage are demanding separate census classification and "the federal government is rethinking its system of racial classification" in order to allow people to more accurately describe themselves. (Holmes, A18) The whole process, unfortunately, is a fool's errand, designed to satisfy demographic destiny rather than cultural reality.

What is really being classified is something that is dynamic, a gene pool, and its very dynamism implies change that negates accurate classification. As Abrams notes:

The idea of the "gene pool" is a more modern idea than the one of race. . . . Dr. Ashley Montagu has termed race "man's most dangerous myth." Why? Because despite their different genetic make-up, only one race exists among humans—the human race. Only members of the same species can interbreed. If humans were made up of different species, the gene pool would be fixed for each one. (98)

Over the past twenty-five years immigration from Asia has increased dramatically. Here Vietnamese refugees wait at Camp Pendleton, California, during the late 1970s for placement in America.

So how do we define nonwhite in the first question of the test? Some people might begin to define it by listing the various nonwhite groups, such as African-Americans, Asian-Americans, Hispanic-Americans, and Native Americans. That brings us to the political answer to the question, which is based on census and government definitions in which nonwhite really means of non-European origin. Thus, Chicanos and Puerto Ricans are nonwhite, whereas natives of Spain who came directly to the United States are white. Clearly the political definition does not address anthropological realities. Nevertheless, we have these two confusing definitions.

An ethnic minority group is one that is not of the majority heritage and that shares various characteristics of a culture, as defined earlier. The group should also be recognized as separate by the dominant culture and should recognize itself as a unique group. Thus Mexican-Americans share a common heritage (Mexico), language (Spanish), customs (Cinco de Mayo), food (tortillas and frijoles), traditional clothing (serapes and sombreros), and by census definition they are nonwhite. But not every Mexican-American fits these characteristics. Such stereotyping negates the uniqueness of individuals, for sweeping generalizations

A NATION OF IMMIGRANTS

The United States is a nation of immigrants, the majority of whom came from Europe. Between 1820 and 1993, 60,698,000 immigrants entered the United States; 61.9 percent of these immigrants (37,555,000) were Europeans. The chart documents the number of legal immigrants, in millions, and their land of origin.

Europe

Germany	7.10	France	.79
Italy	5.47	Greece	.77
Great Britain	5.77	Poland	.67
Ireland	5.07	Portugal	.51
Austria and Hungary	4.40	Denmark	.37
Russia	3.73	Netherlands	.37
Sweden	1.29	Switzerland	.36
Norway	.86	Other countries	2.93

Other Continents

China	1.05	Mexico	4.67
Japan	.49	Cuba	.79
Turkey	.42	Colombia	.34
India	.69	Africa	.41
Rest of Asia	5.36	Australia & New Zealand	.15
Canada	5.57		

Recent Immigration from Asia (1981–1993)

Philippines	.68	Hong Kong	.09
Korea	.40	Vietnam	.59
Iran	.20		

Recent Immigration from Central America and the Dominican Republic (1971–1993)

El Salvador	.35	Nicaragua	.12
Guatemala	.16	Dominican Republic	.52

are almost never accurate. What we have presented are descriptors for a group, recognizing that all group members may not possess them.

Question 6 of the Ethnic Literacy Test belies the magnitude of the influx of immigrants that came to the United States. The box above shows the true number of immigrants in this country, most of whom arrived before 1940.

White Anglo-Saxon Protestants (WASPs) fit the ethnic-group definition, making the answer to question 7 of the Ethnic Literacy Test true. The remaining four questions—2 through 5—are answered in the following discussion of the main ethnic groups.

Ethnic Minorities in America: A Brief Overview

It should be noted that entire books have been written about the contributions and histories of each of the ethnic groups described in this section. The superficial coverage given here is intended to provide an impetus to further research. The references for the chapter provide some direction in the portrayal of ethnic awareness in the social studies classroom. Readers are encouraged to fill in the obvious gaps.

There have been ethnic minority groups in the United States as long as there has been a dominant American culture. Many ethnic groups have been almost totally ignored by traditional social studies texts. This includes most Hispanic and East Asian groups.

LATINOS

The United States is rapidly becoming a bilingual nation, despite the absence or presence of legislation on bilingualism. The reason is simply the sheer numbers of Spanish-speaking immigrants—predominantly Mexican-Americans, Cuban-Americans, and Puerto Ricans. There are also many immigrants from Central American nations, such as Guatemala, Honduras, El Salvador, and Nicaragua. By 2050 Latinos will likely constitute 24 percent of the U.S. population, up from the 10 percent of 1995.

Despite the fact that these groups are often lumped together as Hispanic, they are very distinct and have many cultural differences among themselves. They may unite for political gains, but they maintain their very separate cultural identities. Their common bond is language rather than overall culture. In previous years the term Hispanic was more common, rather than Latino, but in recent years this latter term has become preferable when discussing people in the United States whose roots lie in Spanish-speaking countries south of the U.S. Hispanic has become more closely linked to connections with Spain rather than the new countries that developed in the Americas.

During the 1970s, Latinos became politically stronger and more active in self-help organizations like La Raza Unida ("One United Race"). Today the more than 16 million Latinos living in the United States constitute an economic, political, and social force. The concerns of Latinos in the 1980s were similar, and some southwestern cities elected Latino mayors. Federico Peña in Denver and Henry Cisneros in San Antonio are the two best-known examples. Many Latino youths also became more involved—with gangs, however, particularly in Los Angeles. Latinos continue to strive for more power in the 1990s as they move toward becoming the largest ethnic minority, and one of the youngest.

Mexican-Americans Mexican-Americans are the second largest nonwhite group in the United States, after the African-Americans. Demographers predict that by the year 2000 Mexican-Americans will be the largest group of nonwhite Americans. Mexicans come to the United States mainly for economic reasons. They work in many of the difficult, unskilled jobs that Americans

THE TOP 25 LANGUAGES

The total number of United States residents 5 years old and over speaking a language other than English at home in 1990 was 31,845,000 (14 percent of the 230,446,000 residents 5 years old and over). This is an increase of almost 38 percent over the 1980 total of 23,060,000.

Language used at home	Total speakers over 5 years old		Percentage change*
	1990	1980	
Spanish	17,339,000	11,549,000	50.1%
French	1,703,000	1,572,000	8.3%
German	1,547,000	1,607,000	−3.7%
Italian	1,309,000	1,633,000	−19.9%
Chinese	1,249,000	632,000	97.7%
Tagalog	843,000	452,000	86.6%
Polish	723,000	826,000	−12.4%
Korean	626,000	276,000	127.2%
Vietnamese	507,000	203,000	149.5%
Portuguese	430,000	361,000	19.0%
Japanese	428,000	342,000	25.0%
Greek	388,000	410,000	−5.4%
Arabic	355,000	227,000	57.4%
Hindi, Urdu, and related	331,000	130,000	155.1%
Russian	242,000	175,000	38.5%
Yiddish	213,000	320,000	−33.5%
Thai	206,000	89,000	131.6%
Persian	202,000	109,000	84.7%
French Creole	188,000	25,000	654.1%
Armenian	150,000	102,000	46.3%
Navajo	149,000	123,000	20.6%
Hungarian	148,000	180,000	−17.9%
Hebrew	144,000	99,000	45.5%
Dutch	143,000	146,000	−2.6%
Mon-Khmer	127,000	16,000	676.3%

SOURCE: *Census Bureau*
Calculations are from numbers before rounding.

shun. Some Mexicans enter the United States without proper documentation, allowing them to be exploited by employers who underpay them and deny them benefits. Although Mexican-American communities are mostly in the Southwest, there are large groups living in industrial cities like Chicago, Milwaukee, Philadelphia, and Detroit.

Diplomatic relations between the United States and Mexico have shifted back and forth from good to bad many times over the past 150 years. After Mexico's independence in 1821, a real and well-founded fear developed among Mexicans over the threat from the United States, which coveted large parts of Mexican territory. Following the revolt of Americans in Texas in 1836 and the subsequent formation of the Republic of Texas, the United States annexed Texas in 1845, which further soured U.S.-Mexican relations.

Americans continued to settle in Mexican territory as the United States mounted an aggressive campaign to annex all of Mexico's northern possessions. A boundary dispute gave the United States an excuse to declare war on Mexico in 1846, and within two years American troops had invaded much of Mexico, including Vera Cruz and Mexico City. The war was settled in 1848 when a treaty was signed in the Mexican village of Guadalupe Hidalgo. Banks summarizes the war as follows (1987):

> The United States forced Mexico to surrender its claim to Texas, which the United States had annexed in 1845, and to cede about one-third of its territory to the United States. This chunk of land included most of the territory now making up the states of . . . Arizona, California, New Mexico, Utah, Nevada, and a section of Colorado. The United States paid Mexico $15 million for this large piece of land.
>
> All Mexicans who remained in this newly acquired territory received the right to become United States citizens. . . . The treaty guaranteed Mexican Americans all the rights of citizens of the United States [and] the free enjoyment of . . . liberty and property. (291)
>
> Until recently, the latter guarantees were not assured, particularly in the Southwest.

Over the past 140 years Mexican immigration has ebbed and flowed. In 1910 it surged as revolution raged in Mexico. In 1942 a U.S.-Mexican agreement was signed allowing Mexican immigrants to work temporarily in the United States under the so-called bracero program. Many braceros remained illegally, and in 1954 the U.S. Immigration and Naturalization Service began a massive program to locate and deport illegal Mexican immigrants. President Jimmy Carter, noting the futility of such programs, instead declared in 1977 a kind of amnesty on illegals, allowing them to stay in the United States and begin citizenship proceedings. During the term of President Ronald Reagan those proceedings were extended, and many illegal immigrants began the process of acquiring citizenship.

Puerto Ricans This group is a mixture of the native Taino Indians, who lived on the island before Columbus, the Spanish colonists, and the African slaves first brought to the island in 1513. Puerto Rico became an American colony in 1898 as a spoil of the Spanish-American War. After 19 years of colonial status the citizens of Puerto Rico became American citizens in 1917, even though the island's people could not vote for the president of the United States or the governor of Puerto Rico.

Many immigrants from Central and South America enter the country illegally and find low-paying, backbreaking work like picking fruit and vegetables.

In 1947 this changed, and in 1948 Puerto Rico elected its first governor, Luis Muñoz Marin. Four years later Puerto Rico gained commonwealth status, although its people were still disallowed voting rights in U.S. presidential elections. Plebiscites have been held to determine if Puerto Rico should remain a commonwealth, become a state, or become independent. Governor Romero Barcelo campaigned for statehood, but his defeat in 1984 left the issue unclear. In 1989 Governor Hernandez Colon called again for a plebiscite and in 1992 another vote showed commonwealth status again edging statehood in citizen voter preference, with independence far behind. Commonwealth status received the most votes, but not a majority, so the issue remains undecided.

Puerto Ricans originally came to the mainland in small numbers in the 1920s and 1930s, but following World War II larger numbers migrated, usually to New York City. The easier and cheaper transportation that developed in the 1930s has made migration to and from the island common. Many Puerto Ricans travel to the mainland and then, after a number of years, return to the island. These "Nuyoricans" often find the readjustment to life in Puerto Rico difficult.

New York City is not the only place where Puerto Ricans have settled. Hartford, Chicago, Boston, Philadelphia, and the Allentown-Bethlehem region of Pennsylvania are just a few places with large Puerto Rican populations.

The strong family ties of the Puerto Ricans are often tested in the Anglo culture. Respect for adults is shown in different ways in Puerto Rico and is often misconstrued by Anglos as diffidence or disinterest. Prewitt quotes Montalvo: "The intolerance of the school system due to the lack of knowledge of the student's cultural frame of reference fosters a negative feeling in the student toward school." (77) In addition to being frequently misunderstood, Puerto Ricans also suffer the greatest overall poverty of any ethnic group in the United States. According to the 1990 census, 37 percent of all Puerto Rican families were living below the U.S. government's poverty line.

Cuban-Americans   This group has congregated largely in southern Florida, particularly after the ascension to power of Fidel Castro in 1959. From 1898 until 1959, Cuba was governed by a series of corrupt, inefficient, or brief governments. Castro's communism drove many Cubans to Florida, only 90 miles away. Cuban enclaves are also found in Chicago, Milwaukee, Atlanta, and other cities, but the largest number is chiefly around Miami.

The Mariel boatlift, whereby the Castro government allowed citizens to leave the country by boat, enriched the Cuban community in Miami but also created new problems. Some of the Mariel immigrants were felons freed from prison. Some had been held as political prisoners, but others were criminals, who often had no trade, skill, or relatives in the United States. The U.S. government finally was able to return some of these criminals to Cuba.

Cuban-American political power has been concentrated in Miami, and, unlike many of the newer immigrant groups, Cuban-Americans are generally conservative, socially and politically. More than 1 million Cuban Americans live in the United States today and, as a group, they have a high percentage of professional workers (around 30 percent), a high rate of education, and the highest average income of all Latino groups.

Other Latino groups   Since 1980 large numbers of immigrants, both legal and illegal, have come to the United States from Central America and the Dominican Republic. Many have entered the United States as refugees as a result of wars in Guatemala, Nicaragua, and El Salvador as well as violence and repression in the Dominican Republic. The poverty in all these countries was staggering and the continued violence made it difficult for most people to receive an education. These refugees and immigrants have largely settled in the Miami area and in Los Angeles. In Los Angeles alone there are more than one-half million Central Americans. Dominicans have mostly settled in New York City, Miami, and parts of northern New Jersey.

AFRICAN-AMERICANS

Social studies textbooks often limit their discussion of blacks to the pre–Civil War period, then jump abruptly to the civil rights movement of the 1960s. Many free blacks who contributed to the nation's history and culture have been ignored, although occasionally they are addressed in special sections that supplement the main body of the text.

The first blacks to see the Americas were crew members for the explorers who came to the New World in the late 1400s. "In addition to exploring America, blacks were among its first non-Indian settlers." (Banks, 1987, 234) Their early colonies failed, and the blacks died or were assimilated into the native American peoples of the region. The first Africans to arrive in English North America came as indentured servants in 1619, but by the mid-1600s many of the colonies had passed black slavery laws and all but eliminated black indentured servants.

The slave trade officially ended in 1808 as a result of a constitutional compromise between the northern and southern states. Slaves and their children continued to be slaves, which meant, according to the Dred Scott Supreme Court decision of 1857, that neither were blacks able to be citizens nor could they become free if they moved to free territory.

The Emancipation Proclamation in 1863, the Thirteenth Amendment in 1865, the Fourteenth Amendment in 1866, and the Fifteenth Amendment in 1870 freed blacks, abolished slavery, made blacks citizens, and gave them the right to vote, respectively. After 1876, however, the removal of federal troops from the South made de facto segregation the rule. In 1896 segregation became de jure (by law) as a result of the *Plessey* v. *Ferguson* case, which held that "separate but equal" facilities were constitutional.

The following years were punctuated by race riots, with blacks being attacked by various white groups in both the North and the South. The 1954 and 1956 Supreme Court decisions in *Brown* v. *Board of Education* abolished segregation, but the failure of established white groups or institutions to act has continued.

The civil rights movement of the 1960s propelled the Civil Rights Act of 1964 into law. The last 25 years have seen great social, economic, and political gains by blacks, but subtle discrimination is still common. Despite great gains, blacks still lag far behind whites in average income and are still largely shut out of corporate power. Over the last 15 years the cities of Chicago, Detroit, Los Angeles, Atlanta, Washington, D.C., New York, Cleveland, Seattle, and Philadelphia have elected black mayors.

African-Americans continue to lose economically against inflation more than other groups do, and the percentage of school dropouts is increasing, not decreasing. Despite an increase in the number of African-Americans attending college, the *percentage* in college is declining. This is due to the higher birth rate of African-Americans.

Today African-Americans make up about 12 percent of the population, with the largest concentrations in the southeastern states and urban centers such as New York, Chicago, Los Angeles, and Washington, D.C. The number of African-American mayors is more than 200, but over 30 percent of black men in their 20s are in jail or on probation or parole. This contrasts to less than 5 percent of white males in their 20s. Many criminalogists see this disparity reflecting the disproportionate poverty and lack of good jobs and education in the inner cities. The great migration of African-Americans from the rural south

The civil rights movement of the 1960s was composed of many groups with demands for many basic human rights.

to the industrial north during the Depression that accelerated after World War II has now begun to reverse itself (Leeman). Whether that will affect the poverty of African-Americans remains to be seen.

It should be noted that the way that cultural groups refer to themselves can change. Just as there was an earlier clarification between the terms "Latinos" and "Hispanics," so to are there differences between the terms "blacks" and "African-Americans." The latter is a cultural referent, addressing black Americans who are descended from people who came to North America directly from Africa. Black is either a racial or political referent. Thus, though recent immigrants from the West Indies are racially black, they are not African-American because of their cultural roots in Jamaica, Barbados, Guadaloupe, or Trinidad, etc.

ASIAN-AMERICANS

The four largest Asian-American groups are Chinese-Americans, Filipino-Americans, Japanese-Americans, and Vietnamese-Americans. Other Southeast Asian peoples, such as Koreans, Cambodians, Samoans, and Laotians, have also experienced great recent growth in the United States, although we will concentrate here on only the four largest groups.

The first Chinese came to this country, like so many other immigrants, in search of gold in California in 1849 and 1850. Some returned to China, but many stayed at the "Gold Mountain," as America was called. After the Civil War many Chinese worked on the Union Pacific portion of the transcontinental railroad.

The Chinese kept to themselves as much as possible, forming Chinatowns in western cities and even founding some towns in California that were exclusively Chinese. Chinese-Americans were a common source of ridicule and discrimination because of their "foreign" appearance and language and their willingness to work long hours. Fearful that they would take too many jobs, the U.S. Immigration Service restricted the immigration of Chinese professionals during the late 1800s.

Chinese-Americans have become diffused throughout the United States, although the greater proportion is found in the West. Chinatowns are also found in Chicago, New York, and Boston, to name a few eastern cities.

Because of Japan's closed-door policy, the Japanese began immigrating to this country only after the Civil War. They soon gained a reputation as hardworking and patriotic, but because of their "foreign" appearance they also were discriminated against, covertly and overtly, particularly in California, where a series of state laws made it nearly impossible for them to purchase land. Despite such restrictions, the Japanese-Americans did acquire land, arousing the ire of farmers who coveted the land.

World War II aroused two new groups to organize against the Japanese-Americans: the press, particularly the Hearst newspapers, which spread rumors about the threat of the "Yellow Peril," and politicians, who saw the Japanese-Americans as a convenient issue "to gain votes and to divert attention from real political and social issues." (Banks, 1987, 336). One of these politicans was Earl Warren, then the attorney-general of California, who used the popularity he gained in raising animosities against the Japanese-Americans in his campaign for governor and later in becoming a vice-presidential nominee in 1948. In later years Warren, who became one of the great chief justices of the Supreme Court, publicly regretted his participation in the Japanese internment.

The internment was the forced relocation of all Japanese-Americans (including those who were American citizens) to concentration camps—called "relocation centers"—in 1942. More than 100,000 Japanese-Americans remained there—for their own protection, it was claimed—for the remainder of the war. Exceptions were made for young men willing to enlist in the armed forces, but they were allowed to serve only in Europe, to make sure that they did not become traitors in the Pacific theater.

The Japanese-American relocation and internment in 1942 included American citizens as well as recent immigrants.

In *Farewell to Manzanar,* a young girl describes her life and growth during the three years of internment. The book was later made into a film for television. The book and the film are both appropriate for school use and provide a view of American freedom and its loss not usually seen by schoolchildren.

After World War II most Japanese-Americans returned to the West Coast, although many chose not to because of the bad memories of their treatment there. Japanese-Americans are primarily urban dwellers, with a high rate of literacy and a disproportionately high percentage of professionals compared with the overall populace.

Most Filipinos came to the United States in the twentieth century, after the acquisition of the Philippines by the United States in 1898. Filipinos were not granted American citizenship, however, and were often discriminated against in this country. In 1934 a compromise of sorts was reached in the Tydings McDuffie Act, which promised the Philippines independence in exchange for limiting immigration to the United States to 50 persons per year. Independence did not come until 1946, following World War II.

The Immigration Act of 1965, which allowed more Filipinos to enter the United States, coupled with the suspension of democracy by Ferdinand Marcos in 1972, caused a large influx of Filipino immigrants, including many professionals such as teachers, doctors, and lawyers.

The election of Corazon Aquino as president in 1987 was supported by the United States, but economic troubles still plague the Philippines. Immigration to the United States continues, but at a slower rate. Filipinos, too, have begun to try for more political influence in the 1990s.

The most recent influx of Asian-Americans has been from Vietnam, particularly after the Vietnamese War. After the withdrawal of American forces from what was South Vietnam, many people of that country came to the United States.

At first their numbers were so large that many Vietnamese were detained so that the United States government could help place them in communities. One of the largest camps was at Fort Indiantown Gap, outside Harrisburg, Pennsylvania, which has led to a large number of Vietnamese settling in Pennsylvania, in addition to the Pacific coast states. A number of Vietnamese who had been involved with fishing in their homeland have settled along the Texas Gulf coast, where they have encountered both subtle and blatant discrimination.

The renewed interest in Vietnam, both during and after the Vietnam conflict, has prompted the development of new curricular materials. Berman notes that "there are alternative approaches to the teaching of Vietnam, based on understanding Vietnamese history and culture through Vietnamese literature and poetry." (168) Saul has an annotated list of children's trade books about the Vietnam War available (see end-of-chapter references).

The 1990 census indicates that Asian-Americans are the fastest growing group in the United States, with a 385 percent increase from 1970 to 1990. The 7.3 million Asian-Americans are projected to nearly double (to 13.2 million) by 2005. These immigrants are upwardly mobile; nearly two-thirds of adult Asian immigrants attended college and are proficient in English. In addition, these immigrants started over 70 percent of new small businesses in the United States between 1979 and 1987. (Puente, 4A)

NATIVE AMERICANS

Native American Indians are often studied in textbooks, but that study is usually limited to stereotypes of the colonial era or of frontier settlement. Many textbooks depict Indians as savages who needed "saving," although these texts give little information about the life of contemporary Native Americans. The history of Anglo-Indian relations is rife with broken promises, stolen land, and cultural destruction. Over 2,000 tribal groups once existed in the Americas, most of them in relatively small concentrations so as not to harm the land; Native American Indians sought to live in harmony with nature, a concept unknown to the European invaders.

The Trail of Tears *by Robert Lindneux depicts the relocation of Native Americans from the Southeast to Oklahoma territory in 1838.*

In 1830 the Indian Removal Act allowed for the first major legislative theft of Indian land. Between 1838 and 1839 the Cherokees were forced to move to Oklahoma Indian territory, to be followed by Creeks, Choctaws, and Chickasaws. "During the long march from Georgia to Oklahoma in 1838 and 1839, almost a fourth of the Cherokees died from starvation, diseases, and the perils of the [winter] journey. Their . . . journey is recalled as the 'Trail of Tears.'" (Banks, 1987, 153) Massacres and removals mark the fate of the Indians until the final battle at Wounded Knee Creek, South Dakota, in 1890, in which 300 Sioux were murdered.

The twentieth century brought recognition of such rights for Indians as citizenship, suffrage, and compensation for lost land. Nevertheless, Indian unemployment runs 10 times the national average, and a male Indian's average life expectancy is only 43 years. In recent years self-help groups have been formed by Indians to compensate for the indifference of the government and the general populace to their plight.

EUROPEAN-AMERICANS

This last group constitutes a number of ethnic cultures, all of which have a unique history in this country. Jews, Germans, Irish, Russians, Poles, Italians, Greeks, Swedes, Portuguese—to name only a few—all have ethnic stories to tell. Their influence in America is illustrated by the following facts:

- The second largest concentration of people of Polish ancestry in the world lives in Chicago (first is Warsaw).

FIGURE 5.6

The Changing Face of the U.S.

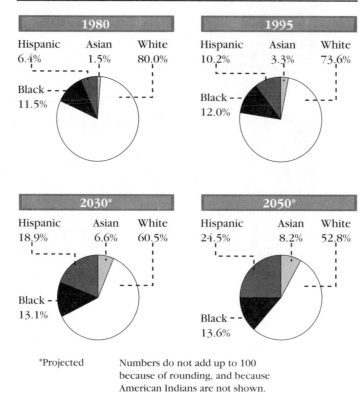

1980		
Hispanic 6.4%	Asian 1.5%	White 80.0%
Black 11.5%		

1995		
Hispanic 10.2%	Asian 3.3%	White 73.6%
Black 12.0%		

2030*		
Hispanic 18.9%	Asian 6.6%	White 60.5%
Black 13.1%		

2050*		
Hispanic 24.5%	Asian 8.2%	White 52.8%
Black 13.6%		

*Projected   Numbers do not add up to 100 because of rounding, and because American Indians are not shown.

SOURCE: Census Bureau.

- The city with the largest Jewish population in the world is New York City (with Tel Aviv second).
- There are more people of Irish ancestry in Boston than in Dublin.
- The southern coast of Massachusetts is known to some as the "Portuguese Coast" because of the large numbers of Portuguese living there.

Historically, Irish-Americans were discriminated against in the mid-1800s, but as their numbers grew and they gained political power prejudice shifted to southern and eastern European immigrant groups—Italians, Slavs, Greeks, and Poles. The treatment of such groups in the late 1800s and early 1900s was deplorable.

Today European groups face less prejudice, but there are still some groups that are subtly or openly discriminated against. The ability to blend in more easily with mainstream society has aided the integration of these European groups, but prejudice remains in many areas.

TEACHING MULTICULTURALISM: GETTING STARTED

Too often ethnic studies and multiculturalism are separated from regular social studies, making ethnic studies seem ancillary to the "real" curriculum. It would be preferable to integrate ethnic studies with the established social studies curriculum. How can this be accomplished?

One way is to include ethnic ideas in the planning of a new unit. For example, in a unit on the newspaper students could learn about William Lloyd Garrison, a pre–Civil War abolitionist who used his Massachusetts newspaper to attack slavery. This would illustrate the power of the press and could be compared with the same power during the Vietnam War era. Another activity could involve student research into current and past ethnic newspapers in the United States. Anna Uhl Ottendorfeer, born in Wurzberg, Bavaria, in 1815, emigrated to the United States in 1836. She and her first husband, Jacob Uhl, bought the newspaper *New-Yorker Staats-Zeitung,* and she shared in the editorial, business, and even composing room and press work. They built the newspaper into a successful institution that was distributed to cities with sizable German communities. It soon became a biweekly and then in 1849 a daily. From the death of her husband in 1852, Anna managed the entire enterprise by herself. Henrietta Szold, born of a German-speaking Hungarian immigrant family, served as a Baltimore correspondent of a New York paper, the *Jewish Messenger.* The *Chicago Defender* and the *Jewish Daily Forward* are two more of many ethnic newspapers that have existed in the United States.

A unit on gold would be an obvious place to discuss immigration, since many people came to the United States from all over the world to seek their fortunes. Even if they did not find gold in California or Alaska, many of these people stayed and contributed to the American culture.

In fifth-grade social studies, there are ample opportunities to integrate the study of various ethnic groups and individuals. In their study of the American Revolution students could learn about the death of Crispus Attucks, a black man, in the Boston Massacre. Without the financial support of Haym Salomon, a Jew, the Revolutionary forces would have been in great peril. Lydia Barrington Darragh, born in Dublin, Ireland, in 1729, emigrated to Philadelphia around 1754 and was credited with saving General George Washington's army. When General Howe commandeered one of her rooms for a secret conference on December 2, 1777, Darragh listened at the keyhole and heard the plan to attack Washington two nights later at Whitemarsh, about eight miles away. She obtained a pass to leave the city and warned Colonel Thomas Craig of the British plan of attack. The British found the Continental army ready to fight, and Howe was forced to return to Philadelphia. These contributions should not be singled out, but should be discussed along with the contributions of Paul Revere, Deborah Sampson, Samuel Adams, Mary McCauley, Benjamin Franklin, and others.

In primary studies about the family, more attention to the extended family might make students whose families include grandparents in the home—unlike the typical nuclear family—feel more comfortable.

The better-developed study of Puerto Rico as a part of the U.S. history course would correct the misconception that Puerto Rico is a separate country, but allow for Puerto Rico's unique culture to be examined.

A science unit on inventors could have an ethnic flavor. Daniel Hale Williams, a black man, was the first to perform open-heart surgery successfully. Gerty Cori, born in Prague in Austria-Hungary (now the Czech Republic) in August of 1896 and who emigrated to the United States in 1922, was a co-recipient of the 1947 Nobel Prize in medicine for her work as a biochemist. Albert Einstein, a Jew, developed the theory of relativity, a great contribution to modern physics. Chien-Shiung Wu, born in China in 1912, who emigrated to the United States in 1936, won the Research Corporation Award in 1958 and was elected to the Academy of Sciences for her confirmation of the Lee-Yang hypothesis. She was considered one of the premier experimental physicists in the world. Often students investigate the lives of Henry Ford or Thomas Edison. Margaret Knight, known as a "woman Edison," had 27 patents to her credit (among them an attachment for paper-bag folding machines that allowed the production of square-bottomed bags) and should be studied as one of the most prolific of women inventors. Students could study other inventors and their ethnic heritages without singling them out as only ethnic group members.

The National Council for the Social Studies (NCSS) has an excellent set of "Curriculum Guidelines for Multicultural Education" available that include a program evaluation checklist. These first appeared in 1976 and were revised in 1991 and were published in toto in the September 1992 *Social Education*. They are available as reprints from NCSS.

WOMEN'S STUDIES AND SEXISM

Over the past 20 years the women's movement has also entered the classroom. The inclusion of more women in social studies courses, the elimination of sexist attitudes and gender-specific language, and the growing body of knowledge about women in contemporary society have all been the focus of school concerns.

Carney has identified the teacher as the key to eliminating sexism in schools. Despite the possible lack of instructional materials available, she notes that:

> Teachers interested in teaching sex equity should not find instructional materials a stumbling block. As they make inroads into this dimension of the program, teachers can adapt the curriculum as needed. (59)

Despite Carney's reassurances, many of the materials available are not academically defensible, so caution is urged.

Ferguson and Smith summarize a number of studies revealing sex stereotyping in children's readers. In one study boys exhibited predominantly active, industrious, and clever traits, whereas girls exhibited mostly passivity. Results of some of these studies are shown in Table 5.2.

TABLE 5.2
Sex Stereotyping in Children's Readers

	NUMBER OF TIMES FOUND IN READERS	
	BOYS	GIRLS
Ingenuity, cleverness	131	33
Industry, problem solving	169	47
Strength, bravery, heroism	143	36
Adventure, exploration, imagination	216	68
Passivity, pseudo-dependence	19	119
Rehearsal for domesticity	50	166
Incompetence, mishaps	51	60
Object of humiliation or victimization	7	68

SOURCE: From Ferguson and Smith, 1976.

Another study cited by Ferguson and Smith focuses on the Hallmark books written by D. Walley entitled *What Boys Can Be* and *What Girls Can Be*.[1] This study revealed the following configuration of occupations by sex:

BOYS CAN BE:	GIRLS CAN BE:
firemen	nurses
baseball players	stewardesses
bus drivers	ballerinas
policemen	candy-shop owners
cowboys	models
doctors	big movie or TV stars
sailors	secretaries
pilots	artists
clowns	teachers
farmers	singers
actors	designers
astronauts	brides
president	housewives
	mothers

[1] The study, by Weitzmann and others, is entitled "Sex Role Socialization in Picture Books for Children," *American Journal of Sociology,* vol. 77, May 1972, pp. 1125–49.

WOMEN IN PROFESSIONS

Since World War II there has been steady growth in the number of women entering professional fields that formerly were seen as the exclusive province of men. That growth has accelerated since 1975. The following statistics illustrate the trend:

Percentage of Medical Degrees (M.D.) Received by Women

1950	1960	1965	1970	1975	1980	1985	1990	1992
.7	.8	.7	.9	3.1	13.3	30.4	34.2	35.7

Percentage of Law Degrees (LL.B., J.D.) Received by Women

1950	1960	1965	1970	1975	1980	1985	1900	1992
(NA)	2.5	3.2	5.4	15.1	30.2	38.5	42.2	42.7

Percentage of Dentistry Degrees (B.S., M.S., Ph. D.) Received by Women

1950	1960	1965	1970	1975	1980	1985	1990	1992
.5	.8	(NA)	.9	3.1	13.3	20.7	30.9	32.3

The authors present guidelines for evaluating instructional materials regarding: (1) visibility of males and females; (2) role models—male and female; (3) behavior regarding active or passive roles; (4) language; and (5) parallel treatment of men and women.

As Carney notes, teachers must aid in teaching in a nonsexist manner. What can they do? Sadker and Sadker suggest a number of strategies, including (1) raising awareness, (2) values clarification and analysis, and (3) intentional nonsexist teaching. An awareness activity might include charting television shows to see if males or females have leadership roles in various programs. A clarification activity might include things like values voting regarding women's roles in society. An action activity could be to produce student-made material filling in the gaps in a social studies textbook in areas regarding women. The authors use this example of the third strategy:

> The difficulties of establishing nonsexist teaching patterns are great, but so are the rewards. It is heartening to observe the reactions of a suburban Maryland first-grade class in which a talented teacher has been working to loosen the stereotypes that confine young minds.
>
> When the six-year-olds were shown *I'm Glad I'm a Boy! I'm Glad I'm a Girl!*, the picture book that announces that boys are doctors, pilots, policemen, and presidents while girls are nurses, stewardesses, metermaids, and first ladies, the effects of nonsexist teaching were apparent in the youngsters' reactions. Most of the students were appalled at a book they clearly saw as inaccurate.

WOMEN'S LITERACY TEST

Indicate whether each of the following statements is TRUE or FALSE by placing "T" or "F" in the space that precedes it.

1._____ Susan B. Anthony and Elizabeth Cady Stanton formed the American Woman Suffrage Association in 1869.

2._____ Frances Wright established a reservation called Nashoba for the gradual emancipation of slaves by purchasing and colonizing them.

3._____ President Abraham Lincoln received Sojourner Truth, an emancipated slave, in the White House in 1864.

4._____ Jane Addams was a co-recipient of the Nobel Peace Prize in 1931 for founding and presiding over the Women's International League for Peace and Freedom.

5._____ Victoria Woodhull was the first female candidate to run for the office of president of the United States.

6._____ "Declaration of Sentiments," patterned after the Declaration of Independence, was issued at a convention of women in Seneca Falls, New York, in July 1848.

- Not true. Girls can be presidents too. And other stuff.
- It's too dumb and telling boys and girls what they can and can't do is wrong.
- This book doesn't tell the truth about what people can do.
- I don't like this book. It gets male chauvinist ideas into kid's minds. (114)

The Women's Literacy Test, part of which is shown in the box above, was developed by Vanessa Curry, a student at Penn State University, to provide a fuller perspective on the role of women in American culture. The first question addresses the suffrage movement and some of its leaders—Susan B. Anthony, Elizabeth Cady Stanton, Lucy Stone, and Julia Ward Howe—and the organizations they formed. Frances Wright's plan (see box) was approved by both Thomas Jefferson and James Madison. Sojourner Truth was an eloquent speaker who was a leader in both the abolitionist cause and the rights of women. Jane Addams did more than found Hull House, the renowned settlement house in Chicago. Victoria Woodhull's name was recalled when Geraldine Ferraro ran for vice-president on the Democratic ticket in 1984; Woodhull ran on the Equal Rights party slate. The Declaration of Sentiments, signed by 68 women and 32 men, highlighted the single most important issue of feminism, that the preamble to the Declaration of Independence should be extended to include both women and men as created equal.

WHAT MAKES AMERICAN CULTURE?

American students today are becoming more and more aware of a cultural perspective in their readings and school materials. Most elementary social studies texts use anthropological concepts in some way to show so-called cultural universals. The study of various world cultures now focuses on all aspects of a culture; in studying Japan, for example, students learn of and may even participate in origami, martial arts, Kabuki theater, bonsai gardening, and so on.

Unfortunately, most students do not get commensurate exposure when they study American culture. Despite the proliferation of movies, television, music, sports, and arts all around them, most instructional materials assiduously avoid legitimizing American culture. The student may feel that what exists in America has no cultural history or impact on society as a whole. Of course, this flies directly in the faces of Madonna, Alex Rodriguez, Tiger Woods, Whoopi Goldberg, Norman Lear, Michael Jackson, Gloria Estefan, Michael Jordan, Jodie Foster, and the *Star Wars* films of George Lucas. These, however, are not recognized by students as an extension of American's cultural development. Instead, they exist as isolated pieces of entertainment.

Ideas for Studying American Culture

Turner suggests a number of activities for studying popular culture that are basically contemporary in approach, whereas Cooper focuses on popular music ideas but presents them both historically and contemporarily.

Much of the research and development of such ideas depends on the teacher. The interest of students makes the time invested well worth it. For example, when using a standard American political history textbook to teach the fifth and sixth grades, a teacher could research material, prepare handouts, overheads, and bulletin boards on the cultural experience of American baseball. For example, one could begin with the rules drawn up by Alexander Cartwright for the Knickerbocker Baseball Club in the 1840s, followed by town ball of the 1860s, the first professional league in 1871, and the National Association of Professional Baseball Players.

The history of American baseball reflects American social history—racial and ethnic discrimination, the popularity among immigrant groups, the Sunday baseball bans, the reintroduction of blacks in 1947 (seven years before the *Brown* v. *Board of Education* decision), and the big business of sport as illustrated by massive player salaries, the shifting of teams, and the reflected demographic shifts in the American population. If one doesn't like baseball, one could study architecture, with a particular focus on the Chicago School of Louis Sullivan, Frank Lloyd Wright, Ludwig Mies van der Rohe, I. M. Pei, and Philip Johnson. Ballet in America is another option. Its history, early pioneers, and leading contemporary companies, like the Joffrey, American Ballet Theater, New York City Ballet, and San Francisco Ballet, could all be studied. George Balanchine, Martha Graham, or another giant of American dance might serve as the focus of study. Obviously there are many possibilities for a unit on American culture. The key here is teacher interest and student interest: one should choose something in which both the teacher and the students can share mutual enjoyment. Throughout these studies, one will find concepts of economics, sociology, geography, history, and anthropology. Such an approach is academically justifiable—even if it is fun.

QUESTIONS AND ACTIVITIES

1. Determine how your state defines gifted. What provisions for educating gifted students are state mandated or recommended?

2. Discuss with a teacher the ways he or she tries to provide different social studies activities for learning disabled, EMR, and hearing-impaired students.

3. Examine a regular classroom in a school. Can you see ways to rearrange the room to better deliver social studies lessons?

4. Do some research on outstanding members of *your* ethnic group. Discuss with your parents any hardships your relatives might have encountered as members of an ethnic group.

5. What are the unique problems that immigrants from Mexico and Central America face in becoming successful in the United States? Where would you go to find answers to this question?

6. Research the politics of Puerto Rico. Are the political parties the same as on the mainland? How is Puerto Rico represented in Congress, and by whom?

7. Obtain census data for the 20 largest cities in the United States. What percentage of each city is "nonwhite"?

8. Examine two or three elementary social studies textbooks to see how ethnic groups, women, different age groups, and handicapped persons are portrayed.

9. Outline a unit that focuses on American culture and list possible resources in your community that would enhance the teaching of such a unit.

10. The Equal Rights Amendment was not passed by two-thirds of the states and therefore did not become law. The amendment is this:

> Equality of rights under the law shall not be denied or abridged by the United States or any state on account of sex.

Is there still a need for such an amendment?

11. A number of states have passed "English only" laws, making English the only language in which governmental activities (not schooling) can be conducted. Congress has been pressured to pass such national legislation. What are your feelings about such laws?

REFERENCES

Abrams, L. *Inquiry into Anthropology.* New York: Globe Books, 1976.

Banks, J. *An Introduction to Multicultural Education.* Boston: Allyn and Bacon, 1994.

Banks, James A. *Teaching Strategies for Ethnic Studies.* 4th ed. Boston: Allyn and Bacon, 1987.

Berman, D. M. "Perspectives on the Teaching of Vietnam," *The Social Studies,* July/August 1986, pp. 165–168.

California State Department of Education. *Social Sciences: Curriculum Guide for Teaching Gifted Children Social Sciences in Grades One through Three.* rev. ed. Ed 152 020. Sacramento, CA, 1977.

Carney, L. "Responses to Sexism: Two Steps Forward and One Back?" In *Racism and Sexism: Responding to the Challenge.* R. Simms and G. Contreras, eds. NCSS Bul. 61. Washington, DC: National Council for the Social Studies, 1980.

Clement, Kim. "Understanding Handicaps." Photocopy. Pennsylvania State University, November 1980.

Cooper, B. L. "Popular Music in the Social Studies Classroom: Audio Resources for Teachers." NCSS How-to-Do-It Series 2, no. 13. Washington, DC: National Council for the Social Studies, 1981.

Curry, V. "Women's Literacy Test." Unpublished paper. Pennsylvania State University, 1990.

Dupuis, M. M., E. N. Askov, B. Badiali, and J. Lee. *Teaching Reading and Writing in the Content Areas.* Glenview, IL: Scott Foresman, 1989.

Ellis, A. K. *Teaching and Learning Elementary Social Studies.* 5th ed. Boston: Allyn and Bacon, 1995.

Ferguson, P., and L. C. Smith. "Treatment of the Sexes in Instructional Materials: Guidelines for Evaluation." In *Teaching About Women in the Social Studies.* J. D. Grambs, ed. National Council for the Social Studies, Bul. 48. Washington, DC, 1976.

Gaston, J. *Cultural Awareness Teaching Techniques.* Brattleboro, VT: Pro Lingua Associates, 1984.

Goldsmith, J., et al. *Teaching Units for Challenging the More Able Student in the Classroom.* Ed. 001 287. San Jose, CA: Cupertino Union School District, San Jose State College, 1961.

Herlihy, J. G., and M. T. Herlihy, eds. "Mainstreaming in the Social Studies." NCSS, Bul. 62. Washington, DC: National Council for the Social Studies, 1980.

Hiernaux, J. "The Concept of Race and the Taxonomy of Mankind." In *To See Ourselves.* T. Weaver, ed. Glenview, IL: Scott Foresman, 1973.

Holmes, S. "U.S. Urged to Reflect Wider Diversity in Racial and Ethnic Classifications," *New York Times,* July 8, 1994, p. A18.

Houston, J. W., and J. Wakatsuki, *Farewell to Manzanar.* Boston: Houghton Mifflin, 1973.

Kuhns, K. "Deafness." Photocopy. Pennsylvania State University, June 1989.

Lee, F. "Intolerance to Be Topic for Students," *New York Times,* September 18, 1989, p. A31.

Leeman, N. *The Promised Land.* New York: Vintage Books, 1992.

McArthur, B. *Enrichment Activities For the Gifted Child in the Regular Classroom—Grades Four Through Eight.* Ed 001 290. Cullowhee, NC: Western Carolina College, 1960.

McCarthy, M. "Inclusion and the Law: Recent Judicial Developments," *Research Bulletin* no. 13, Phi Delta Kappa Center for Evaluation, Development and Research, Bloomington, IN, November, 1994.

Mezzacappa, D. "History? Essay on Puerto Ricans Fails Test," *Philadelphia Inquirer,* February 9, 1990, p. B-1.

Morganthou, T. "What Color is Black?," *Newsweek,* vol. 125, no. 7, February 13, 1995.

National Council for the Social Studies Task Force on Ethnic Studies. "Curriculum Guidelines for Multicultural Education," *Social Education,* vol. 56, no. 4, September 1992, pp. 274-294.

Pregler, H. O. "Social Studies." In *Curriculum Planning for the Gifted.* L. A. Fliegler, ed. Englewood Cliffs, NJ: Prentice-Hall, 1964.

Prewitt, J. "Hispanic Communities." In *Content Area Reading.* M. Dupuis and E. Askov, eds. Englewood Cliffs, NJ: Prentice-Hall, 1982.

Puente, M. "Study: Asian Immigrants Fastest," *USA Today,* March 28, 1996, p. 4A.

Richards, L. "Handicaps." Photocopy. Pennsylvania State University, May 1988.

Rocha, R. M., and G. P. Gregory. "The Resource Room." In *Social Education,* January 1979, vol. 43, no. 1, p. 63.

Ryan, H. "Deaf Awareness." Photocopy. Pennsylvania State University, May 1981.

Sadker, D., and M. Sadker. "Nonsexist Teaching: Strategies and Practical Applications." In *Teaching About Women in the Social Studies.* J. D. Grambs, ed. NCSS, Bul. 48. Washington, DC: National Council for the Social Studies, 1976.

Sanford, H. "Organizing and Presenting Social Studies Content in a Mainstreamed Class." In *Mainstreaming in the Social Studies,* J. Herlihy and M. Herlihy, eds. Washington, DC: National Council for the Social Studies, 1980.

Shaver, J. P., and C. K. Curtis. "Handicapism: Another Challenge for Social Studies," *Social Education,* vol. 45, no. 3, March 1981, p. 208-211.

Trainor, Lois. "A Resource Guide for Third Grade Summer School Acceleration Classes." In *The American Indian.* Ed 00 1850. Sacramento, CA: California State Department of Education, 1963.

Turner, T. N. "Using Popular Culture in the Social Studies." NCSS How-to-Do-It Series 2, no. 9. Washington, DC: National Council for the Social Studies, 1979.

USEFUL ADDRESSES

For an annotated list of children's trade books about the Vietnam War, write Wendy Saul, Dept. of Education, University of Maryland-Baltimore County, 5401 Wilkens Ave., Catonsville, MD 21228.

For supplies, films, videos, books, kits, and other classroom materials on the studies of women in American society, write the National Women's History Project, 77838 Bell Rd, Windsor, CA 95492-8515.

For NCSS materials, write to 3501 Newark St., NW, Washington, DC 20016.

PART III

Teaching Strategies

Chapter Six

INQUIRY, LECTURE, AND GUIDED DISCOVERY

Teachers become predictable to their students long before they realize it. Although many students, particularly young ones, need and feel comfortable with structure, that does not mean a dull sameness day after day. The classroom should not be a static place. Surprising students with an unexpected activity can reap rewards. Teachers should have a direction in mind, however, before they abandon their initial direction in mid-lesson.

This chapter will consider three basic strategies for teaching social studies: inquiry, lecture, and guided discovery. Inquiry teaching is a divergent process in which the teacher serves as a resource but allows students to draw their own conclusions. Because it depends on student responses, the outcome of inquiry teaching can never be predicted.

The second strategy, lecturing, can be useful under certain circumstances in providing background information. The chapter describes a number of factors involved in preparing a lecture—student attention span, eye contact, audiovisual aids, and the arrangement of the classroom.

In guided discovery and concept development, the teacher seeks to elicit a specific response from students through careful questioning, rather than by merely stating what is important. In this sense, guided discovery strikes a sort of middle ground between lecture-recitation and inquiry. Because concept development largely depends on how one defines concepts, several popular views of concept formation are presented.

INQUIRY

It is usually easier to demonstrate the process of inquiry than to describe it. As an experiment, examine these 15 items:

IHOO	SUIRIMOS	DRE
ISLONILI	BLUICOMA	SLACHER
DROOLOAC	MEJAS	ANKES
SHODNU	SARNSAKA	CAMPTOO
MELARH	WALDEERA	ACCIHOG

Now do what you think is necessary to solve this "problem." Well? What is the answer? What is the problem?

To answer these questions, we have to understand what assumptions the person presenting the problem is making about his or her audience. Similarly, the student makes certain assumptions about the teacher's intentions before solving any problem. The assumptions for this problem might be as follows:

TEACHER'S ASSUMPTIONS

- Students can recognize symbols.
- Students can read English.
- Students can spell English.
- Students can recognize scrambled words and reorganize them into English words.
- Students have some background in geography, particularly U.S. geography.
- Students will recognize the American rivers.

STUDENT'S ASSUMPTIONS

- I am rational.
- There is a purpose to this task.
- These are scrambled words.
- These are state names (after unscrambling the first few).
- These are geographic names.
- These are geographic names of U.S. sites
- These are all names of American rivers

Although no instructions are given with this problem, most people who have tried it have concluded that these were the names of American rivers. This conclusion is based on experience with hundreds of students at levels ranging from elementary school through college.

We all know that teachers jumble words, that newspapers print word jumble games, and that most American students have some knowledge of American geography. If we gave this list to non-English speakers or to foreign nationals who speak English, there is no predicting what might happen. In short, I am suggesting that teachers should *know* their students. This should be obvious, but it is not always so.

The method that most people use to solve this exercise is based on the *inquiry model,* a modification of the scientific method. To inquire, a teacher must assume certain knowledge as well as certain attitudes and values. Using this as given, the inquiry method proceeds as follows:

First, a problem is discerned. Second, a hypothesis is formed. Third, the hypothesis is tested. Then additional data are gathered, leading to a new hypothesis, which again is tested. When the hypothesis is found satisfactory, a conclusion is reached. The process is illustrated in Figure 6.1.

Using this method, the answers reached for the exercise on page 160 are:

OHIO	MISSOURI	RED
ARKANSAS	HUDSON	POTOMAC
ILLINOIS	CHARLES	COLUMBIA
DELAWARE	HARLEM	CHICAGO
COLORADO	SNAKE	JAMES

One of the goals of inquiry is to foster divergent thinking and develop creativity in students. Criticism has been leveled against the schools and the educational system because of the emphasis they place on creativity. Teachers claim that they want to instill creativity in their students but that students also have to learn the right answers. This exercise, as described, is clearly not the answer, simply because *most* people would arrive at the same solution. The norm is predictable. Creativity is, by definition, *not* the norm.

Thus the teacher should recognize and foster alternatives to the American rivers answer. In the years that I have used the exercise, only one class has failed to produce some deviance. In most cases, the creative individuals feel frustrated and embarrassed for being different and for not getting the obvious answer. The teacher should strongly support the creative intentions.

The exercise is usually done in pairs. One pair of students went so far as to create a whole cosmology in answer to the assignment, as shown in Figure 6.2. Their explanation of their answers went as follows:

IHOO—Queen grandmother of Waldeera, mother of Camptoo

ISLONILI—Enemy nation of Ihoo

FIGURE 6.1
The Process of Inquiry

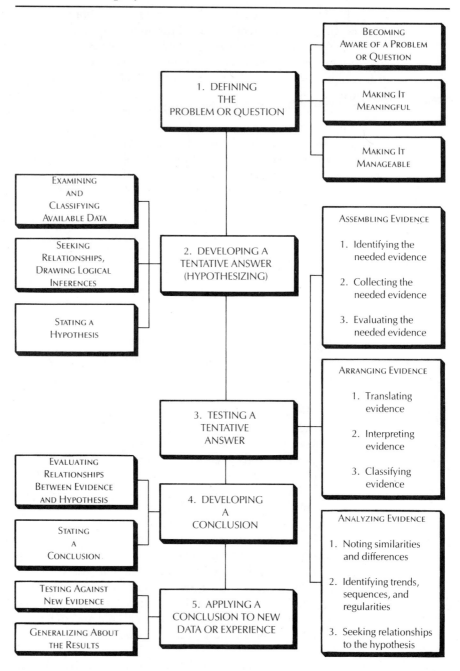

SOURCE: From Barry K. Beyer, *Teaching Thinking in Social Studies.* Columbus, OH: Merrill, 1979. Used by permission.

FIGURE 6.2

One Student Pair's Solution to the Jumbled Word Exercise

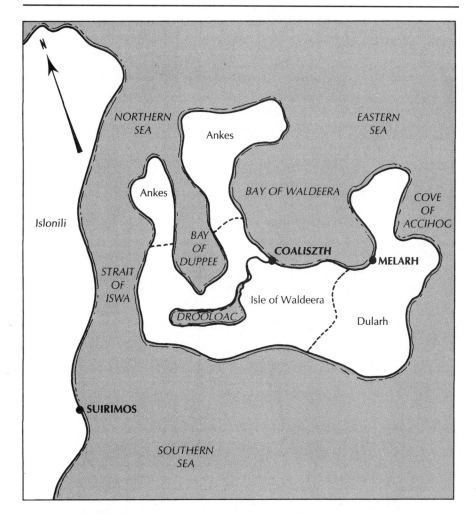

SARNSAKA—One time parliament of Dre; all were killed by Ihoo

WALDEERA—Island country where the Dre rule under Queen Ihoo

DROOLOAC—Only freshwater lake in Waldeera

SUIRIMOS—King, cousin of Ihoo and ruler of Islonili

SHODNU—Southern extended highlands of Waldeera; Melarh is the main city

SLACHER—First man of Waldeera; husband to Ihoo and Camptoo

MELARH—Main town of Dularh, peopled only by males

ANKES—Northern mountainous country of Waldeera; home of Duppee

DRE—Island people (matriarchal); shorter than Duppee, taller than Dularh

CAMPTOO—Queen mother of Waldeera; mother of no daughters of the true king

BLUICOMA—Daughter of Camptoo; illegitimate ACCIHOG—True surname of Ihoo and Camptoo, surname of Dularh

This particular solution incorporates the process of mythology, or the telling of a creation story, something shared by almost all cultures. Going further with this solution could give the students greater insight into a culture's view of the world.

After performing such an exercise, one can appreciate the feelings of frustration and helplessness that students often encounter when given this type of assignment. An assignment that is obvious to the teacher may not always be obvious to children and can rekindle those same feelings of frustration. Some students do not hear well; others do not listen well; still others do not understand oral directions. Whatever the reason, the teacher should try to discern student understanding with a minimum of embarrassment to the individual. We all get confused sometimes.

A Teacher's Role in Inquiry

Many teachers profess to be inquiry teachers, noting disdainfully that they do not lecture to their students. It should be added, however, that inquiry requires *some* prerequisite knowledge, or one ends up inquiring about inquiry. Where does the prerequisite knowledge come from? Any number of sources are appropriate for generating useful knowledge. Take a moment and try to list some.

In doing so, it becomes apparent in how many different ways we gather information yet fail to realize it consciously. Our parents are a source of data, our friends and peers another. People do supply us with knowledge and influence our attitudes. While teaching in Chicago, I discovered that students often argued about the merits of certain baseball players on the Cubs or White Sox team. Their arguments were basically inquiry in mode, with knowledge provided by parents and peers.

A person's knowledge and attitudes are also shaped by the media—newspapers, television, radio. The knowledge base is expanded by films, filmstrips, guest lecturers in class, direct observations, and community participation. Most teachers transmit knowledge through a lecture or "lecturette" at some time or another. Lectures usually comprise the heart of the expository mode of teaching social studies. They will be examined later in this chapter. Inquiry teaching relies on the belief that all of us want to know and understand. We may not all want to know and understand the *same things,* however, so it is up to the teacher to allow students to pursue their own interests based on an initial common problem. For example, a class of third graders is studying their community.

CRITICAL THINKING

A valuable skill that is being rediscovered by educators is critical thinking—the process of thinking critically, being skeptical, digging for answers, not merely accepting information without question.

The idea of teaching critical thinking is hardly new. Back in 1942 the yearbook of the National Council for the Social Studies was entitled *Teaching Critical Thinking in the Social Studies*. Yearbook editor Howard Anderson noted that "critical thinking has long been accepted as a goal of instruction of the social studies."*

The yearbook committee of 1942 asserted that students should develop skills in critical thinking by mastering the subskills of analysis, evaluation, and hypothesis for formulation and by applying these skills in a variety of situations. For the most part, however, teachers have continued to ignore critical thinking. Some 50 years later it is still needed and largely untaught.

Those who advocate critical thinking maintain that students who master these skills and who learn to think independently will benefit both inside and outside the classroom. Such skills can be applied to daily living—in obeying laws, making economic decisions, buying products, interacting with family and peers, and viewing the world and the media.

As a result of the renewed interest, several schools have recently initiated critical thinking programs for students in the sixth through twelfth grades. In Detroit, seventh and eighth graders are being offered a course called "Philosophy for Children" that teaches logic and deductive reasoning. The Detroit schools recently began a special course on decision making for third and fifth graders.

Systematic teaching of critical thinking must be done every day, using variants of the scientific process on inquiry (see Figure 6.1). The biggest obstacle to critical thinking is the fear that it may take too much time from teaching the content that students *must* know. This process-versus-content argument has raged since the time of Aristotle. Is it any wonder that it has not yet been resolved?

* *Teaching Critical Thinking in the Social Studies,* Howard Anderson, ed. Washington, DC: National Council for the Social Studies, 1942.

As a stimulus, the teacher takes the students to a town square or neighborhood. The students then stroll, as a class, around the area trying to formulate questions while they observe the environment. Some questions they might raise:

- How old is that building?
- Has it always been here?
- What was here before?
- Why is that building made of brick but other buildings are not?
- That other building has IOOF above the second-floor windows. What does that mean?

- Why is that house so far back from the street?
- What is under a manhole cover?
- Do the people who own the businesses own the buildings?
- Do they live in the buildings, too?
- Why is there a statue of a soldier?
- Why do some signs say ((P)) rather than "no parking"?

To answer these questions, students could do research, individually or in small groups, about community history, development, economics, resources, and so on. The teacher helps by being a resource, but not by providing answers. Students also need skills in how to use an index and a table of contents before embarking on their research.

The teacher should provide classroom reference materials, such as encyclopedias or magazines. A teacher who sends third or even fourth graders to the library resource center to do research is simply using student time and is shifting the burden of responsibility almost totally to the librarian. Fifth- and sixth-grade students should be able to do this kind of research on their own; primary-grade students need to have their materials available in the classroom, with pages *marked* for use.

Application

A number of small affordable kits that take an inquiry approach and include cultural artifacts from one geographic region or ethnic group have been developed in the past 10 years. They are largely based on a concept first perfected by the most widely known kits, the MATCH kits from the Boston Children's Museum. MATCH (Materials and Activities to Teach Children History) kits are designed and recommended for various grade levels, but they can be adapted to almost any level. The kits, which are expensive but durable, include "Paddle-to-the-Sea," "Indians Who Met the Pilgrims," "Life in the Middle Ages," "The City," "Japan," and "The House of Ancient Greece."[1]

"The House of Ancient Greece" consists of artifact reproductions modeled after those found at the site of a villa excavated by archaeologists in the 1930s. The team of archaeologists, led by David Robinson of the University of Chicago, spent years at the site, Olynthus, a resort city of ancient Greece. The city flourished around 400 BCE, and the site is wonderfully preserved.

The reproductions, handmade to scale by Greek craftsmen, add great authenticity to the kit. Also included are diagrams, floor plans, reference books, two filmstrips, and two *actual* artifacts (a pottery shard and a coin).

The kit is self-contained and includes suggestions for at least 11 separate activities, which would allow for two or three weeks of unit study using the kit as a key element. The first suggested activity is excavating a wastebasket,

---

[1] "The House of Ancient Greece" kit costs about $500 but will last at least 10 years.

which introduces students to the study of archaeology. The most important message here is that conclusions can be wrong because of insufficient data or inaccurate interpretation.

ACTIVITY 1: EXCAVATING A WASTEBASKET[2]

Description: The children take one thing at a time out of a full wastebasket. Using these clues, they try to discover which room the basket stood in, what went on in the room, and what kind of people used it.

Objectives: To introduce children to the methods of archaeology. To show that much can be learned about people from what they leave behind. To demonstrate that what is learned from people's leavings depends on careful observation, precise record keeping, and thoughtful interpretation.

Materials: A full wastebasket from another classroom, the teachers' lounge, or the principal's office that contains provocative clues. You might want to borrow a basket from another familiar source—such as the local candy store, a bank, or the post office.

Procedure: Do not tell the children where the basket comes from. They should discover this by themselves in the process of excavating the basket.

1. Place the basket so all can see it. Appoint one student (a lively one!) as excavator. The excavator's job is to remove objects from the basket one by one and describe them carefully so the class can discuss them. Important clues should be passed around.

    Appoint another student as cataloger. The cataloger's job is to draw a cross-sectional view of the basket on the blackboard and note the position of important items as they are dug up by the excavator.

2. Excavate the basket, piece by piece. Ask the students to give evidence for their conclusions about the contents. Explain that they need to be good detectives to do this job well. From the clues in the basket, help the children find answers to questions such as:

What is each item? (Careful detective thinking is necessary at every moment, or final conclusions may be wrong.)

Who might have thrown it in?

How long ago was it thrown in?

Has the basket been filled up quickly, or are there some fairly old, stale things in it?

Which items give the best clues?

Where does the basket come from?

---

[2] Used by permission. Boston Children's Museum (1965).

Following are several important points about excavating that may be brought out during the activity:

A. Once the basket has been excavated, it is easy to forget where items were. Unless careful notes are kept the first time, there is no way of rechecking the position of each object.

B. We can feel quite sure about some things but can only make guesses about others. For example, if we find math papers identified with the names of fifth-grade students, we may feel fairly sure that the basket comes from the room where that math class is held. But several half-eaten apples do not tell us definitely if a group ate lunch in the room with the basket or if a few passing people just happened to throw away their apple cores there.

C. It is possible to come to the wrong conclusions or to be fooled by what we see.

Note: Procedures (1) and (2) introduce students to the process of archaeology. You may prefer to use just one of these to ready your class for "excavating" the villa or to do both activities the same day. Keep these activities short; stop before students get bored.

Following this activity, or independent of it, students may examine the materials of "the House of Ancient Greece." The artifacts are in six boxes, each corresponding to one of the room areas shown in Figure 6.3 (alpha, beta, gamma, delta, zeta, and epsilon).

Over a period of two to three days, students should examine each artifact from their "room" as well as pictures of other artifacts found in that room. They should attempt to determine the function of the various objects and of the individual rooms through the process of inquiry, much as an archaeologist would.

Students working in groups of four to five should then compare their hypotheses and conclusions with the "archaeologists' notes" for each room and see how accurate their assumptions are.

The rooms of the house had various uses, but generally the functions are discernible without great difficulty. The exercise itself allows students to apply their conclusions to new data, a vital step in the process of inquiring.

LECTURE

As noted earlier, the assembling of evidence requires a variety of information sources. Lecturing is one of those sources. Many people scoff at the idea of lecturing to young children, but one need only visit any primary grade classroom to note that lecturing can and does occur at this early grade level. Teachers must like lecturing to some extent, or they would not do it so much, would they?

A lecture should be well organized, not just a series of facts thrown together with "and," "or," and "but." When dealing with children, organization is especially vital. Some good questions to ask *before* choosing a lecture approach include:

FIGURE 6.3
Plan of the Villa of Good Fortune

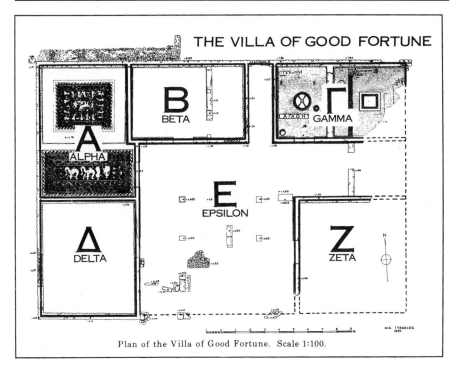

Plan of the Villa of Good Fortune. Scale 1:100.

SOURCE: From "The House of Ancient Greece," Boston Children's Museum (1965).

- What is the purpose of this lesson?
- Is there important information on it accessible to students and me?
- Is the topic interesting?
- Is this the *best* way to impart the information? Why? (Time, shortage of materials, assurance that all students will receive the same information.)
- Are there alternatives to this approach, and have they been considered?
- Can my students sit and listen to a lecture for the required amount of time?

If the answers to these questions are all "yes," then a lecture should be organized for class presentation. In preparing a lecture, a teacher should consider factors other than content. These include:

Vocabulary	Student attention span
Audiovisual aids	Concept use
Room arrangement	Individual student needs

When choosing a lecture topic, the teacher also should consider how long students generally will retain their interest. For very young students five to 10 minutes may be the maximum length of time, but for sixth graders a lecture of 40 minutes might be possible. Although five minutes may not seem like a lecture to a college student, it surely does to a five-year-old, particularly when many new terms are introduced.

The vocabulary of students also should be considered. If new terms are not necessary, do not use them, or use only a few. If new terms *are* necessary, they should be defined and illustrated as they are introduced. Many terms may be familiar orally but not in written form and vice versa, so all new terms should be written on the board.

My own experience serves as an example. For years I thought that the word "facade" was two different words. The oral version was pronounced "fasahd." The other was written "facade" and, in my mind, pronounced "fakayd." It was only later that these versions merged in my mind—I had never been introduced to the word in an organized, planned context.

Audiovisual aids should be used if a term or concept is particularly complicated or unfamiliar. For example, a slide showing the facade of a building would help clarify a lecture on architectural styles in the local community. Slides, overheads, models, and other tangible items make a lecture come alive. A lecture on world hunger would be enhanced by having a small bowl of rice handy—the amount of food consumed daily by the average Cambodian, for example.

Years ago most classrooms had fixed seating. Desks were bolted to the floor, and the arrangement of the seating was a nonissue in classroom presentations. This is no longer the case. The arrangement of the room gives a message to students. If desks cannot be moved, the message is that order predominates, even at the expense of learning. Desks are not mobile merely for the convenience of the building custodian; they are meant to be moved to meet the educational needs of the students.

During inquiry teaching, desks are best arranged in groups of three, four, or five in various sectors of the room (Figure 6.4). This arrangement gives students the opportunity to work together, while being separated from other groups dealing with similar but different tasks. During a lecture the teacher may wish to move all students close to the board. If this is not feasible, desks should be arranged like the seats in an amphitheater, to reinforce the notion that students' attention should be directed toward the lecturer (Figure 6.4). This reduces the number of students in the rear of the room, maximizes student attention, and improves sight lines.

Individual student needs during a lecture may vary. For example, some may require longer eye contact for reinforcement of listening. The teacher may also want to address a student directly, or use that student's name in an example when answering his or her questions or concerns. In addition, students with special needs, such as the hearing impaired or visually impaired, should be seated to allow them access to the teacher.

FIGURE 6.4
Alternative Arrangements of Classroom Seating

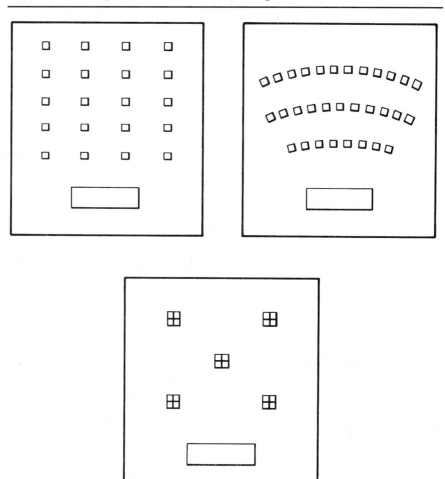

A lecture should be accompanied by a handout summarizing concepts, dates, or names, so that students don't have to scramble to write down all this information. In most elementary grades (kindergarten through fourth grade), note taking during lectures should be discouraged, if not forbidden. Only in the upper grades, when it can be undertaken seriously, should note taking be required during a lecture. The elementary school lecture, unlike the college lecture, should not emphasize or highlight detail. The lecture should be a story. This does not mean all details are omitted, only that minutiae should not be related for their own sake. Concepts should be the greater concern of the elementary school lecture, and they can be taught by accentuating and illustrating them clearly.

Why are some lectures better than others? Or, more important, why are some *lecturers* better than others? Over a number of years I have observed and have asked students these questions. Some characteristics of a good lecturer stand out.

1. Well prepared—knows the material. There is no substitute for preparation.
2. Has a good speaking voice and varies the tone. Both qualities can be worked on to improve them.
3. Knows the students. Can personalize content for the class, the community, or the school when examples or illustrations are sought.
4. Varies the pace. No machine-gun pattern, or any dragging either.
5. A sense of humor. This should come naturally in the lecture; if it is forced, students can tell and will resent being patronized.
6. Eye contact—does not keep the head down all the time.
7. An interest in the material. If there, it shows; if not there, that shows, too.
8. Use of audiovisual aids if warranted. This is not vital, but if the aids fit, fine. Do not use audiovisual material just to do so.
9. Good introduction and good conclusion. Like a good book, a good lecture should suggest directions and intentions. A conclusion should provide a recap and closure.

CONCEPT-GUIDED DISCOVERY

Weil et al. describe the process of concept development and attainment as being adapted from the work of psychologists like Jerome Bruner. During concept development, teachers guide students, often through a series of yes-no questions, toward an understanding of a particular concept. For example, suppose the teacher puts two columns on the board, labels one "Yes" and one "No," beneath the first column writes "Mississippi River," and beneath the second writes "Long Island." If students could hypothesize about the concept involved in this exercise, they might guess that the "Yes" column represents bodies of water and the "No" column represents land masses. The concept is revealed through the "Yes" column.

The teacher could then present another yes-no pair, "Ohio River" and "Chesapeake Bay." Students might guess that the concept here is river, which should be illustrated, but the teacher might be looking for a more specific concept. If "Yes" is the Sacramento River and "No" is the Susquehanna River, the concept might be *navigable* rivers, which would be important for understanding geography and commerce. Table 6.1 provides an example of what the teacher's completed columns might look like.

The process of concept attainment, which might be part of the preparation for a lecture, is similar to inquiry. One important difference, however, is

JEROME BRUNER AND THE PROCESS OF EDUCATION

Jerome Bruner, a psychologist at Harvard University, has long been identified with concept development in education. Bruner's seminal work, *The Process of Education,** led to much of his identification with concepts in learning. The book grew out of a conference held at Woods Hole, Massachusetts, in September of 1959, where more than 30 scientists, scholars, and educators gathered to discuss how science education in American schools might be improved. Many viewed the curriculum as "in crisis" following the Soviet launching of the Sputnik satellite.

Participants spent 10 days in various work groups, which were entitled "Sequence of a Curriculum," "The Apparatus of Teaching," "The Motivation of Learning," "The Role of Intuition in Learning and Thinking," and "Cognitive Processes in Learning," and there was an executive committee with Bruner as chairman. The conference was supported by the National Science Foundation, the U.S. Office of Education, the Air Force, and the Rand Corporation.

Each work group offered progress reports on new curriculum projects, position papers on requirements in the curriculum, and appraisals of work being done in the schools. These reports were not written as final statements, however. It fell to the chairman, Bruner, to prepare a report that encapsulated the major themes, principal conjectures, and conclusions. Bruner's "sense of the conference" became *The Process of Education.*

In his book Bruner identified the most general objective of education: that it cultivate excellence and that "each student achieve his optimum intellectual development." (9) Four themes constitute the bulk of this volume. First is the role of structure in learning and how it may be made central in teaching. The second is concerned with readiness for learning. The third involves the nature of intuition, and the fourth theme, the desire to learn and how it might be stimulated through motivation.

The Process of Education inspired an interest in education among a whole generation of scholars, the effect of which is still being felt today.

* Cambridge, MA: Harvard University Press, 1960.

that inquiry is for the most part a *divergent* process, and guided discovery is a *convergent* process. That is, inquiry can lead to a variety of answers, some of which the teacher had not anticipated, whereas guided discovery leads to an answer or answers known to the teacher and intended for student discovery. Thus guided discovery emphasizes concept formation.

Chapter 2 presented such concepts as culture, self, and norm in conjunction with the social sciences. But the question still remains: how are concepts formed, and how can one teach a class in that manner? The best-known model of concept formation for social studies teaching is that developed by Hilda

TABLE 6.1

**Concept Formation Columns
(Concept of Navigability)**

YES	NO
Mississippi River	Long Island
Ohio River	Chesapeake Bay
Hudson River	Lake Michigan
Sacramento River	Susquehanna River
Missouri River	Maumee River

Taba. Her *Teacher's Handbook for Elementary Social Studies*, which is under 150 pages, is still the most cited work for explanations and examples of concept formation through guided discovery. One example of concept development for second graders used by Taba concerns the following idea:

> The supermarket needs a place, equipment, goods and services. The owner must be able to pay for these goods and services. (43-45)

Taba offers 29 activities based on this concept, ranging from a list of items Mr. Smith will need to open a supermarket to the daily weighing of fresh produce. Each of these activities fits into one of the categories shown in Table 6.2.

Each of the three steps in Table 6.2 is a necessary prerequisite to the next step, and teachers must guide students along. Because many groupings are possible, teachers should encourage the direction desired but should not discourage inappropriate, though correct, groupings. For example, Taba observed that when second graders were asked if they saw items in a grocery store that belonged together, she got responses other than the expected category groupings. Groupings such as "peaches and ice cream" or "potatoes and gravy" were functionally grouped because they are eaten together. These groupings are neither right nor wrong, but reveal only that children are operating at the functional level.

Following concept formation, teachers should guide students through more complex tasks of interpreting, inferring, and generalizing. These additional steps are summarized in Table 6.3. As Taba notes, these steps are more difficult because students "often have had years of conditioning against going beyond what was given on the printed page." (102) This is demonstrated in the discussion among a group of schoolchildren in the box on page 177.

According to Taba, concept development requires the student to predict consequences, explain those predictions, and then verify them. Much of the process of guided discovery relies on the ability of teachers to ask good questions. In Chapter 12, we will consider questioning skills in more detail.

According to John Lee, concept development varies depending on the type of concept. Lee presents four kinds of concepts to demonstrate this theory. First is the concept of objects, defined as persons or things in one's environment. As Lee notes, "When a child can group objects into classes and when

TABLE 6.2
Three Steps Required in Concept Formation

OVERT ACTIVITY	COVERT MENTAL OPERATIONS	ELICITING QUESTIONS
1. Enumeration and grouping	Differentiation	What did you see? Hear? Note?
2. Grouping	Identifying common properties, abstracting	What belongs together? On what criterion?
3. Labeling, categorizing	Determining the hierarchical order of items. Super- and subordination.	How would you call these groups? What belongs under what?

SOURCE: Taba, p. 92.

those objects have some meaning for him, then he has begun to develop a concept." (34)

A second concept, Lee notes, is that of activities, such as hiking, planning, working, or thinking. By engaging in an activity, one develops a behavioral definition of that activity.

A third concept concerns the *quality* of an activity. Playing basketball is an activity, but the quality of that activity is a different concept. What constitutes good basketball playing? It is more than shooting baskets. The most important qualities are playing good defense and cooperating with teammates. Basketball is a team sport, and success comes from performing with the team. Part of cooperating with one's teammates involves such activities as handling the ball well and passing the ball. Good shooting alone is not necessarily quality basketball, particularly if one never passes the ball and plays poor defense.

A final concept noted by Lee is that of abstractions, which is closely related to the social science concepts described in Chapter 2. Abstract concepts can be dealt with at all levels if teachers use appropriate examples that "translate abstractions into experiences with concrete objects, actions, situations, or questions. The teacher who will not attempt this or cannot do it is reduced to leading children to manipulate words without meaning." (40)

Thus guided discovery and concept development are partners in developing children's thinking and, ultimately, their decision making. This decision-making process will be examined in Chapter 8.

TEACHING AND LEARNING STYLES

In recent years there has been concern expressed about "learning styles" and trying to match such student learning preferences with the teacher's "teaching style." Learning style inventories abound, but despite research derived from

TABLE 6.3
Interpretation of Data

OVERT ACTIVITY	COVERT MENTAL OPERATIONS	ELICITING QUESTIONS
1. Identifying points	Differentiating	What did you notice? See? Find?
2. Explaining items of identified information	Relating points to each other. Determining cause and effect relationships.	Why did it happen?
3. Making inferences	Going beyond what is given. Finding implications, extra-updating.	What does this mean? What picture does it create in your mind? What would you conclude?

SOURCE: Taba, p. 101.

using them, there are no findings to suggest that students are consigned to learning in only one way. Rather than an absolute limitation, a learning style is "a preferred way of using one's abilities. . . . Hence, learning styles are not good or bad, only different," notes Robert Sternberg, a noted psychologist. (36) Determining learning styles, then, does not require elaborate examination by outside individuals. A teacher can do such an assessment without any formal questionnaire or other instruments. A teacher, knowing his or her own class, could simply "analyze the types of instructional and assessment activities" that a student prefers. (Sternberg, 37) Once that occurs, however, it is necessary for the teacher to vary her or his teaching styles in order to both capture various student preferences and to train students to be more interested in learning in other manners. As Sternberg notes, "the key is variety and flexibility using the full range of styles available. . . ." (38) Rather than conceding that some students only learn in certain ways, the creative teacher is obligated to vary her or his teaching, relying on group work, lecture, projects, inquiry, guided discovery, in-class work, and other modes in order to allow each child to display her or his talents and to succeed.

QUESTIONS AND ACTIVITIES

1. Visit a class at your college or in a public school. If the teacher is giving a lecture, try to think of ways it could have been presented as an inquiry lesson or as a concept-guided discovery. If the class is inquiry oriented, try to restructure it as a lecture or a concept-guided discovery lesson.

2. What advantages or disadvantages can you think of that might make the various teaching strategies preferable under different conditions?

INTERPRETING DATA: GRADE THREE

Here is a discussion among a class of third graders who are contemplating the storage of personal funds in a less-developed nation. Note that their interpretation reveals examples of ethnocentricity within the context of the data given.

TONY: They put the money right in the middle of the floor. They build this place in the floor.

TEACHER: Why do you suppose they put it there?

TONY: So no one would steal the money.

TEACHER: Why do you suppose they keep their money in their home?

LEE: They put the money in the pot and then they make a hole in the ground and put the pot in the ground and put sticks over it.

TEACHER: Can you guess why they want to keep that pot in the floor safe?

LEE: So nobody will see it.

TEACHER: Yes, but why—can you guess why they put that pot in their home?

SALLY: Same reason we do.

TEACHER: What is our reason for keeping money?

SALLY: So no one could take it.

TEACHER: Yes, there's another reason I think, too.

SANDA: Because they haven't any banks.

TEACHER: Yes, and when you don't have any banks in the village, you have to find some safe place to put it, don't you?

SUE: And if someone's babysitting they can find the money, but if you put it in the floor they can't.

SUE: They may forget where they put it if they put it outside.

TEACHER: That's true. Why?

ANDY: They don't trust the banks so they have their own bank.

SOURCE: Taba, p. 104.

3. Visit a local museum, courthouse, or historical site. How would you organize an inquiry lesson for a class visiting such a site? What information would have to be made available beforehand, through a lecture or some other expository means?

4. Watch an educational program on television, like *Nova* or a *National Geographic Special* or a special on the History Channel or the Discovery Channel. What kind of inquiry lessons could you develop using one of these programs as the primary source of initial information?

5. Outline one or two lectures for an intended unit of study. Include the special factors listed in the chapter, such as vocabulary, room arrangement, and audiovisual aids. What accommodations should be made to keep the interest of students not "preferring" lectures?

6. Think of two or three concepts and prepare the kind of concept formation columns presented in Table 6.1. Ask a classmate to examine your columns, pair by pair, to determine if the concepts are clear.

7. See if one of your concepts in question 6 can be broken down in the manner described by Taba on pages 174–176 in this chapter.

8. Think of qualities that are appealing in a good lecturer. How do they compare with those on p. 172?

9. Interview a principal, another teacher, a parent, or a local business person to find his or her views on this statement: "It is more important to learn how to learn than to acquire content."

10. If you could design the ideal classroom for your teaching, how would it look?

REFERENCES

Beyer, Barry K. *Teaching Thinking in Social Studies.* Columbus, OH: Merrill, 1979.

The House of Ancient Greece Teacher's Guide. Developed under the MATCH Project, Boston Children's Museum. Boston: American Science and Engineering, 1965.

Lee, John. *Teaching Social Studies in the Elementary Schools.* New York: Free Press, 1974.

Sternberg, Robert J. "Allowing for Thinking Styles," *Educational Leadership,* vol. 52, no. 3, November, 1994, pp. 36–40.

Taba, Hilda. *Teacher's Handbook for Elementary Social Studies.* Palo Alto, CA: Addison-Wesley, 1967.

Weil, Joyce, Bruce Weil, and Marsha Weil. *Models of Teaching.* 2nd ed. Englewood Cliffs, NJ: Prentice-Hall, 1980.

ADDITIONAL CONCEPT REFERENCES

Brownell, W. A., and G. Hendrickson. "How Children Learn Information Concepts and Generalizations," In *Learning and Instruction,* N. B. Henry, ed. 49th Yearbook of the National Society for the Study of Education. Chicago: University of Chicago Press, 1950.

Vencicke, W. E. "Concept Formation in Children of School Ages," In *The Psychology of the Elementary School Child,* A. R. Binter and S. N. Frey, eds. Chicago: Rand McNally, 1972.

Chapter Seven

TEXTBOOKS AND SOCIAL STUDIES TEACHING

INTRODUCTION

As a student, I found a lot of things I liked in my social studies textbooks, particularly the maps, charts, and tables. As a new teacher, I found the books badly written and poor depictions of the world, but I was compelled to use them.

Almost every new classroom teacher is asked to teach from a textbook. Some of these books are quite useful; others may be actually detrimental to the goals of learning. What makes the difference? Teacher training programs devote surprisingly little time to examining *and* assessing textbooks and their use. It is true that most beginning teachers are told what texts to use, but some of them may have a choice, and over time many teachers will serve on textbook selection committees for their school, district, or county.

This chapter looks at textbooks and their use in the social studies class-room. The focus is not on reading, however. Though there are a few passing notions regarding reading procedures, it is assumed that most teachers have had a separate course in reading methods with application to basal use in content areas. Thus, the chapter does not cover that subject.

What will be discussed are larger questions of textbook use in social studies, beginning with the question of why one should use a textbook at all. The chapter examines the advantages and, later, the disadvantages of using a textbook in social studies.

Another area of concern is the selection and assessment of a textbook. How does one judge a textbook's quality? What kinds of problems are likely to arise in textbook selection? How will a given textbook fit with other readings in the classroom?

Textbooks, particularly those in social studies, have come under fire from a variety of critics in recent years. Many observers have closely scrutinized textbook use and content and found them wanting. The sources of those criticisms will be addressed, as will suggestions for the improvement of textbooks. To illustrate these issues, examples from a number of textbook publishers appear throughout the chapter.

The chapter closes with an examination of the possible effect on textbooks of various commission reports, technological innovations, and changing ideas about schooling.

Why Use a Textbook?

The most pressing reason for teachers to use textbooks is that their principals expect them to, and they are evaluated on the basis of how well they implement the requirements of the school district. But there are less threatening reasons for using a textbook to teach social studies. The first reason is organization. The textbook constitutes a prearranged approach to the curriculum, which relieves the teacher of the chores of planning units, overall course structure, and, in some cases, individual lessons. Use of the same textbook and the same organizational approach also assure greater curriculum continuity, which, according to Evans and Brueckner, "facilitates cooperation among the instructional staff to work together to achieve specific learning goals." (265) For example, if all third-grade classes are using the same book, questions about curriculum that may arise from the use of that text can be discussed knowledgeably and pragmatically by all the third-grade teachers in the school or district.

Another reason to use a text, as cited by Evans and Brueckner, is a corollary of organization: the use of the text as an instructional tool. It provides data and teaching suggestions that teachers assume are accurate and reliable, and they do not have to research the data for themselves. Unfortunately, such a reliance on textbook accuracy is not always well founded.

One year when I taught in Chicago I had a choice of two social studies books, neither of them very impressive. I chose to use one and kept the other on hand for occasional reading. I especially liked my students to read both when the books contradicted each other. This considerably shook the students' reliance on a text for the answers. My little foray into cognitive dissonance was a useful lesson in getting them to ask questions, but not in developing respect for their textbooks. Nevertheless, "against the authority of the lone teacher, textbooks are a hard lure to resist." (Christenbury and Kelly, 77)

A first-year teacher may opt to use a textbook because it will help him or her to manage the classroom. The ideas, activities, lessons, and sequencing that textbooks provide allow the class to be divided into groups for separate assignments, and the teacher can then move from group to group.

Sometimes a textbook is used because it is part of an entire textbook series that a school or school system has adopted. The book for grade three, for example, recognizes that students will have had the prerequisites to certain material if they used the same textbook series in grades K–2. Similarly, the third-grade teacher knows what to teach students to prepare them for grades 4–6.

The prevalence of series has led to a situation that some educators like more than others—the standardization of the school curriculum, or a de facto national curriculum. In a highly mobile society, parents view this as advantageous because their children, theoretically, can move from place to place and find similar curricula and textbooks everywhere. Some publishers have extolled the virtues of increased standardization. One editor argued that it led to the improvement of elementary social studies textbooks because more standardization left more money to spend on features rather than on curriculum development. This in turn would attract more publishers and lead to a better product. Even though "programs are becoming more and more alike," the contention was that "publishers are not imposing a curriculum on educators. . . . [Publishers] try to match as many [curricula] as they can to maximize profits. . . . Textbook publishing is big business." (Graham, 55) And that big business aspect carries over into economies of scale. It is often cheaper for school districts to adopt texts than to reproduce other materials themselves. Christenbury and Kelly note that "The duplication and supplementary materials budget of most schools are not equal to what it would take to substitute for textbooks." (77)

Another reason to use a textbook is for purposes of student evaluation. Because a textbook provides a core of knowledge and because publishers commonly supply test items and other evaluation materials, it is ostensibly easier for teachers to evaluate their students' knowledge and understanding of the standardized material they have studied. It is also easier to make comparisons across classes or schools in a district.

Finally, the reason many teachers choose to use a textbook is convenience. They simply do not have the time to write separate curricula or to research a substitute curriculum.

THE TEXTBOOK AND THE CURRICULUM

Ideally, textbooks are selected according to how well they fit with the curriculum of the school district. Unfortunately, this does not always happen because of the sometimes awkward process of textbook adoption. In at least 20 states (as of 1996), textbooks are adopted on the basis of how well they meet state criteria and guidelines for particular grade levels and content areas. Only books that are on the state-approved list can be considered by the schools in those states, and this usually leaves them with fewer books to choose from. In the last few years many of these "adoption" states have loosened their regulations a bit and have state-*recommended,* rather than -required, textbooks. Nevertheless, for their part, the publishers still tend to tailor their textbooks to the criteria of the larger adoption states, since getting on a state-approved list means almost certain adoption by a large number of districts.

Adoption states wield a disproportionate influence on the content of elementary social studies textbooks. The director of the Schomburg Library, one of the largest research collections of African-American material, made this observation about the process:

> What we learned . . . is that content of textbooks is determined by the politics of the adoption states and the two main states are Texas and California, Texas representing the conservatives, and California, the liberals. This is just a simple matter of markets. Textbooks are not about education, but making money. (Schomburg, 1988, 4)

A district may seem to have independence in its adoption policies, but the adoption states will have shaped the textbooks before the district ever sees them. Also, other factors influence the independent districts that determine adoptions in the remaining 27 states. Muther asserts that "offering the best deal (usually a combination of free material) sways 20 to 70 percent of district decisions nationwide, according to estimates of several publishing executives." (5) She goes on to note that "adoption states, special interest groups, and readability formulas have all contributed to produce textbooks designed by a committee, written by a committee, and selected by a committee, to please all and offend none." (7)

It is no surprise, then, that most textbooks are innocuous. But not all are, and they need not be.

The textbook-curriculum fit is a constant problem. As noted earlier, the ideal is for teachers to develop and approve a social studies curriculum and then search for a textbook that matches the curriculum. This in itself is a challenge, and it becomes even more of a challenge when a district adopts social studies textbooks by series rather than individually. That has become the normal procedure, usually preceded by visits of publishers' representatives to present their material.

Except in the most unusual circumstances, the teachers in a district will likely find that *parts* of a series—the primary-grade books, for example—mesh better than the whole series, and primary-grade teachers may choose one series while the teachers in the intermediate grades want a different series.

This raises the question: Why not just adopt *books,* rather than a whole series? The most obvious reason is money. As Muther notes, many district decisions are based on "perks," on what more the district can get by adopting a series. It gains little advantage from adopting only a few *parts* of a series.

Another argument for a series adoption is continuity. Certain strands, either cognitive or affective, are presumably woven into the series fabric on the K–6 level, and disjunctive use of the books may not allow for thorough learning and understanding. Though I find these arguments specious, particularly in a classroom with a rich diversity of materials and teaching approaches, my views are clearly in the minority. Some critics feel that the textbook has become the total program, with between 70 percent and 95 percent of class time spent on the textbook or on textbook activities. (Muther, 8)

The adoption process can be very frustrating to teachers who have worked to develop a meaningful curriculum and gain broad support for it in the district, only to find that the right materials are not available. Some districts have therefore approached the curriculum-textbook problem from the opposite direction.

These districts first decide on a textbook series and then fit the curriculum to the parameters of the series. In other words, despite the protestations of publishers, there are instances in which the textbooks *do* impose a curriculum on schools, even though the schools may willingly accept it.

I once worked with a prominent school district over a long period of time on the revision of the curriculum for social studies. The teachers on the district team were intelligent, experienced, and diligent, and the task of revision, while tedious, came easily to them. But when intellectual conflicts arose between what they thought should be covered at a particular grade level and what was covered in the textbook series the district had adopted, the contents of the series always won.

The reason was not simply convenience. The situation was more complex. First, the district had just adopted the new series. If the curriculum guide did not reinforce the series content, the teachers might be seen as encouraging the waste of time and money. These teachers were far too conscientious to put their district in the position of having to defend the purchase of new materials that were not being thoroughly used. A second reason was that the teachers on the district team were quite experienced and realized that teachers like themselves could teach effectively despite the apparent cognitive dissonance of the textbook and the curriculum. Newer teachers, however, would need to have consonance. Feeling obligated to provide it, the team opted for the textbook whenever questions of content inclusion arose in the development of the curriculum guides.

SELECTING AND ASSESSING A TEXTBOOK

It should be obvious by now that textbooks do have a prominent place in most elementary social studies classrooms. Until alternatives to textbooks are available (some of these are discussed later in the chapter), teachers must have clear notions of how to judge a textbook for quality and usability.

Content

The first concern in textbook selection is content. The book must deal with the content the teacher wishes to cover and must do so fairly and equitably, in a manner that does not perpetuate myths or stereotypes.

In recent years there has been greater acknowledgment that textbooks cannot be comprehensive (and never have been). This has led to renewed questions about breadth versus depth in content. Newmann has asserted that depth is preferred for real learning. On the other hand, Mehlinger has noted: "As long as teachers must cover the history of the world or the history of America in a single year, it will be difficult to avoid superficiality." (33)

Of course one wants up-to-date information and thus might select a textbook or a series with the most recent copyright date. Sad to say, this does not necessarily ensure the most recent or reliable data. Publishers may issue basically the "same" book over a number of years, changing only the pictures, the cover, or the order of presentation but making few substantive text changes. This is possible because copyright laws allow a book to be called "new" when as little as 10 percent is changed, and that can include graphs, charts, photos, covers, and ancillary material. (Muther, 6)

In assessing textbooks one must also guard against being influenced by form over substance. Woodward, Elliott, and Nagel have recognized this problem:

> Many of the books resemble travelogues that adorn coffee tables in many households. On the surface, the texts appear to be attractive, enticing and excellent learning tools; beneath the surface, they leave much to be desired as high quality, comprehensive instructional materials. . . .
>
> Any social studies expert looking at elementary social studies series must be dismayed by their wide breadth and lack of depth. (51)

The situation is not surprising, considering everything that the textbook is required to include. Such requirements often call for an even distribution of major populations, ethnic, gender, and age based; omission of sexual overtones; no obscene words; no violence; no murder or anything "downbeat." As Muther notes, few pieces of good literature meet all these criteria, and textbooks tend to give a sanitized version of real life.

In their annotated bibliography, Woodward et al. cite some of the areas in which researchers have sought equity (or at least decency) in the way groups are represented in textbooks. These include images of Australia, Central America, Japan, Russia, the Arab world, the U.S. presidency after Watergate, the family, Africa, and various ethnic minorities in the United States.

The representation of U.S. ethnic minorities has probably received the most attention and study. Chapter 5 presented a great deal of information on both ethnic minorities and sexism that can be helpful in scrutinizing a textbook not only for misrepresentation, but also for lack of representation of some groups.

William Patton identifies three key concerns for evaluators to bear in mind with regard to minority representation: tokenism, omissions, and balance. Are minorities or minority group members presented fairly, in text and in pictures, as individuals and as groups? Are there significant omissions? Is the portrayal balanced? "When a social studies textbook presents a composite picture of events that make up the past, present, and future for ethnic groups and which reflects the positive and negative dimensions of roles, traditions, and values, it will have balance." (53)

On the depiction of women, Patton discusses several criteria for identifying sexist elements. Language is the first, and he uses occupations, illustrations, and roles as additional criteria. Sexist language is often apparent through, for example, the use of male gender pronouns when gender is not specified. The second criterion, occupations, can be analyzed by viewing careers as instrumental (involving production and the use of equipment) or expressive (nurturing and service roles). Are women largely depicted in the latter category and men in the former? The third criterion, illustrations, involves the ratio of male depictions to female depictions and the mode—whether they are photos, paintings, drawings, or cartoons. Finally, the most difficult of the criteria, roles, is discussed. Are there sexist patterns? Is the presentation of females as main characters disproportionate to that of males?

These are not simple criteria to apply. In order to make an intelligent judgment, a text must be examined thoroughly with some thought given to the purpose of the presentation and its accuracy (in historical perspective, if appropriate).

Other groups that may be examined for stereotyping should not be overlooked. Most prominent are children, who often seem to be depicted either as "super kids" or as vacuous dolts deserving of any mishaps they fall into. Professions, too, have stereotypes to overcome, some of them tied to the gender or ethnic stereotyping just mentioned.

Some critics object to such an "inclusion process." Recently the New York State Regents discussed the possible revision of curriculum guidelines and materials that had been designed to make social studies more ethnically diverse. "Less powerful" groups in America's story were being depicted, and some critics saw this as diluting the strength of the American character, rather than improving it. Detractors say that giving all ethnic groups an equal place at an educational round table "could distort history"; others are concerned "that the breakdown of American society into only five cultures, including the neologism, 'European-American' will gain acceptance. The writing of a curriculum, like that of a textbook, is as much a political process as an academic one." (Berger, 1990, 5)

Readability

If a book is not readable, the content does not matter very much. Thus, some educators assert that the basic approach to textbook writing should be to ensure that the book will be read. In this approach, the content is fitted to readability formulas. As noted earlier, this often makes for a dull, lifeless volume. In the interest of "readability," the pulse of the book is sacrificed; it is "dead on arrival."

Obviously, there are strong arguments for having a textbook that is readable. "While there may be people who believe that students should be able to learn from just about anything, a number of researchers have found that the more organized and readable a text, the more students will learn from it." (Osborne et al., 12)

Savage and Armstrong identify a number of readability issues, most of them not unique to social studies texts. These include different ways of reading, the use of study guides, and vocabulary difficulties. The latter problem is well illustrated in an overreliance on readability formulas, like the Fry or Fogg methods discussed in Chapter 12. Most such methods rely on some mixture of sentence length and number of syllables in randomly selected passages. A teacher may select passages from a textbook, test them using, for example, the Fry method, and determine that the book is "on grade level." Nevertheless, "simply because a teacher might know that a given story is at the fourth grade reading level does not assure that all youngsters in a particular fourth grade classroom will be able to read *and learn* [my emphasis] from the material." (Savage and Armstrong, 275)

In addition, since the Fry formula does not consider vocabulary, it is possible, indeed probable, that unfamiliar words in short sentences might be interpreted as appropriate. Examples of short words that would be virtually unknown to fourth-grade students but might be deemed appropriate in a fourth-grade text could include *credo, plateau, mesa, ecology, system, veto,* and *norms.* Similarly, a number of words that would seem difficult, according to the formulas, might be commonly used by students. Examples are *legislature, diversity,* and *ethnocentricism.*

Teachers need to scrutinize textbook readability using more than formulas. Savage and Armstrong identify three kinds of words to be alert for— unfamiliar vocabulary, out-of-date words and phrases, and specialized vocabulary.

An important aspect of readability is how user friendly the textbook is. Is the table of contents laid out clearly and easy to use? Are there chapter summaries or some other form of advance organizers to alert students to upcoming problems or issues? Is the index clear? Does it combine all terms, or are there separate subject and name indexes? Is there a glossary, and is it understandable? What information is included in the appendixes, and are the appendixes referred to in the text? The responses to these questions might indicate how difficult the book will be for children to use.

If there is time, a teacher might consider having a small group of his or her students examine a text under consideration and compare it with the one they are using. The first responses are likely to be superficial, with students choosing the current text because they are comfortable with it or the new one because it is different. Once these predictable responses are out of the way, however, it should be possible to gain some insight from the children into the qualities of a new textbook—although it will not be intellectually deep commentary. After all, this is a new experience for the children, and they will be as much concerned with doing well as with being insightful.

Many districts use a textbook evaluation form to collate staff opinions about various books. Figure 7.1 shows one such form of four pages, which is succinct and clear in its directions.

Page 1 provides general information—why a new text is being considered and what ones are being examined. Page 2 continues with general questions, including readability and the availability of supplementary materials like a study guide, teacher's edition, and other additional components.

Page 3 applies the school district's criteria on issues similar to those raised by Muther, Woodward, Patton, and others. The first concern is readability and layout. Print size, spacing, and the use of graphics all have an effect on a student's ability and desire to read. These are not covered by a readability formula, nor are levels and styles. In addition to vocabulary, the concepts that are introduced and developed must be considered. And a part of readability is the author's style. Is the book interesting, thoughtful, fun? Many texts are criticized for their lifelessness, and teachers should be alert to this problem.

Next on the form is an assessment of content in relation to the intended age group. The book may be judged as excellent for sixth graders but has been written for fourth graders. It might seem to be a simple solution to use a fourth-grade book at the sixth-grade level. Unfortunately, most older students are likely to see what is being done and will rebel against using a book designed for fourth graders ("a baby book").

The next criteria refer to the equitable, responsible presentation of people, especially as related to race, color, creed, national origin, gender, age, and handicap. Obviously teachers should be able to document their assertions, even though the form asks them only to rate the criteria for appropriateness on a declining scale.

The last page of the form lists other criteria that enter into the mix. These include price and hard or soft cover, factors that have nothing to do with quality education but that are important concerns of a school district. The form also asks for the copyright date, but it does not specifically address any other measures of topicality.

This district also wants to know what unit(s) the textbook would be appropriate for, and the form includes a question about suitability for the unit.

FIGURE 7.1

TEXTBOOK EVALUATION FORM

DIRECTIONS: Please complete the following questionnaire.
Your comprehensive review of the textbook is
essential to the selection process.
- Directions vary among the sections. Please
follow all directions carefully.
- If you believe you do not have sufficient
information to answer some of the questions,
please contact the coordinator.

I. GENERAL INFORMATION

A. Teacher(s) submitting _____ Building _____

B. Statement of need to adopt a new textbook:

C. Other Textbooks Examined in Addition to the One Being
Recommended.

Title	Publisher	Edition
_____	_____	_____
_____	_____	_____
_____	_____	_____

- 1 -

D. This book is intended for:
1. What grade/division? _____
2. What unit or course of study? _____
3. What level? _____
4. Approximate number of students? _____

E. Please complete the following information

Title _____

Preferred Edition (publisher, edition, copyright date)	Type of Binding	Cost
_____	_____	_____

Alternate Editions
_____
_____

F. The approximate readability level of this book is _____

G. 1. Is there a study guide and/or teachers' edition
available? _____ cost _____

2. List additional components supplied.

Item	Cost
_____	_____
_____	_____

H. Is the book in use elsewhere in the curriculum (or in
other content areas)? _____
If so, where? _____
Number of students involved? _____

- 2 -

TEXTBOOK REVIEW COMMITTEE
RECOMMENDATION FORM

DIRECTIONS: Please submit this recommendation with the completed textbook selection form.

Review Committee Members:

Department/Division: _____

NAME _____   BUILDING _____

Please complete the following information:

Textbook Title _____

Edition _____   Copyright Date _____

Publisher _____

THE TEXTBOOK IDENTIFIED ABOVE:

☐ is approved for recommendation to the State College Area Board of School Directors for adoption

☐ is not approved for recommendation to the State College Area Board of School Directors for adoption

Comments:

_____
Curriculum Coordinator's Signature

II. DISTRICT CRITERIA

A. The textbook is readable with an appropriate format including:
   1) size of print
   2) spacing on page
   3) number of pages
   4) use of color and graphics

B. The textbook is readable and understandable for intended students, including:
   1) concept level
   2) author's style
   3) vocabulary level
   4) syntax

C. The subject matter is appropriate for the intended age group, in reference to
   1) values presented
   2) interests developed
   3) maturity needed

D. The textbook presents similarities and differences among individuals sensitively and responsibly especially as they relate to:
   1) race
   2) color
   3) creed
   4) national origin
   5) sex
   6) age
   7) handicap

E. The textbook deals accurately and fairly with the problems and contributions of women, ethnic and racial minorities, handicapped and all others as recommended by the Task Force on Understanding Others.

	VERY APPROPRIATE	APPROPRIATE	SOMEWHAT APPROPRIATE	INAPPROPRIATE	NOT APPLICABLE	NOT INCLUDED

- 3 -

SOURCE: State College Area School District

Patton's book shows another district's evaluation form, which includes questions about charts, maps, diagrams, and the author's competence in the field. (76) No such forms can or should be exhaustive; rather, they are guideposts on the textbook assessment trail. Chambliss suggests graphic organizers in text evaluation and also indicates that familiarity, interest, and structure are key factors in increasing comprehension of textbook writing. She suggests that these important factors be strongly considered in textbook evaluation.

USING A TEXTBOOK

There is no one right way to use a social studies textbook. It is a tool to be fitted to the curriculum and the classroom, and its use may—in fact, should—vary from classroom to classroom.

The most common manner of using a textbook is sequentially, in the order in which the chapters appear in the text. This assumes that the order coincides with that in the curriculum guide, which, as noted, may have been written with the textbook in mind.

But even if one follows the organization of the textbook, all chapters need not receive the same amount or type of attention. Although most children like some ritual, simply reading the chapter and answering the questions at the end of it is not a ritual many of them are fond of. Instead, the teacher should examine each chapter, along with the corresponding sections of the curriculum guide, the recommended ideas, and the teacher's edition that may be a part of the textbook package. Evans and Brueckner caution that a "teacher's guide is useful and dependable, but should be used less as you are more perceptive of students' needs." (278) They recommend using the guide to supplement text ideas and to find resources. Easy as it is to let the textbook lead one's curricular decisions, one need not organize precisely as the text does if it seems inappropriate. The textbook can be used more selectively, perhaps in sequential order but skipping chapters that seem less appropriate and spending more time on chapters with richer material. A variation on this theme might be to use only certain chapters and to present them in the order that the teacher finds most productive. This can be planned, or at times a teacher may alter the curriculum to take advantage of what is referred to as a "teachable moment." For example, in both 1995 and 1996 hurricanes devastated parts of the east coast of the United States, causing major damage to port cities in the southeast. For third graders studying communities and using, for example, the Holt, Rinehart & Winston social studies series, it would have been a good chance to wed those current events to the study of port communities (part of the fifth chapter of the textbook) rather than simply moving through the text, ignoring the events that could have made the subject more timely and meaningful. The teacher could have used the chapter as a springboard to examine the difficulties faced by living in some types of communities and the importance of friends and neighbors in rebuilding a community.

A third way to use a textbook is as a reading book. This is more often the case when the curriculum has been developed prior to the adoption of a textbook. In such situations, the textbook may be used only sporadically to provide general information, augment other views, or tie ideas together. The flow of the curriculum may come from readings in trade books, from teacher-made activities, or from a combination of stimuli of which the textbook is merely one part. For example, a unit on medieval times for sixth graders might have the book *Robin Hood,* by Walter Pyle, as the common reading book. In their research for papers, presentations, or plays the students might use the textbook, or portions of the textbook might be assigned as background reading before the students begin *Robin Hood.* Fitting in trade books is an excellent way to combine literature and the language arts with social studies. Some literary classics may seem a bit daunting, and many have been issued in abridged versions, but one should not reject outstanding writing because it seems too difficult. Teachers can read to children and have them reread parts for themselves or read on their own afterward. Often this can be the impetus for students to exceed expectations. A number of children's books can enhance the conceptual goals of curriculum guides. The *Frog and Toad* books by Arnold Lobel are useful in the primary grades for their focus on friendship, human emotions, and adversity. The Dr. Seuss books often focus on neighborhoods or responsibility—for example, *And to think that I saw it on Mulberry Street* or *Horton Hatches the Egg* or *The Grinch.* Ezra Jack Keats portrays neighborhood life in many of his books, such as *The Snowy Day* and *Goggles.* These are only a few of the authors that could be chosen, and the textbook would then augment the views taken from literature.

Similarly, the textbook can be used in conjunction with such print materials as magazines, newspapers, and teacher-made handouts. For younger children, magazines and newspapers written for them, such as *Weekly Reader, Ranger Rick, Dolphin Log,* and *Boys' Life,* are good places to find ideas. Stories from *Dolphin Log* on topics like ocean pollution, life on a barrier reef, or traveling up the Amazon could complement fourth-grade textbook chapters on world resources or regions. Or a unit on "Life Under the Sea" might use that magazine and others, with the textbook providing background information.

For sixth graders, topics of study might be generated by using *Newsweek* or *Time,* again with the textbook providing historical or geographic background. The drama and excitement of 1989, 1990, and 1991 as Eastern Europe evolved into separate political entities were unprecedented in my lifetime. That was a unique and, one would hope, unforgettable opportunity for lessons about the real world, augmented by the textbook. Instead, for reasons discussed earlier, most teachers continued to move through a textbook-based curriculum.

As for teacher-made materials, these could lead the curricular focus, but because of the great time involved they will most likely stay as supplements. When I taught sixth grade, the textbooks contained many references to the monolithic model of communism. But it was hardly explained and was always presented in an aura of doom and a tone reminiscent of President Ronald Reagan's characterization of the Soviet Union in the early 1980s as an "evil empire." Rather than rely on my deficient sixth-grade texts, I produced a series of handouts that highlighted dates, facts, and tenets. Meant only as background, they provided a context for student understanding. Today, of course, I could just write to the Russian tourist office or embassy and get a variety of useful materials to go with the improved coverage in today's textbooks, but that was not the case in the early 1970s. Many textbook areas need similar augmenting and updating. In his article "Updating the Outdated in Textbooks," Patton suggests updating through maps, graphs, charts, photos, cartoons, and other illustrations, in addition to updated factual information. (Patton, 1–8)

There *are* times when a dated textbook can be useful. Take, for example, a 1980 text on regions of the United States that discusses the booming economy of Wyoming because of the need for uranium and "clean" coal for energy. That could be compared with the realities of today's Wyoming—a stagnant economy and a shriveled energy industry. That kind of updating can help students learn to ask good questions, do research, and rely less on a blind belief in everything they read in their textbooks.

THE PROBLEMS OF TEXTBOOKS

This chapter has already addressed a number of problems associated with the use of textbooks. Some of these problems—among them the process of developing and producing a textbook—need further discussion here.

As one of the sample textbook evaluation forms showed, the author is an important consideration in choosing a text. Is he or she well known in the field of social studies or in one of the social sciences? However, it is erroneous to assume that someone noted in the field will write a dependable textbook. Unfortunately, most of these books are not written as novels or histories are; they tend to be the peculiar product of a system of group writing. Chambliss aserts that a text series staff may often exceed 60 people. (Chambliss, 360)

> Textbooks are usually produced by a team of authors under contract with a publisher. . . . The authors then generate a manuscript, and the editors at the publishing firm apply their skills—readability, illustrations, design maps and charts, study aids, end of chapter questions, index, supplementary reading lists all are examined. The authors whose names appear on the cover may have contributed a little or a lot to the final product. (Mehlinger, 34)

Because of the stiff competition among publishers, most of them want to publish textbooks that are pretty much like those of their competitors. Originality is not necessarily a virtue in textbook publishing. Rather, each publisher seeks to set its product apart by emphasizing the ancillary parts of the "package."

But publishers are not solely to blame for the failings of textbooks. Downey asserts that the scholarly community has not taken enough interest in school text-

DRAWING BY THE (ETHNIC) NUMBERS

Irene Trivas, an artist, stopped accepting assignments to illustrate children's readers four years ago, partly out of frustration over publishers' efforts to "be everything to everybody," as she put it. Here is her account of the instructions she received for one book:

It's etched in acid in my mind. They sent 10 pages of single-spaced specifications. The hero was a Hispanic boy. There were black twins, one boy, one girl; an overweight Oriental boy, and an American Indian girl. That leaves the Caucasian. Since we mustn't forget the physically handicapped, she was born with a congenital malformation and only had three fingers on one hand.

One child had to have an Irish setter, and the setter was to be female.

The Hispanic kid had two parents. The father has a white-collar job. The mother is an illustrator and she works at home. At one point, they are seen through the kitchen screen door making dinner, having spaghetti and meatballs and a salad. The editor appended a note that said, "Make sure it's not iceberg; it should be something nice like endive."

They also had a senior citizen, and I had to show her jogging.

I can't do it anymore. (S. Chria, 1990)

books and that academics should show more concern over what the books convey to students and how. For example, for years social studies textbooks talked about the three (or four) races of man (not humans), a view that reputable anthropologists had discarded by the 1950s. Unfortunately, textbook authors were not anthropologists and vice versa, so the misinformation lingered. Evans and Brueckner (263–83) discuss several other disadvantages of textbooks. The first of these, alluded to throughout this chapter, is overdependence on the textbook. The text works best in conjunction with a clear set of curricular and classroom goals.

A corollary to this disadvantage is unrealistic expectations regarding the textbook. Some teachers believe it should contain everything; as this and other chapters have shown, that is simply not possible, nor is it desirable.

Another disadvantage to a reliance on texts, as we have seen, is the impossibility of doing justice to current events. Some books will add new chapters at a late date or provide a supplemental chapter. In presidential election years, a publisher might prepare two versions of its American history textbook revisions for the eighth and eleventh grades. One version assumes the victory of the Democratic candidate and the other version the victory of the Republican candidate. As soon as the election results are in, the correct version is quickly rushed into print, making this publisher's textbook appear the most up-to-date when it is exhibited at the National Council for the Social Studies conference held annually in mid or late November.

Though cute, all these schemes are more public relations hype than substantive examinations of current issues. No matter how hard they try, publishers cannot produce texts that are less than a year out of date by the time they are published. Current issues can be covered only by not using the text, or by using it simply for background information when appropriate. Bettex sees the textbook as "an instrument of resistance to change, the ally of an old-fashioned way of teaching, perpetuating, for example, the habit of teaching from the front of the class. . . ." Texts also allow, he notes, "for manipulation by economic powers and (thus) soon become dated so that they can be replaced as soon as possible." (47)

Evans and Brueckner also find that textbook formats are too inflexible. Again, alternatives to such inflexibility have been discussed previously, as have the problems of stereotyping and dated materials.

The final disadvantage identified by Evans and Brueckner is the limitations inherent in textbooks that provide only low-level questions. This is true of most textbooks, particularly for the lower grade levels. Younger students tend to think in concrete rather than abstract terms, but this does not mean that they are incapable of analyzing or evaluating in some way. For all their enhanced beauty, many social studies texts offer few opportunities for thoughtful questioning. The teacher's guide sometimes points to higher-order questioning, but not always. Figure 7.2 shows the teacher's text of one second-grade book. The student book asks, "What do the people in this neighborhood like to do?" The teacher's text gives this answer: "they enjoy the out-of-doors; they like to raise horses and go horseback riding." What it ignores is the possibility that the people in this "neighborhood," as it is called, may have an interest in attracting tourists and making money. Or that the residents may regard riding as a necessity, not a pleasurable activity. Many teachers' guides present potential higher-order questions (see Chapter 12), but they usually do so in a lower-order manner, by means of specific answers and directions.

Elliott et al. question the legitimate usefulness of any social studies textbook in the elementary classroom. Like Evans and Brueckner, they see major problems with textbook series and have identified six of the problems of social studies series as follows:

1. They are loosely related collections of separate texts, not really a series as such.
2. Study of the United States is dominant.
3. Most series are similar in content, methodology, and scope/sequence. ("If you've seen one, you've seen them all.")
4. They are superficial in their coverage of topics.
5. Representations of women and minorities are unrealistic (ranging from no representation to almost everyone being a doctor, a lawyer, or a top business executive).
6. Skill strands are limited to map and globe skills (and even these are not integrated in the text).

FIGURE 7.2

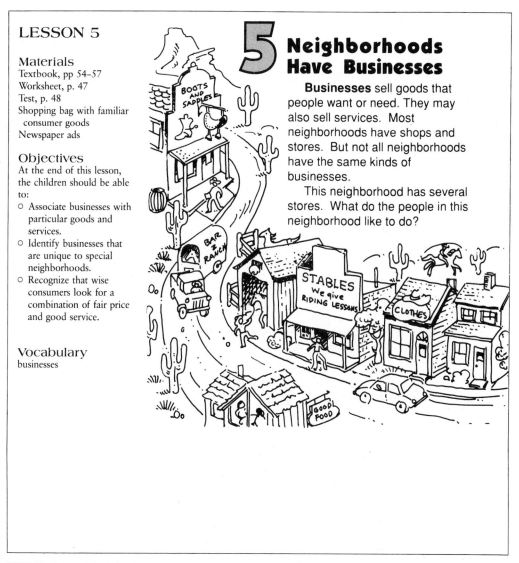

LESSON 5

Materials
Textbook, pp 54–57
Worksheet, p. 47
Test, p. 48
Shopping bag with familiar
consumer goods
Newspaper ads

Objectives
At the end of this lesson,
the children should be able
to:
○ Associate businesses with
particular goods and
services.
○ Identify businesses that
are unique to special
neighborhoods.
○ Recognize that wise
consumers look for a
combination of fair price
and good service.

Vocabulary
businesses

5 Neighborhoods Have Businesses

Businesses sell goods that people want or need. They may also sell services. Most neighborhoods have shops and stores. But not all neighborhoods have the same kinds of businesses.

This neighborhood has several stores. What do the people in this neighborhood like to do?

SOURCE: Cangemi, J. *Neiborhoods.* Holt, Rinehart & Winston, 1986.

IMPROVING TEXTBOOKS

For all their problems, textbooks continue to be widely used, and therefore a word about how to improve them is necessary. A major concern is the adoption process of states and school districts. An individual teacher can do little to *change* that process. However, teachers should be attuned to the particulars of the process—time lines, evaluation instruments, adoption lists, and the like—in order to have some say regarding which textbooks are chosen for their districts or classrooms.

One should make a thorough assessment of the book. If it is unsatisfactory but must be used, the teacher can stockpile an arsenal of supplementary material in the form of trade books, magazines, videos, pictures, artifacts and realia, audio tapes, and a list of resource persons. Of course, this is what a resourceful teacher always does when teaching any unit (see Chapter 3).

Teachers should try to get on textbook review committees and work to develop a useful textbook evaluation instrument.

If a text is reviewed but not selected, tell the publisher what the personal or district concerns were. One can do this through the publisher's representatives, but their main concern is selling the product they have, not planning a new one. Thus, it may be more advantageous to contact the publisher directly (a list is in the Appendix) with suggestions. Most publishers welcome thoughtful input and may ask for additional comments. This is unlikely if the original remarks were perjorative, inaccurate, or sketchy, however. To have one's feedback acknowledged and/or utilized, rationales must be clear, well developed, and accurate.

SOME TEXTBOOK EXAMPLES—PATTERNS, PROBLEMS, AND PROSPECTS

An examination of a few popular textbook series from the larger publishers confirms many of the critical comments made in this chapter. The sameness of organization and content (particularly the expanding-communities model) is evident when one examines series titles.

	MACMILLAN/MCGRAW HILL	SILVER BURDETT/GINN	HARCOURT BRACE
K	Here I Am	No formal text	No text
1	My World	Families and Friends	All About Me
2	People Together	People and Places	My World
3	Communities	Communities Around the U.S.	Meeting Many People
4	Regions	Regions and Resources	States and Regions
5	United States	Our United States	America's Story
6	Our World	The World and its People	Our World's Story

Textbook "packages" are more than just textbooks—but this is not a new phenomenon. As early as 1929, the Ginn social studies materials by Harold Rugg included a teacher's guide, a student workbook, and the textbook, which Rugg referred to as the reading book. Almost all publishers now provide a teacher's edition of the textbook, usually including the pages of the student text accompanied by lesson objectives, suggested resources, vocabulary, advance organizers, activities, and bibliographies (see Figure 7.2).

Some publishers provide student workbooks, along with teachers' editions of the workbooks that give answers to the puzzles, games, questions, and map exercises. One can hope that the teachers already know the answers or how to find them, but the teachers' editions do make things more convenient. Unfortunately, they are highly dependent on low-level answers. A teacher's edition of the workbook usually is not automatically included with each shipment of a classroom set of books, but one will be sent at the request of a teacher or administrator. This makes the teacher's edition one of the negotiable "perks" Muther refers to.

Some publishers compile a teacher's resource book, that includes workbook materials, tests and answer keys, and "home letters" for each unit. These letters summarize the content and skills of the unit and suggest ways in which students' learning can be reinforced by the parents outside the classroom. One of these is reproduced in Figure 7.3. Again, while this may be convenient for the teacher, it is one more way for publishers to teacher-proof their materials—even letters to parents are provided, to reduce the margin of teacher error (Harcourt Brace supplies them in both English and Spanish). Some resource books contain posters and photos. For its Grade 2 Neighborhoods book, the Holt social studies program offers posters of (1) all the U.S. presidents, (2) a picture of goods and services with space for classroom input, (3) a poster with space for safety rules to be added, (4) an outline map of a neighborhood to be filled in, (5) a simple map showing changes over time, (6) pictures of people working called "People Long Ago," (7) a holiday-cards poster with space for student input, (8) pictures of people in different homes called "Neighborhoods in Other Places," and (9) a blank map of the western hemisphere with only the borders of the continental United States outlined.

Some publishers are now including computer software to go with each unit or lesson (discussed below and in Chapter 10).

The textbook itself is relatively easy to characterize, as Woodward et al. have noted. It is colorful, graphically impressive, and filled with references to a diverse number of social groups. Many textbooks append extensive sets of data following the text. *Our Country's Communities,* a third-grade text from Silver Burdett/Ginn, extols this fact: "With an Atlas, Gazetteer, a glossary, and other references right in the book, *Our Country's Communities* provides all the tools students need for success in social studies." (Loftin & Ainsley, T2) The teacher's edition of the textbook contains an overview of the complete series, reviews the organization of chapters and lessons, and lists the contributors. The Silver Burdett/Ginn series lists 24 authors, seven contributors to the series, eight workbook authors, and 49 teacher reviewers—lending credence to Mehlinger's comment about the extent of the authors' actual contributions to the final product.

FIGURE 7.3
Sample Parent Letter

DEAR PARENT OR GUARDIAN:

I would like to tell you about our social studies program in the coming year. Through discussion and worksheet activities, your child will become more aware of himself or herself and the world around us. We will talk about how people learn, communicate, change, and interact with other people.

In the first part of the year, your child will discover how our five senses help us learn, how people have a variety of feelings, and how people change and grow.

Here are a few suggestions for ways in which you can encourage your child's interest in social studies.

   Draw attention to things that affect any of the five senses. Help your child identify textures, colors, shapes, sounds, smells, and tastes.

   Call attention to your child's growth by keeping records of changes in height and clothing sizes.

   Look at family photographs together, and discuss ways in which family members have changed and grown.

   Call attention to your child's achievements by pointing out things he or she has learned or is learning to do.

   Above all, ask your child often about what he or she is learning. Offer to help any way you can. With your support and encouragement, your child will learn a great deal in the coming year.

SINCERELY,

A skills index is included in most series. As Woodward et al. note, these are mostly map and globe skills. Silver Burdett/Ginn gives little attention to chronological skills; the McGraw Hill series does somewhat better. Skills are not discussed in the chart but are briefly mentioned in the program rationale. The chart does not separate skill development into introductory, reinforcement, and mastery (see Chapter 11), but merely identifies where in the grade-level texts these skills exist.

Most textbooks are divided into units, which are then divided into chapters. Figure 7.4 shows part of the table of contents of *States and Regions,* one book in the 1997 Harcourt Brace social studies series. The listing indicates a similar pattern for most chapters—content, making social studies relevant (a boxed section having some relation to the content), various skills, and occasionally a featured lesson highlighting some children's literature (another boxed item, but longer and linked to the unit in which it appears). Maps and globes are also listed; *States and Regions* contains over 100. It also has around 60 charts, graphs, diagrams, and time lines. The book is not dependent on historical interpretation for its organization; rather, it is organized by geographic regions, which could be reasonably recombined in several other manners. Inserted within the chapters are historical stories that add variety to the lengthy geographic narrative. The pictures, drawings, graphs, and maps are all impressive and colorful, but the narrative seems to be lacking in transitional quality and shows little attempt at linkage within or between chapters. This book is no worse than most others and may, in fact, be better than many. Nevertheless, it demonstrates that textbooks will never be the reading book of choice among teachers or students.

THE FUTURE OF TEXTBOOKS

What does the future hold for textbooks in the social studies classroom? Critics like Woodward hope that they will improve significantly (which he doubts) or will disappear (which also seems unlikely). Such concern for textbooks has not always been seen as much of an issue. In 1899 the Committee of Seven of the American Historical Association (AHA) observed that "unless supplemented by other work, the textbooks used are likely to furnish an insufficient mental pablum." (144) The Committee of Eight of the AHA felt that textbooks were unsuitable and that historical readers should be used in the early elementary grades. Only in grades seven and eight were textbooks to be utilized more, and then "the class should not confine its work to one textbook." (99) But historical readers were still preferred over textbooks, which were always confined to condensed statements. (Committee of Eight, 99–100)

The 1916 report of the Committee on Social Studies believed that the textbook would become "less and less a compendium of information and more and more a manual of method and illustrative material for the teacher and a guide to observation and study for the pupil." (Committee on Social Studies, 62)

FIGURE 7.4

Table of Contents

Later studies saw similar problems with textbooks and voiced similar hopes for their improvement, as well as for less dependence on them—criticisms strikingly like those of recent years.

In the early 1960s came predictions that television would partially replace the classroom teacher. When that did not happen, there was speculation that television would replace the textbook, and the television-as-textbook notion grew as instructional television shows mushroomed in number. Instructional television was in evidence at all school levels, and shows were produced in all content areas. Professionals in instructional television contend that the problem is not the lack of enough content materials for school use, but, rather, the problem of producing good instructional materials that will be used profitably in the schools.

Instructional television shows are available that cover map use, geographic understanding, famous persons in history, economic concepts, cultural groups, governmental structure, and current issues. "National Geographic Explorer," "Smithsonian World," the Jacques Cousteau specials, and many other shows produced on an irregular basis could all be made a part of the social studies curriculum. Yet none have replaced the textbook.

Today, microcomputers and their myriad software—data bases, games, simulations, word processing—are being seen as the textbook replacement. Many textbook companies include software packages with their other materials. Often the software consists of data bases more suitable for detailed study in the higher grades, but some of the software gives feedback to students on their text reading, as a means of review.

Some schools have adopted "The Voyage of the Mimi," a science package with many social studies connections, as the centerpiece of a portion of the elementary curriculum. While few other software packages have the breadth and depth of this program, it shows that in theory it is possible for computer software to replace textbooks. But costs, convenience, and tradition all weigh against this occurring, at least in the near future.

Interactive video by means of CD-ROMs (see Chapter 10) is another recent entrant in the replace-the-textbook sweepstakes, but this, too, is unlikely to gain primacy over the textbook any time soon. Some critics predict a new generation of textbooks, one intended for use within a new kind of teaching environment where the texts "will look like a kind of guide, providing suggestions, enticing ideas to motivate personal research, together with examples or models that are on the student's level." (Bettex, 48)

Thus, the future of textbooks appears uncomfortably secure. Despite protests, complaints, insensitivity, overindulgence, repetitiveness, and dullness, the textbook continues to be the predominant teaching factor in most elementary classrooms. And that appears to reflect the future for elementary social studies. Textbooks may change, although not very much, and when they do change, most will change in the same manner. I do not characterize this as either good or bad (though I certainly find it uncreative), merely descriptive.

In 1970 Robert Sherrill published a book entitled *Military Justice Is to Justice as Military Music Is to Music.* So, too, with textbook publishing. Creative, original works written in a lively, readable style are always in demand, whether they are fiction or nonfiction. Only in textbook publishing are these canons violated. Originality gives way to mimicry, lively writing is sacrificed for readability, and character development yields to ethnic balance. With so much stacked against them, it is a wonder that textbooks are as good as they are. Nevertheless, teachers should not complacently accept textbooks as they are; rather, they need to be more active consumers. Even with the restrictive parameters imposed on textbooks, they can be better. It is the obligation of educators both to demand that they be better and to aid, thoughtfully, in the process of making them so.

QUESTIONS AND ACTIVITIES

1. In groups of two or three, examine two or three textbooks for the same grade level. Which do you prefer? Why?

2. Read a textbook chapter and examine the notorious "questions at the end of the chapter." What questions would you ask instead of these? Which questions would you *not* ask?

3. What different slant might you take in rewriting a textbook to make it more interesting?

4. Obtain a copy of the adoption guidelines for social studies in your state or a neighboring one. What do you like and dislike about the guidelines?

5. How are minorities and women depicted in the textbook you examined? If either are depicted unfairly, how could that be rectified most easily?

6. Compare textbook topics with the Appendix *of this book.* Which resources listed could be used to provide materials to augment the textbook?

REFERENCES

Berger, J. "Now the Regents Must Decide If History Will Be Recast," *New York Times,* February 11, 1990, p. E5

Bettex, M. "Textbooks—Prospects for the Technological Era," *Educational Media International,* vol. 32, no. 1, March 1995, p. 47-50.

Cangemi, JoAnn, ed. *Neighborhoods.* New York: Holt, Rinehart & Winston, 1986.

Chambliss, M. "Evaluating the Quality of Textbooks for Diverse Learners," *Remedial and Special Education,* vol. 15, no. 6, November 1994, p. 348-362.

Chria, S. "Writing Textbooks for Children: A Juggling Act," *New York Times,* January 17, 1990, p. B8,

Christenbury, L., and P. Kelly, "What Textbooks Can—and Cannot—Do," *English Journal,* vol. 83, no. 3, March 1994, p. 76-80.

Committee of Eight of the American Historical Association. *The Study of History in the Elementary Schools.* New York: Charles Scribner's Sons, 1910.

Committee of Seven of the American Historical Association. *The Study of History in Schools.* New York: Macmillan, 1899.

Committee on Social Studies of the National Education Association. "The Social Studies in Secondary Education," comp. A.W. Dunn. Bureau of Education Bul. no. 28. Washington: Government Printing Office, 1916.

Downey, M. "Speaking of Textbooks: Putting Pressure on the Publishers," *History Teacher,* vol. 14, 1980, pp. 61-72.

Elliott, D., K. Nagel, and A. Woodward. "Do Textbooks Belong in Elementary Social Studies?," *Educational Leadership,* vol. 42, no. 7, April 1985, pp. 22-24.

Evans, J., and M. Brueckner. *Elementary Social Studies: Teaching for Today and Tomorrow.* Boston: Allyn and Bacon, 1990.

Graham, Alma. "Elementary Social Studies Textbooks: An Author-Editor's Viewpoint," *Social Education,* vol. 50, no. 1, January 1986, pp. 54-55.

Haas, M. E. "An Analysis of the Geographic Concepts and Locations in Elementary Social Studies Textbooks Grades One Through Four." Unpublished, 1988, ED 305 309.

Communities. Orlando, FL: Harcourt Brace Jovanovich/Holt, Rinehart & Winston, 1991.

States and Regions. Orlando, FL: Harcourt Brace and Company, 1997.

Loftin, R., and W. F. Ainsley, Jr. *Our Country's Communities.* Morristown, NJ: Silver Burdett and Ginn, 1988.

Mehlinger, H. D. "American Textbook Reform: What Can We Learn from the Soviet Experience?," *Phi Delta Kappan,* vol. 71, no. 1, September 1989, pp. 29-35.

Muther, C. "What Every Textbook Evaluator Should Know," *Educational Leadership,* April 1985, pp. 4-8.

Newmann, F. "Beyond Common Sense in Educational Restructuring: The Issues of Content and Linkage," *Educational Researcher,* vol. 22, no. 4, March 1993, pp. 4-13.

Osborne, J., B. Jones, and M. Stein. "The Case for Improving Textbooks," *Educational Leadership,* vol. 42, no. 7, April 1985, pp. 9-16.

Patton, W. E., ed. *Improving the Use of Social Studies Textbooks.* Washington, DC: National Council for the Social Studies, 1980.

Savage, T. V., and D. G. Armstrong. *Effective Teaching in Elementary Social Studies.* New York: Macmillan, 1987.

"Schomburg Library Chief Discusses the Development of the New CIBC History Book," *Interracial Books for Children Bulletin,* vol. 19, nos. 1 and 2, 1988, pp. 3-5.

Woodward, A., D. L. Elliott, and K. C. Nagel. "Beyond Textbooks in Elementary Social Studies," *Social Education,* vol. 50, no. 1, January 1986, pp. 50-53.

———*Textbooks in School and Society: An Annotated Bibliography and Guide to Research.* New York: Garland Publishing Company, 1988.

Chapter Eight

ROLE PLAY, GROUP DECISION MAKING, AND CASE STUDIES

THE PERSONAL TOUCH

There are a number of ways to enhance student involvement and interest in social studies classes, although many of these methods cater more to language arts, science, or even mathematics. This chapter will examine three general strategies for enhancing student involvement, including role play, group decision making, and case studies. All these strategies are student centered rather than teacher centered; both students and teachers share responsibility for the effective functioning of the class.

Sociodrama is a type of role play that seeks to improve citizenship and to help students understand others. The stimulus for sociodrama may be a story, an assigned reading, pictures, or a film, all of which end without resolution. The students then must try to recognize and solve the perceived social problem. Dramatic play is less structured than sociodrama and seeks to improve student understanding of content. As with sociodrama, effective planning is vital to its success.

The second strategy, group decision making, offers advice and rationales for establishing small groups and encourages equal status interaction between members in small-group decision making. The third strategy, case studies, uses real-life situations or fictionalized ideas to encourage the examination of fewer ideas in more depth. Case studies are a lively, effective way to truly digest material, not just sample it.

This section is entitled "The Personal Touch" because the teaching strategies presented here require even greater consideration of student sensitivities and capabilities than almost any other format. They require quick, subtle decisions from the teacher to ensure student participation, support, and direction in the classroom.

An appropriate strategy is one that meets the situational needs, the students' needs, and the teacher's ability. The latter point is vital. No matter how much one likes a strategic teaching mode, it cannot be effective without able teacher demonstration. How good a strategy may be theoretically will make no difference to a class of young children. Finding and choosing the best strategy is often a matter of trial and error. This should not lead to discouragement; part of good teaching includes failing once in a while. It helps one learn the parameters of one's abilities and keeps a teacher humble.

ROLE PLAY

Everyone plays roles, in school and out, intentionally and unintentionally. We all have expectations for the way roles should or should not be fulfilled, and we modify our behaviors depending on these expectations and the behaviors of others. A few of the many roles a person might assume in a day are son or daughter, friend, parent, employer or employee, counselor, and colleague. Some more specific roles include gardener, cook, garbage collector, and housekeeper. These examples illustrate the variety and breadth of the roles we play out every day, whether we acknowledge them or not.

Many types of role playing can be carried out in the classroom. One type that this chapter examines extensively is *sociodrama,* which can be used in solving social problems. Another type of role play used in the classroom is *historical role play,* in which students assume the roles of historical figures in order to better understand what those people did and why. A third type of role play, called *psychodrama,* attempts to solve individual psychological problems. (The psychological problems of *students,* however, should not be considered the province of the classroom or of the classroom teacher. Such students should be referred to a guidance counselor or the school psychologist.) Finally, role play functions as a learning method for disadvantaged children and as a means of learning special skills. Thus, depending on the teacher's purpose, the nature of role play exhibits different intents and characteristics. For example, role play could be used in the classroom to improve understanding of content, to solve problems (individually or in groups), or to understand the feelings of others faced with social or moral quandaries.

Sociodrama

Solving social problems is one of the most useful and popular functions of role play. Probably the most influential person in the development of sociodrama is Fanny R. Shaftel, who is credited with taking others' ideas concerning role play and psychodrama and shaping them into a useful form for schoolchildren. As Shaftel views it, role playing should strive to promote education for citizenship as well as provide group counseling for children as they encounter the pressures of growing up, including peer pressure, parental expectations, societal rules, and understanding the problems of others. According to Shaftel, role playing "is a group of problem-solving procedures that employs all the techniques of critical evaluation implied in the terms, 'listening,' 'discussion,' and 'problem solving' and is akin to the research procedures which behavioral scientists term simulation and theory of games." (1982, 9) This is discussed more in Chapter 10.

Sociodrama is used to help students and teachers recognize and solve problems together, understand how to solve problems together (even if they are unsolvable), and stress empathy while analyzing problems.

The books and papers cited at the end of the chapter offer the theoretical background for further application, and readers are strongly urged to read at least one of these selections. But, more than anything else, sociodrama needs to be *practiced*. Its effectiveness in the classroom needs to be developed over time. The nearly instantaneous decisions about what to do next are always subject to second-guessing. With practice comes confidence that one's decisions will be good ones for student growth; they may not always be the best choices, but they will always be ones that ensure student empathy and understanding. Sociodrama does not always work immediately. It requires certain behaviors on the teacher's part and a positive environment for student discussion and risk taking. The teacher must learn to recognize factors that will inhibit initial responses to sociodramatic episodes. Most of these factors will reflect previous classroom experience. Some of them might be: (1) a teacher who recognizes only *right* answers and leaves little room for doubt, (2) a teacher who holds few discussions, (3) a teacher or parents who overemphasize grades at the expense of student growth, and (4) a belief among students that sociodrama is acting and that they themselves are not good actors.

As discussed in Chapter 1, some teachers need to have the *right* answers to questions, and they convey that need to their students. After sufficient exposure to this method, students are bound to be timid about responding unless they feel that they know precisely what the teacher is after. Because sociodrama encompasses much ambiguity, it is unlikely that right answers will be obvious—thus student response will be very tentative.

A photograph can be used to stimulate sociodramatic episodes. What seems to be going on in this picture?

Discussion also will be tentative, because younger students will not necessarily want to be identified with a position that is not the teacher's, since the teacher's position is, of course, the "right" one.

As children get older, they will often *reject* the teacher's position, simply because it represents the authority that they are questioning or testing. Among sixth graders, for example, the peer group's opinions will have more influence than the teacher's. Facing such a rebellion should not "throw" a teacher. The teacher who is reluctant to take a position makes a discussion even more uncomfortable for students.

An emphasis on grades will also lead to inhibition, because students will want to do well but will not initially be able to discern the standard by which a good performance is determined. Some students may have become so jaded (even by the third or fourth grade) that they will not participate in an activity unless they believe they will be evaluated and graded.

Student concerns with whether they are good actors reflect their concerns with how their peers view them. By junior high school, peer influence may be as great as or greater than parental influence. In the middle and upper elementary grades the need to please or at least acknowledge the influence of peers may discourage students from participating in sociodramatic enactments. To offset this, the teacher should practice behaviors that promote the proper climate for sociodrama. Hunt and Shaftel emphasize that

> it is the teacher's role to give the student the opportunity to learn (from his or her mistakes) in a supportive, nonthreatening environment. The teacher is an interested listener or seeker of information rather than a participant in the decision making. (1–2)

To create this atmosphere, the authors suggest the following:

1. The teacher should establish a positive climate through example and discussion.
2. The teacher should select for exploration through role playing those issues that are genuinely of concern to the group and which permit emotional involvement.
3. The teacher should remain cognizant of those student behaviors which lead to desired outcomes of role playing and should not enter into the decision-making process. Rather, the teacher may assist by reflective listening, problem focusing, exploring consequences, testing for reality, developing feelings for others, exploring complexity, and generalizing theories.
4. The teacher should be tolerant of occasionally lengthy silences while students are thinking, which can occur at any time, but this is particularly acute when considering generalizations.

Rather than listing the steps for sociodramatic role play, the following incident demonstrates one of the many ways a teacher could introduce sociodrama into a classroom:

> Mr. Barnard is beginning his first year of teaching at the Lemont School, which is also his first year of teaching anywhere. He was hired because of his excellent recommendations, his fine student teaching performance, a very positive series of interviews, and a good knowledge of the subject areas.
>
> Barnard's methods are less traditional than those of many older teachers, some of whom have been at the school more than 20 years. Two of these older teachers are Ms. Rishel and Ms. Fagan. Both are well respected in the school and community, still enjoy teaching, and believe that they have learned a great deal from their years of experience.
>
> On this particular day, Ms. Rishel and Ms. Fagan are relaxing in the teachers' room at lunch, which is empty, as they are invariably the first ones in the teachers' room each day. Ms. Fagan is talking to Ms. Rishel, who is listening or nodding in agreement.
>
> "I'll tell you, Betty, I don't know how much longer I can take it. Today's version of 'new educational practices' consisted of pounding on the walls. I

half expected to see a little fist pop through the wall any second. It was driving me crazy! My kids were supposed to be reading, but I'm sure half of them couldn't get a thing done."

"What did you do?" asks Ms. Rishel.

"What could I do!? Nothing. If he's so lost control of the class that they're pounding on the walls, my saying anything wouldn't make any difference. I'm going to *have* to go to Caroline [the principal] to see what she can . . ."

At that moment Mr. Barnard steps out of the small alcove in the room where the coffee pot is. He clearly has heard every word they have said. He looks from Ms. Rishel to Ms. Fagan and then . . .

At this point the teacher stops and asks the class a series of questions about the situation. For example, the teacher might ask:

"How do you think Mr. Barnard feels?"

"How do you think Ms. Rishel or Ms. Fagan feels?"

"What do you think is going to happen?"

These questions should not be asked all at once; rather, the teacher should solicit answers from the class on each question and mentally note who contributes and seems interested in the questions.

Student responses might be something like "Mr. Barnard is angry; he'll tell her off," or "He's upset but won't say anything." Concerning Ms. Fagan, they might say, "She is embarrassed and will try to apologize" or "She'll speak right then to Mr. Barnard and try to bring the situation out in the open."

After the selection of students to assume each role, an enactment of the scene takes place, with the audience acting as observer-participants. Following the enactment, a class discussion could take place, leading to subsequent enactments and discussions. As the final step, the teacher-leader would encourage students to share their own similar experiences and try, if possible, to generalize about them. Students who offer to share experiences they have encountered like this one may advise others to be ready to forgive, to apologize, or to compromise. By admitting one's mistakes, a person learns something.

Another generalization that might be derived from such an experience could be "get someone before he or she gets you." This may seem harsh, but if students honestly believe it is true the teacher should allow it to stand. If the teacher interferes unduly, it will imply that right answers are determined only by the teacher, and students will go back to getting the teacher to tell them the answer.

Some generalizations also dissatisfy youngsters, and they may opt to reopen the sociodrama proceedings the next day. The teacher may hear students discussing the reenactment at recess or during lunch. Sociodrama encourages students to talk, think, and recognize that social problems require everyone's efforts to solve them. The sociodramatic process is outlined further in the box on pages 210–212.

THE SOCIODRAMATIC PROCESS

The following material, adapted from Shaftel and Shaftel (1982), clarifies the steps and procedures used in a role-play episode.

1. SETTING A CLIMATE FOR ROLE PLAY Prepare the class to face a problem. This is an important key to realistic role play. The vehicle for such a warm-up varies. The teacher could describe an unresolved incident or read students an unfinished story. The Shaftels' book presents over 40 problem stories, that can be updated and adapted for particular classrooms. A teacher could also shut off a film before it ends or could show a film that presents a problem with no solution (although this could be difficult to do with primary grade youngsters). Another vehicle would be to display a large picture that students could describe and use to make predictions based on their observations. This may be most appropriate for the primary grades, although it also could be used for higher grade levels. The vehicle in sociodrama will depend on the student concentration level and on the approach with which the teacher feels most comfortable.

   In setting the climate, the teacher "guides the group to think of 'what *will* happen' rather than 'what *should* happen.' We want the *should* aspect to emerge from the group's growing insight as they role-play the situation." (Shaftel, n.d., 1)

2. SELECTING ROLE PLAYERS Try to select as role players "people who evidence impulsive or socially poor solutions so that these may be opened up and explored for their consequences. Save the positive and socially apt solutions for final enactments so that the entire gamut of behaviors may be exposed to the group for evaluation." (n.d., 1)

   Do not use students volunteered by others because they would "really be good in that role." When a student is asked to play a part and refuses, ask again if there seemed to be some hesitancy on the student's part. Sometimes students may refuse initially because they do not want to look too eager to please the teacher. This is particularly true with upper elementary and middle school students. After two refusals, however, ask another student.

   With primary grade students the problem is usually one of too many volunteers rather than too few. Since younger children often cannot sustain an enactment for very long, the teacher may decide to let *everyone* get a turn at it, with each enactment lasting from 30 seconds to a minute.

3. PREPARING THE AUDIENCE Once the role players are selected, they should describe their roles as they see them. This helps

(continued)

(continued from previous page)

the audience and the role players to better comprehend why the actors behave as they do. This stage setting goes beyond the initial descriptors given in the warm-up. One person playing Ms. Rishel might describe her as "fifty-three years old with graying hair and two grown children. She is patient and hardworking. She doesn't read as much as she used to; she's just so tired when she gets home."

The audience should understand that sociodrama is a *class* exercise, not a performance put on by two or three people. To reinforce that, the audience should be given an assignment to carry out during the enactment. The audience should scrutinize each role player (or only one) in an attempt (1) to assess how realistic the person's actions are and (2) to consider possible alternative solutions. This helps prevent the audience from losing interest, by making it an important part of the sociodramatic episode.

4. THE ENACTMENT The teacher could help the enactment along somewhat by asking when it takes place and where, if there is a choice to be made. As Shaftel notes:

An enactment does not have to go to completion. The leader may stop it when the role players have clearly demonstrated their ideas of what will happen. However, sometimes the teacher may want to allow a situation to be played out to the bitter end— so that the consequences become dramatically clear to the group. (n.d., 2)

5. DISCUSSING AND EVALUATING The teacher must be careful not to be judgmental and should ask any number of open-ended questions to further discussion, such as:

"What is happening?"

"How does _____ feel?"

"Could this *really* happen this way?"

"Why did _____ act like he did?"

"Are there other ways that this could have ended?"

The teacher might also ask students whether the sociodrama enacted could happen to them and have them apply the various roles to their own lives.

6. THE REENACTMENT Further enactments could give other students the chance to reinterpret the roles, providing alternative solutions or behaviors. This is an area that requires quick, decisive judgment from the teacher. As students in the audience comment on different aspects, the teacher must decide how to go forward, with whom, and for how long. There may be no opportunity to return to someone's suggestion if it is not seized on immediately, as the class mood and intentions may shift rapidly. Each choice

(continued)

(continued from previous page)

made by the leader means a distinct direction to the role play.

7. SHARING EXPERIENCES AND GENERALIZING With younger children, generalizations will be conceptually difficult to understand, although they may be able to share their experiences, focusing on a similar incident or similar feelings. For example, a teacher could show the Shaftels' "Trick or Treat" film, in which two boys who go out trick-or-treating are followed by younger boys. Annoyed, the older boys persuade one of the younger ones to perform a trick on a man that results in great property and human damage. The younger boy is caught; the older boys escape unrecognized. The older boys then discuss what, if anything, they should do.

After viewing the film, students might share some of the things they once got away with and how they felt about it. The teacher might add his or her own experiences, some dating back to childhood. With older students, generalizations like "Better to be honest than live with guilt" come fairly easily. Younger children are often too concrete in their thinking to provide such an abstract statement, however.

Chesler and Fox also provide brief scenarios that may be appropriate for role playing. Some of these are:

Your friend has asked you to go skating. Your mother says you must stay home.

You do not want to hurt your friend. Mother is standing near.

A shy schoolmate has returned to school after a sickness of several weeks. You want to make him feel at home in school again.

You want to help a friend who is unsure of himself and shows off and talks loudly.

You see one child teasing another.

You see two children fighting.

A classmate jumps on you or hits you in trying to say hello.

You and a classmate are walking through a department store. He tries to get you to steal something.

You've never played with a particular classmate, but you'd like him to be your friend.

Another student has just torn up the homework you spent all last evening doing.

You meet a friend after you've heard that he has said unpleasant things about you. (67)

Children's literature lends itself to many situations for sociodrama, particularly among younger children. Leo Lionni's *The Six Crows* or Don Freeman's *Dandelion* are two of hundreds of possibilities for sociodramatic situations.

Role play can be a profitable, enjoyable learning experience when used to examine social issues. If overused, however, it can become predictable. Scheduling a sociodrama every day or every week may not have the excitement of a surprise drama. As in all strategies, sociodrama should be only one part of the teacher's repertoire, to be used when appropriate.

Dramatic Play

Dramatic play is another form of role play, although it reflects different intentions and obtains different results. According to Merritt, "dramatic play is the free playing out of familiar roles and activities." (202) There is no plot or story line in dramatic play. Rather, events are improvised by students who are familiar with the roles or incidents. Students should not memorize dialogue, although they may need background information, particularly if the dramatic play draws on an area of historical or cultural study.

Corbin suggests that teachers who use drama in the classroom can (1) provide students with a genuine sense of participation, (2) allow them to truly empathize with others' conditions, (3) transcend ethnocentrism, and (4) address international situations more objectively while retaining the sense of complexity of global issues. (45)

The following example, found in John Lee, illustrates how basic a dramatic play can be:

> The first-grader reads, "Look at the horse walk. Clomp, clomp, clomp! Now look at the horse run. Clippity, clippity, clippity!"
>
> The teacher says, "Show me how the horse walks. Show me how the horse runs."
>
> The third-grader says, "Watch me; I'll show you how they get into the lunar module."
>
> The fifth-grader says, "I got a dead fish and some corn. This is what the Indians showed the Pilgrims."
>
> The seventh-grader puts on his wig and says, "The delegates from the Colonies assembled here in Continental Congress will put out their pipes and come to order." (269)

Lee offers many other examples, but certainly a teacher should encourage students to pursue the dramatic play themselves, drawing from material that is currently being studied. Dramatic play reflects what students know. Through discussion following each round of play other students in the classroom can clarify misconceptions or misunderstandings. Corbin provides some useful procedural steps for a teacher who wishes to present a historical personage:

1. Choose a character.
2. Research the character's life using children's and adult's biographies.
3. Wear a simple costume or have a significant appropriate prop.
4. Stay in character while presenting the role.
5. Involve the students through a "press conference" or discussion.
6. Have students prepare through readings of the historical period or geographic area. (46–47)

Dramatic play can be enhanced by making it an integral part of unit study, complete with props, costumes, and sets. Once all these have been assembled, students can return to the set as new concepts are introduced and practiced. A teacher's role in dramatic play shifts from leader to facilitator. Some planning and evaluation guidelines for teachers provided by Merritt are both appropriate and useful:

Plan understandings to be developed through dramatic play.

Plan learning resources that may be used when the need for them arises.

Plan possible construction materials and activities that will further dramatic play.

Arrange an environment conducive for play.

Help children connect the previous day's planning and evaluation with today's plans.

Help children organize for play.

Encourage children to talk about their play activities, bringing to the group any problems they have faced.

Help children focus on concepts that need clarification and on information, materials, and procedures that will make the next play session more interesting.

Help children record plans for future action. (206)

Dramatic play is fun for students and can be used by teachers as an informal evaluative device. It also provides insightful learning: students are able to see beyond action without deliberation and to consider underlying causes for action. But, as in sociodrama, the teacher must feel comfortable in the facilitator role in order to ensure some degree of success with the technique.

SMALL-GROUP DECISION MAKING AND COOPERATIVE LEARNING

Many activities in the classroom require groups to accomplish various tasks. There are many ways to group students in order to enhance a group's effectiveness. A teacher's method of grouping can sometimes make the difference between a student who feels neglected and one who believes himself or herself to be a vital part of the group. This section is primarily concerned with small groups (consisting of about three to seven students) that work cooperatively. "Evidence has mounted documenting the effectiveness of cooperative learning strategies for a wide array of outcomes, from enhanced achievement to improved intergroup relations and acceptance of mainstreamed classmates to self-esteem and positive attitudes toward school." (Slavin, 1990, xi) Although they receive less recognition from teachers and college instructors, small groups can make learning more meaningful. They operate best when all parties treat one another as equals. In groups of more than eight persons, the most aggressive members tend to dominate.

Historical role play gives students a sense of history, understanding, and involvement.

Establishing a functioning small group is not an easy task, nor is it an endeavor from which immediate success can be expected. Cohesiveness is more likely to be maintained in the classroom when small groups are formed frequently. However, bringing small groups together three or four times a week will not necessarily produce cohesiveness. A teacher must consider other factors, such as the attitudes expressed by students.

According to Schmuck and Schmuck (94), children tend to reject four types of student peers: (1) those who are limited in physical ability, (2) those who have difficulty in developing meaningful social relations with others, (3) those who have intellectual limitations, and (4) those who have mental health difficulties. Recognizing these students and integrating them into all groups is an initial step in developing cohesion within groups. A small group will be only as effective as the efforts of teacher and students to build and maintain it. Some major requirements cited by Bradford (45) for building and maintaining an atmosphere conducive to group work are:

1. Sharing in decision making about group goals and behavior whenever possible
2. Sharing diagnosis of group difficulties and analyses of group successes
3. Sharing in analyses of teacher and student roles and functions
4. Accepting all individuals as members of the group

5. Developing an accepted standard of working on individual and group problems, one that affirms the group's task of learning
6. Agreeing to be experimental in procedures, clarifying or changing goals and modifying group behavior
7. Making an effort to utilize members' resources

Each member brings his or her unique experiences to a group. "In essence, then, varying backgrounds, attitudes, and emotional responses are brought into the group by each participant, which can either enhance or inhibit the group decision making." (Nelson and Singleton, 145)

Slavin sees three concepts as central to all student team-learning methods —team rewards, individual accountability (toward team success), and equal opportunities for success. (1990,3) Many times a teacher will establish small groups to help students develop cooperative decision-making skills. The teacher may decide to focus the group's efforts on decision making in order to improve the overall ability of the group to work toward a goal. A wide range of techniques is available for developing both routine and creative decision-making skills. Pfeiffer and Jones offer a myriad of ideas in their annual handbooks on human relations training (see References).

Cooperative group work seems to be successful because it is motivational, that is, because students want to do well for and with their peers and because of the cognitive experiences it provides. Of particular impact is the learning gained by both explainer and explainee when one student explains material to another.

Equal Status Cooperation

One of the keys to group cooperation is equal status interaction in the small-group setting. Each member of the group should recognize the need for every member to contribute. In a cooperative small-group setting, equal status provides a viable means of making legitimate decisions through the equal distribution of power.

> Small group experiences reflect the power structure evident in the larger classroom setting. The use of power in the classroom setting will directly influence the degree of open cooperation small groups are able to achieve. By virtue of position, societal mores, and school rules, the teacher is perceived by students as a source of power. The teacher's attitude toward the use of power is an important aspect of trust development in small groups. (Nelson and Singleton, 154-55)

Four essential ingredients are needed to establish cooperative groups based on trust. First, each individual in the group must be strongly committed to reaching the group's goal. Second, each individual must realize that he or she cannot reach the goal without the help of other members. Third, the individual must realize that other members are depending on his or her help to reach the goal. Fourth, each individual must realize that all members are mutually dependent on each other. (Nelson and Singleton, 157)

Students meet to compare work and ideas for a class project.

In light of the importance of clear goals and the ever-present threat of group conflict, it may be helpful for the teacher to establish a checkpoint system along the way. The teacher who has several small groups in operation at the same time will probably spend much time going from group to group, observing and monitoring. Using the checkpoint system, the teacher responds to each group at regular intervals, both encouraging and monitoring its progress through the use of a mental checklist. This would alert the teacher to special problems, such as lack of progress, off-task behaviors, and group anxieties. The teacher could also note whether some group members exhibit the following skills: an ability to evaluate hypotheses, an ability to recognize a problem, speaking skills, and listening skills. (Nelson and Singleton, 158) The more aware of and involved in the group process experiences the teacher is, the easier it will be to recognize approaching decision points.

Johnson and Johnson have developed a paper-and-pencil checklist of cooperative experiences to be used by teachers in developing and monitoring small groups. The list is reproduced in the box on page 219. The ideas of Johnson and Johnson have been used and adapted by Nelson and Singleton.

At this point it may be useful to summarize the preparation for small-group decision making. The following guidelines are from Nelson and Singleton (167–68), who also provide a brief rationale for each guideline based on research findings.

1. Brainstorm when time is limited and the problem or task is simple.
2. Continue to use task groups in later activities, such as simulation games.
3. Determine (examine) roles in the group by keeping an anecdotal record of group interaction, member roles, and task orientation.
4. Foster a social climate helpful to group work.
5. Try to break up previously established patterns of familiarity: friendship groups, bus groups, ethnic groups, and sociocultural groups should be discouraged.
6. Use established student leaders to aid in group formation and development.
7. Shift group members after a series of tasks.
8. Clarify the task explicitly.
9. Try to discourage autocracy and encourage status interaction.
10. Aim toward consensus without unjustified acquiescence.
11. Discourage conflict among ad hoc groups.
12. Be a silent, nonobtrusive listener.
13. Encourage conflict among established groups.

Although brainstorming is often helpful in solving simple problems, it may be less so for solving complex ones. Indeed, most researchers have found that group participation in brainstorming may *inhibit* creative thinking because individual members tend to conform to group boundaries and suppress divergent thinking.

The determination or examination of individual student roles in the group is of primary importance. Teachers should note the leadership choices and role developments that occur, as well as the structure and evolution of a group. This will not only aid the teacher in better understanding the complexities of group process; it may also aid in classroom management. Observing the students' potential in equal status confrontations may help a teacher in planning future student tasks and programs in other areas.

The teacher's decisions regarding social climate may also be vital to task completion. In group problem solving, a permissive social climate will often prove superior to a traditional climate for students with high levels of intelligence. In an equal status situation, however, most groups are of mixed intelligence. Therefore, a permissive social climate with relatively visible parameters is usually most effective in facilitating group decision making and task completion.

Once a group has performed a series of tasks, it may become so stable that it loses its creativity. Shifting group members will break up stultifying cliques or embattled rivalries and minimize the possibly erosive effects of social "crassness." After a time students seem to enjoy working in new groups. Do not rush to break up small groups, however, until you see that their creativity and efficiency are diminishing.

Clarifying a group's task may seem patently obvious, but it is important. A group that is confused over its task assignment may devote its time to destroying the task rather than performing it. Thus it is imperative to clarify the task to the satisfaction of group members. Repeat the instructions later, if necessary, but *do not* direct the group's progress. In ad hoc groups, conflict is

TEACHER CHECKLIST FOR COOPERATIVE SMALL-GROUP EXPERIENCES

1. What are the desired outcomes for the experiences?
   A. Cognitive
   B. Affective
2. What is the identified task goal of the small group?
   _____ A. Are the students aware of the group goal?
   _____ B. Are the students aware that the group reward will be based on quality according to announced, fixed criteria?
3. Does the classroom arrangement provide a means of:
   _____ A. Open communication for students clustered in small groups?
   _____ B. Freedom to move about in the quest for information?
   _____ C. Sharing of both verbal and written information within small groups with relative ease?
4. Are students aware that they should:
   _____ A. Interact with each other within the small group?
   _____ B. Share ideas and experiences as well as materials and information in a helping fashion?
   _____ C. Divide tasks as well as integrate individual findings into a group product?
   _____ D. Demonstrate an acceptancy attitude, limited or mutual respect for the status of each member of the group, and encouragement of further contributions as in an atmosphere of genuine friendliness and warmth?
   _____ E. Speak and think in terms of the cooperative group rather than in the individual sense?
   _____ F. Explore various avenues in an attempt to classify or expand particular contributions while continuing to maintain an awareness of the task as the major focus?
5. Do students know and understand the teacher's role:
   _____ A. As facilitator, observer, and supporter of the group?
   _____ B. As a strong supporter of group cooperative effort in which the capabilities of each member are utilized to the greatest degree possible?

SOURCE: From Johnson and Johnson, pp. 54–56.

often disruptive and should be discouraged. In established groups, however, a wide variety of opinions is often stimulating, so conflict should not be discouraged. The rationale for this appears to be that when group members know each other well, they do not take attacks on ideas personally. Ad hoc group members often feel threatened and possibly embarrassed by disagreements with persons they know only casually.

Throughout the process of small-group decision making, the teacher should be as unobtrusive as possible, maintaining the role of patient listener. The teacher should float from group to group, should sit and listen for a time and answer questions, but should discourage students from appealing for help too often. Do not volunteer information unless there has been an obvious discrepancy in the task assignment. In such cases, provide the correct information to the entire class before fading again into the background.

Slavin has identified a number of cooperative learning outcomes other than achievement. These include (1) the fostering of intergroup relations, (2) the acceptance of mainstreamed academically handicapped students, (3) growth in student self-esteem, (4) an increase in the internal focus of control (that is, students feel in control more than they feel they are being controlled), (5) an increase in time on the task, (6) an increase in positive feelings toward the school or class where cooperative learning takes place, (7) the recognition of pro academic peer norms (that is, students perceive that their peers want them to work hard and succeed in the class). (1990)

Slavin also identifies various forms of cooperative learning. Group investigation and equal status interaction have already been described. Four others are major components of Slavin's presentation. Two of those, Team-Assisted (or Accelerated) Instruction (TAI) and Cooperative Integrated Reading and Composition (CIRC) are more subject specific to mathematics and reading/language arts, respectively. (1990)

The remaining two, Student Teams—Achievement Divisions (STAD) and Teams—Games—Tournaments (TGT), are variations of the same format. STAD has five major components for teacher-selected cooperative groups. The first is the teacher's class presentation of a topic to introduce and direct the students to their work. Step two involves teams working together to prepare all the team members to do well on quizzes. This may be fostered through worksheets and team study. When teams are sure that all teammates will get perfect grades on the quiz, they move to step three, the quiz.

Quizzes are individually taken and scored by the teacher or other students. The teacher must compile team scores in order for the groups to move to step four, team recognition. This comes in the form of award certificates or other rewards to high-scoring teams. Scoring is done on the basis of improvement over past quizzes (a base score) and an overall excellence on the quiz. Types of recognition can include bulletin board displays listing the week's outstanding teams or photos of successful teams, special buttons to wear, or special privileges, like first to line up for recess or lunch or first choice on classroom jobs for the week.

As noted earlier, teams should be rotated regularly, about every six weeks, to keep the program fresh, allow students to work with other classmates, and give students on low-scoring teams a new chance.

"TGT is the same as STAD in every respect but one: instead of the quizzes and the individual improvement score system, TGT uses academic tournaments, in which students compete as representatives of their teams with members of other teams who are like them in past performance." (Slavin, 1990, 66)

In the past 10 years cooperative learning has become more commonplace in schools. A 1993 "national survey found that 79% of all elementary teachers and 62% of middle school teachers reported making some sustained use of cooperative learning." (Slavin, 1996, 43) It is heartening to hear these findings but it must be noted that groups are not necessarily better than individuals in problem solving. They may not be better in all aspects of decision making. Small groups are, however, a superior way of making *certain* decisions, particularly those of a social-action nature. Most decisions in our society are considered by small groups, making small-group decision making a worthwhile skill to develop and encourage, both in and out of the classroom.

CASE STUDIES

A case study is an in-depth analysis of an event or series of events that can be used to illustrate certain concepts. Although case studies may ultimately cover less content than a textbook, what is covered is examined in depth and is more likely to be understood and retained.

The case study approach was originally borrowed from the study of law. In extolling the virtues of case study, Lee states:

My observations over the past half-dozen years indicate that cases are probably the single most effective new teaching procedure with fourth- through eighth-graders. Pupils clearly build understandings from cases, and there is considerable evidence that cases influence attitudes and overt behaviors in highly favorable ways.

A case can be short or long; it can be historical or contemporary. It can deal with a grand principle or with the most fleeting of relevant problems. But the real beauty of a case is that pupils must respond to it by reasoning rather than by memorizing or identifying an answer. (301)

The case study method can be used in a variety of ways with various grade levels and subject areas. Cases may cover a historical era through events or biography, geographic concepts, the problems anthropologists face, political issues and their backgrounds, or some single economic, social, or political issue. To clarify the method a bit, we will consider two case studies and how they might be approached in the classroom incorporating various teaching strategies and materials.

A case study can be fictional or based on fact. With younger children, it may be easier to develop an appropriate case from material you happen to be working with than to find data that are appropriate in content and of interest to youngsters. Some of the strategies that can be applied to case studies include role play, simulation, group decision making, individual research, field trips, and community surveys. Two very different examples of case studies follow.

Case 1: Playground or Mini-Mall

For weeks, the members of a city council have been debating what should be done with a plot of land in the downtown area. Members agree that because the downtown area lacks greenery, the land should not be used to erect another building. As the city owns the property, the council has decided to seek public opinion as to what should be done with the land.

A number of people have suggested that the land be used as a playground. Many apartment dwellers in or near the downtown area who have young children say there is no park within walking distance. In spite of its size, the plot would be a veritable oasis for parents and their young children.

Another group, strongly supported by the downtown merchants' association, has suggested that the land be made into a mini-mall, with flower boxes, benches, a small fountain, and possibly a gazebo. They argue that there is no place to sit and relax downtown and that the mini-mall would have the same function as a town square in many other communities.

There is not enough land for both groups to have what they desire. It is up to the eight-member city council to decide on a solution.

There are the raw facts of the case, although more information could be given as to initial expenditures, upkeep, insurance, and so on. A teacher could probably spend a week with second or third graders studying this case in more depth.

Some activities that students might engage in during this period are: (1) research on city life and planning (what do communities need to provide?); (2) a community survey on the question; (3) a field trip to their own downtown area to assess what provisions are made and how they work; (4) research on the costs of building such areas by checking with local contractors; (5) a field trip to a city council meeting to see how such questions are handled; (6) a simulated city council meeting, with eight students posing as council members. Many other activities could be added to fill a week of class time. Although the time spent on this case would take time away from textbook study of the community, the trade-off seems more than worthwhile, considering the conceptual depth of such work.

Case 2: The Impeachment Trial of Andrew Johnson

Rather than a week or more spent on the textbook study of Reconstruction, an in-depth study of the impeachment trial of Andrew Johnson would give students the opportunity to assess the depth of feeling in both the North and the South following the Civil War. Students could do biographical research on Sec-

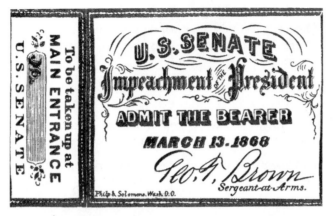

Facsimiles of artifacts, like this ticket to Andrew Johnson's trial, can be useful in a case study.

retary of War Edwin Stanton, President Johnson himself, or key congressmen like Thaddeus Stevens of Pennsylvania, Charles Sumner of Maryland, and John Bingham of Ohio. They could assess economic conditions by using old newspapers or encyclopedias. Finally, they could examine the geography of the United States in 1868, leading some researchers to the Treaty of Guadalupe Hidalgo, the Missouri Compromise, and the differences between rural and urban America.

Recreating the impeachment trial would require research, planning, and design, but after such work students would more clearly understand the animosities between North and South than if they had only read about this era. This exercise is most appropriate for fifth graders or middle school students.

Case studies require time and preparation, but they also can be deeply rewarding for students and teachers alike. That is true of all the strategies discussed in this chapter. Teachers have to invest more effort and creativity in preparation, but the dividends in student interest, enjoyment, and learning make it a high-yield investment.

QUESTIONS AND ACTIVITIES

1. Think of an incident that occurred in your elementary school years. The incident probably impressed you or you would not still remember it. Try to put it in story form, omitting the ending.

2. One part of sociodrama that often requires further development is characterization. Try to add to the following characterizations to make the individual more real:
    a. a stout fourth-grade boy with few friends
    b. a sixth-grade girl who is a head taller than anyone else in the class

    c. a boisterous third-grader who cannot read

    d. James, a second-grader, whom everyone likes

    e. Karen, a fifth-grader, who has been the smartest student in her class for years

3. Develop one or two of the incidents of Chesler and Fox listed on page 212.

4. What problems, if any, do you anticipate having with sociodrama? What could you do to deal with these potential problems?

5. What incidents in American or world history might be fun to dramatize? Try to reenact them with friends or classmates.

6. Visit an elementary school classroom and devise ways to group the students based only on your observations.

7. Ask an elementary school teacher about the different ways that he or she groups students.

8. Study your local newspaper for a week or two and develop a case study similar to Case 1 (p. 222).

9. Organize and present a press conference with a noted person from American or world history.

REFERENCES

Bradford, L. P. "Developing Potentialities Through Class Groups." In *Forces in Learning.* Selected readings, ser. 3. Washington, DC: National Training Laboratories and National Education Association, 1961, p. 34–47.

Chesler, M., and R. Fox. *Role-Playing Methods in the Classroom.* Chicago, IL: Science Research Associates, 1966.

Corbin, D. "Using Drama in the Classroom," *The Councilor,* Illinois Council for the Social Studies, vol. 48, October, 1988, p. 6–11.

Hawley, R. C. *Value Exploration Through Role-Playing.* New York: Hart Publishing, 1975.

Hunt, B., and F. Shaftel. "Teacher Behaviors Which Create the Proper Conditions for Role Playing." Mimeo. Stanford University, School of Education, n.d.

Johnson, D. W., and R. T. Johnson. *Learning Together and Alone.* Englewood Cliffs, NJ: Prentice-Hall, 1975.

Lee, J. R. *Teaching Social Studies in the Elementary School.* New York: Free Press, 1974.

Merritt, E. P. *Working with Children in Social Studies.* San Francisco: Wadsworth, 1961.

Nelson, M. R., and H. W. Singleton. "Small Group Decision Making for Social Action." In *Developing Decision-Making Skills,* D. Kurfman, ed. 47th Yearbook of the National Council for the Social Studies. Arlington, VA: Ness, 1977, p. 141–172.

Pfeiffer, J. W., and J. E. Jones, eds. *A Handbook of Structured Experiences for Human Relations Training,* vol. III. La Jolla, CA: University Associates, 1974. (Subsequent volumes published annually to date.)

Schmuck, R., and P. Schmuck. *Group Processes in the Classroom*. Dubuque, IA: Brown, 1975.

Shaftel, F. R. "Role-Playing Suggestions for the Teacher." Mimeo. Stanford University, School of Education, n.d.

Shaftel, F., and G. Shaftel. *Role Playing for Social Values*. 2nd ed. Englewood Cliffs, NJ: Prentice-Hall, 1982.

Siks, G. B. *Creative Dramatics*. New York: Harper and Row, 1958.

Slavin, R. E. *Cooperative Learning—Theory Research and Practice*. Englewood Cliffs, NJ: Prentice-Hall, 1990.

Slavin, R. E., "Research on Cooperative Learning and Achievement: What We Know, What We Need to Know." *Contemporary Educational Psychology*, vol. 21, no. 1, January, 1996, 43–70.

Stephenson, N., and D. Vincent. *Teaching and Understanding Drama*. Windsor, Great Britain: NFER Publishing, 1975.

Chapter Nine

COMMUNITY RESOURCES
IN THE SOCIAL STUDIES

This chapter is devoted to the most available resource that any teacher has—one's own community. By their very nature, the resources of each community are unique. Thus the examples and ideas expressed in this chapter may not be directly applicable to every community. But generic ideas should emerge from the discussion that can be modified for use in any setting.

During the progressive era of the 1930s and 1940s the community was a primary source of study. But as textbooks became standardized, community study was considered less important, particularly in the middle and upper elementary grades. There are, however, a number of reasons for studying one's community, including the pride it instills in youngsters, the ties that bind school and community, and the exploration of a more active learning mode. This chapter will attempt to rekindle the enthusiasms teachers once had for community study. Now that many school districts have less money to spend, community study offers a learning bargain, providing unique insights into social studies at very low cost.

The first part of the chapter outlines the many advantages of community study, as well as some of the ways to develop community resources, from the location and training of resource personnel to the preparation of one's class and the planning of field trips. Some of the drawbacks of action learning, and the contrasts between urban and rural community resources, are also noted. Finally, the chapter offers some specific ideas on the many areas of the community that could be investigated and on ways to organize such study.

OUT OF THE CLASSROOM AND INTO THE STREETS

Community study is sometimes referred to as action learning, because learning goes on outside the classroom and requires a more active role on the part of learners. Five of the most compelling reasons to use the community for study are:

1. Communities provide a unique, rich resource of materials.
2. Community study brings the school and the community closer together, both physically and mentally.
3. Community study promotes a sense of pride and fulfillment in youngsters.
4. Theories developed in the classroom and tested or observed in the community make learning more directly relevant to students' lives.
5. Community study allows for diversity of learning modes as well as a degree of student choice.

The following section examines these reasons one at a time.

For years, the community or community helpers have been studied as topics of interest in the second or third grade. Although this illustrates the *potential* for community study, it hardly demonstrates the depth and breadth of possibilities on all levels.

Every community has something unique about it, if only the fact that it may be hidden in peaceful isolation. In a busy, noisy world, that kind of peaceful existence is rare. Rather than bemoaning the fact that their community doesn't resemble those depicted on television, students should gain strength and pride from their unique hometowns. By studying their community, students will realize how much it has to offer. This sense of community pride has a positive effect on the egos of all youngsters, increasing and enhancing their self-esteem. According to Mehaffy, Atwood, and Nelson,

> action learning can contribute to a sense of industry and identity by focusing on tasks that the student sees as relevant, ones over which the student has some control. Action learning can further the process of psychological maturation by providing students with varied opportunities for role experimentation in the company of many types of people. (194)

The community also benefits from action learning. Paul Hanna suggested over 60 years ago that a goal of education is to "harness the energy of youth for the task of progressively improving conditions of community life." (21–22) According to Mehaffy et al.,

> Such a philosophical position remains popular with some educators even today. They suggest that students assume projects for the good of the community. . . . In many societies youth are expected to contribute importantly to the goals and programs of the society. . . . Educators in such nations believe that children who participate learn while contributing to the good of the society, and in the process acquire wholesome attitudes toward social obligations. (194)

Some additional outcomes of using community resources are cited by Collings:

- Students demonstrate greater proficiency in problem-solving. Experiences in real situations such as selecting the appropriate visit, making arrangements, and carrying out the follow-up activities are actual living, not playing at living.
- [Students who operate in] groups show superior ability in getting along with others. Better human relations are demonstrated.
- An increased interest in school is evident. Pupils are rarely absent on the day of a trip. General attitude is better.
- Students are increasingly aware of the ability of many groups to contribute to the total community goal.
- Increased cooperation results in better understanding on the part of parents and others in the community.
- Students acquire greater knowledge of the functions of civic and governmental agencies and the specific services of these agencies to the total community.
- Students gain firsthand experiences in determining available job opportunities, necessary qualifications, working conditions, remuneration, existence of employee benefits, and retirement plans.
- Students acquire the concept of giving something to their community through participation in appropriate volunteer service activities and membership in community organizations. They obtain enriched understandings of the possibilities within the community for profitable use of leisure time. (6–7)

All of these very serious rationales obscure another excellent reason for the use of the community—it is enjoyable. Somehow many people have become convinced that if learning is painful, it is more effective. Such specious logic has prevailed in many circles, a carryover from the old belief that the brain was a muscle that required stretching.

Neither Dewey nor Piaget promotes this analogy. In fact, interest in a subject *promotes* learning, and enjoyment in learning promotes interest. Because community exploration is enjoyable, students will learn more. They may not necessarily learn precisely what the teacher had planned, however. In action learning, the effects of collateral interest, or serendipity, become much more pronounced. This is not necessarily bad, but it should be taken into account. The following example serves to illustrate the phenomenon:

> A class of third graders at the Hillview School is studying a unit on inventions and technology. Local fire fighters offer to let the class tour the fire station to observe how technology is used in alerting the fire fighters to a fire as well as how the equipment works. Afterward, the fire fighters have volunteered to demonstrate a number of old pumpers for contrast.
>
> While touring the station, a couple of students notice that all the photos of fire fighters on the wall are of men. Not one woman is depicted. This gets them interested in two areas: sex discrimination in employment and women inventors.
>
> The teacher obviously did not anticipate that this would occur, but the action learning that promoted this collateral interest can be pursued with the teacher's encouragement and guidance.

Utilizing Resource Personnel

The first step in utilizing resource personnel is finding appropriate candidates for a class to use. Once these people are located, the teacher may invite them to the classroom to explain or demonstrate their knowledge. Some of these resource people must be viewed in action because of the nature of their work, their busy schedules, or the great benefit the visit would have for the students.

> Children are often keenly interested in occupations that may hold less appeal for adults. For example, most students would like to meet a garbage collector and inspect his [or her] truck; talk to an "eye-in-the-sky" traffic controller and sit in the helicopter; inspect an 18-wheel semitractor truck and visit with the driver; and meet a police [officer] with a K-9 dog. All of the speakers and others would fit easily with primary-grade study units on "community helpers." (Mehaffy et al., 196)

One of the best ways to find people is to ask other teachers and friends if they know of anyone who can speak about a particular topic. It is amazing how effective that simple procedure is in generating a pool of possible resource people.

If this method proves unsuccessful, or if the people suggested do not work out, check with the high school counselors. Many of the representatives and recruiters who appear at high school career days may also interest elementary students. Chapin and Messick note that:

> parents and grandparents are sources of learning about cultures which teachers often hesitate to tap. . . . The payoff of parent presentations is multiple. Parent and child feel valued and included. Other children begin to see similarities between their ways and those of their classmates. Having parents in the classroom provides face-to-face contact between parents and children from different groups. We know that this kind of contact reduces fear of the unknown for all. (161)

The telephone book is another excellent resource, although if someone is identified through the *Yellow Pages,* an invitation to that person should be sent in writing first and followed up with a telephone call. Hardly anyone likes to be put on the spot with a phone call out of the blue asking for an appearance in Ms. Cable's fifth-grade class to discuss his or her collection of Civil War memorabilia. Common rules of courtesy should take precedence over educational zeal.

Senior citizens are another excellent community resource and are frequently willing to contribute their time and talent. Indeed, senior citizens may be the most underused resource in a community. They can be great sources of oral history (see Chapter 12), often can provide materials for demonstration or observation that are no longer readily available, and usually are willing to take the time to explain things to large or small groups. The mutualistic relationship of the senior citizen and schoolchildren is well documented. The senior citizen acquires renewed purpose in this role and receives love and attention; the children gain the benefit of wisdom and insight packaged in a generally patient and folksy manner.

HOW TO USE RESOURCE PERSONNEL

Once resource personnel are identified, how can they be used in an educationally sound way? Most resource people need guidance, not having spoken to a group of young people very often. It is up to the teacher to provide some general guidelines to potential classroom visitors. For example:

1. Give the resource person a time limit. The visit may be only part of your day's plan, so don't be caught short or become overcommitted.
2. Clarify precisely what you want presented and why.
3. Give the content background of your students, so that the resource person can start a discussion at an appropriate place rather than wasting time and boring the students.
4. Indicate the ability of the class to understand abstract thought and technical language.
5. Ask if the resource person can suggest some advance reading that would better prepare the students for his or her presentation.
6. Help the resource person by providing or suggesting audiovisual aids if none are already available.

Obviously a teacher could make further suggestions. These general guidelines will make the resource person more comfortable by knowing what is expected of him or her.

Preparing the Class

The class also must be attuned to a resource person's presentation. It would be useless and embarrassing to have an excellent resource person visit the class-

Interviewing an older person can be a rewarding experience for all concerned.

room and have the students display no response whatsoever. Some resource people may not notice such a lack of response, but a good teacher will find it educationally unacceptable. If a class is well prepared, this is much less likely to occur. Some useful guidelines for class preparation are:

1. Do not contact the resource person until you are sure that the class is ready for such a visit, both maturationally and cognitively. If students know the material but cannot conduct themselves well, the presentation is likely to be of little value.
2. Discuss with students the resource person's background and why the visit is appropriate for what is being studied.
3. Encourage individual students to explore specific areas of knowledge that the resource person might have viewpoints about. This exploration might come through encyclopedias, newspapers, or personal interviews with friends or parents.
4. Outline generally what the resource person will cover and the time allotted for the visit. Find out if there is anything else students want to know about the topic.

5. Schedule a brief mock presentation, with the teacher playing the part of guest. This "pump priming" may lower student anxieties about questions to ask or comments to make.

Despite extensive preparation of students and the resource person, the presentation may not readily be seen as relating to the unit at hand. It is up to the teacher to act as synthesizer and translator, making the presentation both meaningful and understandable.

FIELD TRIPS

Many of the preparations we have just talked about apply to field trip planning as well, but since a field trip also involves leaving school, it must be even more carefully planned.

A field trip may be appropriate at one of three points in a unit. First, it may serve as a stimulus activity. A trip to a science museum might get students interested in various aspects of inventors and inventions. If the teacher is willing to let some individuals pursue the unit on their own, an initial field trip would be appropriate.

A field trip may also serve as a culminating activity to complete a unit. A trip to a large baking company, for example, would be an appropriate choice for a unit on bread. Unfortunately, the activities seen at the baking company cannot be researched further because the unit has ended—although they could be discussed in a post-trip evaluation (see page 234). A third type of field trip, one that comes *during* the unit, would allow for the possibility of further research.

Before deciding where to go, you may want to seek the advice of other teachers, to find out what field trips they have taken that were exceptionally useful. Even if these places seem inappropriate for the unit at hand, they should not be immediately rejected. After all, a good teacher is able to shape the environment into a more usable, understandable form, and a good site may have great potential for many units.

Field Trip Preparation

The most important key to a good field trip is to visit the site personally beforehand. There is no shortcut for this. "Thoughtful consideration of goals, on-site activity possibilities, outcomes, and potential problems are a necessary part of educationally sound field trips." (Mehaffy et al., 199)

One should time the drive to the site, noting potential traffic bottlenecks that might occur on a weekday afternoon or morning. Once at the site, check the business hours; they may be subject to seasonal or daily changes. Investigate whether any type of tour materials are available or mandatory for visiting the site. If they are optional, find out how long a tour would take using these materials, where they take visitors, and how the information is presented. One should also note attractive side trips that are available. For example, if a small museum is located near a large auto assembly plant, the two places might be combined into one trip.

Dates for the field trip should be submitted well in advance of the trip—as much as six months ahead. This helps school administrators in planning bus use, coordinating when classes are absent, and checking on liability of the site to be visited. Once a trip is approved, the time and date should be posted so that other teachers will not plan a trip on that day, and to note when certain students will be absent.

Liability and safety regulations should be checked thoroughly by the teacher. One should not assume that the school district has everything under control, although this is usually the case. The teacher is responsible for the students' welfare and should not pass that responsibility on to others, although it can be shared.

Permission slips should be sent home well in advance of the trip, to allow for follow-up if students lose them or forget to have them signed. Permission slips should tell the parents precisely where the trip will be, how long the students will be away, and what they need to bring or wear. Do not deviate from this. It is *possible* that the school's liability can be nullified if the teacher decides to take the class somewhere other than where he or she had told parents and administrators.

SETTING OBJECTIVES

Part of the discussion in the previous section on resource personnel applies to field trip preparation, but with additional suggestions covered here. Because the teacher has already visited the site, he or she should conduct a discussion of it prior to the trip. Rules for bus safety and on-site regulations should be presented and, if necessary, spelled out in a handout.

Trip objectives should be drawn up by the teacher and, to some extent, by the students. Background reading will make the trip much more understandable, although the same materials need not be read by every student.

One potential problem might be money. In some districts students may not be required to pay for anything, even field trips. If a small fee is required (one dollar, approximately), this should be collected voluntarily or come out of class funds raised from activities like bake sales or magazine sales. The class should decide early in the year how the money is to be used. The teacher then can act discreetly and avoid embarrassing students whose families don't have much money.

While driving to the site, or upon arrival, the teacher could have students examine a map to familiarize themselves with the area. The teacher could also highlight significant areas to view. If groups are to be formed headed by adult chaperones, the teacher should organize them before leaving the school. Students should not be allowed to wander around on their own, although they may lead the way, accompanied by a chaperon. To be assured of returning to school on time, tell students to be back at the meeting place one-half hour *before* the bus is to leave, as some students are inevitably late.

The teacher should stay in the background during a field trip. Too often I have seen students loaded down with so many worksheets and directions that they "miss" the field trip. They are so concerned with filling out papers and finding the required answers that they neither notice much about the site nor enjoy the trip. If the students are well prepared, they will not need the teacher's guidance, which could, in fact, prevent them from noticing things that the teacher missed or was not interested in. As Bye notes:

> On a field trip we do not educate people, we set the stage or situation so that they will educate themselves. Propaganda of any kind has no place on field trips. Let students observe what is there and draw their own conclusions. Superficial observations or hasty and irrelevant conclusions can be ironed out in discussion periods after the trip. (6)

POST-TRIP EVALUATION

In order for students to digest what they have learned, the teacher should conduct a post-trip evaluation, both formally and informally. The students should write down what they enjoyed most about the trip, or compose a picture or a story related to their experience. In-class discussion might focus on what was exciting or boring about the trip. Students should be encouraged to express *their* thoughts rather than just nodding in agreement with others. The class should also compose a letter of appreciation to those responsible for the trip— the people who led the tour as well as the chaperons.

The teacher should keep a record of all trips taken, with information about the site as well as an evaluation of the site as an educational resource. A copy of that evaluation should be kept in a master file in the school or district office. Teachers should also query parents (through notes, by phone, or in personal conversations) as to what students have said directly or indirectly about the field trips. These might include specific comments pertaining to the site or general opinions (such as "boring," "fun," "not as good as last year," and so on). From all this, a teacher can draw up a relatively accurate evaluation of the trip in terms of learning and simple enjoyment.

URBAN AND RURAL RESOURCES

Although urban and rural areas have many resources in common, there are also many differences. In general, urban resources will be determined by the unit at hand, although some excellent materials focus specifically on this area. One of the most useful (and inexpensive), *The Yellow Pages of Learning Resources,* is concerned with "the potential of the city as a place for learning." In the introduction, R. S. Wurman, the editor, states that

A museum visit allows students to become actively involved with what they have been studying.

the city is education—and the architecture of education rarely has much to do with the building of schools. The city is a schoolhouse. . . . The graffiti of the city are its window displays announcing events; they should reveal its people to themselves, tell about what they're doing and why they're doing it. Everything we do, if described, made clear and made observable—is education: the "Show and Tell," the city itself. (1)

The Yellow Pages of Learning Resources recommends many people and places to visit in a city as well as what can be learned there and how. The goal is to "create in a student the confidence that will enable him to develop the criteria that might be used in the evaluation or creation of his own environments." (1) One rationale given for using this book can be viewed as a rationale for all action learning:

Very often things can best be learned by experiencing them firsthand. Why read about how a port operates when there is one a short bus ride away? Why read a book about how steel is made if there is a steel plant nearby? Does it make sense to study about crime and police protection services without even visiting a real police station? Any place where special things happen or that possesses unique characteristics . . . can be a rich learning resource. (2)

The book suggests 71 specific people and places to visit. Some examples of these are:

airport	hospital	real estate broker
architect	hotel	restaurant
bakery	journalist	road building and repairing
bank	junkyard	social worker
butcher	library	taxicab driver
carpenter	lumberyard	television station
cemetery	museum	theater production
city hall	newspaper plant	union boss
clergy	orchestra member	upholsterer
computer programmer	prison warden	vacant lot
construction site	pharmacist	weather forecaster
courtroom	photographer	x-ray technician
dry cleaner	polling place	zoning board
food distribution center	post office	zoo
gas station	psychologist	
greenhouse	race track	

Many resources—including hospitals, telephone repair, quarries, gas stations, teachers, garbage collectors, and insurance agents—are as much a part of rural life as of urban life. Still, rural communities will have greater access to natural resources than to urban resources. This does not necessarily make one type of community better or more interesting; it only indicates one of the many differences between urban and rural lifestyles. McCain and Nelson's *Community Resources for Rural Social Studies Teachers* provides some excellent ideas for the social science disciplines as well as law-related education. Although the book provides ideas for resource location, the authors note that the real work begins for teacher and students after the appropriate resource has been located. One suggestion, for example, involves a visit to the county extension office to observe the testing of soil types.

Soil types and climate are environmental factors which exert a significant influence upon any community. Each state has county extension agents who usually work in cooperation with the land grant university . . . to provide agricultural leadership within the state. The county agent is a source of expert advice about the most efficient use of land for agricultural production in local soil types and climate. He or she can demonstrate how soils are tested to determine which are suitable for crops appropriate to the climate conditions of a particular locality. . . .

Identification of soil type is an important factor in land use planning and is becoming increasingly critical as much of our nation's prime agricultural land is being taken for residential purposes. Soil type is also an important factor in problems of water pollution. Without proper sanitation systems, the possibility of sewage seeping into surface and underground water sources is often directly related to the types of soils involved.

The county agent can provide information about the climate history of the community in terms of precipitation and temperature. (8–9)

Regarding rural law-related resources, McCain and Nelson suggest a number of possibilities. For example:

Occupational health hazards in industry are the prime concern of the Occupational Safety and Health Administration (OSHA). That agency's representative can focus on laws affecting workers in various rural areas. Brown lung, black lung, and cancer are some of the health hazards from which OSHA strives to protect workers. OSHA also inspects places of work for potential safety hazards.

The majority of migrant workers in American find seasonal employment in rural areas, most of them in agricultural jobs. Recently, migrant workers have been offered increased protection under the law. Legal services or community service agencies that represent migrant workers can provide individuals to discuss the legal problems of migrants in education, housing and discrimination. (20)

These excerpts give the flavor of rural community resources, just as the selection from *The Yellow Pages of Learning Resources* captures the urban flavor. Examples like these should stimulate the teacher to focus on the uniqueness of his or her own setting.

DRAWBACKS TO ACTION LEARNING

The drawbacks to action or community learning should be noted, although they are generally offset by the benefits. The most significant drawback is time: the time of students, administrators, secretaries, parents, resource people, and others. A teacher must also invest additional time to make action learning successful. "Teachers need time to prepare for an action-learning experience, as their training has likely ignored action-learning approaches." (Mehaffy et al., 195) Second, action learning costs money. Transportation, insurance, meals, and incidental expenses require funds that could be used in other ways.

Finally, there are risks involved when children travel away from school, with parents wondering if there is adequate supervision and protection. Parents and other may become critical of the type of community work students are engaged in, especially if that work is of a political nature. "Student participation in political campaigns may lead to criticism of school participation in partisan politics." (Mehaffy et al., 195) Parents may also become concerned about safety if students are to visit a site in a rough neighborhood. Some parents might even object, on personal or religious grounds, if students were to visit a hospital or a medical clinic.

WHAT DOES ONE STUDY IN THE COMMUNITY?

Almost any approach to community study will be governed by the age of the students. A second grader's view of the community is obviously limited. Children in the upper grades, however, can readily examine the issues their community faces or the historical development of the community. In either case, it is up to the teacher to encourage students to see the community they live in as something more than, say, a town that surrounds the local college campus.

To begin, a teacher might assign each student two street names—one on campus, one off—and require them to determine after whom or what the streets were named. This simple exercise encourages students to study old newspapers, oral history, local library archives, and campus archives—making the community a living, dynamic place.

HISTORY

Suppose one wished to study the history of a community. Where would one begin? The local historical society could provide data on the community's founding and first settlers; family histories could supplement that. Old newspapers and the other sources just mentioned could be used by younger students as well.

Metcalf and Downey suggest many possibilities for using local history in community study. These include family study and economic, social, and political history. Other ideas include walking tours of a neighborhood and the recording of cemetery data (see page 239). Another useful book in this vein is *Who Put the Cannon in the Courthouse Square?* The box on page 240 shows one section of Manhattan and highlights a walk through American labor history. Students could create similar maps of their own communities' histories.

A town or village serves as a good unit for intermediate or upper-level students, starting with the layout of the town. Most northeastern towns—especially their older, downtown areas—are laid out in a grid pattern. One notable exception is Washington, DC, which has a rotary, or circle, pattern. Chicago and Cleveland have diagonal streets designed—before expressways—for swifter urban travel. Still other cities and towns have used a grid pattern in the most inappropriate ways. San Francisco, for example, should have streets built into the sides of the hills, to allow for less strain on people, animals, and machines. But the city's founders wanted to emulate the east—making San Francisco's streets among the steepest grades in the world.

A community's style of architecture also reveals a lot about its history, ethnic groups, and natural resources (see LeClerc for good ideas about

A VISIT TO THE CEMETERY

A cemetery can be a fascinating place to visit, although the initial student reaction may be fear or distaste. Usually such feelings are superficial, but if there has been a recent death in the family these feelings may be very real, and a teacher should probably defer a trip until a later date or spend some time talking with students about coping with their feelings about death.

Cemeteries can offer glimpses into the history, geography, economics, and sociology of a community from its founding until the present day. The cemetery in Virginia City, Nevada, for example, is the resting place of people from all over the world who arrived seeking their fortunes; the headstones and the different materials they are made of reflect the success or failure of the silver mines the community depended on. In Boston, the names on the Old Granary Burying Yard's headstones transport visitors back in time to the Revolutionary War, as many early patriots are buried there.

Exploration of a rural Pennsylvania cemetery may reveal that nearly half the occupants have the same last name. Trac-

ing generations through the headstone dates of birth and death is interesting detective work for student and teacher alike. Deducing the ethnic origins of a community's members may shed light on the town's history and suggest which languages may have been spoken there—indicating waves of immigration and the like.

During their visit students might take rubbings of old headstones, much as brass rubbings are done in various churches in England, or might examine dates of death to see if there was some calamity (a war or epidemic, for example) that took the lives of many people in a brief period of time. Students might even find the graves of distant relatives, which could arouse an interest in their family history and lead to interviews with other relatives or a study of courthouse records and local newspaper archives. Styles of headstones are also interesting to note—including the use of Latin inscriptions, phrasing, depictions of angels or other carvings, and so on.

A visit to a cemetery is an interesting walk through the past, for the gravestones provide a record of events that, unlike the paper of files and registries, lasts.

architecture). For example, Chicago's homes are predominantly red brick because the materials are available locally. San Francisco, for all its eastern influences, has few brick buildings because of the lack of those same materials; its homes tend to be made of wood or, more recently, stucco, because of nearby resources and Spanish influence. Occasionally one can be misled by architecture. The German settlers of the Amana colonies in Iowa imported stone from Europe to build many homes—not knowing this could lead one to make specious assumptions about the resources available in that community.

The architecture of a city can reveal when it was built, too. San Francisco's wooden homes are mostly late Victorian in style because they were

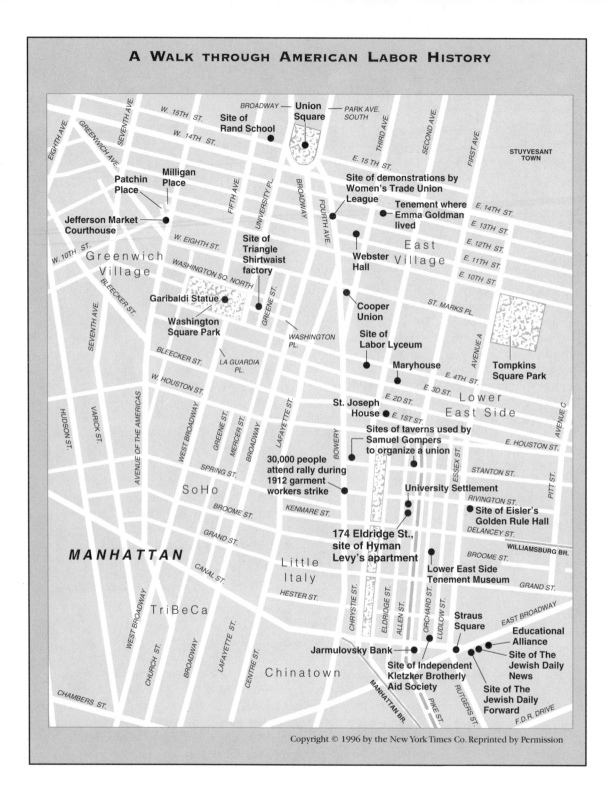

A WALK THROUGH AMERICAN LABOR HISTORY

BROADWAY — **Union Square**

W. 15TH ST.

PARK AVE. SOUTH

Site of Rand School

W. 14TH ST.

STUYVESANT TOWN

E. 15TH ST.

Patchin Place

Milligan Place

Site of demonstrations by Women's Trade Union League

Tenement where Emma Goldman lived

E. 14TH ST.

E. 13TH ST.

Jefferson Market Courthouse

W. EIGHTH ST.

E. 12TH ST.

E. 11TH ST.

E. 10TH ST.

East Village

W. 10TH ST.

Greenwich Village

Site of Triangle Shirtwaist factory

Webster Hall

WASHINGTON SQ. NORTH

Garibaldi Statue

ST. MARKS PL.

Cooper Union

Washington Square Park

WASHINGTON PL.

Site of Labor Lyceum

Maryhouse

Tompkins Square Park

BLEECKER ST.

LA GUARDIA PL.

E. 4TH ST.

Lower East Side

W. HOUSTON ST.

E. 3D ST.

E. 2D ST.

St. Joseph House

E. 1ST ST.

E. HOUSTON ST.

Sites of taverns used by Samuel Gompers to organize a union

SoHo

SPRING ST.

STANTON ST.

30,000 people attend rally during 1912 garment workers strike

KENMARE ST.

University Settlement

RIVINGTON ST.

Site of Eisler's Golden Rule Hall

BROOME ST.

DELANCEY ST.

WILLIAMSBURG BR.

GRAND ST.

174 Eldridge St., site of Hyman Levy's apartment

BROOME ST.

MANHATTAN

CANAL ST.

Little Italy

Lower East Side Tenement Museum

GRAND ST.

HESTER ST.

EAST BROADWAY

Straus Square

TriBeCa

Educational Alliance

CHAMBERS ST.

Jarmulovsky Bank

Chinatown

Site of Independent Kletzker Brotherly Aid Society

Site of The Jewish Daily News

Site of The Jewish Daily Forward

F.D.R. DRIVE

A community's architecture says a great deal about its history. Shown here are Victorian houses in San Francisco.

built between 1906 and 1926. The 1906 earthquake and fire also help date homes there, as much of the city had to be rebuilt. Chicago's famous Prairie School of architecture flourished in the late 1800s and early 1900s, and the homes from that period are easily identifiable. The great Chicago fire of 1871 acts as a temporal "base"; homes built before then are less likely to have survived. Investigating how the community is designed gives clues to the people who originally settled there. Some architecture may show distinct ethnic influences and give clues to the former (and possibly present) ethnic composition of various neighborhoods. Public buildings can be studied to determine schools of architectural style or the work of individual architects like Frank Lloyd Wright, Louis Sullivan, Ludwig Mies van der Rohe, Philip Johnson, Eeno Saarinen, and I. M. Pei.

WATER RESOURCES

Water resources are another potential area of study. Where does a town get its water, and how does the water get to the residents? Some towns have a convenient lake; some utilize underground streams; some, like Los Angeles, pump water hundreds of miles from mountain ranges. A trip to the local water filtration plant can be edifying and useful. Students can hear and see how their water is purified, fluoridated, and treated as waste. What effect does rainfall have on the water supply? What is a water table? An aquifer? What constraints are there on the water supply? Have any use restrictions been imposed in recent years? Has there been any ground-water pollution in the region? All these are questions to be pursued and answered.

FOOD TRANSPORT

How does the community get its food? Many urban children have no idea of how food appears in grocery stores. For someone who has never seen vegetables grow, this kind of logic is not unusual. The transportation of food to community stores via rail, truck, or ship illustrates the interdependence necessary to survive in the style to which we have grown accustomed. Students might survey stores to find out how many tons of food are sold in a day or week, or could keep track of the amount of food consumed in their own families per day or week. This could be compared with data on world food consumption. They might visit a nearby public market or farmer's market and weigh the advantages of fresher produce at lower costs, recognizing that such a market can exist only in good weather and when the sale of all food is virtually assured.

HEALTH CARE

The health of a community is often related to the number of doctors per capita, the number of specialists among those doctors, the number of dentists, specialized nurses, hospitals, clinics, and other health care facilities available. Does a community practice preventive dentistry and medicine, or is it mostly reactive? Many rural communities are having difficulties attracting and retaining physicians. What have these communities done to address the problem? Are new parents able to learn about baby care and parenting? Are there facilities to deal with mental as well as physical illness? Have local or state health ordinances prevented serious outbreaks of disease? Are people in the local community healthier than those in neighboring areas or in towns across the country? Students could answer some of these questions by visiting the director of the county health department or some other local health care official. A Health Maintenance Organization staff, for instance, should be able to answer questions such as these.

EDUCATION

We all have a vested interest in a good education. Students should attempt to assess the quality of education in their community by surveying the number of schools, the number of teachers, and determining the student-teacher ratio. The local district office as well as the local teachers' union should have these data. The latter should also have comparative data on student-teacher ratios in other districts.

How old are the school facilities, and how good is the education in the community? This latter point is very subjective, but students could survey parents, store owners, and other townspeople for their opinions. What is the tax rate? Should it be higher or lower? Obviously most people want lower taxes, but wouldn't they rather have continually improving schools? As the teacher population becomes older and more stable, it may require tax increases merely to maintain the status quo. This is because a veteran teacher population will be more highly paid than a less experienced one. To meet normal salary increases, taxes may have to be increased.

Do the schools in the community prepare students for their future social and career roles, or do students learn mostly about the past? To what extent do citizens and parents have the opportunity to give their input about the school system? What type of people make up the school board? Students could sit in on at least part of a school board meeting to try to determine how the schools operate.

INDUSTRY

What type of work is done in the community? Is it heavily dependent on one plant or industry? Was the town built where it is for economic reasons, such as supply of a natural resource, location of a transportation medium, or accessibility of a power source? Cities like Pittsburgh, Chicago, and Fall River, Massachusetts, were all founded for economic reasons and grew with the economy. Unfortunately, a heavy reliance on one or two industries can create economic casualties during depressions or recessions.

Do people work within their community, or do they live in a bedroom community, which releases commuters in the early morning and reclaims them in the evening? Some suburban areas exist solely in this manner, with almost no industries within the community.

TRANSPORTATION

Transportation is important for the distribution not only of food but of heavier materials and of people. Does the community have a local airport? If not, how far away is it? What about rail service and bus lines? Is the community near navigable waters, and are they used? How good are the roads, both in quality and in variety of destinations? Is the terrain such that travel becomes difficult at certain times of the year?

COMMUNICATION SYSTEMS

A community must have contact with the rest of the country, if not the world. Students should determine if there is a daily local newspaper. If not, does a large regional newspaper provide local coverage of the community? How expansive is the coverage? Does one get a good idea of what is going on in the community by reading the newspaper? Are there local radio stations? How do they fulfill their commitment to public service and access? Is there a local television station, and, if so, does it provide locally produced shows or segments? How good is the telephone system? There are hundreds of small phone companies nationally, some with just a few hundred subscribers. In some cases, the phone service is more personalized and effective with small companies; in others, it is abysmal.

ENTERTAINMENT

A community is more than a place to work; it is also a place to play. How much entertainment is available in the community? Students could compare the number of movie theaters to the number in other communities, or determine if there are local theater, symphony, or opera associations and sports teams. If professional sports, opera, or theater is not available, how far must one travel to see them? Students could survey some community members regarding their musical preferences. Are the generations markedly different in their tastes? What magazines or books do people in the community read? How many libraries are there, and what can librarians reveal about the community's reading preferences?

For those who wish to participate in sports for recreational purposes, what facilities are available? Does it matter if the person is young or old? Is there a local Y, youth center, or senior citizens' center where people can participate in activities? Students might like to determine how much opportunity there is for joiners in the community. They could find out if organizations like the Elks, the Moose, the Rotary, the Kiwanis, the Sierra Club, the Chamber of Commerce, the Veterans of Foreign War, the Daughters of the American Revolution, the American Association of University Women, the NAACP, church groups, the League of Women Voters, political parties, unions, or cooperatives exist in their community. These organizations could all be visited by teams of students to see what each actually intends to do and ultimately carries out. Is there land in the community set aside as green space for relaxing and enjoying nature? Or, if the community is more rural, does the region have good places to hike, fish, hunt, climb, or camp?

LOCAL GOVERNMENT

Visits to local government offices are always interesting. Before doing this, students need to examine how the community is governed and how the work of different officials overlaps by design. Are there open town meetings on a regular basis? How does the community raise money to run the town? How does this compare with what other communities do? A trip to the courthouse, the city hall, the tax office, or the city registrar can be interesting, especially if students have had previous exposure to local government and have good questions to ask.

Attending a school board meeting will give students an idea of who is in charge of the local schools and how they seem to operate. Students might take

Tombstone rubbings allow students to read a headstone more easily and may provide a direction for further inquiry.

a position on an issue of importance to them and present it to the school board for consideration or comment. Individual students or a small group might visit an office or a judge's chambers to find out more about people in various positions or about the company's (or government's) history. This could then be reported to the larger class.

CEMETERIES

Another excellent, although unusual, community resource is the local cemetery. The history of the community, its ethnic composition, economic status, medical health, and population growth can all be assayed by studying headstones (see page 239). These visits never fail to provide fascinating insights and anecdotes regarding American community life.

QUESTIONS AND ACTIVITIES

1. Community study is mostly found at the first- or second-grade level. How could it be incorporated at the third- and sixth-grade levels of an expanding-horizons model of curriculum?

2. Imagine that a local architect is coming to your class to answer questions and talk about the community's design. What five areas would you want to help your students discuss with the architect? How would you prepare them for the visit? What advice or direction might you give the architect?

3. Make a list of at least five places that a class could visit on a local field trip, and then combine your list with those of three other class members. A larger class sharing and discussion of ideas might also ensue.

4. What was the best field trip that you ever took as an elementary school student? What was it that made the trip so memorable?

5. How much do you know about the community in which you grew up or the one of which your college is a part? Investigate the historical background of one of these communities. When was it first settled, and how did it come to be located where it is?

6. Investigate the history behind the names of some of the streets in your community (excluding obvious ones like Main, Elm, or Maple).

7. Examine your community for answers to some of the questions raised in the "What Does One Study in the Community?" section of this chapter.

8. What are the best things about living in your community? What should the community change to become a better place to live and how can elementary-aged children be a part of that change?

REFERENCES

Bye, E. C. "How to Conduct a Field Trip." NCSS How-to-Do-It Series, ser. 1, no. 12. Washington, DC: National Council for the Social Studies, 1967.

Chapin, J., and R. Messick, *Elementary Social Studies: A Practical Guide.* 2nd ed. New York: Longman, 1992.

Collings, M. R. "How to Utilize Community Resources," NCSS How-to-Do-It Series, ser. 1, no. 13. Washington, DC: National Council for the Social Studies, 1967.

Cooper, K. *Who Put the Cannon in the Courthouse Square?* New York: Walker and Company, 1985.

Hanna, P. *Youth Serves the Community.* New York: Appleton-Century, 1936.

LeClerc, D. C. "Architecture as a Primary Source for Social Studies." NCSS How-to-Do-It Series, ser. 2, no. 5. Washington, DC: National Council for the Social Studies, 1978.

McCain, A. E., and M. Nelson. *Community Resources for Rural Social Studies Teachers.* Las Cruces, NM: ERIC/CRESS, January, 1981.

Mehaffy, G., V. Atwood, and M. Nelson. "Action Learning in Social Studies." In *The Social Studies,* 80th Yearbook of the National Society for the Study of Education, Part II. Chicago: University of Chicago Press, 1981, p. 190–202.

Metcalf, F. D., and M. T. Downey. *Using Local History in the Classroom.* Nashville, TN: American Association for State and Local History, 1982.

Wurman, R. S., ed. *The Yellow Pages of Learning Resources.* Boston: MIT Press, 1972.

Chapter Ten

COMPUTERS, SIMULATIONS, GAMES, AND THE MEDIA

The majority of readers of this book will spend most of their teaching careers in the twenty-first century, which will be markedly different from this one. Historians will point to the fact that the twentieth century marked the end of the industrial revolution and the beginning of the information revolution.

The machine that heralded the beginning of the information revolution is the computer. Since its invention in 1946, the computer has dominated the growth patterns of industrialized societies in the latter half of the twentieth century. The first computers occupied several hundred square feet and were built around vacuum tubes that constantly burned out. Over the years computers have become many times smaller and more efficient. They now use an infinitesimal amount of energy and literally never wear out.

Computer workers, environmentalists, and others have become increasingly concerned about the health hazards of computers caused by long-term exposure to video display terminals (VDTs) and by the creation and disposal of silicon chips. These latter processes cause dangerous chemicals to be released into the air and the water.

It is too early to tell what the overall effects of the computer revolution will be on our society. The computer cannot replace human mental energy the way the machines of the industrial revolution replaced human physical energy. However, the computer has the potential to *extend* our mental energy in ways we never thought possible.

Because computer technology is developing so rapidly and because computers behave in ways that appear mysterious to some people, it has become natural to glorify or to fear these machines. However, as the computer becomes more and more common, people are beginning to realize that it is nothing more than a sophisticated tool that can be used to improve the quality of life.

Because the computer is above all an information-processing machine, it makes an effective tool for instruction and has become common in education. Most schools in the United States have at least several computers. In addition, the growing popularity of home computers has brought both students and teachers into greater contact with the computer's many uses. Through the Internet the computer can now bring various forms of media directly to consumers on their personal computers. Even more advanced technology allows for the internet to be accessed through one's television.

The media is rarely a subject of study in elementary schools, which is both surprising and disturbing when one considers the amount of exposure that children have to media outlets like newspapers, radio, television, and Internet links every day. An examination of the media should be undertaken with the intention of making students critical consumers and viewers. Critiques of the news and of advertisements, music, and television programs are all potential areas of study. Although students have enormous media contact from an early age, few are exposed to such critical media study until early adulthood. Students can and should study the media rather than just be absorbed by them.

The purpose of this chapter is to examine the effect of the computer and simulation games on the social studies curriculum and to provide a better understanding of the media and current affairs.

COMPUTERS AND SOCIETY

One of the purposes of social studies is to examine the current social scheme. Another purpose is to prepare students for their introduction into society. Thus it is entirely appropriate for teachers and students to examine the impact of the computer and the effects of the information revolution on society.

For instance, there are moral dilemmas that come with the use of such a powerful tool. Who has access to computers? They are relatively expensive—does this make the rich more powerful? Another moral dilemma concerns the right to privacy. As more and more information is fed into computers, the proportions of the revolution and the resulting changes in our society and economy can be seen. These questions and others are all relevant to the social studies curriculum.

How has industrialization changed the simple notion of instruction in this country over the years? For many centuries, the family was the social institution that carried out the education of the young. The industrial revolution gave people more free time and the ability to pursue a formal education. During the latter part of the twentieth century, schools have been supplanted as a source of information by an electronic source—television. Most of today's students will have spent more time in front of a television than in front of a teacher by the time they are 15 years old. Eventually, however, the computer is likely to supplant both school and television as the main information source.

The most common use of the computer today in social studies education is computer-assisted instruction, the use of the computer to store information and present it to the student in the form of lessons. Some 2,000 firms in the United States produce computer-assisted lessons, many of which are devoted to social studies. The vast majority of these lessons operate on a very simple level. A few others make use of the computer's simulation abilities, which are discussed later in this chapter.

Computer-based instruction involves tutorial instruction and self-contained learning packages. These may include pre- and post-tests, higher-order thinking practice, and opportunities for "looping," or directing learners back to a similar area of learning until the area is mastered.

The use of the computer as a support resource will probably have the greatest effect on the teaching of social studies as students gain access to data bases. Students will be able to contact various data bases by telephone and obtain information that they need for their own social and individual decisions.

Until now, social studies teachers have trained students how to *answer* questions. As data bases become more available and sophisticated, however, students will have to learn how to *ask* questions. They must learn how to search through masses of data and how to bring all this information together in creative ways to help them solve particular problems. Today the development of data bases is expensive. However, the cost of such technology will probably decrease in the future. Many encyclopedias and library resources are already on line or on video disks as well as in books.

It is, however, in the higher-level strategy of problem analysis and decision making that computer-assisted instruction really comes into its own. The techniques of simulation and game playing have been applied in social studies instruction for some years and have allowed fuller utilization of the computer's potential. A student may be presented with a simulated situation in which the computer provides the necessary generalizations and situations. The student must analyze this information and come to a decision. This decision can then be "played out" by the computer so that the student can determine whether the decision is viable. Thus, during simulation the computer allows the student to go through the decision-making process and to test the results of a decision in a simulated situation rather than a real one.

When something as new and revolutionary as the computer comes into the classroom, it presents educators with many new questions. Some of these questions revolve around the machines themselves. Others concern the type of material put into the computer. When considering lessons that might be appropriate for the computer, we might look at the social studies textbook as a model. More and more major textbook publishers are providing interactive software—computer programs that can be used along with their textbooks. Many other computer lessons are being written by new software firms that have sprung up specifically for that purpose.

In the early 1990s many children became much more capable of dealing with various kinds of computer simulations. This was directly due to the advanced technological development of video games, both in commercial video arcades and for home use. Sega and Nintendo have produced intricate and exciting software simulations of various sports as well as variations on themes of war, combat, and violence. In many cases, the more simulated gore, the more popular the simulation. Most of the time, however, game popularity is directly linked to the challenge of winning or of advancing to higher and higher levels of achievement.

It is this level of computer software sophistication that educators must compete with in order to capture student interest. It is clear that educational simulations will not be able to have as many "bells and whistles" as commercial products, so a piece of educational software must compete on a different plane. In order to have appeal to students, the game must be user friendly so that students less facile with microcomputers can participate easily. The simulation should be challenging, drawing on student knowledge and skills, but also informational, with a strong emphasis on decision making or problem solving. The software should also be colorful, include sound effects, if possible, and be playable within an hour. This latter requirement is because of limitations on software or hardware use. If that is not a problem, a good piece of software might take a few hours of intermittent use to work through.

In the 1990s there was an explosion of materials that were more and more elaborate and that many children found greatly interesting. Tom Snyder, a former social studies teacher, formed Tom Snyder Productions in the 1980s and has produced outstanding software for school use, some of which is described in the references at the end of the chapter. Microsoft, the behemoth of the microcomputer industry, has weighed in with its school software, and the list continues to grow. The software is available on CD-ROM (computer disk read-only memory) disks that can not be altered interactively, and some educators are predicting the decline of CD-ROMs as more schools and homes get on-line, that is, linked to the Internet and the wealth of resources available via that avenue. This view, however, is not yet prevalent.

Many publishers are also providing CD-ROMs that have Internet access capability to expand their breadth. Ayre notes that "reports on the death of the

CD-ROM . . . or the brave new world of on-line access should all be treated with caution." (Ayre, 132) He also notes that new high-density digital video/versatile disk (DVD) technology is becoming available that "can deliver increased data capacity and outstanding audio and video quality which on-line services will have difficulty matching. . . ." (128)

CD-ROM capability continues to grow in depth and presentation. The 1995 award winner "Destination Vietnam," for example, introduces three-dimensional formats in both pictoral presentation and accessibility to disk "avenues." The color photos and sound are also highly superior to most previous CD-ROM offerings.

Also more available and increasingly more sophisticated in their content are on-site data bases. As Budin, Kendall, and Lengel note, "There is a great deal of interest in using data bases in the Social Studies, and much of the current work in software development is being done in this area." (41) Data on politics, geography, and history with various cultural or economic emphases can now be accessed on one or two disks. Off-site data bases are also of great use; a useful organization schema is seen in Table 10.1. (Use Table 10.2 as the key to Table 10.1.)

THE INTERNET

The future, it seems, lies on the Internet. Every day more businesses, organizations, and individuals make their own web pages available. The growth and change on the Internet has been, and continues to be, dramatic. The Internet is an enormous electronic "highway" that makes incredible volumes of data available swiftly and without the cost of paper. Many publications now make their product available on-line, and there are magazines that are solely published in virtual form, that is, in cyberspace.

This may be very intimidating for teachers and students. In fact, I have found many teachers who are highly technophobic. It is a common fear. The combination of fear of the unknown, fear of change, and loss of control makes some teachers go out of their way to avoid using the Internet. This is not a wise course of action. Many states have already provided the resources to link all school districts of the state to the Internet. This is a trend that should reach all states within five years of the millenium. New teachers should do their utmost to become familiar with the Internet and its riches since this familiarity can only be helpful in both finding a teaching position and working in the schools.

The Internet was originally created so that researchers and the U.S. military could share information worldwide. Since 1990 the Internet has grown in use exponentially, and by 2000 a new more powerful system "known as the National Research and Education Network (NREN)" may be in place. (Martorella, 338)

Access to the Internet is most commonly made through the Worldwide Web (www) using popular interfaces like Netscape and Mosaic. Once a user is linked to such an interface, one can "browse and navigate among documents by clicking on a highlighted piece of text that contains hyperlinks to a related

TABLE 10.1
Social Studies Databases

AMERICAN HISTORY

Academic American Encyclopedia
    On-line Availability: 4, 8, 15, 17, 41, 46, 55
Almanac of American Politics
    On-line Availability: 34
America: History and Life
    On-line Availability: 9, 30
American Statistics Index
    On-line Availability: 30
The Boomer Report
    On-line Availability: 33, 34
Historical Abstracts
    On-line Availability: 9, 30
Living History Forum
    On-line Availability: 6
Social SciSearch
    On-line Availability: 16, 29, 30

WORLD STUDIES

AP DataStream
    On-line Availability: 6, 13, 22, 30, 33, 50
Newsearch
    On-line Availability: 9, 30
U.N. Demographics
    On-line Availability: 22
UPI News
    On-line Availability: 2, 9, 30

GOVERNMENT AND LAW

Census Information Service
    On-line Availability: 3
Congressional District and State Profile Report
    On-line Availability: 34
Congressional Records Abstracts
    On-line Availability: 11
Criminal Justice Periodical Index
    On-line Availability: 30
LEXIS
    On-line Availability: 32
Legal Resource Index
    On-line Availability: 4, 9, 29, 32, 52
PAIS International
    On-line Availability: 9, 19, 28, 29, 30, 36, 37, 40, 44
Various News Services
    On-line Availability: 6, 30

SOCIOLOGY, PSYCHOLOGY

American Statistics Index
    On-line Availability: 30

Applied Social Sciences Index & Abstracts
    On-line Availability: 29
Current Contents Search
    On-line Availability: 16, 29, 30, 40
PsychINFO
    On-line Availability: 9, 10, 16, 24, 29, 30, 35, 36, 37, 40
Social Sciences Abstracts
    On-line Availability: 30, 38, 45, 49, 53, 54
Sociofile
    On-line Availability: 40
Sociological Abstracts
    On-line Availability: 9, 16, 29, 30, 35, 36, 37, 40
WESTLAW Social Sciences and Humanities Library
    On-line Availability: 52

ECONOMICS

ABI/INFORM
    On-line Availability: 1, 4, 5, 9, 20, 21, 23, 25, 27, 29, 30, 34, 36, 37, 39, 40, 47
Canadian Press Information Network
    On-line Availability: 26, 27, 43
County Personal Income, Population, and Employment
    On-line Availability: 51
Datastream Economic Series
    On-line Availability: 14
Dow Jones News
    On-line Availability: 18, 20, 21
EconLit
    On-line Availability: 9, 30, 35, 36, 37
U.S. Economic Statistics
    On-line Availability: 22

CURRENT EVENTS

AP On-line
    On-line Availability: 3, 6, 41
Ethnic NewsWatch
    On-line Availability: 17, 32, 34, 42
Information Please Almanac
    On-line Availability: 6
New York Times Abstracts
    On-line Availability: 12, 29, 31
Newsearch
    On-line Availability: 9, 30
NEXIS Various News Libraries
    On-line Availability: 33
U.S. News & World Report
    On-line Availability: 12
UPI News
    On-line Availability: 2, 9, 30, 33

TABLE 10.2
On-line Availability (Key for Table 10.1)

1. Ameritech Library Services, Vista
2. AT&T EasyLink Services
3. BT North America, Inc.
4. CARL Corporation
5. CitaDel Service
6. Compuserve Information Service
7. Compuserve Information Service (AP Online, AP Online Weather, AP Sports Wire)
8. Compuserve Information Service (ENCYCLOPEDIA)
9. Compuserve Information Service, Knowledge Index
10. Compuserve, Inc. (IQUEST)
11. Congressional Quarterly, Inc.
12. DataTimes Corporation
13. DataTimes Corporation (AP)
14. Datastream International Ltd.
15. Delphi Internet Services Corporation (GROLIER)
16. DIMDI (Deutsches Institut fur Medizinische Dokumentation und Information)
17. Dow Jones & Company, Inc
18. Dow Jones & Company, Inc. (DJNEWS, WIRES)
19. EBSCO Publishing
20. European Space Agency (ESA), Information Retrieval Service (IRS) (DOW JONES NEWS DATABASE)
21. FT PROFILE
22. GE Information Services
23. Gesellschaft fur Betriebswirtschaftliche Information mbH
24. HealthGate Data Corporation
25. HRIN Corporation
26. Infomart Assistant
27. Infomart Online
28. Information Access Company
29. Knight-Ridder Information Ltd., DataStar
30. Knight-Ridder Information, Inc., DIALOG
31. KR Information OnDisc
32. LEXIS
33. NewsNet, Inc.
34. NEXIS
35. NlightN
36. OCLC EPIC
37. OCLC FirstSearch Catalog
38. OCLC Online Computer Library Center, Inc.
39. ORBIT QUESTEL
40. Ovid Technologies, Ovid Online
41. PRODIGY
42. Profound Inc.
43. QL Systems Limited
44. Research Libraries Information Network
45. SilverPlatter Information, Inc.
46. StarText
47. STN International
48. The Canadian Press
49. UMI
50. Videotel, Inc.
51. WEFA Group
52. WESTLAW
53. WILSONLINE
54. Wilson Company
55. Youvelle Renaissance Group, GEnie

document." (Martorella, 342) One can search by topic or www address by using powerful search engines such as Yahoo! or Alta Vista. With millions of pieces of data on the Web it is far easier to find a specific document if one knows the www address, but sometimes serendipitous searches can be more fun and, ultimately, may yield the same result. The Web, however, can be almost addictive; it accesses a vast storehouse of knowledge like a library and one can "surf" for hours, losing all track of time.

The Web has made available to students materials that could not have been made accessible previously. The Library of Congress, for example, has digitized and made available thousands of documents with a goal of five million items by the year 2000. "Already accessible are materials documenting 100 years of black history in America, including fliers seeking the return of runaway slaves and 351 pamphlets by writers such as Frederick Douglass and Booker T. Washington; Civil War photographs taken by Matthew Brady; 99 early motion pictures; 167 items documenting women's suffrage; and photographs by Carl Van Vechten of celebrities prominent in the 1920s and 30s as well as photos from the Depression and World War II." (Smith, 8)

The Web is truly an international experience, both in sites that can be accessed and in users. In 1994 there was an 81 percent increase worldwide in computer systems providing access to the Internet. Argentina had an 8,167 percent increase and Ukraine a 994 percent increase which, though astounding, also indicates how few connections there were prior to 1994 in those countries. The United States, with only a 38 percent increase, is still the biggest presence on the Web, accounting for 63 percent of all host computers (Time OnLine).

So what does all this mean to elementary schools and teachers? First, it indicates the growth of the Internet, and second, it illustrates the international aspects of Internet growth. For a teacher or class with Internet access the number of Web sites are nearly unlimited. The key is knowing how to find and use such sites. There is no table of contents on the Internet and with over 3.5 million documents (as of 1996) available, searching can be time consuming and frustrating. In addition, sites move frequently and an address may be outdated within months.

Many Internet guides are appearing in stores, on-line, and in journals. A few useful ones are listed at the end of the chapter, though again, it should be noted that by the time this book is in print these volumes are likely to be outdated. What may be easier and more up to date are on-line directories of resources.

Though they may have already changed addresses, here are a few interesting Web sites that a teacher might find useful.

http://www.csulb.edu/gc/libarts/am-indian/
American Historical Images On File

Native Americans in photos, drawings, and pictures organized by time period, region, and activity.

http://www.utexas.edu/world/lecture/
University of Texas-Austin World Lecture Hall

Too complex for most kids but a wealth of instructional uses of the Web for teachers from accounting to zoology.

http://www.ushmm.org/education/ed.html
United State Holocaust Memorial Museum

Photos and documents from the Museum. Powerful and thought provoking, but unsettling for unprepared youngsters.

http://www.nj.com/yucky/
Cockroach World

Prides itself as the "yuckiest site on the Internet," but has lots of information, quizzes, multimedia shows and a mascot, Rodney Roach, who guides users through the site.

http://www.sandiegozoo.org/
Zoological Society of San Diego

This great site offers a virtual tour of the zoo and the Wild Animal Park. Games, photos of baby animals, and exhibits are included.

http://www.randomhouse.com/seussville/
Welcome to Seussville

Dr. Seuss stories, information on the late Theodore Geisel (Dr. Seuss), and items for sale. All ages (including teachers) will enjoy these familiar characters.

http://www.osprey.unisa.ac.za/o/docs/southafrica.html
South Africa Tour

Includes a travel map, links to facts and figures, cultural documents, and more.

http://.rs6.loc.gov/cwphome.html
Civil War Photograph Collection

Maintained by the Library of Congress, this site contains more than 1,000 images of military personnel, preparations for and the aftereffects of battle, and portraits of enlisted men.

http://www.accuweather.com/web/welcome.htm
AccuWeather

The largest private weather company in the world offers great graphics, tours of the atmosphere, and weather information.

http://www.mapquest.com/
(also tripquest.com/) MapQuest and TripQuest

Provides maps for anywhere in the world and helps with planning trips to these various spots with road maps of countries, regions, and cities right down to large street maps, though it takes a while to get to the smallest inset maps.

COMPUTER USE

When something as new and revolutionary as the computer comes into the classroom, it presents educators with many new questions. Some of these questions revolve around the machines themselves. Others concern the type of material put into the computer. When considering lessons that might be appropriate for the computer, we might look at the social studies textbook as a model. More and more major textbook publishers provide interactive software—computer programs that can be used along with their textbooks. Many other computer lessons are being written by new software firms that have sprung up specifically for that purpose.

There are very few really good examples of interactive software. One of the better computer games is called "Lemonade Stand," which was developed

The computer often brings students together to work and learn cooperatively.

by the Minnesota Educational Computer Consortium (MECC) for Apple II and Apple II-compatible computers. In "Lemonade Stand," students simulate the simple entrepreneurship of owning a lemonade stand set up on the sidewalk. The object is to maximize profits. They must weigh the factors of costs, potential foot traffic, and weather in determining how much lemonade to produce and what to charge for it. With a good teacher follow-up, "Lemonade Stand" can provide an experiential, analytical understanding of basic economic concepts.

Other excellent simulations include "Oregon Trail" (MECC), which recreates the overland trip west from Missouri to the Oregon Territory in 1847, "Geography Search" (McGraw Hill), which creates the New World explorations of the late 1400s and early 1500s, and the various Carmen Sandiego adventures (see box). The 1990s promise to be a golden age for social studies software as capable social studies educators (such as Tom Snyder) become more adept at developing software for commercial distribution.

Writing a complete lesson using the computer is a time-consuming task. Many of the lessons that teachers write are so simple and straightforward that they do not even merit the use of the computer. Some 30 years ago, after the introduction of the mimeograph machine and other forms of reproduction, people were predicting that teachers would begin writing their own textbooks and that the textbook publishing companies would go out of business. As

WHERE IS CARMEN SANDIEGO?

Since 1985 a series of computer software games has excited and entranced users from the proverbial seven to 70. The first game was "Where in the World is Carmen Sandiego?" followed by "Where in the U.S.A. is Carmen Sandiego?," then "Where in Europe . . . ?," "Where in Time . . . ?," and the latest, "Where in America's Past . . . ?" Carmen Sandiego, the central character, is a shadowy woman who leads a gang of international criminals like Gypsy Rose Lasagna, Sven Gali, and Benny Hana. They set out to pull off the most daring and outrageous adventures, such as stealing the Empire State Building or Hoover Dam.

The object of the game, ostensibly, is to find and apprehend this gang of thieves, culminating in the successful arrest of Ms. Sandiego. The player's persona is that of a detective (with various ranks such as gumshoe or inspector) assigned by the Acme Detective Agency to solve the various crimes. The actual objective is to delight users with the pursuit of geography or history. To assist in both objectives, each game comes equipped with a special edition of a useful reference book like the *Rand McNally Concise Atlas of Europe,* the *Fodor's U.S.A.* travel guide, or the *New American Desk Encyclopedia.*

The game begins with the statement that a crime has been committed, say the theft of the Eiffel Tower. The player then tries to track the thieves through a series of clues offered by traveling to places around the world or through time. At each destination more clues are offered, and a suspect's modus operandi is put together. When one is confident of one's clues, a warrant can be issued for someone fitting that description. Time is a factor; the player has about a week to solve each crime, and the computer week goes by in about 45 minutes.

If a crime is solved and the criminal apprehended, one can go on to pursue other characters until Carmen Sandiego is the object of the search. This is a rare occurrence, but hardly a deterrent. The fun and the knowledge gained from Carmen Sandiego has caused Broderbund Software, the publisher, to employ eight to 10 people to create a Carmen Sandiego program. Each piece of software "involves music and 1,200 to 1,500 clues per game."[*]

One of the authors has noted that "you don't get to interact with Carmen without learning something, whether it's the capital of France or when false teeth were invented."[†]

Schools have had "Carmen days" and, needless to say, the response has been overwhelmingly positive.

CARMEN SANDIEGO VITAL STATISTICS

Publisher:	Broderbund Software
Address:	P.O. Box 12947, San Rafael, CA 94913-2947
Cost:	$54.95, plus $10 for teacher's guide
Compatibility:	All Apple Power Macs, Performas, LCII and LC IIIs and all IBM or similar machines with Windows 95 or 3.1

Games include a teacher's guide, maps, and an appropriate reference book.

---

*Rogers, M. "Crime Doesn't Pay: It Teaches," *Newsweek,* March 19, 1990, pp. 72–73.
† Rogers, pp. 72–73.

every teacher knows, this prediction certainly never came true. The same predictions could be made for computer-assisted instruction. However, it will be a long time before teachers are given the freedom, the time, and the money to create their own lessons. It seems more likely that commercial publishers will soon be producing enough disks that teachers will be able to find a selection acceptable to them.

Interactive Video

One of the most exciting developments in computer-based education has been interactive video. Through the use of a CD-ROM, vast amounts of information can be put on a large record-type disk that is read by laser. Great diversity in direction is possible. For example, ABC News has been a pioneer in developing materials for school use. Drawing on its video footage, ABC has put together packages on Vote 88, Vote 92, Martin Luther King, Jr., and other subjects.

In Vote 92, the menu allows the user to examine the 1992 election from the preprimary posturing to the results in November that gave Bill Clinton the presidency. The Iowa caucuses can be called up and speeches and results seen and heard. A student might want to examine all the speeches and coverage given to the late Paul Tsongas of Massachusetts, including his withdrawal speech in the spring of 1992. A campaign issue such as the environment can be presented, with each candidate speaking to that issue. All this and, to coin a phrase, much more is possible with a minimum of searching. The key, as noted earlier, is the students' ability to ask insightful questions.

Hardware for the Classroom

Another series of questions for educators revolves around the machinery itself. For example, what computers should be used and how should they be organized in the classroom? Most computer manufacturers do not produce interchangeable parts—equipment made for one computer usually cannot be used with another. Another question concerns funding. Computers are expensive, although they are becoming less so, and to equip a school with computers requires substantial funding and a great deal of wisdom. Still another question is: how many computers or computer terminals should one have? Experience has shown that not every student needs to have his or her own computer. Generally, if 15 students sit down in front of 15 computers to write and work on 15 projects, within a few minutes they will have grouped together in clusters of two, three, and four to help each other through the programs they are working on. Thus the computer is not necessarily an isolating machine. Rather, it can bring students together in cooperative ventures and promote a great deal of peer instruction.

An illustration of this, as well as of the differences in individual use, can be drawn from "Oregon Trail II," a piece of software from MECC described earlier in this chapter. In "Oregon Trail II" students take the role of settlers heading to the Oregon Territory in the 1840s or 1850s. A student could work alone and learn content as he or she strives to achieve the goal—a safe arrival in Oregon on the overland trail from St. Joseph, Missouri. The same goal could also be attempted by a group of four or five students, thereby adding the dimension of cooperative learning (see Chapter 8) to the mix.

There are many future possibilities for the computer. Given the proper circumstances, it is reasonable to assume that the computer could radically change the appearance of the classroom and, more important, the way in which a student learns. For now, the computer can lead the student through a body of material at the learner's own pace until the student masters that particular material. The computer also can be used as an instrument for calculation and as an information-storage device that will allow students to find information they need.

Thus the computer should be viewed as a liberating tool for teachers. It frees them from being repositories of knowledge, from training students how to answer questions, and from being drillmasters. It will, in other words, allow the teacher to do those things that a human can do best. The teacher will be free to act as a counselor and guide for students, to answer questions that a computer can't, and to help the students cope better with the complicated world in which we live.

A list of computer-related software appears at the end of the chapter.

LOW-TECH GAMES

There are many educational games that can be played without a computer. A game, according to Eric Berne, is "an ongoing series of complementary ulterior transactions progressing to a well-defined, predictable outcome." (48) In other words, a game has rules, opponents, and a payoff. We all play games, whether we realize it or not. Students play "let's get the teacher to tell us the answer." This occurs when students guess or ask the teacher "what do you mean?" or say "I don't understand." With proper prompting, a teacher can be taught to provide the information asked of students in a few short weeks. Throughout his book, *Games People Play,* Berne details other everyday games. For example, "Kick Me Hard" is played by people who constantly get themselves in a position to be "dumped on" in order to arouse the sympathy of others. Berne mostly refers to social interaction games, but there are other types, some more appropriate to educational settings.

Simulation Games

Games are either zero sum or nonzero sum. In the former, the number of winners or the amount won must equal the number of losers or the amount lost. Poker is such a game. If five people play poker and four people win a total of $11, then the other player must have lost $11. Money won must equal money lost. A nonzero sum game might be a scavenger hunt, in which each team gets a certain amount of time to find the items. Unless it is stated that the first team to find all the items wins, it is possible for *all* teams to be winners.

THE DUMP GAME

Simulation games needn't be complex to be useful. A simple but effective example is "The Dump Game," originally created over 20 years ago but even more appropriate today. In this game students share roles in the town of Middleboro as it decides where to locate its incinerator. The brief instructions are as follows:

Problem: Where do we build the incinerator?

The town of Middleboro has a rubbish disposal problem. Until now, people have taken care of their own trash, with the result that the town lands, the marsh, the quarry, the pond, the streams, the beach, and the forest have become littered, polluted, and unattractive. The shopping areas are dirty and infested with rodents. Individual burning of trash is becoming a health hazard.

Money has been assigned for the construction of a town incinerator. A town meeting is to be held to decide where it is to be built, and the location must have the approval of four fifths of the members of the community.

Each child is to pretend to be the owner or representative of one of the properties lettered A-Z on the map in Figure 10.1—dairy, golf course, garage, lumberyard, gas station, school, and church. He or she is to lightly shade in this property on the map.

Tomorrow, after each child has worked out solutions that reflect his or her own interests, the students will go to a town meeting where they will see whether the residents can agree on a single solution.

Parents can help their children by having them consider various locations of the incinerator and what the locations would mean to the people of Middleboro, but parents should not work out the problem for the students.

This simulation, as you can see, is very simple. The directions, written for elementary-age students, can be modified to fit any age level. The game has proved useful in getting students involved in the following kinds of questions:

1. How did you actually make the decision? Was this a democratic way to decide? How does it compare with the way decisions are made in real town meetings, in the U.S. Congress, by the President, and so on?
2. What kinds of things motivated your actions? What role did information, personalities, or alliances play in the decision-making process? Do you think these things influence other decision-making situations?
3. How was power distributed and used? What kinds of power were there?

A simulation is something that resembles reality in structure or format. The simulation may have rules, but it need not. Airline pilots learn some of their flying on a simulator that never leaves the ground. Since it is costly to lose enormous airplanes during pilot training, the simulation of actual flight problems is a much safer and more practical alternative.

Figure 10.1
Town of Middleboro

Figure 10.1
Town of Middleboro

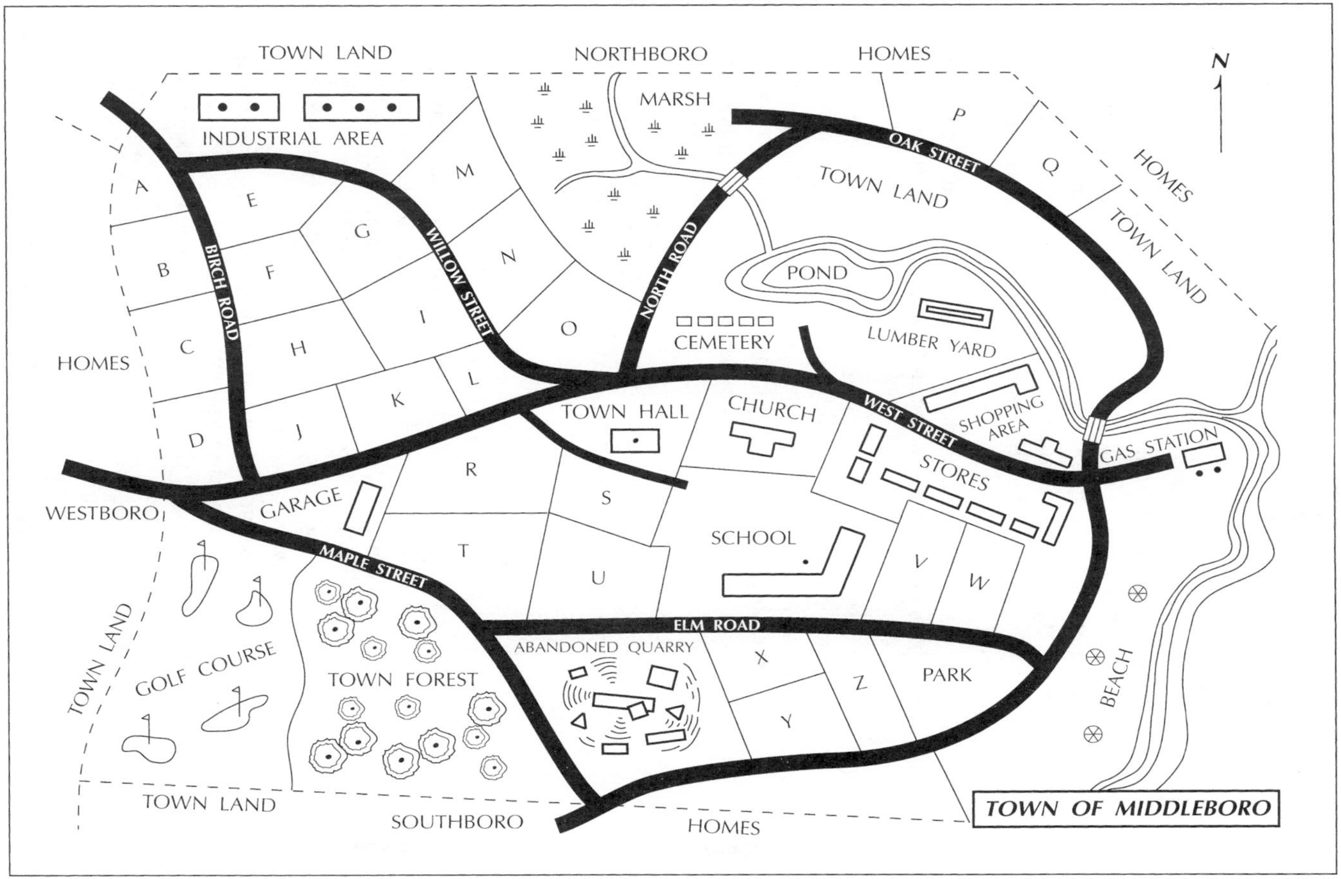

A simulation game, then, is a game that resembles reality. There are three general types of simulation games, which differ structurally. First, there is the board game, like Monopoly. Second, there is the role-play game, in which participants are assigned parts to play and act in a manner commensurate with their assigned roles (see Chapter 8). Third is the role-play board game. No one type of game is better or more complex than the other. One's choice of a simulation game should be based on one's objectives regarding the game usage. For example, if the teacher wishes to have students understand the mental anguish and strain of farming, then the "Game of Farming" found in *Geography in an Urban Age* would be most appropriate because of its role-play emphasis. A game like Risk! (Parker Brothers) emphasizes a strategy more appropriate to its board-game design.

At this point readers might ask: Why play games at all? Of what use are they? There are many good reasons to use simulation games; 10 are listed below:

1. *Active Learning.* By allowing students to get more fully involved, a teacher can more accurately assess student learning.
2. *Self-Development.* Simulation games stress rational decision making, understanding, cause and effect relationships, and the rewards of self-restraint. Teachers may encourage students to follow these suggestions, but in a game students can actually see the rewards and consequences of their actions.
3. *Communication.* In a game, students become less withdrawn because they can take roles and avoid the risk of reality. As in sociodrama, students are protected by their roles, and they must act in order for the game to continue.
4. *Time Perspective.* Simulation games allow students to see events occur over accelerated time. Children often have difficulty sequencing and predicting. Simulation games ameliorate this problem.
5. *Abstract Ideas.* Concepts are more easily understood when they can be broken down and examined in a simulation game, like a rerun of a successful football or basketball play. Highlighting key blocks and fakes makes the complex play more understandable and shows the teamwork involved in success.
6. *Immediate Reinforcement.* In a simulation game, there is immediate feedback. Students can see immediately if what they do is good or bad. They do not have to wait days to determine their success or failure, as on a test.
7. *Discipline.* This becomes less of a problem during simulation games. Because movement and small-group discussion are acceptable, there is greater diffusion of pent-up mobility.
8. *Cooperative Competition.* Students work together toward a common goal, rather than attempting to improve at the price of another's success.
9. *Gain Information.* Students may prepare for a game by reading much more than a teacher might assign. Students also gain information about processes involved in game playing.

10. *Examination of Values.* Students become more aware of their own values as they support or fail to support certain game issues.

THE TEACHER'S ROLE

In a simulation game, the role of the teacher changes significantly. Rather than being the "sun" around which all the "planets" revolve, the teacher becomes more of a coach, a guide, or an expeditor. While the game is being played, the teacher should fade into the background unless a student requests his or her services.

The teacher should make some preparations before students begin the game (Gordon, 106–10). First, the teacher should determine whether all the necessary props are on hand, how the room should be arranged, how long the game will last, whether or not any background reading is necessary, and if the game is truly appropriate. If for some reason the game cannot be played ahead of time with other teachers or friends, then the teacher should work through it alone from start to finish. This is less useful, but is better than just assuming that the game is adequate.

In some cases roles will need to be assigned. The most obvious choice for a role is not always the best. If possible, the teacher should balance the role requirements with the needs of individual students. For example, if a student needs to show a bit more responsibility, he or she should be given a role that calls for responsibility but without assuming the *most* responsible role in the game.

DEBRIEFING

This is probably the most important segment of game playing (Gordon, 118–20). It gives students an opportunity to discuss what they have really learned from the game. Little can be said about *precisely* what questions to ask when leading a debriefing session. There is a general hierarchy of questions, however, that may prove useful. First-level questions are used to determine what happened in the game—including actions, reactions, and procedures. Second-level questions focus on causes, feelings, and alternatives: "Why did you do such and such?" "What *could you* have done?" "How did you feel when someone else did such and such?" Third-level questions focus on any applications or generalizations that students might offer after playing the game. Fourth-level questions focus on what individual students learned from the game—about themselves, others, the game, game playing generally, the content of the game, and so on.

NEWSPAPERS

Almost everyone encounters newspapers at a young age, first as an observer of parents or older siblings reading the paper, next as an occasional participant, as news photos or comics are pointed out or read to the younger child, and finally as a real participant—although that may be limited to the comics, the mini-page of activities for kids, and specialized articles. As a child's reading level and interest grow, newspaper involvement increases.

Newspapers, of course, vary in size, distribution, content emphasis, and reporters' styles and abilities. Some papers are national or even international in scope, whereas others are regional or even more localized. Regional biases may be found in some local papers, despite the journalistic goal of objectivity. These biases are discussed briefly below. The *New York Times* has for years been seen as a paper with a national as well as a New York City emphasis. The newspaper can be purchased daily in all the major cities in the United States. Its extensive business news and its foreign and domestic news are the main reasons for its recognition as a national paper. The *Christian Science Monitor* and the *Wall Street Journal* also have national scope, with their own particular limitations on coverage.

In recent years other newspapers have attempted to attract a national audience. Both the *Los Angeles Times* and the *Washington Post* have tried to broaden their sales bases and reputations as national papers. In 1982 the first issue of *USA Today* appeared, advertised as this country's "first national newspaper." It is sold throughout the United States and throughout the world and makes full use of satellite communication in the transmission of stories.

Since 1970 many major urban newspapers have gone bankrupt, reducing the number of newspapers in large urban areas. This has reduced competition in some geographic areas and *may* have led to less objectivity. Teachers and students should be aware of this when examining newspapers.

In "How to Use Daily Newspapers," Cummings and Bard list a number of points that readers should consider when assessing a newspaper's quality or objectivity (5–6). They suggest asking the following questions:

1. Publishers and owners: who are they? Is the paper part of a chain or a purely local enterprise? Are the publishers local or do they live in another city?
2. History: how long has it been in existence? Has it always been owned by the present publishers?
3. Expressed policies: for example, "All the News That's Fit to Print," the motto of the *New York Times*. Is there a stated political affiliation or an independent status? Are there widely held beliefs regarding the newspaper's affiliations?
4. The staff: who writes the editorials? What are their educational backgrounds? What events are covered? What news comes from wire services' publicity people, or "stringers?"[1]
5. The plant: where is it? How modern is the equipment?

---

[1] Independent reporters who report on a single and/or local event and then try to sell their reports to newspapers.

6. Circulation: what is it and what percentage is home delivery?

7. Income: what is the profit margin of the paper?

Newspaper Programs

Not all elementary schools or middle schools can examine newspapers in depth. Because of reading difficulties, it is unlikely that a newspaper in the classroom program will be very effective until *at least* the third grade, and probably not until the fourth or fifth grade. This does not mean that the newspaper cannot be utilized, however, merely that its utilization is severely limited until students reach a certain age.

Newspapers in the Classroom (NIC) is a program sponsored by state and regional newspaper publishers to promote the greater utilization of daily newspapers in school classrooms. At reduced rates, the publishers make sets of papers available for classroom use. It is not only big-city papers that operate such programs; many smaller papers do also. One should check with the local paper about such a program; perhaps if enough teachers inquire, a publisher may decide it is worthwhile to begin such a program.

Once a class embarks on a newspaper program, various things can be studied. A unit on the newspaper might be an appropriate introduction. Following the unit, the newspaper could be used to augment other social studies units. Here are some useful guidelines that will help an NIC program to succeed.

First, all students should have their own newspapers, just as they have their own textbooks. If the reduced rate offered through NIC is still too expensive, there are other alternatives. Some newspapers make day-old papers available to schools at a minimal "pick-up" cost. Since the publishers recycle the newsprint, the day's difference does not matter to them, and the public relations feature is attractive to a community-minded institution. Teachers should check out all possibilities before rejecting an NIC program out of hand.

A second point to remember is the newspaper's "renewableness." Each day brings a new newspaper, so teachers need have no reservations about having students mark up the paper, tear out articles or pictures, and redesign ads or layouts.

Third, the teacher should clarify the sections of a newspaper and how they are organized. Most daily papers contain the same sections, although the arrangement and emphasis vary from paper to paper. Almost all newspapers contain an index on the first or second page to help readers locate the different sections of the paper. Thus the use of the newspaper can reinforce the referencing and researching skills taught for dictionary, encyclopedia, and textbook usage.

Organization of a Newspaper

Newspapers divide their coverage of "hard" news among national, international, and local stories. The size of the paper determines how many stories are written by its own reporters, how many are picked up from wire services like

United Press International (UPI) or Associated Press (AP), and how many are bought from newspaper chains like Knight-Ridder, Gannett, or the Chicago Tribune News service.

Every newspaper contains advertisements; their presence represents the financial health of the newspaper, which is largely supported through ad payments. Display ads are larger and more costly, whereas classified ads are smaller and cheaper. The editorial page contains letters to the editor and columns written by local people (not necessarily journalists), as well as purchased opinion columns by syndicated columnists like Ellen Goodman, William F. Buckley, or Art Buchwald. Almost every paper has a sports section, with some coverage of national or international sporting events and heavier coverage of local or regional sporting events and personalities. The *San Francisco Chronicle,* for example, will have in-depth articles on the San Francisco Giants and Oakland A's during the baseball season, while the *New Orleans Times-Picayune* may carry just a brief account of all major league contests from the previous day. The business section of a newspaper may accentuate local commercial interests while also covering stock market trends and averages. The larger the city, the more extensive the business holdings and the more coverage devoted to business.

With all these sections, how can a newspaper be used as a renewable textbook? Let us examine some possibilities in a number of subject areas.

LANGUAGE ARTS

Because the newspaper is a communications medium, this may be the most obvious area to explore. Rather than making up special worksheets for grammar or reading, a teacher could use the newspaper as a daily worksheet, for highlighting different parts of speech—circling nouns, underlining verbs, and so on. Reading for the main idea or for more specific comprehension could also be accomplished by using a newspaper article rather than a textbook.

We all recognize the individuality of students and express a desire to individualize course work. We also recognize the extra work that individualized instruction entails. Using the newspaper makes this task much simpler. Have students pick a story to read for comprehension. If they are interested in science, let them read about the space shuttle. If it is sports, there is plenty to choose from, as well as in other areas.

For writing practice, students could rewrite articles or write descriptions of photos, ads, or comics. To learn to write, one must practice *daily* (see Chapter 2). There are no shortcut, how-to-do-it-in-five-days techniques.

Advertisements are another potential learning tool. Students could describe an ad in writing, presenting the main argument briefly, or they could practice writing their own ads as they study the use of persuasive language. Students organizing a class or school newspaper might try to design ads that pertain to their school, such as an advertisement for the school cafeteria (usually a *real* challenge). Creating ads also gives students a chance to practice their artistry in design. This project could be coordinated with the school's arts program.

MATHEMATICS

Advertisements, of course, provide a myriad of problems in mathematics. The level of mathematics study will determine the type of problems drawn from display ads. Almost any elementary math problem can be seen there—addition, subtraction, multiplication, division, fractions, percentages, story problems, weights, and measures. For example, if a display ad says 30 percent or one third off, students could calculate how much money shoppers are saving and how much they are spending for an item.

SOCIAL STUDIES

Not surprisingly, there are many uses for the newspaper related to the social studies. Almost any news story can be examined for concepts. This conceptual reductionism could be performed as an analytical exercise. Teachers could also present a synthesizing exercise in which they present several concepts and ask students to write a news story. For example, the concepts of colonialism, war, revolution, property, and equality could be shaped into a story explaining the threat of revolution in central Africa. This is not an easy exercise, so teachers should carefully consider the concepts they present for synthesis. So many news stories concern events around the country and the world that they could easily be used as a starting point for map or globe study. Students could simply locate the places mentioned or, as they become more sophisticated in their map use, could plan how they might get to such a place to cover the story as a reporter would.

For example, students in Pittsburgh might be interested in the headline and story, WINTER STORMS THREATEN NATION'S SALAD BOWL, referring to the Imperial Valley of California. For third or fourth graders the location of San Diego in relation to Pittsburgh would be of initial interest. Reading the story might arouse the students' interest in climatic differences nationwide, differences that require them to wear down parkas while lettuce and tomatoes are growing in California.

Older students might plan a trip to California by air or land, using road maps and train and airline schedules. Mathematically they might also try to plan the most cost-effective trip for what they will be doing (reporting or simply vacationing). If they choose to drive or take the train, a topographic map could be used to predict the terrain they will encounter. Any news story could be developed in this manner; the only limitations are time and the teacher's or students' imaginations.

The ability to read graphs and charts is another social studies skill. These appear in newspapers on subjects ranging from the cost of living, unemployment, and tax revenues to public opinion polls. Some students, particularly those with reading problems, may understand the visual information more easily than the written word, but all children should learn how to read both.

Sports and entertainment provide a variety of contemporary American cultural experiences (see Chapter 2) and a modicum of career education as students test their dreamlike aspirations for fame against the adversities of struggle in professional sports or the arts. Reading about a painter who could not sell a painting for years, or about an actress who worked as a waitress while auditioning three days a week for parts, is bound to tarnish a few dreams. The sports section also reveals the darker side of celebrity life—including injuries, drug and alcohol abuse, and extensive and wearying travel. Unfortunately, such realities rarely tinge a child's romanticism. Of course, they find the eye-popping salaries of the sports pages exciting, but reality can be inserted—for instance, during baseball season, when many Sunday newspapers carry the ballplayers' batting averages. Almost all the players in the major leagues can be listed in two or three columns; with team populations that small, what are the odds of becoming a professional ballplayer? The same applies to dancers, artists, musicians, actors, and others in the arts. How many do you know from your own hometown—maybe one or two? This kind of examination is not intended to deflate students' aspirations, just to temper their ideas with some reason. By reading a newspaper, as opposed to teen or sports magazines, students can put the world of entertainment and sports into a cultural and career perspective.

Another important aspect of newspapers is their treatment of law-related issues. This subject will be examined in Chapter 13.

In spite of reporters' professed objectivity, values are discernible throughout a newspaper. As noted in Chapter 4, all writing is bound to be value laden, simply because facts are seen through the filter of prior knowledge and understanding. Moreover, no news story can present *all* the facts. In choosing what information to present, the reporter is making a value decision. Thus stories can be read by students for their explicit or inherent values, like the textbook exercises in Chapter 4 (pages 98–100).

Another good example of expressed values is the comic page. The authors of comics are sometimes subtle and sometimes blatant in their lampooning of the left or the right or of specific people or issues. For example, "Dick Tracy" has become symbolic of so-called law-and-order policies, whereas "Doonesbury" is more illustrative of the political left.

Comics often mirror societal changes. A strip like "Cathy," which expresses all the singles' hang-ups of the 1980s, is in stark contrast to the single life of "Winnie Winkle," a comic from the 1950s, or "Brenda Starr" (premarriage, of course). The Canadian comic strip "For Better or Worse" contrasts with "Blondie." Both are humorous; they just have different perspectives on family life. Even children's perspectives of family life can be contrasted in the comics. The view in "Family Circus, for example," sharply contrasts with that of Calvin in "Calvin and Hobbes."

Current fads are often lampooned in the comics. For younger students, who may not understand the transience of fads, the joke may be lost. Although analysis of humor often spoils the joke, the exercise is a valuable one for school use. Students might even put their talents to work by creating a comic strip of their own, thus illustrating the application of their study.

These ideas certainly are not exhaustive. Many of the newspapers participating in NIC or NIE (Newspapers in Education) programs provide materials or workshops for school use. Several general publications on using the newspaper in school are listed at the end of the chapter.

CURRENT AFFAIRS

One of the primary reasons for studying newspapers is to comprehend more fully the world in which we live. A textbook cannot do this; it will be one to two years out of date before it is even published. Thus students and teachers must rely on the news media to provide views of current events for public benefit.

How important are current events, really? This question is often raised by both students and preservice teachers. Should it really matter to students who controls the West Bank of the Jordan River? When phrased this way, the answer may be no; that is, if people do not care about something, then you cannot force them to care. For the most part, however, students in elementary classrooms *and* college classrooms are saying in essence, "I want to see the importance of this, but I just don't. Can you help?"

Part of the answer reflects what education, schooling, and social studies are for. In this country, the purpose of education is to impart knowledge and understanding and to help members of the society live lives that are as rewarding as they can be. A chief prerequisite of this is a populace that can make decisions as citizens.

An understanding of the situation in the Middle East affects all of us in many ways. Economically, instability in the Middle East can affect the price of oil. Governmental decisions on the use of American foreign aid may mean less money for domestic programs or other foreign programs. Thus economic decisions are also social decisions. Knowing the historical precedents for such decisions can help determine the course of action the government takes. The government is composed of politicians who, for the most part, either want to serve their constituents for purely altruistic reasons or just want to be reelected. Either way, they will respond to the demands of an informed constituency. Not everyone may believe this, but even a cynical view of politics is more convincing with adequate knowledge.

Determining what is news is not always easy. Students can gain some insight into the question by listening to their parents, listening to the television or radio news, reading a newspaper, or using the current events periodicals available in many schools, such as *My Weekly Reader, News Ranger,* or *Junior Scholastic.* Even so, current events study in school can be dull and predictable. See if the following scenario sounds familiar:

Children's periodicals can stimulate or develop interest in current affairs.

It's Friday morning around 8:15, and a fourth-grade student, Mark, is frantically combing the previous day's newspaper in a desperate search for an "appropriate" article. What, however, is appropriate? To the teacher, it is probably an article that means something to Mark—an article that he has thought about, that can be built upon in the coming weeks, and that will stimulate continued interest in the news. To Mark, "appropriate" means an article that is short, incidental (a one-time experience, a "man bites dog" type of story), easy to read, and maybe even has a picture. He will probably not think about the news until he thinks of the assignment. His concern is to pick an article fast, read it fast, tell the class about it fast, and get it up on the current events bulletin board *fast.* Mark sees the assignment as a task to be completed, whereas his teacher sees the experience as a process to be explored.

The problem here lies in communicating the teacher's goals to the students so they can make those goals their own, rather than playing more of the game "Tell me what to do and I'll do it." Why does the purpose of such a task become so distorted in moving from the teacher's mind to the student's? One reason is that the teacher may not really believe in what he or she is doing—which is easily transmitted to students. For example, if current events are so vital, why does the teacher address them only on Friday? If a student asked this question, the teacher's response might be "Because we have other things to do, too." In other words, current events are not really as important as spelling, mathematics, or penmanship.

WHAT'S IN THE NEWS

In 1972, "In the News," a locally produced instructional television program from WPSX-TV in State College, Pennsylvania, designed for 4th through 6th graders to have a better grasp of current events, began broadcasting statewide on the Pennsylvania Public Television Network. Teacher response from around the state was enthusiastic and the response at various educational broadcast conferences held around the United States was so positive that in the Fall of 1978 "What's in the News" (the name had been changed to avoid confusion with a short-lived show broadcast on one of the major networks) became the first instructional television show to be broadcast using the aid of a communications satellite, now a common occurence. By 1985, stations in more than 20 states had decided to carry the show and as of 1998, "What's in the News" was being shown in 36 states and the American School in Reykjavik, Iceland on a regular basis.

Despite the plethora of news shows and channels, there are few media outlets that are concerned with children's understanding of the news, rather than their mere access to it. "What's in the News" tries to present the news to its audience in a explicatory manner while neither boring nor talking down to the viewers. Judging by research surveys and independent teacher and student comments, the show succeeds admirably in that goal. Respondents in a 1997 survey of teachers who had viewed the show rated "What's in the News" 9.9 on a 10.0 scale regarding the value of the series.

The show's format consists of news summaries every other week focusing on the major events of the previous two weeks and a feature show in the intervening weeks which take an in-depth look at some major story in the news that seems to need further development and discussion in order to aid student appreciation and understanding. Some of these stories have included recent AIDS research, India and Pakistan's 50th anniversaries, the presidential election process, South Africa, the continuing conflict in the Middle East, the American labor movement, media literacy, and education issues. Two of these shows per year have been set aside for student responses to a write-in topic which draws upwards of 5,000 participants.

The series has recently teamed up with the National Aeronautic and Space Administration (NASA) to allow kids to participate in a number of experiments both on and off the Space Shuttle, but which all have some impact on the understanding of the effects of space on the growth and development of life forms in space, chemical bonding in space as well as how physical properties are affected by weightlessness and changes in gravitational force.

With the advent of the "What's in the News" web site, even students and teachers that are in states that do not carry the series can have access to the teacher utilization tips, the write-in-topics, questions and suggestions and the home page of the writer and cohost, Katie O'Toole. The address is http/www.witn.psu.edu and the email address is witn@psu.edu.

What's in the News
WPSX-TV/Penn State University
115A Wagner Building
University Park, PA 16802-3899

CHILDREN'S EXPRESS

In 1976 a reporter named Gilbert Giles informed his newspaper that Walter Mondale was Jimmy Carter's choice as his vice-presidential nominee. Gilbert, who was 12 at the time, scooped the *New York Times*, the *Washington Post*, the Associated Press's Walter Cronkite, and the rest of the journalistic establishment. His newspaper and organization, *Children's Express* (CE), went overnight from a curiosity *to* a group of accepted reporters doing their job.

Today CE continues to function as a press service, publishes a bimonthly newsletter, and holds occasional hearings on children's issues. The organization has published four well-received books, has broadcast a 13-week series on PBS during prime time, has an on-line Web site, and is now about 25 years old, with news bureaus in the United States and overseas.

Clearly *Children's Express* illustrates that children have a great interest in media and can produce a quality journalistic product. Admittedly, most of these children are above average in intellect, but that should not preclude any child from pursuing his or her interest in media. It is that keen interest that seems to drive these young reporters and editors; that and a real sense of justice and fairness for all—including children.

Officially, *Children's Express* is a private, nonprofit news service reported by children who are eight to 13 years of age. The reporters work in teams led by editors who are 14 to 18 years old. The weekly CE column is distributed worldwide from CE's six news bureaus, in New York City, Washington, DC, Indianapolis, Oakland, Marquette, MI, and London, England.

CE reporters are responsible for the content of all the columns; the teen editors are responsible for news-team leadership, management, training, and research. Adults are responsible for business management, final editing, and story assignments.

Since its inception in 1975, *Children's Express* reporters have covered the Republican and Democratic political conventions of 1976, 1980, 1984, 1988, 1992, and 1996. CE's main focus, however, is on issues that directly affect children—including child abuse, divorce, hunger and malnutrition both here and abroad, the incarceration of children, day care, education, and alcohol and drug abuse.

Children who live near one of the CE news bureaus and meet the age requirements can contact the bureau directly and apply for training as a CE reporter or editor. Those who do not live near such a news bureau can contribute through access on-line.

Children's Express is located at 19 West 21st St., Suite 1001, New York, NY, and the following bureaus: 3000 N. Meridian St., Indianapolis, IN 46208; 1440 New York Ave. N.W., Suite 510, Washington, DC 20005-2111; c/o Center for Urban Family Life, 685 14th St., Oakland, CA 94612; c/o Upper Peninsula Children's Museum, P.O. 384, 129 West Baraga, Marquette, MI 49855-3911; Exmouth House, 3.11 Pine St., London EC1 OJH, ENGLAND. Web address is http:\\www.ce.org\.

Understanding our daily lives should be as important as these basic disciplines. It would not take long to address current affairs *every* day, either directly or obliquely, by relating current issues to the unit topic at hand. If a child is studying a unit on Japan, some current issues that could be examined are import restrictions, tariffs, Japanese influences on the American workplace, and the treatment of Japanese-Americans in World War II.

Thus, to convince students that current affairs *are* important, a teacher should encourage discussions of the news and should relate current ideas to various topics of study. A teacher does not always have to be totally prepared if a student raises a question about some current issue. Ideally, that is what a teacher should strive for—unsolicited questions from students about important issues. Unfortunately, teachers may put off such questions because they are off the subject. But when is violence between Hindus, Muslims, and Sikhs in India *ever* going to be on the subject? Students today see and hear much more of the news, but they are still puzzled over how to interpret it. They are concerned about answers to questions like "Why are people dying in Rwanda?" Ignoring such questions makes us lesser teachers.

Creating Media

The study of current events may motivate students to develop their own newspapers or radio or television news scripts. Generally students should use a standard adult newspaper as their initial model. The class must delegate responsibility for the project. Not everyone can be a reporter—nor does everyone want to be one. Editors, layout artists, and circulation coordinators are also needed. Some jobs could be doubled up, but the newspaper should be a cooperative effort, not a series of individual efforts held together by coincidence.

Before embarking on such an adventure, students should spend some time studying and examining how a newspaper is put together. The key question that will emerge as the students begin their project is "What is news?" In order to establish some consistent editorial philosophy and policy, the newspaper staff must address this question. Is it news when a student gets dressed and comes to school? No, not usually, unless that student comes dressed as a gorilla. Is it news if a new student enters Room 116? Probably not, but what if that student is a Laotian immigrant who has fled with her family from a totalitarian government? That would probably be news.

Thus students will come to understand that many factors govern what is news. The setting of an editorial policy will help, but it will not necessarily answer all questions regarding what is news. With the teacher's guidance, the students must set parameters of coverage and publication. Realistically, how often can such a paper be written, edited, compiled, and distributed without totally dominating classroom activity? A weekly paper is probably the most ambitious goal; a bimonthly or monthly paper may be more realistic.

It would seem most logical to limit the scope of the newspaper to events within the school, but there may be some local event that deserves coverage

Students can produce their own newspaper on a computer terminal.

also. Wider coverage than that would leave the students unable to report their stories firsthand and would force them to rehash the stories from a secondary or tertiary source.

The assignment of "beats" to reporters would stem from the general coverage decision. A reporter might be assigned to cover each classroom in the school, or possibly each grade level. Another reporter or two might cover administration of the school (principal, guidance counselor, office secretaries), and another might report on school maintenance personnel (custodian, bus drivers, crossing guards, cafeteria workers, nurses). An ambitious reporter might wish to meet with a school board member.

Before the reporters are let loose, they should have some idea of how to conduct an interview. Their questions should be written out before hand and shown to the teacher so that they can be checked for clarity. This may sound like censorship, and in a sense it is. But because this is a *class* enterprise done under the supervision of the teacher, the teacher should always be aware of what is going on—not to censor the students so much as to be informed.

Too often an interview ends up being no more than an introduction to the interviewee. Student reporters should be encouraged to keep their ears open to determine what issues are of local or school importance in the community that might lead to an interview. They should practice by interviewing each another, so that they will learn to organize their thoughts and questions, as well as to modify their questions depending on the interviewee's response.

RADIO

For many intermediate students one of the most popular media is radio. For many primary-grade youngsters, listening to the radio is more common than looking at a newspaper, particularly if they have older siblings. Classroom use of the radio is superior to the use of television in that radio requires only listening skills. Also, because the radio allows for much more visual imagery, students are limited only by their imaginations, rather than by a small screen.

So what can one do with radio? To begin with, radio could be the focus of a unit topic. The unit might cover radio history, technological changes, the science of radio transmission, the evolution of radio regulations by the Federal Communications Commission, Radio Free Europe and other propaganda uses, and, if possible, actual radio broadcasting. Radio also could be assessed in terms of the media industry or to contrast radio news with television or print news.

A more expeditious unit would examine radio from the perspective of a consumer. This corresponds to the goal outlined earlier in this chapter: to encourage students to think critically about the media and to make them better-informed citizens.

MUSIC

Most students listen to radio for the music, and most radio stations promote music as their primary product. Decision making about music is clearly based on values more than on factual criteria. Despite different preferences, students should acquire some knowledge of how music is classified and how each classification is characterized. Students could chart the music played on various stations and begin to understand how stations target a particular audience for certain periods each day and how that affects their decisions on marketing certain products on the air.

A study of popular radio music might lead to a study of the place of music in the broader scheme of American culture. As suggested in Chapter 2 by writers like Lee Cooper, popular music is a worthwhile subject for student analysis and discussion.

NEWS

Radio news presents a sharp contrast to newspapers and television news in that it is briefer, more general, and limited to aural stimulation. One clear advantage of radio news, however, is its frequency—airing every half-hour or hour, and with interruptions for news flashes. In analyzing news or current affairs, a student might compare the range of topics and the depth of coverage on the radio, on television, and in newspapers.

ADVERTISEMENTS

As mentioned earlier, radio ads are aimed at a target audience for a specific program. During the day there are more ads for household products than during the evening. On evenings or weekends a classical music station might advertise a cultural magazine, a bookstore, a restaurant, or a local theater group, as well as more general items like gasoline, food, furniture, clothing, or travel arrangements.

Radio ads could be studied in the same way as newspaper or television ads. Students could categorize the ads (celebrity endorsement, bandwagon approach), dissect the advertiser's message, and decide whether they find an ad effective or believable. If the message is obscured by the delivery, then the ad has not met its objective. Ideally, all advertisers want people to buy their products and want their messages to be clearly communicated. This kind of analysis can be applied to television as well, although with television there is much more to study and much more attention paid to it by students.

TELEVISION

NEWS

Many of the study ideas from newspapers and radio lend themselves to television. One that is unique to television, however, is the use of film to report the news. Viewers often become so caught up in the entertainment aspects that they miss the intent of the film. Clearly this is an example of McLuhan's the "medium is the message," whereby the images on film may send a message quite different from or similar to the announced commentary. The images carry much more impact.

According to James Dick, viewers analyzing a television news story should ask themselves the following questions:

1. Is this really news or did the reporter's presence make this news?
2. Was the film "accurate" in keeping with the story or was there undue sensationalism?
3. Was the report or reporter biased? Did he have an obvious point of view?
4. Did the reporter induce people to participate in the story through promises of notoriety, confidentiality, or some sort of "reward"?
5. Is the story clear and effective?

Much can be done with television news study, including analyzing the people in the news, the events, the lengths of stories, the extent of coverage,

Home Improvement, *starring Tim Allen, is viewed as an excellent television program conveying a positive home life.*

and the types of stories covered in local broadcasts compared with the network news offerings. Dick's pamphlet expands on these topics (6-7).

Thus a study of television news should not be limited to older children. Young children can and do watch the news—though certainly with a different perspective than adults. One of my children declared at age three that she intended to marry Walter Cronkite, the anchor at that time on "CBS Evening News," which she watched faithfully each night. She also named one of her stuffed animals Richard Threlkeld, after a television news correspondent. Clearly, even young children are affected by the news. The object of the teacher is to exploit and expand that interest into comprehension and understanding.

TELEVISION ENTERTAINMENT

Recent studies contend that by age 15 the average child will have spent more hours in front of the television than in school. (See, for example, Minow and LaMay, 1995.) Yet children between the ages of two and 11 are actually spending less time watching television, dropping 18 percent since 1984.

Computers and videocassettes have eaten into television time but it still averages almost 22 hours per week, more than almost any other activity (Fabrikant, D8). Another study shows that children are portrayed on television in an unrealistic manner. "The children on television, the study found, are mostly motivated by friendship, sports, romance and self improvement. Family relationships, performance in school, useful community roles or earning money are less often the reason for children's actions." (Lewin, B8) In addition, children shown are overwhelmingly white. These findings have been the cause for alarm among many educators, who advocate turning off the tube and placing books in the hands of all students. Although noble, this approach is neither realistic nor ultimately effective. Forbidding use of the television will probably not work, and even if it did, students would miss the opportunity to view excellent television programs as well as those with little or no redeeming value. After all, other recent studies also indicate that educational television benefitted preschoolers in preparation for school and later performances in math and verbal tests (Mifflin, B8).

What seems more realistic is to cultivate children's television viewing *skills*—to make them critical consumers of television. Many children are inclined to watch television merely because the set is on; the moving images can become mesmerizing in spite of the shallow content. Television viewing skills involve analyzing what makes some programs shallow and others educational. After making this gross distinction, more subtle criticism is necessary. Elliot Eisner advocates that teachers be educational connoisseurs; the same can be done for students with regard to television. Recent television industry ratings for programs imposed by the industry itself under threat of government regulation may help students and adults view television more critically. The six rating categories, however, still left many people critical as they do not differentiate for sex, violence, or language.

Being a critical viewer is a skill that needs to be developed. As with news program analysis, the teacher should present questions and guidelines to students to help them critically appraise the programs they see at home. An analysis of television could include prime-time network television, Saturday morning children's programs, and reruns of older programs, most of which used to be prime-time programs.

The average half-hour program spends approximately 24 minutes on the program itself. In that time a story must be introduced, characters developed, and some problem resolved. What can students look for as critical viewers? A useful activity might be to assign students to watch a show (their choice) and record their responses on a worksheet. (See Figure 10.2 for an example.) Here are some additional questions to ask of students to deepen their critical viewing skills (not all will apply to every program):

1. What is the story about? Is it believable? Does it even *attempt* to be? Shows like *Third Rock from the Sun*, *Mighty Morphin Power Rangers*, and *ALF* immediately set a premise of fantasy, making realism less important.
2. Are the characters believable? Even in an unrealistic setting, good character development is possible and certainly preferable.

FIGURE 10.2
Worksheet on a Television Show

Name of show _____ Date viewed _____

Name of reviewer _____

1. Was the story believable?   yes   no

2. Were the characters believable?   yes   no

3. What made them (story, characters) believable or not so?

	None portrayed	Stereo-typed	Fairly presented	Super-women	Super-heroes
4. Treatment of women:					
Treatment of minorities:					

5. Was there violence?   yes   no

   Did it add to the story, or was it unnecessary?

6. Did the characters drink, smoke, or use drugs?   yes   no

7. What occupations were depicted?

---

3. What is the purpose of the show? Is there any goal perceivable beyond simple entertainment? *M*A*S*H* sought to visualize the horrors of war and to sensitize viewers to the value of all human life.

4. How are minorities and women portrayed? Are all the women in traditional female roles? If ethnic minorities or senior citizens are portrayed, are stereotypes perpetuated? Television networks have become especially sensitive to criticisms about stereotyping, claiming that their job is to entertain and that they should not be responsible for social change at the risk of losing viewers. Do you believe this is so?

5. What about the setting of the show? Do the seasons change? Do the inside shots reflect a believable living situation?

6. How much violence is there—particularly on Saturday morning cartoon shows? Is the violence necessary, and could students misinterpret the results of the violence? For example, many cartoon characters

have guns go off in their faces. Their faces are blackened, but the characters heal almost immediately. Might children come to believe that a firearm injury is not very serious?

7. Are the various social classes portrayed on television—from *Home Improvement* to *The Simpsons* to *Roseanne*—stereotyped?

8. Is drug use glorified, particularly drinking alcohol and smoking? Some studies have shown that these substances are used much more on television than in society generally.

9. Are the jobs portrayed representative of a cross section of the population? Studies have shown this not to be the case. Students surveying a number of programs could provide data on occupations for the class to compare with the jobs of their own parents.

10. How much lawbreaking is done on television? Is it justifiable when it is in the interests of justice?

These questions are only a beginning. Many others could be raised by critical student viewers.

ADVERTISEMENTS

Much of what was said about radio advertisements applies to television, with the exception of television's added visual dimension. A good project for critical consumers is to try to re-create commercials for children's toys with the toys in hand. A number of classes have done this and have discovered that the ads were misleading in portraying the capabilities of dolls, toy motorcycles, certain athletic equipment, and building sets.

A teacher could attempt to cultivate a degree of skepticism among students for "hidden camera" personal-testimony ads. Do they believe that someone would refuse three boxes of another detergent in favor of one brand? Do they believe it when someone says, "I'm going to use _____ from now on?"

Based on their observations, students might create their own commercials, thereby demonstrating their understanding of selling techniques. This could serve as a small-group project. The commercials could be written, performed, and even taped if the school has facilities for doing so.

Instructional Television and Current Affairs

Some television stations offer special programs for children that attempt to analyze and interpret the regular news media. Currently, there are at least two such programs on public television: "Assignment: The World," produced in New York, and "What's in the News," produced in Pennsylvania. These programs are designed to be discussed in school by students and their teachers.

"What's in the News" is aimed at students in the intermediate grades, although some teachers have adapted the program to the primary grade level and to the junior high or middle school level. The news is reported in a style and vocabulary that students can understand. The programs demonstrate that the news can teach students more about the world in which they live. By watching "What's in the News," students learn to think of the news as a means of developing new interests or of pursuing interests they already have. The show carries a news summary every other week, alternating with in-depth features on a current topic in the news. These topics range from the Middle East to medical breakthroughs, from Africa south of the Sahara to federal regulations and agencies. The news summaries carry "hard" news, explained in a style, pace, and vocabulary geared to the intermediate grade level, as well as "soft" news—lighter stories on topics like famous people, sports, cultural events, or kids in the news.

Such a program could be used in the classroom to augment current events study. The program itself could provide the foundation for at least a week's worth of discussion and research. For example, a story on the Middle East might send fourth graders in various directions. Some might want to read a bit more about one or more of the nations or peoples of that region. The teacher might lead a discussion on the treatment of various groups in the Middle East over the past 30 years. Other students might like to discover where Middle Eastern immigrants live in their state or town. They might present an oral history of Middle Eastern immigrants, illustrated with a map tracing their route from the Middle East to the Americas.

These are ideas generated from just one story that appeared on a children's current affairs program. The other five or six stories on the same program could provide similar ideas, all contributing to a better understanding of current issues. A teacher may also select stories from a current affairs show that complement or enrich a unit the class is studying. Instructional television (ITV) differs in a number of ways from network television. First, ITV is primarily concerned with learning. Second, most shows are broadcast during the day for use in the classroom. Third, ancillary materials are often available to schools in the form of teachers' guides or newsletters. Fourth, most ITV series are repeated, and many have taping rights that allow programs to be taped off the air and shown at a more convenient time. Fifth, ITV shows are usually designed for a particular grade level or levels and include some academic or educational consultants.

One can be a critical consumer of ITV, but the kinds of questions asked may be less appropriate, because most ITV directors will have already asked themselves those same questions.

ITV programs are also aired by the Public Broadcasting System (PBS) during prime-time hours. Shows like *Nova* and *Odyssey* are examples. Both of them have accompanying teacher's guides that are quite useful. Teacher's guides for many PBS shows are available through local PBS stations or local broadcasting councils. Some states, like Pennsylvania, acquire the rights to some PBS shows after their initial broadcast and then make them available to school systems at almost no cost. Upon receipt of a blank videotape from a school, the Pennsylvania Department of Education will tape certain programs and send the tape back to the school. In this way, excellent "evergreen" (always usable) shows can become part of a school's permanent collection of materials. In many of today's schools and homes it is the era of the VCR. The prime-time shows of public or network television reappear in classrooms across the country. In many cases teachers tape only those shows that they have the legal right to use, but in other cases they may not know or care about such "details." Unquestionably, one should check with the district media specialist or a curriculum coordinator to make sure it is all right to use a video program before taping it for classroom use.

Most people recognize the ease and flexibility that the VCR adds to teacher planning and presentation. VCRs are also quite affordable for most schools (though reserving the VCR is not always easy). The use of video is growing, but teachers need good modern equipment and training in using it in the classroom (Carlisle, 3).

Cable Television

In recent years, as cable television has entered more homes, cable broadcasters have turned their attention to educational and instructional programming. *CNN Newsroom*, begun in 1989, is one example of current affairs instructional programming offered on cable. Broadcast in the early morning hours, *CNN Newsroom* is designed to be taped off the air and used later in the day. It is geared to junior and senior high school students, but an elementary version has been discussed. The program reviews the day's top stories and has special reports that deal with a different theme—global issues, international issues, business, science, editorial features—each day. Feature segments and other film are drawn from regular CNN broadcasts. A daily classroom guide summarizes the program and suggests teaching activities. *CNN Newsroom* is shown without commercials and is distributed free to schools.

Another show, *Channel One*, which first aired in the spring of 1989, aroused tremendous controversy when it took to the air. *Channel One* had commercials, and many educators and state legislators found this educationally indefensible. *Channel One* could also be seen only through satellite pickup, and the owners of *Channel One gave* schools the equipment necessary to receive the signal and present the show. Some educators found this trade-off—commercials in exchange for video equipment—too attractive to pass up. Others denounced it as selling children out. As of 1996, *Channel One* had over 12,000 schools viewing the program, though at least two studies had attacked the show as being biased and having a commercial rather than an educational function (Honan, B7).

Cable's exponential growth has meant that whole new "networks" exist for children's learning or mislearning. The Discovery Channel has become the rival of public television in providing excellent shows on aspects of nature and cultures throughout the world. The channel offers lesson plans for a number of its shows.

Nickelodeon has established children as its prime audience and provides children's news, new shows, and reruns of classic television shows (Nick at Night). One of its most popular shows is the 1950s show, *I Love Lucy*.

There are a number of sports channels, food channels, old movie channels, and the Weather Channel, which broadcasts *The Weather Classroom* for student use. Cable television has established "niche" viewing with smaller, more loyal viewers whose demographics allow advertisers to appeal to the specialized audience. A creative teacher can now draw from a myriad of television resources for school use.

CABLE TELEVISION CHANNELS
WITH USEFUL EDUCATIONAL ASPECTS

Discovery
7700 Wisconsin Ave.
Bethesda, MD 20814
(301) 986-1999

Nickelodeon
1515 Broadway, 20th Floor
New York, NY 10036
(212) 258-8000

The Weather Channel
2600 Cumberland Parkway NW
Atlanta, GA 30339
(770) 434-6800

QUESTIONS AND ACTIVITIES

1. What social studies ideas discussed in previous chapters might be made easier through the use of a computer or word processor? Keep this question in mind for subsequent chapters.

2. What are some ways that computers make a student's job easier or more difficult?

3. Examine some computer software designed for social studies use. In what areas is the software deficient? In what areas is it helpful to students?

4. Assuming that you have the programming ability, what would you like to see computer software teach regarding social studies?

5. A major computer company once proposed to donate a microcomputer to every elementary school in the United States. Why would it make such a generous offer? Why would a school district refuse such an offer?

6. What games do you play as a student, as a family member, as a friend? Are the rules always clear to all participants? Do the rules ever change?

7. If simulation games are so useful, why don't more teachers use them?

8. Design a lesson or series of lessons that focus on utilizing Internet resources. How would you assist students in finding such resources?

9. How can teachers and parents work with students to "harness the Internet" for educational purposes?

10. Visit an elementary school classroom and ask the teacher or students which sections of the newspaper the students like to read best.

11. In what ways could a study of the newspaper or of the media be integrated within an expanding-communities model of the social studies curriculum?

12. To what extent should teachers be experts on current events? How many newspapers should they read a day? Should they read a weekly news magazine? Should they watch the network television news daily?

13. What advertisements on the radio or television are most memorable, and why? Would your answers agree with those of a third or fourth grader?

14. The parents of most children in school today grew up with television. How might they respond to an intended unit of study on television?

15. What reservations would you have about showing televised commercials in your classroom?

16. Follow a news story through the newspaper and through television. Is the information the same? Is it better to have less information and more visual stimulation or more information and little or no visual aids?

17. People often lament "there is nothing on TV," even when cable delivers over 50 channels. What is meant by such a comment and do you agree with it?

REFERENCES

Ayre, J. "Off-line and On-line: Scenarios for CD-ROM Formats in the Late 1990s," *Educational Media International,* vol. 33, no. 3, September, 1996, pp. 128–132.

Berne, E. *Games People Play.* New York: Grove Press, 1964.

Budin, H., D. Kendall, and J. Lengel. *Using Computers in the Social Studies.* New York: Teachers College Press, 1986.

Carlisle, R. D. B. *Video at Work in American Schools.* Bloomington, IN: Agency for Instructional Television, 1987.

Cooper, L. "Popular Music in the Social Studies Classroom: Audio Resources for Teachers." NCSS How-to-Do-It, ser. 2, no. 13. Washington, DC: National Council for the Social Studies, 1981.

Cummings, H. H., and H. Bard. "How to Use Daily Newspapers." NCSS How-to-Do-It, ser. 1, no. 5. Washington, DC: National Council for the Social Studies, 1964.

Dick, J. "Using Television News, Documentaries, and Public Affairs Programs in the Social Studies." NCSS How-to-Do-It, ser. 2, no. 12. Washington, DC: National Council for the Social Studies, 1981.

Eisner, E. *The Educational Imagination.* 3rd ed. New York: Macmillan, 1994.

Fabrikant, G. "The Young and the Restless Audience," *New York Times,* April 8, 1996, p. D8.

"The Game of Farming," *Geography in an Urban Age* (formerly *The High School Geography Project*). New York: Macmillan, 1972.

Gordon, A. K. *Games for Growth.* Chicago: Science Research Associates, 1972.

Honan, W. "Scholars Attack Public School TV Program," *New York Times,* January 22, 1997, p. B7.

Lewin, T. "Children on TV Out of Touch, Study Finds," *New York Times,* February 27, 1995, p. B8.

Martorella, P. *Teaching Social Studies in Middle and Secondary Schools.* 2nd ed. Englewood Cliffs, NJ. Merrill/Prentice-Hall, 1996.

McLuhan, M. *Understanding Media.* New York: McGraw-Hill, 1965, 1964.

Mifflin, L. "Study Finds Educational TV Lends Preschoolers Even Greater Advantages," *New York Times,* May 31, 1995, p. B8.

Minow, N. and C. LaMay. *Abandoned in the Wasteland: Children, Television and the First Amendment.* New York: Hill and Wang, 1995.

Postman, N. *Teaching as a Conserving Activity.* New York: Delta (Dell), 1980.

Smith, L. "Click on to Our Nation's History," *Parade Magazine,* September 29, 1996, pp. 8–10.

Social Education, November, 1972, vol. 36 no. 7

Time On-Line and CIESNET, May 23, 1995.

Zuckerman, D. W., and R. E. Horn. *The Guide to Simulation Games for Education and Training.* Cambridge, MA: Information Resources, Inc., 1970.

Handy Internet Print References

Barron, A. and K. Ivers. *The Internet and Instruction: Activities and Ideas.* Englewood, CO: Libraries Unlimited, 1996. Just what the title implies, including chapters on Internet activities for students and on-line projects for teachers. Resources and activities are divided into four chapters—science and mathematics, language arts, social studies and geography, music and art.

Gilster, P. *The New Internet Navigator.* New York: John Wiley & Sons, 1995. Covers all aspects of the Internet, with two chapters on using electronic mail, one on listserves, and one on the web. Also includes a useful appendix of dial-up Internet service providers.

Hahn, H. and R. Stout. *The Internet Complete Reference.* Berkeley, CA: Osborne-McGraw Hill, 1994. Comprehensive guide with chapters on various aspects of using the Internet as well as a brief explanatory chapter on the web and its use. Lengthy catalogue of Internet resources (likely to be outdated by the time you read this!)

Maxwell, B. *Washington Online: How to Access the Federal Government on the Internet. Washington Congressional Quarterly* (latest year). Useful, up-to-date information, particularly for those education web sites aimed at teachers and school access.

White, C. "Special Section: Technology and Social Studies," *Social Education,* vol. 61, no. 3, March, 1997, pp. 147–175.

Television Shows

"Assignment: The World." Produced by WXXI, Rochester, NY.

"Channel One." Produced by Whittle Communications, Knoxville, TN.

"CNN Newsroom." Produced by Turner Broadcasting System, Atlanta, GA.

"What's in the News." Produced by WPSX-TV, Penn State Television, University Park, PA.

Exciting and Useful Social Studies Software, pp. 197–199

Ancient Lands, 1995, Microsoft, grades 4 and above. One Microsoft Way, Redmond, WA, 98052-6399

More of a database than anything else, this disk focuses on ancient Greece, Rome, and Egypt with legends, stories, guided tours of various sites, and pictures. Well researched, lovely graphics, and easy to use. $29.95

Decisions, Decisions Series (seven titles), 1986, 1987, Tom Snyder Productions, grades 5 and above. 80 Coolidge Hill Road, Watertown, MA 02172.

Simulates various content and concept areas—the budget process, colonizing the new world, American foreign policy, American immigration, Revolutionary War, television and media ethics, urbanization. $120 per disk

Ellis Island, 1995, Microsoft, grades 4 and above. One Microsoft Way, Redmond, WA 98052-6399

Provides reams of documents, pictures, and personal accounts of the immigrant experience, primarily from the late 1800s to the 1950s. $98

History and Culture of Africa, 1995, Queue, Inc., grades 6–9. 338 Commerce Dr., Fairfield, CT, 06432

Introduces the diversity of life on this vast continent of which most Americans are quite unaware. Program has four sections—people, history, maps, and reading material (much of which is also available in Spanish).

Kids and the Environment, 1994, Tom Snyder Productions, grades 2–6. 80 Coolidge Hill Road, Watertown, MA 02172

Simulation of a local pollution crisis that kids address by studying about and making decisions regarding recycling, landfills, and civic responsibility. $99.95

Maya Quest, 1995, Minnesota Educational Computer Consortium, grades 5 and above. 3490 Levington Ave., St. Paul, MN 55126

Combines multimedia resources and a simulated bike trip game to learn about the ancient Mayas, their culture, and their use of archaeology. Fun, but difficult at times to escape from the sites in the system. Includes an Internet connection to expand the material. $59.95

Neighborhood Mapmachine, 1997, Tom Snyder Productions, grades 1-5. 80 Coolidge Hill Road, Watertown, MA 02172

Enables students to make their own maps and reinforces early map reading skills with a variety of activities. A number of ready-made maps are available for solving mysteries and for editing and exploring. $99.95

Only the Best, by S. B. and G. W. Neill, is an annual guide to the highest-rated educational software. There is a cumulative 1985-89 guide and an annual guide for each subsequent year. New York: R. R. Bowker Publishing.

Oregon Trail II, 1995, Minnesota Educational Computer Consortium, grades 5 and above. 3490 Levington Avenue N., St. Paul, MN 55126

This "old chestnut" continues to be updated and improved. Excellent problems to solve, better photographs, and some three-dimensional images. Still one of the best pieces available. $74.95

Passage to Vietnam, 1995, Against All Odds Production/Total Research Corp., grades 4 and above. P.O. Box 1189, Sausalito, CA 94966-1189

A travelogue and, to a degree, database on modern Vietnam. Beautiful photographs by noted photographers and interesting music combine with fascinating three-dimensional graphics to produce a lovely package. Unfortunately, it is very slow and may lose impatient students before they get interested. $39.95

Picture Atlas of the World, 1995, National Geographic Society, grades 4 and above. 1145 17th Street NW, Washington, DC 20036

A beautiful database with all the resources of National Geographic behind it. Students can explore the world, create their own tours, and revel in the sparkling photographs. $69.95

The Ripple That Changed American History, 1987, Tom Snyder Productions, grades 5-12.

This is a game in which students try to pinpoint and stop disturbances that are disrupting historical events. Using the accompanying *Encyclopedic Dictionary of American History* for help, they search for the elusive ripple through clues on history. A bit hard to master at first, but fun to travel through time. $70

Sim Town, 1995, Software for Kids, grades 4-7. 2 Theatre Square, Orinda, CA

Students can work together or alone in building a town. Easy to use with important conceptual issues presented. $36.95

SkyTrip America, 1996, Discovery Multimedia, grades 4-8. Discovery Channel, Box 55742, Indianapolis, IN 46205

Students "tour" panoramous of the American landscape, learning about events, places, and people from history. There are 12 panoramas divided by geographic regions. $39.95

Where in _____ is Carmen San Diego? Broderbund Software, all grades. P.O. Box 12947, San Rafael, CA 94913-2947

Now includes a junior detective edition for grades K-2 that is easy to use and enjoy. Wildly successful series of software is described more on page 257. $49.95

These are not the only good pieces of software, although there isn't a huge number. These, though, are rewarding, educational, and fun, and the publishers are reputable and educationally concerned.

Chapter Eleven

MAP AND GLOBE SKILLS

Educational disciplines like mathematics and reading have certain fundamental ideas that serve as the foundation for all further learning. In the social studies, however, it has been very difficult for educators to agree on what such fundamentals might be. Nevertheless, it could be argued that a basic understanding of maps and globes is vital in the social studies curriculum. With an understanding of the locations of the earth's great land and water masses, all other areas of social studies can be placed in a workable, unambiguous frame. The land and water masses provide a common beginning that is not subject to reinterpretation based on new historical or economic discoveries.

Without the basic geographic frame, economic conditions, drought, war, historical events, and political divisions become muddled. For example, if a student reads the newspaper or sees a news story on television, a rudimentary knowledge of the globe will help place the incident. From here, the student can surmise what problems might be inherent in the location of the incident.

Economic problems are often as much a reflection of difficult terrain and climate as of human intransigence. Issues such as crop failures or marketing difficulties can be at least appreciated, if not fully understood, through geography. Therefore it is essential that the skill of working with maps and globes be reinforced on a regular basis from the primary grades through high school.

As discussed in Chapter 2, geography has become a source of great educational concern since 1985. This is as much a political issue in education as it is an intellectual one, but the concern here is with teaching and learning. Using the guidelines for geographic education discussed previously will make this chapter even more useful. This chapter addresses three concerns: (1) teaching and using the globe; (2) using maps; and (3) sequential development of map and globe skills.

Directional mastery is vital for any study of maps or globes. The chapter discusses ways to develop directional skills in young children, along with an understanding of simple map terms and symbols. Throughout the chapter, different kinds of maps are presented, including political maps, road maps, Landsat maps, special purpose maps, and puzzle maps. Finally, because map and globe skills are cumulative, the chapter presents a possible sequence for teaching the use of map and globe skills and geographic terms.

THE GLOBE

The first part of the chapter deals with globe study in isolation; later in the chapter map and globe studies intertwine.

Ideally, a globe should be available in every classroom for students to handle or play with informally. Too often globes are out of reach, to be used only with permission. The globe often sits gathering dust until some appropriate exercise is devised that requires its use. What does this say to children? First, it says that globes are not toys. Second, it says that globes should be used for a specific purpose only. Third, it says that geography is not fun; it is serious business. That may not be the teacher's intention, but it is the message that comes through. Many teachers clearly value an orderly classroom, with everything in its place, more than they do children's creative exploration. Order is certainly superior to classroom chaos, but how far must a teacher go to ensure it? Holding a globe hostage may be going too far in maintaining orderliness.

Teaching Globes

For the primary grades particularly, and even for older students, a teaching globe should be used. What makes a globe a teaching globe? First, it should clearly differentiate land and water, and little else. The globe should ideally be in two colors—one for land and the other for water. The water should consist of ocean areas, although some of the larger rivers may be depicted.

Photos from space provide a thrilling view of the earth, a spinning globe.

Second, a teaching globe should be nonpolitical. For children, especially young children, most globes are too busy. They include countries, states, rivers, cities, capitals, inland bodies of water, and islands, to name just a few items. The extensiveness of the globe may overwhelm and confuse children while providing little understanding of geography. Finally, a teaching globe can be manipulated in a variety of ways. It can be removed from its cradle to allow students to alter the angle of the globe's axis or to view all areas of the globe without obstruction. Some teaching globes can be marked with various media, like chalk, tempera paint, or clay (for building mountains). Finally, manipulation may refer to tactility; a topographic globe can be kinesthetically appealing.

With a teaching globe, students can discern the two halves of the world: the water half (Southern Hemisphere) and the land half (Northern Hemisphere). This should be pointed out and the globe examined individually by all youngsters. The most important part of the examination should be the initial exposure to the great land masses and the great water masses. This must be constantly reinforced in the primary grades, but it should be introduced in kindergarten, along with good photographs of the planet taken from space. A teacher should also deal with the position of the sun when first introducing and working with the globe. Students need not know that the earth is tilted at 23.5 degrees, but they should know that the earth is tilted and that this is what causes the change of seasons, *not* how close the sun is to the earth. Many students (and some adults) erroneously believe that the sun is closest to the earth in the summer and farthest away in the winter. This lack of understanding may lead students to believe that the sun actually sets somewhere, rather than this being merely a convenient expression to describe our ability to see the sun only about half the time during a 24-hour period.

A variety of sun activities can be done with younger students to prove that the sun is always in the southern sky in our part of the world and that in the Northern Hemisphere the sun is at its lowest point in the sky on December 22. Some good ideas can be found in James and Crape's *Geography for Today's Children.*

A popular exercise is to turn off the lights, draw the shades, and shine a flashlight on a globe cradled at the proper angle. Students will see that the angle of the earth's axis causes more or less light to be absorbed by the earth, warming the ground much more in summer. To test this, students can use a shadow stick to show the seasonal path of the sun. James and Crape describe this exercise:

> A shadow stick can be made by fastening a stick the size of a pencil or a long nail to a flat piece of wood about six inches square. Place the shadow stick on a desk or table near a window where the sun will shine on it during the day. Under the board, place a large piece of paper on which the class can mark the length of the shadow and the date. The observation must take place at the same time of day each time the record is made. September 22 is a good date to begin recording the length and position of the shadow. Thereafter, make monthly observations and records. Summarize the observations made so that the children will understand the significance of what they are observing. (37)

WIRE MESH AND BALLOON GLOBES

A globe is a model of the earth. With satellite photos this is easier to explain than it once was, but students may still need reinforcement. A toy car or a dollhouse can be used to represent the idea of a model. Measurements and comparisons can be made between the toy car or dollhouse and a real car or house. Students can see that the car or house is not real but represents a scale model of the real thing. The globe is similar in that respect.

To reinforce this further, teachers may wish to build their own working globes for further student manipulation. This can be done in a number of ways, but two useful ideas are the wire mesh globe and the balloon globe. The first involves fine-mesh chicken wire wound around a small pole, such as a sawed-off broom handle, which serves as the axis of the globe. The mesh can be manipulated to resemble the earth's shape; different colors of tissue paper can be put into the wire mesh to form the various land masses. This obviously is not terribly accurate, but it allows students to manipulate and practice with a sphere to further their understanding.

The balloon globe, which has the same function, requires a thick, large balloon. After it is inflated, strips of wet tissue paper can be used to cover the balloon. Different thicknesses of tissue can make the globe more topographically accurate. When the paper has dried, the globe can be painted to reasonably reflect the great land and water masses of the earth.

INFLATABLE GLOBES

An excellent and low-cost globe that is also fun is an inflatable globe. These are sold as beach balls or simply as inflatable globes through travel stores, discount stores, and some teacher resource stores. Though the globes are often too crowded with information, their ready availability, low cost (under $5), and fun aspects make them a handy item for teachers to purchase and use. They can be used in the classroom or on the playground.

Directional Mastery

Three terms are important for student understanding about the globe: axis, equator, and hemisphere. According to James and Crape, the axis can be demonstrated by piercing a rubber ball with a long knitting needle. The teacher can then rotate the ball counterclockwise on its axis just as the earth rotates.

The equator should be introduced by its root word—equal. Cutting an apple into halves can be used to introduce and accentuate the idea of equal and the words derived from it—equidistant, equality, equator. What would an equator divide if we had one on our globe? The imaginary line that divides the earth into the Northern and the Southern Hemispheres is called the equator.

Hemispheres can be examined by dividing rubber balls or oranges in half. Together the two parts form a sphere, or round object. Dividing them in two makes two half-spheres, or hemispheres. It should be noted that the earth is sometimes divided into eastern and western hemispheres by an imaginary line running from the North Pole to the South Pole.

All this requires the introduction of cardinal directions at the primary level. How can this be done?

First, children must feel oriented within the classroom, the school, and their immediate environs. Children in grades K–1 should feel comfortable and familiar with the classroom setting and the objects within it. Simple items like the flag, the various areas of the room, and the cupboards or cabinets should be labeled, identified, and introduced. Only after establishing that kind of familiarity should the relatively complex question of direction be introduced.

What is so hard about directions? Directional mastery requires listening skills, the ability to differentiate, and the ability to apply differences. These complex place-location skills must be mastered before further globe or map use is attempted.

When students are asked to move or to trace certain directions, the teacher can minimize listening problems by asking students to repeat the directions or requests before they are carried out (see Chapter 12). This method also helps the teacher focus more discreetly on specific learning problems.

Before mastering the cardinal directions, students need to know right, left, forward, and backward. Forward and backward should be no problem, but for most kindergarten students and many first graders discrimination between right and left is still difficult. To introduce the concept, the teacher should stand in the front of the room facing *away* from the children, who should stand by their desks facing the *same* direction as the teacher. This eliminates the confusion that inevitably occurs when the teacher faces the class, making the children's perspective of right and left the opposite of the teacher's. This technique should be repeated daily for *at least* a week until there is relative mastery among a majority of the students. Additional techniques for mastering right and left can vary. Testing and application techniques might include the "Simon Says" games and the "Hokey-Pokey" song ("You put your right foot in," and so on).

From there the teacher might make a series of large-group or individual assignments so that students can apply the principles at hand. For example, a group of students could stand together and move on the teacher's command in a kind of synchronized movement. Small groups of four or five could be given a worksheet of exercises like these for their members to carry out:

1. Tell a group member to take four steps to the right. Did the person do it right or not?
2. Tell someone to go six steps left, two backward, and one to the right. Was everything okay?
3. Tell someone to touch his or her right hand to a chair with that person's left foot off the ground.

Can all of you do this?

The teacher also could organize a scavenger hunt in the classroom or on school grounds with clues based on following directions of right, left, forward, and backward. Students could participate individually or in small teams.

CARDINAL DIRECTIONS

Once the basic directions are mastered, the teacher can introduce the cardinal directions—east, west, north, and south. This can be done and reinforced in many ways. Some of the techniques are similar to those already mentioned, with the substitution of east and west for right and left, and so on. Some teachers like to label the walls of the room with the directions, but because many buildings do not squarely face in a cardinal direction, this can mean labeling the corners of the room.

A good orientation is to take students outside in the morning to track the sun from its generally easterly direction across the sky to its generally westerly direction. Because the students should have mastered right and left by now, the relationship between the directions should be emphasized. If one is facing due east, north will always be to one's left and south to one's right. Thus knowing only *one* direction allows one to know all directions. Students can then see the importance of a compass and can test its use in small groups.

Caution should be taken not to confuse north with up or south with down. A globe can be used to clarify this problem somewhat by illustrating that "up" refers to *away from* the earth and "down" is *toward the center of* the earth.

Introductory globe study should teach introductory rules of climate and weather. Defining the location of the poles and the equator is a natural introduction to a discussion of climate. This could be supplemented by pictures or filmstrips of life at the equator and at the poles. The relationship of climate to the equator should be *introduced* in the primary grades and *developed* in the intermediate grades. As one moves north or south from the equator, temperatures grow gradually colder. There are, of course, other factors that affect weather generalizations, most notably altitude and ocean currents.

Remember that globe and map study should be used to illustrate how people live. The object of social studies is to understand people better—both ourselves and others. Map and globe study reinforce this and can be made more interesting by keeping it in mind. Without playful speculation, globes may become tedious and boring.

Playing with the Globe

Left to their own devices, students will spin a fixed-axis globe or run their hands over a cradled globe, topographic or not. This should not only be allowed but encouraged. It should *not* be required or assigned, since that takes the fun away, but encouragement can come in the form of participation. A child whose hands are crawling around a globe may be imagining what it is like in the place where the hands stop.

Imagine the following situation: Three students—Paul, Maria, and Lester—are playing with the globe before class begins. Paul has his eyes closed and runs his hand over the globe. He stops his hand and looks where he is—Kenya. (At least he did not drown at sea!) Paul could just go on, but stimulating low-pressure questions from his teacher, Ms. Chernik, encourage him to think about how climate is determined. (This kind of activity might be appropriate at a third-, fourth-, or fifth-grade level.)

Ms. Chernik:	What do you think Kenya is like?
Paul:	I don't know; I never heard of it.
Ms. Chernik:	But it's near the equator—what could that mean?
Maria:	That it's hot?
Ms. Chernik:	Yes—and what else?
Lester:	I don't know.
Ms. Chernik:	If you wanted to find out, where could you look?
Lester:	The encyclopedia? Or an on-line site?

Ms. Chernik:	Okay. Let me just add that many of the world's wild animals are found in Kenya. What else might you say about it?
Maria:	That there are jungles.
Ms. Chernik:	Maybe—but what would there not be as much of, compared to, say, our state?
Paul:	Cars? Roads?
Ms. Chernik:	Maybe. If you look for information on Kenya, I'll be glad to help you if you need it.

Note that although Ms. Chernik has applied no pressure, the application of research to basic knowledge of climate can be seen already.

Longitude and Latitude

Two concepts that are best taught by using a globe, *not* a map, are longitude and latitude. Although they require similar skills to master, longitude and latitude must be taught separately. Until one is mastered, the other should not even be introduced, or great confusion may result. Many geographers feel that latitude should be dealt with first because the area described by lines of latitude is roughly equal around the globe, whereas lines of longitude are uneven—wider apart at the equator and reduced to nothing at both poles. On the other hand, longitude is an easier concept to introduce to students because it can be related to time zones, which most students have some knowledge of already. Either way, it is imperative that they be taught separately.

LONGITUDE

Longitude should be introduced at the fifth- or sixth-grade level, or at the fourth-grade level at the earliest. The easiest way to introduce this concept is by discussing the time zones. Why do we have them? How did the whole world agree on them? Ask students how many time zones the world has. (The answer: 24, because there are 24 hours in a day.) The earth, as we know, is shaped like a huge ball or globe. In fourth-grade mathematics, most students learn that a circle has 360 degrees. If we wanted to make 24 time zones, how many degrees would be in each zone? (Answer: 15.) Longitude measures in degrees around the earth from east to west.

In the 1800s, distances in our nation were measured with Washington, DC, as the point of reference. In Italy, Rome was the point of reference for distance; in France, it was Paris. All these measurements made trade and travel by sea particularly confusing for ships crossing the ocean to these countries. It became obvious to the governments of a number of countries that some sort of standardization was needed, so in 1884 the members of an international conference held in Washington agreed to have one reference point for measuring all distances around the globe; that point was Greenwich, England. The imaginary line running north and south through Greenwich is called the prime meridian, and thus all distances would be east or west of Greenwich. Today,

Greenwich is a district of London, so we essentially measure from London. Some teachers use London as a mnemonic device to remember what longitude represents. Thus the distances east and west of LONdon are LONgitude. Another device is to remember that LONG lines represent LONGitude.

How many degrees can we measure east from London? This is similar to the riddle "How far can a dog run into the woods?" The answer: "Halfway— then he starts running out." So it is with longitude. One can measure halfway around the earth (180 degrees) in an easterly direction. After that one is closer to west of Greenwich, so measurements are made in a westerly direction.

To reinforce concepts of longitude, it may be appropriate to assign additional work in mathematics with circles and the measurement of angles. One additional concept that makes longitude somewhat easier to work with is the fact that as one moves east or west of the prime meridian in a straight line, climate is seen as generally the same.

The concept of longitude is dealt with again in Chapter 12 with regard to chronological skills.

LATITUDE

Latitude is measured from the equator: How many degrees north of the equator can be measured? (Answer: 90 degrees, which puts us at the North Pole and one quarter of the way around the earth.) To introduce latitude, the teacher might draw chalk lines of latitude on a teaching globe. What might students notice about them? That they are the same distance apart around the world and that, unlike the lines of longitude, the lines of latitude never meet.

Degrees of latitude are about 70 miles apart. Students can identify cities of the world and then estimate how far they are from the equator by counting the lines of latitude between them. After determining distance, students could reflect on the climate of these cities, the clothing people might wear, and what their houses might look like.

As we move farther from the equator, the hours of daylight will be more unevenly distributed. For example, Reykjavik, Iceland, has about 20 hours of daylight on June 21, whereas Pittsburgh has about 14 hours. In late December, Pittsburgh has about 10 hours of daylight and Reykjavik has only about three hours. Despite these disparities, every place on the earth receives the same number of daylight hours over the course of a year. The difference lies in the uneven distribution of the hours of daylight.

We have talked of climatic changes due to latitude. Other effects of latitude are length of growing season, type of precipitation, type of crops, and overall differences in lifestyle. These are fertile areas for student research, either individually or in small groups.

The concepts of latitude and longitude are made meaningful only by continued application. Latitude and longitude can be made fun for students through combined search parties. Give students a measurement and ask them to find out what is located there and to hypothesize what it would look like if they visited there. Students could also use the newspaper to find places of interest and then determine their longitude and latitude. Longitude and latitude can be reinforced with a map, but they should be introduced only with a globe. In addition, they should not be pointed out on the map unless they are already clearly understood by the class.

MAPS

The use of maps rightly starts with an understanding of direction and of what a map represents. The globe is presented as a model of the earth, but a map is somewhat more abstract. For example, most maps are distorted because they fail to account for the curvature of the earth.

Many children and adults see maps as a foreign language and thus do not ever attempt to master map skills. They convince themselves that there is something mystical about these spatial representations that will never be revealed to them.

Map use should begin with the simple representation of what a map is. Imagine that one is a fly on the ceiling looking down at a student's desk in the classroom. The direct overhead angle will alter the way things appear, but generally all objects will be identifiable. If a student wished to show others what his or her desk looked like, an overhead view would be preferable. Such a view is shown in Figure 11.1.

Students should see that a map is a picture of reality, one that is reduced to some degree so that the picture can include all necessary data. Because students can just walk around the classroom looking at desks, a map of this type may have no real use other than as an exercise. But if one wanted to let one's parents or pen pals in another town know what one's school desk looked like, this kind of map might be useful.

ACTIVITY 1: MAKING A CLASSROOM MAP

As a group project, the class could make a map of the classroom itself, or possibly the school and grounds, on a large piece of butcher paper. The map should be small enough to fit into a corner of the room, yet large enough for youngsters to walk on in following map directions.

Time: 1–2 weeks.

Materials: Butcher paper (about one eighth to one fourth the size of the classroom); chalk or crayons.

Procedure: To make a classroom map, students must know the four basic directions (left, right, forward, and backward) and must be able to follow them. Before making the map, students must examine the classroom closely, noting the location of objects in relation to each other. The teacher should designate the front, back, inside, and outside walls on the map. Then the teacher should ask, "What is in the front of the room? How close to the front is it, and where should it be drawn on our map?"

To test locations, students should be encouraged to go from the map to the classroom itself in order to place objects on the map in their proper perspective. The teacher should use the map on a regular basis to develop and reinforce the basic map skills and directions.

As a more advanced project, teachers might consider a school map that would include the general area surrounding the school. Before they begin, students should take a walk around the area to note trees, landmarks, and adjacent buildings. Students should be encouraged to note other landmarks of the area they observe on their walks to and from school, such as businesses, traffic lights, or an empty lot.

Again using a large piece of butcher paper, the map of the school area should be drawn and checked as in Activity 1. A school map contains the additional message that learning does not occur just in the school building alone. Time should be allowed for students to test their directional knowledge using the map. It can be filled in with as many personal landmarks as desired. For example, all students should draw their homes, or the directions to their homes, if they are not included on the map. Police and fire stations, the public library, parks, and popular stores all can be put on the map, as well as other important landmarks. Students can test each other on map use when they have free time. For example, Alex could ask Yvonne in what directions she would go to reach school from Michael's house. Her answer could be tested on the map by walking on it and noting the directions.

FIGURE 11.1
An Aerial View of Mark's Desk

FIGURE 11.2

Examples of Symbols That Might Be Used on a School Environs Map

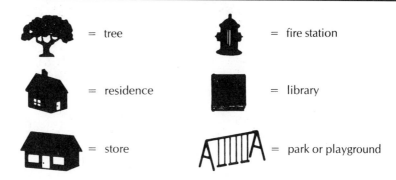

Map Symbols

Part of drawing a map is the use of symbols. The teacher should explain that drawing each house or tree in detail is time consuming and unnecessary. Remember that a map is a picture conveying a place to others in an abbreviated way. Thus symbols are adequate if they represent objects all students are familiar with. For example, the symbols shown in Figure 11.2 might be used on the school environs map. These need not be the only symbols used; more could be added as students desire. Map symbols and terms should be introduced early because their functions grow more complex as maps become more abstract.

A symbol can be more abstract than a caricature of a tree. Colors, for example, are often symbolic—the color blue often represents water and the color green vegetation. Although there is nothing that says water must be represented as blue, it is so commonly done that it seems appropriate to follow this convention most of the time. A teacher might want to represent water in red or yellow after students are comfortable with map use just to see how alert they are in reading map keys.

Special Purpose and Political Maps

Special purpose and political maps usually have a number of symbols, many of which reflect the special purpose of the map. Thus, not reading the map key or legend carefully can make map reading an exercise in futility. An example of a special purpose map is shown in Figure 11.3. This map of the world highlights oil, natural gas, and coal regions with symbols. These are uncommon symbols on a common map. Without an understanding of key and symbol use, the whole point of the map is lost. Another type of map (Figure 11.4) shows the projection of how congressional seats may change from state to state based on population shifts that will be shown in the Census of 2000. This type of map is common in American history and political study.

FIGURE 11.3
Map of the World Showing Oil, Natural Gas, and Coal Regions

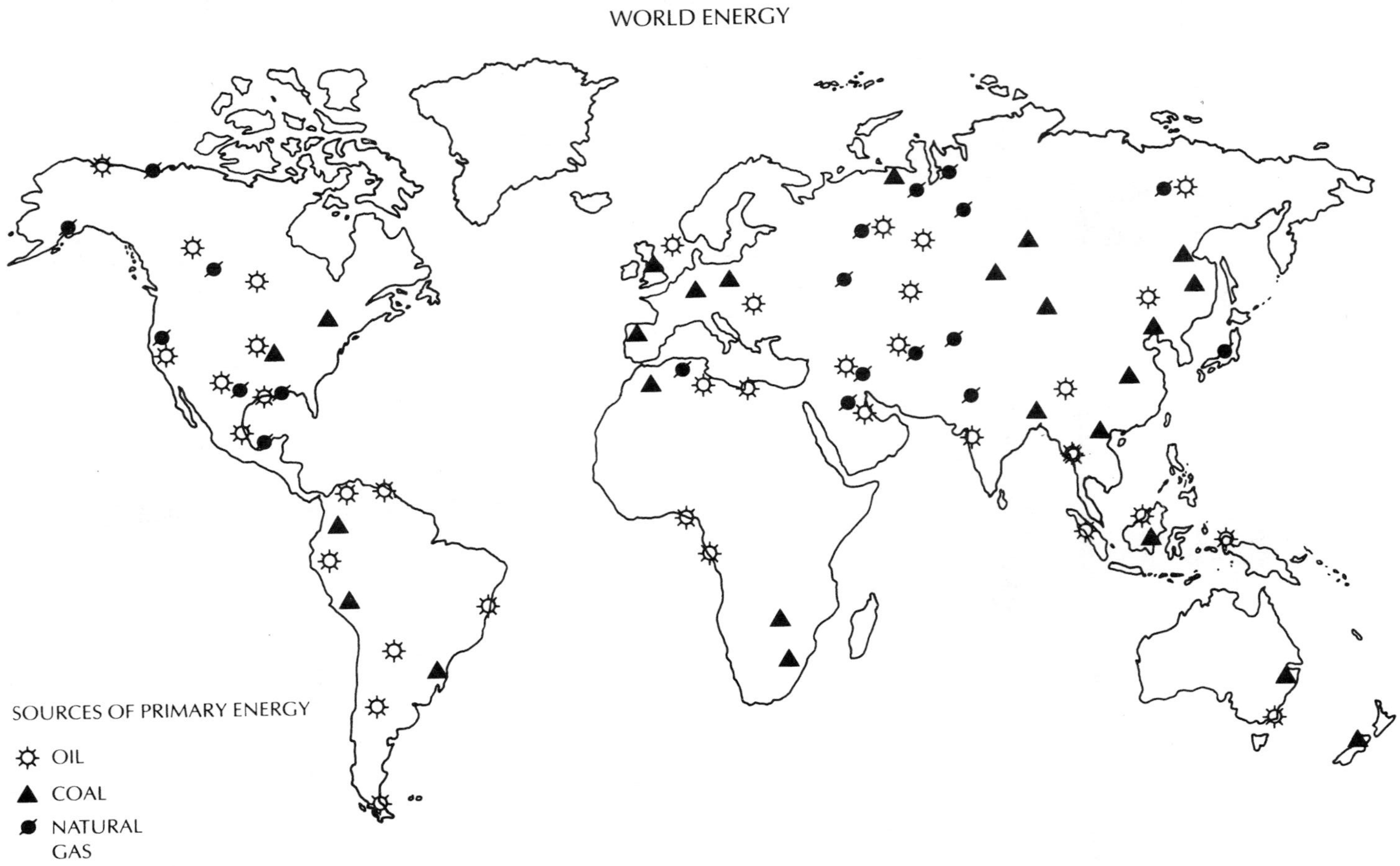

WORLD ENERGY

SOURCES OF PRIMARY ENERGY

☼ OIL
◄ COAL
● NATURAL GAS

FIGURE 11.4

Which States May Gain, Lose House Seats

Based on the latest Census Bureau projection of the United States population in 2000, released in 1994, the Congressional Research Service has projected which states may gain or lose seats in the House of Representatives.

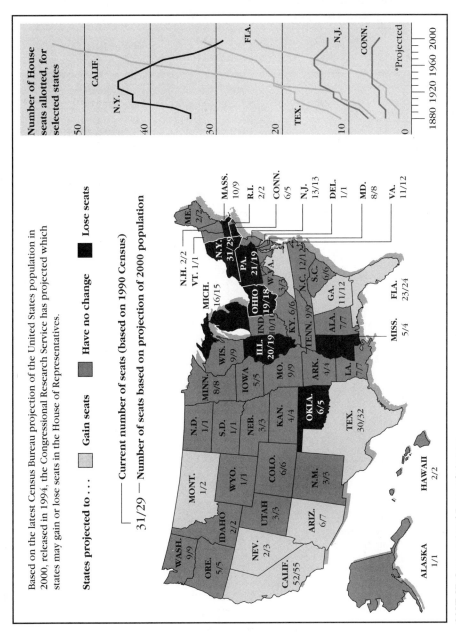

SOURCE: Congressional Research Service

FIGURE 11.5

Pictorial and abstract symbols for roadways, airports, and schools. Also represented are point, line, and area symbols

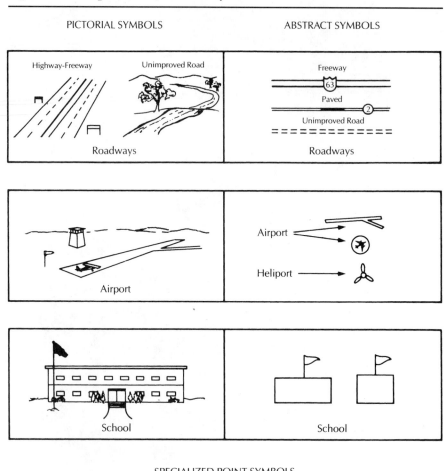

PICTORIAL SYMBOLS

ABSTRACT SYMBOLS

Highway-Freeway

Unimproved Road

Roadways

Freeway

Paved

Unimproved Road

Roadways

Airport

Airport

Heliport

School

School

SPECIALIZED POINT SYMBOLS

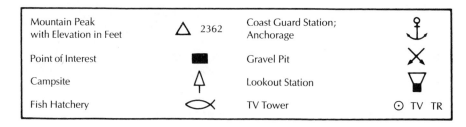

Mountain Peak with Elevation in Feet	△ 2362	Coast Guard Station; Anchorage	⚓
Point of Interest	■	Gravel Pit	✕
Campsite	△	Lookout Station	▽
Fish Hatchery	⊶	TV Tower	⊙ TV TR

Symbols can be used for a variety of features. Cultural features might be shown pictorially or abstractly, as in the symbols for school, airport, and roadways shown in Figure 11.5. Other cultural features that might be depicted in this manner are churches, buildings, railroads, bridges, docks, pipelines, and cultivated fields.

Natural features such as lakes can also be displayed in a pictorial or abstract way. Other natural features that can be shown in this manner are islands, waterfalls, river mouths, deltas, mountains, valleys, deserts, and marshes.

Specialized point, line, and area symbols are shown in Figure 11.3

Geographic Terms

Symbols, of course, are useless without an understanding of what is being symbolized. So, along with studying symbols, students must study map terms. Table 11.1 lists 34 important map terms and a number of symbols, along with the approximate grade level for introducing, developing, and reinforcing each concept. Some of the most common terms are mountain, island, peninsula, continent, cape, ocean, river, lake, valley, plateau, bay, gulf, mesa, plain, canyon, isthmus, and desert.

When one turns from simple maps to more complex maps, the key to understanding is the student's ability to *read* the map, not to have memorized the concept depicted.

Nevertheless, there are a few things that all students must recognize and be able to name in order to establish a general understanding of maps throughout the elementary *and* secondary school years. These are the continents and the ocean areas.

THE CONTINENTS

Depending on the geographer, there are either six or seven continents—North America, South America, Australia, Africa, Antarctica, Europe, and Asia, or Eurasia, which combines the latter two. What constitutes a continent? A continent is a huge land mass—at least one million square miles—separated from other land masses usually by water, although a mountain range is the natural divide between Europe and Asia. Often students will look at a world map and ask, "Why is Australia a continent and Greenland is not?" If one looks at the globe, the answer is obvious: Australia dwarfs Greenland in size, but because maps distort global representations near the poles, it *appears* that Greenland is larger. To alleviate this, emphasize that the globe is the accurate representation of the earth, and use the globe for learning the continents. If students prefer their answer in statistics, give the respective areas of Greenland and Australia. Obviously, there is no comparison.

TABLE 11.1

Sequence for Introducing Map Terms and Symbols*

MAP SYMBOLS	K	1	2	3	4	5	6
Land and water colors	I	D	R	R	R	R	R
Semipictorial symbols	I	D	R	R	R	R	R
Conventional abstract symbols			I	D	D	R	R
Tracing routes		I	I	D	D	D	R
Keys and legends			I	D	D	R	R
Political maps			I	I	D	D	R
Special purpose maps				I	D	D	R
MAP PROJECTIONS							
Understanding projections					I	D	D
Using projections					I	D	D
MAP AND GLOBE TERMS							
Mountain	I	I	D	D	D	R	R
Island	I	I	D	D	R	R	R
Continent		I	I	D	D	R	R
Cape		I	I	I	I	D	D
Peninsula		I	I	I	I	D	D
Ocean	I	I	D	D	R	R	R
Lake	I	I	D	D	R	R	R
River	I	I	D	D	R	R	R
Valley			I	I	D	R	R
Canyon					I/D	D	D
Isthmus			I	I	D	D	R
Bay				I	D	D	R
Gulf				I	D	D	R
Mesa					I	D	R
Plateau					I/D	D	R
Plain				I	D	D	R
Fjord							I
Glacier					I/D	D	R
Desert		I	D		D	D	R
Mouth					I	D	R
Source					D	D	R
Sea	I	I	I	D	R	R	R
Crater					I		D
Estuary					I	D	D
Current					I/D	D	R
Continental shelf						I	D
Sound					I	I	D
Delta					I	I	D
Strait					I	I	D
Tributary					I/D	D	D
Steppe							I
Altitude/elevation				I	D	D	R
Tundra					I	I	D
Tropic					I/D	D	R

*Approximate grade levels for introducing (I), developing (D), and reinforcing (R) each term.

SOURCE: From curriculum guidelines of the Marple-Newton, PA, School District, 1981.

THE OCEANS

The Atlantic, the Pacific, the Indian, and the Arctic oceans really constitute one interconnected ocean, which for the sake of convenience is divided into four ocean areas. The questions often arise, "Why is there no Antarctic Ocean?" and "Why is there no Arctic continent?" The answer is relatively simple. We know that if the icecaps at the poles were somehow to melt, we would find land underneath the ice covering Antarctica and only water under the north polar cap.

Scale

An important skill to master in map reading is decoding the scale of miles (or, in the large classroom map, the scale of feet). This is another type of symbol that is essential to map study and is extremely complex.

The classroom or school map activity (pages 297–298) could be used to introduce scaled distance. The teacher might establish that one foot on the map is equal to four feet in actuality. A map of this size is useful in the classroom, but a bit awkward to carry around the school or to children's homes. To alleviate this problem, students should attempt to reduce the scale of the map further. If the dimensions of the room have been determined and the initial scale of measurement established, it should be relatively easy to establish a new scale to fit the space requirements of a sheet of paper.

Once this exercise is understood by all the children, the teacher may wish to introduce the scale of miles, or could postpone this step until the next grade level. This decision cannot be made by one teacher alone; it demands coordinated curriculum development among the entire school staff.

A good exercise for introducing the scale of miles requires a map with measured lengths of string attached at one city or town—preferably the students' hometown. A six-inch length of string might stand for 50 miles; twelve inches, 100 miles; fifteen inches, 125 miles; and so on. If we were to use State College, Pennsylvania, as the point of attachment (nearly the exact center of Pennsylvania), we would note that the distance from State College to Harrisburg is eleven inches (90 miles); from State College to Pittsburgh is seventeen inches (140 miles); from State College to Philadelphia is twenty-two inches (180 miles); and from State College to Erie is twenty-four inches (200 miles).

This exercise, as noted, is a way to *introduce* the scale of miles. Mastery comes only through continued practice—which is relatively easy when a minimum effort is needed to prepare materials.

Travel Maps

Until students have mastered the scale of miles, travel maps cannot be used in any meaningful fashion. Nevertheless, children can follow route markings while riding in a car, can note the next town to be encountered, and make some estimate of the time between towns.

Once the concept of scaling is understood, however, much can be done with road maps, airline route maps, and shipping maps. These kinds of maps can be easily obtained, often free, from travel agencies or from transportation companies like airlines or shipping firms. Some gasoline companies still provide free road maps, and almost all state bureaus of travel and tourism make their maps relatively easy to obtain.

Travel maps demonstrate to students that maps have a practical function. Students can also have fun planning imaginary trips to various places. This kind of planning involves many other areas of study. It also clearly illustrates to students and teachers that social studies is central to any type of study. To plan a trip, students need reading skills to read the maps, travel literature, and background material. Mathematics skills are needed to calculate the distance and travel time as well as the fuel to be consumed and the amount of cash necessary to cover the costs of the trip. Some knowledge of science is needed to determine weather patterns for planning travel routes and clothing.

ROAD TRAVEL

Travel maps, particularly road maps, describe the various surface roads. Unless the differences in roads are understood, students may take much longer than planned on their trip. Teachers can heighten excitement by making the route planning into a game, with teams competing to determine the fastest, safest route from point A to point B. With the help of state police or an American Automobile Association (AAA) representative, the teacher can determine the "right" answer and award points based on various criteria. Road maps often include inset maps of cities and of the mileage between map points, but these distances are usually based on interstate routes, sometimes negating the aesthetic value of traveling. Such maps also include the locations of state forests, mountains, and parks that might make the trip more interesting. After all, if a traveler is interested only in arriving and not in traveling, the trip will be tiresome rather than an adventure.

AIR TRAVEL

Airline maps cover a much wider area than road maps, which adds a different dimension to trip planning. Good air trip planning requires good consumer skills as well as map skills. Students should consult a newspaper that carries many airline ads or a travel agent in order to see the options available. For example, it may be cheaper to fly from Chicago to Atlanta to Houston rather than directly to Houston; in addition, one has the opportunity to see the capital city of Georgia. Of course, time is another factor to be considered. For some people, the financial savings may not be worth the extra time.

Travel planning does more than just give students skill practice in map use; it also lets them see that maps can be used to add to our enjoyment of the world. Using a map or a globe can impart knowledge about how people live in other parts of the world.

Landsat map of New Orleans.

PUZZLES

To reinforce map use *and* cultural understanding, a teacher can use another kind of learning tool: the jigsaw puzzle. At least two kinds of puzzles are useful—the map puzzle and the geographic scene. The geographic puzzle illustrates life in another country, like any photograph from a social studies book. The puzzle, however, requires closer study, which encourages students to question what is happening in the picture and why. Working on such a puzzle may inspire them to investigate life in another country.

The map puzzle obviously aids in geographic location skills. Most students begin to solve the puzzle (usually in groups of two or three) using the trial-and-error method. The state of Idaho, for example, in a map puzzle of the United States might be tried in all coastline places but rejected. Pieces are fit-

FIGURE 11.6

Landforms of the Continental United States

ted together through luck or shape recognition, not knowledge. Two or three students might take 15 minutes or more to complete the puzzle. Within six weeks, however, almost every student should be able to do the puzzle by himself or herself in less than five minutes. What is even more important is the transference of this knowledge to real maps, real issues in the news, and real history study. If students can picture where Kansas is in relation to Iowa or Washington, DC, they will no longer see Kansas as an amorphous floating land mass located somewhere on the North American continent. With practice, students may get a relatively accurate picture of the geography of Kansas, too.

I have procured puzzle maps of China, Iceland, and the Philippines. Completing them was trial-and-error for me for about the first dozen times, but after that I became somewhat knowledgeable about the provinces of China, the regions of Iceland, and the main islands of the Philippines.

Satellite Maps

In recent years a dramatic new type of map, called the Landsat map, has been created through the technology of satellite transmission. The images are taken from space by using sensing techniques that capture light reflected from the earth's surface. The information sent to earth is stored as digital information on tape and then used to make images on film. Landsat data can identify pollution,

FIGURE 11.7
Native American Lands and Communities

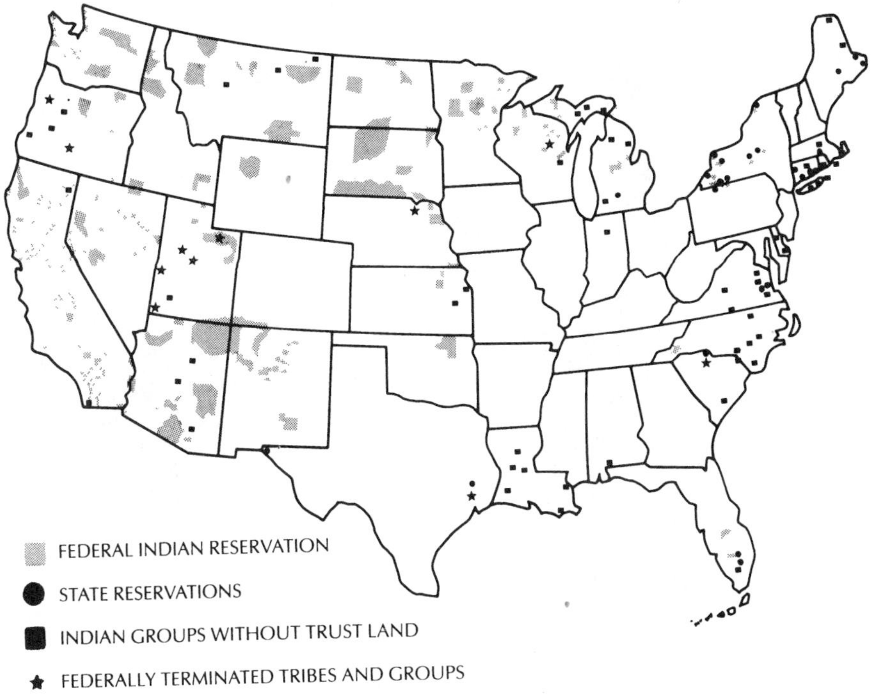

FEDERAL INDIAN RESERVATION

STATE RESERVATIONS

INDIAN GROUPS WITHOUT TRUST LAND

FEDERALLY TERMINATED TRIBES AND GROUPS

ground water, minerals, ecological changes, snow pack, population density, crop growth, and fault lines. Landsat photos and the information obtained from them are available from the U.S. Geological Survey (see References).

Map Use in Inquiry

Once all these different maps are introduced, they must be used correctly. Special purpose maps—including product maps, mineral resource maps, vegetation maps, maps of public lands—may be used to develop and enhance map skills as well as to better understand particular concepts and ideas.

For example, suppose a teacher wished to illustrate the status of Native Americans to a group of gifted fourth graders. The teacher could present a series of map overlays on the overhead projector, using the maps shown in Figures 11.6, 11.7, 11.8, and 11.9. These special purpose maps could be used to illustrate (1) where native American groups are located today; (2) how the forests and vegetation of the United States have altered over 300 years; (3) where different natural resources are located; (4) to summarize, how all these changes have affected Native American lifestyles over the years.

Forest Regions of the Continental United States

OUR FOREST REGIONS

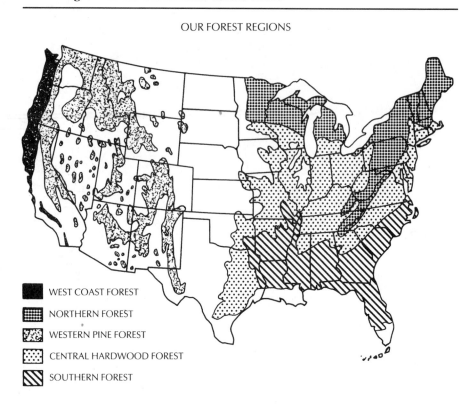

■ WEST COAST FOREST

▦ NORTHERN FOREST

▨ WESTERN PINE FOREST

▨ CENTRAL HARDWOOD FOREST

▧ SOUTHERN FOREST

When these maps are overlaid they form a new picture. Thus, at its best, map use can become inquiry work. Students could raise and answer their own questions. The teacher could pose questions for group discussion or research. These few maps could serve as the basis for days of research, study, discussion, lecture, films. This demonstrates the use of a map as a tool, not an end in itself. Once students master the rudiments of map skills, they can go on to apply and utilize those skills meaningfully and pleasantly.

Sequencing

The use of the skills outlined in this chapter is cumulative and developmental. There are no shortcuts. Table 11.1 offered some general ideas on a realistic sequence for map and globe terms. However, teachers may find they need to modify this sequence if their students are not ready to move on to more complex maneuvers. Like any other skill, one learns simple maneuvers first, then moves to complexity. Babies learn to walk, then to run. There are no ways to reverse this process. Thus teachers must know the level of their students and develop globe

FIGURE 11.9

Average Rainfall and Temperatures for the Continental United States

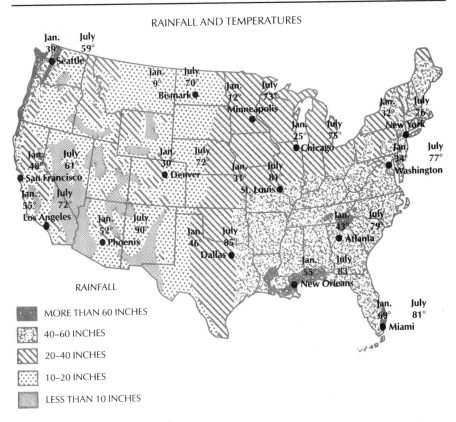

RAINFALL AND TEMPERATURES

RAINFALL

- MORE THAN 60 INCHES
- 40–60 INCHES
- 20–40 INCHES
- 10–20 INCHES
- LESS THAN 10 INCHES

or map mastery sequentially. Some useful notions on sequencing are contained in the books already cited (Hanna et al. and James and Crape). The scope and sequence chart shown in Table 11.2 is adapted from the Marple-Newton, Pennsylvania, School District curriculum guidelines for social studies. The school district, in turn, used the ideas of several map companies, like Rand McNally and Nystrom, as well as the ideas of teachers and consultants.

The sequenced ideas are based on both developmental theories and the practical experiences of teachers and cartographers (map makers). A number of map and globe companies provide ideas and materials for map use. Some are listed in the References.

RECENT FEATURES

Both National Geography Standards and technology software have emerged with more prominence since 1992. The Standards, discussed in Chapter 2

TABLE 11.2
Scope and Sequence Chart for Globe and Map Use*

| | GRADE LEVEL | | | | | | |
SCALE AND DISTANCE	K	1	2	3	4	5	6
Globe as model of earth	I	I	D	R	R	R	R
Maps represent earth	I	I	D	R	R	R	R
Map scale			I	D	D	D	R
Relative distance	I	I	D	D	D	R	R
Determining distance			I	D	D	D	D
Relative size	I	I	D	R	R	R	R
Comparing maps and photographs	I	I	I	D	D	R	R
DIRECTION							
The equator		I	I	D	R	R	R
North and South poles		I	I	D	R	R	R
North arrow		I	I	D	R	R	R
Cardinal directions	I	I	D	D	R	R	R
Intermediate directions			I	D	D	R	R
Latitude and longitude					I	D	D
LOCATION							
Grid system			I	I	D	D	D
Land masses			I	D	D	R	R
Political divisions			I	D	D	D	R
Distributions				I	D	D	D
Relative location	I	I	I	D	D	D	R

*I = Introduce/Explore; D = Develop/Major Instruction; R = Reinforce/Master.
SOURCE: From curriculum guidelines of the Marple-Newton, PA, School District, 1981.

provide vivid pictures, maps, and directions for addressing geography in schools. There are many pieces of software, some described in the previous chapter, but most still have real shortcomings. Many Macintosh computers come with a MacGlobe package that is an acceptable reproducer of national and international maps. There are a number of key omissions, but the package is relatively easy to use.

On-line sites will become more popular both for school and home use. Sites like TripQuest and MapQuest, though useful, may run into school snags because of their inclusive advertising, which is the manner in which these for-profit sites are able to be offered "free" on the Internet.

All these may help to make map and globe skills more exciting and user friendly. So much information can be presented in a succinct manner through the medium of a map. It is a teacher's responsibility to convey that while maintaining the type of enthusiasm that children show when they are eager to spin a globe and imagine where they'll live or visit.

QUESTIONS AND ACTIVITIES

1. This chapter suggests that the teaching globe is the most useful of the globes available. Think of one or two activities that could be substituted if the only globe available is an outdated political globe.

2. What are some of the ways that models could be used to enhance the understanding of the globe, in addition to those mentioned in the chapter?

3. Assuming a student in your fourth-grade classroom has displayed a lack of understanding of cardinal directions, how might you help that youngster to master the concept at this late date?

4. What differences would there be in longitude if the prime meridian ran through Des Moines, Iowa, and St. Louis? What adjustments would teachers, geographers, and others have to make?

5. Design and draw three or four different symbols for a map. Then share your symbols with a colleague to see if they can be understood.

6. Try to locate on a map or globe the geographic formations listed in Table 11.1. What reference materials might help you do this more accurately?

7. Imagine that you have been awarded a travel scholarship to India for the summer. You are to meet with your group in London, but you must get to London on your own. What information would you need to get to London on time and at the least expense?

8. How can maps be used to explain immigration patterns in America or migration patterns within this country?

9. How can maps be used to predict the winner of the next presidential election?

REFERENCES

Hanna, P., R. Sabaroff, G. Davies, and C. Farrar. *Geography in the Teaching of Social Studies.* Boston: Houghton Mifflin, 1966.
James, L. B., and L. Crape. *Geography for Today's Children.* New York: Appleton-Century-Crofts, 1968.

Map and Globe Companies

Department of the Interior
U.S. Geological Survey

Eastern Distribution Branch
1200 S. Eads St.
Arlington, VA 22202

Western Distribution Branch
Box 25286 Federal Center
Denver, CO 80225

George F. Cram Company, Inc.
P.O. Box 426
Indianapolis, IN 46206

C. S. Hammond, Inc.
515 Valley St.
Maplewood, NJ 07040

A. J. Nystrom and Co.
3333 Elston Ave.
Chicago, IL 60618

U.S. Map and Book Company
3504 Fieldcrest Court
Williamsburg, VA 23185

Rand McNally and Co.
8255 N. Central Park Ave.
Skokie, IL 60076

PC Globe, Inc.
4700 South McClintock
Tempe, AZ 85282

Chapter Twelve

CHRONOLOGY, QUESTIONING, AND LANGUAGE SKILLS

"All animals are equal, but some animals are more equal than others." This famous quotation from George Orwell's *Animal Farm (1954)* appears here for two reasons. It covers a multitude of sins and situations, and it provides an analogue for this section on skills. Skill development may be the most vital, far-reaching aspect of social studies instruction, if not of school instruction generally. Skills provide the tools and the practice to master familiar situations and to face new ones with confidence. Of course, one has to continue to practice skills to keep one's edge. The main part of this chapter is devoted to skills in chronology, questioning, and oral history. The final part outlines skills in reading, writing, listening, and graphing, although more in-depth coverage may be found in other chapters of this book and in other areas of elementary teacher training. Reading, writing, and listening apply to all disciplines, but because of the great reliance on reading in social studies they are especially vital to the social studies curriculum.

Although the map and globe skills discussed in Chapter 11 are the most critical to global understanding and citizenship, the skills outlined in this chapter are also vital to student growth. They are discussed together in the interests of both space and complexity. They do not demand the same lengthy time and effort to master as place-location skills, but a failure to come to grips with them will severely hamper the teacher and deprive students of vital foundational techniques.

Social studies must be skill oriented as well as content oriented. The skills in social studies are dynamic and extremely useful. Mastery of them means fuller exploration of one's abilities in and out of school. Without these skills, a student is condemned to simplistic views of a complex, articulated world.

CHRONOLOGY SKILLS

We can all remember the problems of learning to tell time, of asking what time it was when the little hand was on the two and the big hand on the eight. This ability comes to most children by the second, third, or fourth grade. It is quite possible that this skill will become more difficult to master as digital clocks proliferate and clocks with hands become a thing of the past. Nevertheless, the knowledge of how to tell time comes through practice. Students may see the measurement of time as immutable and universal among all cultures. This is clearly *not* the case, however. Time is an abstraction, and its measurement depends on who is doing the measuring. Perception of time is culturally based and culturally biased. "As time passes, so does a child's concept of change. If children are to gain a sense of history, they must have some understanding of the concept of change." (Seefeldt, 146)

The Calendar

A calendar is only one of many ways of measuring the passage of time. Our new year starts in January. The Chinese new year, however, begins in February, and the Jewish new year in September. Other examples include the calendar of the Russian Orthodox and Greek Orthodox churches, of American Indians, and of the ancient Mayans (See Figure 12.1.)

The calendar we use today derives from the Roman Julian calendar, based on the decree of Pope Gregory XIII in 1581. It was originally developed by Julius Caesar, who standardized a 365-day cycle based on the solar year. The Jewish calendar is luni-solar; the others mentioned are lunar.

Why the calendar was reformed is a fascinating story. The World Calendar Association still struggles for worldwide calendar standardization. The books by Watkins *(Time Counts: The Story of the Calendar)* and Wilson *(The Romance of the Calendar)* listed in the references are good sources for further study.

Most students have no idea where the days of the week originated. As Watkins notes:

The seven-day sequence of days that we call the week goes back to very ancient times and appeared in many cultures and religions. It was known in India, Babylonia and Palestine from extremely early days. . . . Ancient Romans observed an eight-day week, and there is evidence that the early Britons knew a five-day cycle. (42)

This may be hard for children to digest; how could there be a week without Friday, for example? Even in the primary grades children should begin to realize that different cultural beliefs prevail around the earth and throughout history. Understanding each culture is not the goal here, but, rather, cultural appreciation and awareness.

The seven-day week is generally accepted as being of Semitic origin—that is, from the Book of Genesis. By the fourth century AD it had been introduced into the Roman calendar. According to Watkins, the seven-day week is "an arbitrary division of time, having no relation to natural phenomena, except the approximation to the moon's phases. Moreover, it is an illogical arrangement, since it will not divide into equal half-weeks." (43)

The names of the days of the week, usually taken for granted by students, also reflect cultural influences, mostly those of the Norse people as derived by

FIGURE 12.1
Another Way to Tell Time: a Mayan Calendar

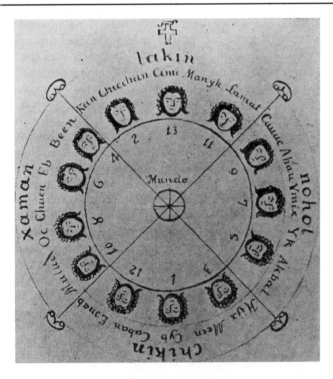

the Saxons of England. Sunday and Monday are named after the most prominent celestial objects. Saturday is named for Saturn, the Titan father of the first
gods in Roman mythology.

What about the other days? The answer to this question is an interesting
one that deserves more study. Tuesday is Tyr's day, named after a Norse deity.
Wednesday is named after Odin, the king of the Norse gods, who was also
known as Wodin—thus Wodin's day. Thursday is Thor's day, and Friday is
Freya's or Frigga's day, after a Norse goddess. Not every culture uses these
names; they illustrate the cultural influences on our view of time. What about
the names of the months? These are a combination of mostly Julian or pre-Ju-
lian Roman views of the year. At one time the Roman year began in March; vestiges of that are seen in the months from September to December, formerly the
seventh through the tenth month, respectively. The months July and August
were named after the great Caesars, Julius and Augustus, replacing the months
of Quinctilis (five) and Sextilis (six).

The months of March and June were named after the deities Mars, the god of
war, and Juno, goddess of light and beginnings. The Roman emperor Numa Pom-
pilius, who reigned from 716 to 673 BCE, balanced March by dedicating a month
to Janus, a peacemaker and a representative of Diana, the goddess of the hunt and
of childbirth. January, the first month, was named after Janus and his twin deity,
Jana, who were seen as looking both forward and backward (Figure 12.2).

May is named after Maius, the goddess of growth. April is the month of
openings (from the Latin *aprere,* "to open"), when buds appear. February, according to Watkins, is a Sabine word for cleanliness. "Can it have been that even
in Sabine homes they celebrated Spring cleaning?" (93-94)

The calendar is sometimes linked to the signs of the zodiac, a cultural artifact of Egyptian origin discussed by Nelson (1978). Most of the signs relate to
the stages of the Nile River, as well as to flooding, harvest, and planting. For example, it is believed that Leo, the lion, was named for the time that lions appeared on the banks of the Nile. The whole sky has shifted in the 4,000 years
since the zodiacal signs were allied with earthly actions; the symbols remain
fixed in what are now inappropriate times of the year. Astrology has outgrown
reality.

Thus the calendar is a true cultural artifact that deserves more attention
than the cursory flipping of a page every 30 days. Various cultures measure the
divisions of time in different ways. Time is an artificially created cultural instrument. For more information, see the references at the end of the chapter.

The International Date Line

Before mass communication and mass transportation became a way of life,
there was no need for time zones or time agreements. People of a particular
city or nation set their own time. No one cared if it was radically different from
the schedules of other nations or cities, simply because messages between two
locales took so long to travel.

FIGURE 12.2
Janus, the Roman God of Beginnings

Technology has changed this. The telegraph, the railroad, and the steamship all had to operate on set schedules in order to provide rapid communication. So in 1884 a standardized measurement of time and distance was established around the globe. Most students become aware of the various time belts in the United States through television, which broadcasts program schedules for eastern, central, mountain, and Pacific time (Figure 12.3). It is relatively easy to figure the time of day in different areas of the world on a globe by counting every 15 degrees and moving up or back an hour, depending on which direction one is heading.

The international date line established in 1884 is located exactly opposite the prime meridian, at 180 degrees west and east of Greenwich (Figure 12.4). If one crosses the international date line heading west, one loses a day, and if one heads east, one gains a day. Of course, one cannot really gain or lose a day, because time is an agreed-upon abstraction. So the date line is basically an imaginary standard with the purpose of achieving world chronological order.

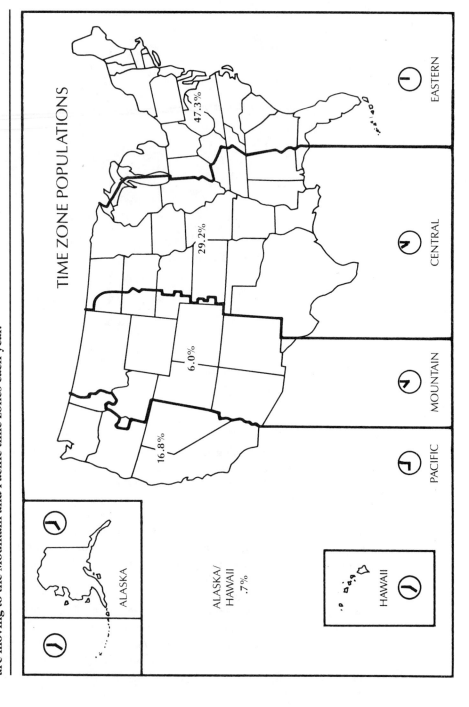

FIGURE 12.3

Despite relatively equal land masses in each time zone, the number of people living in each area varies. More people are moving to the Mountain and Pacific time zones each year.

FIGURE 12.4

The international date line was established in 1884 by international agreement.

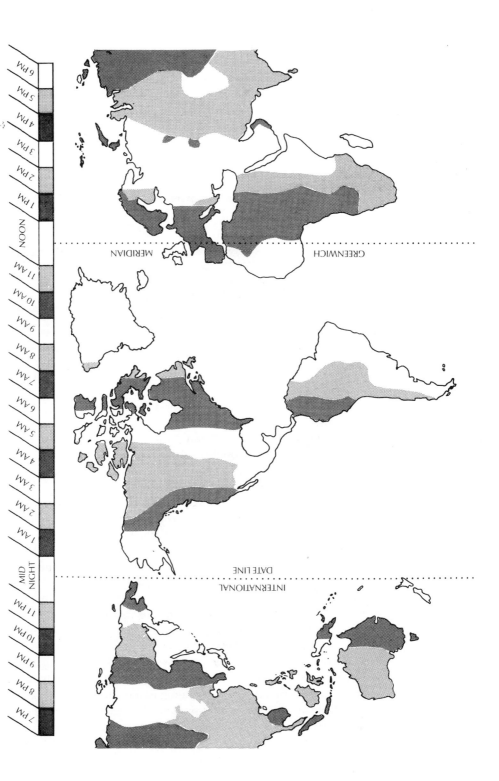

TIME ZONES OF THE WORLD

FIGURE 12.5

Time and space graph projects a child's ability to conceptualize these abstract concepts.

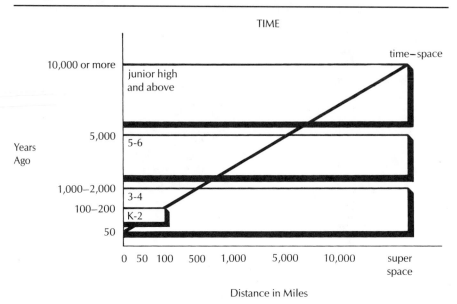

It is often difficult to mix time and space conceptually with young children. At the primary level, it is easier to deal with one or the other, mixing the two concepts only as the children grow older. This is more a developmental process than a strict chronological grade-level process. The graph in Figure 12.5 illustrates the general ability of children to conceptualize time and space from kindergarten through junior high school.

Generally, students need to stay within the area described above or below the time-space (t-s) axis in the graph. For example, most children in the first and second grades have difficulty conceptualizing time spans of more than 200 years and distances of more than 100 miles. A student who goes to the limits of both time and distance at once will only gain confusion. After a certain point, all history runs together—"when Grandpa was young" or "when Grandpa's daddy was a little boy" are as far back as a young child can understand.

If this is so, then why do children love to study dinosaurs? The answer is that, although they love dinosaurs, the difference to young children between the time of the birth of Christ and, say, the Jurassic period is negligible. They both occurred a long time ago—one was just a bit longer ago than the other. Eventually this time gap will be resolved, although it probably should not be attempted in the primary grades. Creating islands of knowledge is not unusual in school; later knowledge usually provides linkages between the gaps. A comprehensive curriculum for a school district should provide a plan for narrowing such gaps.

Third and fourth graders can comprehend approximately 1,000 to 2,000 years back in time, to the birth of Christ, while junior high or middle school students can understand historical time frames about as well as adults can. Many of us still have difficulty imagining that the first hominids appeared five million years ago.

Less research exists on a child's ability to comprehend the future, although it appears there may be fewer distinctions between the young child and the adult in this area. In other words, futurism is as tangible to first graders as to fifth graders. The limits are not ones of a temporal nature, but of interest.

Chronological Terms and Concepts

We have already discussed the month and the week as cultural artifacts. Additional concepts that should be defined and exemplified in the primary grades include day and night and year and season. A year, for example, should be defined as the time it takes the earth to complete one revolution around the sun, not as 12 months, since a month is a relative concept, depending on the type of calendar used and the number of days in any given month.

A season has two definitions, one astronomical and one meteorological. The former divides the seasons by the sun's light. Both the vernal and the autumnal equinox indicate days of equal night and day, whereas the summer solstice marks the longest day of the year and the winter solstice the shortest day. These differences often lead to heavy snow and below-zero temperatures in many places in spring and 100-degree heat in autumn. The meteorological season is more specific. In central Pennsylvania, for example, spring runs from April to June, summer from July to August, fall from September to November, and winter from December to March. Teachers should check with their local meteorologists or the U.S. Weather Bureau to determine their meteorological seasons.

A.M. AND P.M.

These two terms are often thought by students to mean "past midnight" and "something else." We know that they refer to morning and afternoon or evening, but the abbreviations are from the Latin expressions *ante meridian* (A.M.) and *post meridian* (P.M.). Meridian refers to "middle"—in this case, the middle of the day. *Ante* means "before," and *post* means "after."

Two other abbreviations, BC and AD, are also often confused. Although BC means "before Christ," AD does not mean "after death," as many children believe. If this were true, there would be a gap in time measurement during Christ's life. The abbreviation AD is from the Latin *anno Domini,* for "in the year of our Lord," marking the years after the *birth* of Christ. The initials CE, for common era, are sometimes used to denote the years starting with the birth of Christ. BCE, before the common era, designates the time before the birth of Christ.

FIGURE 12.6

The correct sequence for these pictures may be obvious to adults but a challenge to many kindergarteners or first-graders.

SEQUENCING

The simple concept of sequencing is important, as are the words describing such a process; before, present, after. Children in the primary grades need to practice sequencing in order to master the concept. One method is a verbal or pictorial out-of-synchronization test. For example, the teacher could rearrange a group of pictures, like those in Figure 12.6, in sequential order and ask students how one knows the order is correct.

Minutes, hours, and seconds all need to be conceptualized when studying chronology. In later grades (fourth and higher), terms like eon, era, century, and decade can be studied. Table 12.1, reprinted from a pamphlet by K. C. Friedman called *How to Develop Time and Chronological Concepts,* gives a good summation of the capabilities of various youngsters regarding chronological concepts. This should be seen as a kind of scope and sequence table similar to the map and globe tables in Chapter 11.

Another abstract concept that often confuses students is the meaning of relative expressions like "a long time ago" or "a short time ago." Is two weeks a long or a short time? If you are three years old, two weeks is an excruciatingly long time, but if you are 33, two weeks is a very short time. Teachers should recognize the semantic differences that these phrases have for various ages of youngsters. In order to minimize confusion, one should avoid using these phrases without giving some complementary, more precise time frame. Seefeldt notes that temporal sequencing concepts are learned more readily than quantitative temporal concepts such as telling time accurately. (146)

Thornton and Vukelich have summarized some work on chronology acquisition in addition to Friedman's, as shown in Table 12.2. It is less extensive but more eclectic. It might be an interesting exercise to compare these tables.

TABLE 12.1
Sequence of Chronology Concepts

SKILLS IN DEVELOPING A SENSE OF TIME AND CHRONOLOGY	EARLY ELEMENTARY PUPILS BEGIN TO:[a]	LATER ELEMENTARY PUPILS BEGIN TO:[b]	SECONDARY PUPILS BEGIN TO:[b]
To tell time by the clock	Tell time of regular daily activities of the school program Tell the hours, half-hours, quarter-hours, and five-minute intervals	Tell time to minutes Familiarize themselves with time zones, daylight savings time Figure time allotments for specific jobs	
To use the vocabulary of time	Use simple definite terms (e.g., hour, minute, day, week, month, today, yesterday, tomorrow) Use simple indefinite terms (e.g., a long time ago, later, a few years ago)	Use more advanced definite terms (e.g., decade, annual, generation, A.M., P.M.) Use more advanced indefinite terms (e.g., presently, shortly, recently)	Use terms of historical implication (e.g., ancient, era, modern, medieval, dynasty)
To use the calendar in reckoning time	Find the current day or week on the calendar Find dates on the calendar (e.g., holidays, birthdays) Use the names of the months Know the current year Associate seasons with the calendar	Distinguish between BC and AD Familiarize themselves with the effect of the rotation of the earth on day and night Familiarize themselves with the effect of the revolution of the earth around the sun on the seasons of the year	Express centuries as dates Express dates in centuries
To acquire a chronological perspective of history	Sense the passing of time (e.g., since school started, when I went away) Recognize sequence of regular daily activities Distinguish between experiences of the past and events of the future Arrange a list of events in sequence according to time	Figure the number of years between two given dates Interpret a time line Construct a time line Relate dates and periods of time with more familiar historical happenings	Regard certain dates as milestones in history Associate the cultures of peoples with different historical periods Perceive sequence, duration, and the change in the development of social institutions and movements Understand the place of the present era in the history of humankind

[a]Some of the skills listed should not be introduced until the third grade.
[b]Skills introduced in early grades that should continue to be developed.
SOURCE: Friedman, pp. 11-12.

TABLE 12.2
Acquisition of Time-Related Concepts or Skills

AGE	CLOCK AND CALENDAR	HISTORICAL
4–5	Describes the sequence of a day's activities Uses terms before and after, now and then Uses past and future verb tense	
6	Labels blocks of time as lunchtime, playtime, naptime Reads clock hour time correctly Recognizes time and distance as two different dimensions	
7	Recognizes hours as being the same length of time Recites days of week, months, and seasons in order	Places family members (self, parents, grandparents) in correct age sequence
8	Names recent holidays Uses terms like night, tomorrow, morning to describe a point in time Names months, weeks, days	Uses year dates but cannot accurately match year to person or event Given the dates 1750, 1850, and 1950, or 1970, 1980, and 1960, correctly orders them Begins to match dates to significant persons or events
9	Orders the holidays in a calendar year	Uses general terms such as a long time ago, way back when, once upon a time Uses a specific number of years, for example, about 100 years ago, as a time referent Matches significant people with events
10	Realizes that seconds, minutes, hours are the same length everywhere	Labels periods of time, for example, colonial times, the Civil War years
11	Demonstrates mastery of clock and calendar time	
12–13		Matches dates with appropriate historical event, person, or period
14		Uses adult time vocabulary and concepts, for example, century, generation, Pilgrim forefathers
15		Distinguishes between parts of centuries
16		Uses the sixteenth century and the 1500s interchangeably

SOURCE: Thornton and Vukelich, pp. 72-73.

FIGURE 12–7

Time Line for Daniel, Age Eight

	$1\frac{1}{2}$	2	4	$5\frac{1}{2}$	$6\frac{1}{2}$	7	8
Born	Moved to Pennsylvania	Talked	Began preschool	Got a puppy	Played on t-ball team	Joined Cub Scouts	Learned to ski

TIME LINES

Anyone who has traveled frequently expresses distance in terms of time; knowing one implies knowing the other. For example, when asked how far it is between New York and Philadelphia, many people reply, "About two and a half hours." We asked for distance; we received time. Students should understand that time and distance intersect when surface, air, or sea mileages are discussed.

Time lines are a popular way to demonstrate the connection between time and space, particularly when describing a long period of time, like the age of the earth or the span of civilization on our planet. Before introducing these more advanced concepts, however, one should introduce the notion of time lines in simpler terms. Children as young as six or seven, for example, could highlight four or five events in their lives. Such an example is shown in Figure 12.7.

Students could make time lines for their parents' lives (encouraging useful parent-child interaction) or even create time lines for inanimate objects—the family car or the school building. This also reinforces the sequencing skills mentioned earlier. One note of caution, however, is voiced by Thornton and Vukelich:

> Many social studies educators assert that a time line assists in sequencing skills or in ordering events and persons in time. Yet few articles dealing with time lines are available, and none, to our knowledge, are empirically based. Little can be confidently claimed about the effects of time lines on children's understandings. (79)

FAMILY TREES

Following the success of *Roots* by Alex Haley in the 1970s, family trees have become a popular topic in school. The project involves a child's parents and grandparents and encourages cross-generational discussion and understanding (Figure 12.8).

Despite its advantages, there may be drawbacks to this exercise for some families. A student who is adopted and does not know his or her natural

FIGURE 12.8

A Family Tree Diagram

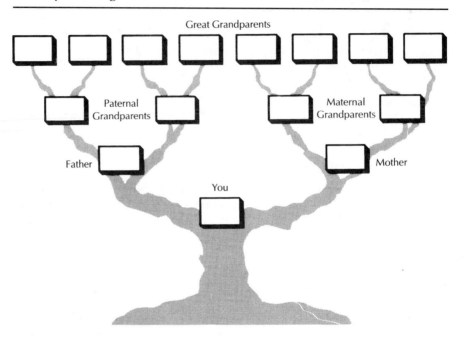

parents may feel embarrassed by the family tree experience. If a child has a stepparent, does he or she trace the stepparent's family or the natural parent's? Still other families have changed their names and do not wish to publicize their family history. Other families may be recent immigrants and hesitant to relive their memories of life in their former country.

To guard against any of these potentially negative situations, the teacher should check with parents before getting students involved in such a project. If some parents find the project objectionable, the teacher will have to weigh the family's position against the potential for learning. If there is only mild opposition, then perhaps these families can be won over. But if the family is vehemently opposed to the idea and perhaps threatens to complain to the principal, the teacher must decide whether such interference represents a potential infringement on academic freedom or is just an inconvenience regarding an issue that is not worth fighting over.

Before the exercise is carried out, certain information must be elicited from students through oral questioning. For example, the teacher might ask: "Where were these people born and where did they live?" "What occupations did they have?" "What was going on in the world, in their country, and in the United States when they were young?" "Which relatives did you know personally?"

Family trees and oral history help depict life in an earlier era in a way that textbooks simply cannot duplicate. They help to bring that complex concept, time, into human terms.

QUESTIONING

Questioning is largely taken for granted by teachers. Most recognize that questions are important, and they ask their students many questions, but more often than not the sequence of questions is unplanned and the questions are of a procedural nature. Research on questioning in the classroom has revealed some interesting findings. First, teachers ask a lot of questions. Second, teachers do not wait very long for answers. Students who have the opportunity to answer higher-order questions will become more independent critical thinkers. Higher-order and lower-order questions refer to distinctions made by Meredith Gall and Norris Sanders, among others, in tying levels of questioning to Bloom's taxonomic levels. Benjamin Bloom and his associates at the University of Chicago developed three different hierarchies (called taxonomies) that describe levels of learning in the cognitive, affective, and psychomotor domains. Other similar hierarchies have been developed, but they do not differ radically from Bloom's, which is the best known and most used. A summation of the cognitive taxonomy is shown in Table 12.3. Lower-order questions ask for direct recall of information or some simple application of information, whereas higher-order questions require students to analyze, synthesize, or evaluate the information given.

Most classroom questions, if not lower-order, are procedural in nature, having little to do with the discussion at hand. Preservice teachers who sit in on elementary school classes will find this out for themselves if they chart the types of questions asked and note how many come from students rather than teachers.

A study by Rowe found that the average wait-time—that is, the time a teacher waits before answering a question himself or herself—is one second in elementary school. Teachers, like nature, seem to abhor a vacuum and fill the silence with more talk. It is amazing that students answer *any* questions in this short amount of time.

The conscious development of a discussion should be part of a teacher's questioning strategy. Avoid starting a discussion with evaluative questions. Simple lower-order questions can be followed by more subjective evaluative questions. The teacher need not feel that a discussion means that students are locked in as answerers and the teacher as questioner. These roles could be reversed, or, better yet, students could assume both roles, using the teacher for clarification.

Cornbleth offers some useful guidelines on moderating, pacing, and reacting to student responses (6–7). Most important, a teacher should keep in mind

TABLE 12.3
Classification of Cognitive Categories

1.00   Knowledge

    1.10   Knowledge of specifics

    1.11   Knowledge of terminology

    1.12   Knowledge of specific acts

1.20   Knowledge of Ways and Means of Dealing with Species

    1.21   Knowledge of conventions

    1.22   Knowledge of trends and sequences

    1.23   Knowledge of classifications and categories

    1.24   Knowledge of criteria

    1.25   Knowledge of methodology

1.30   Knowledge of Universals and Abstractions in a Field

    1.31   Knowledge of principles and generalizations

    1.32   Knowledge of theories and structures

2.00   Comprehension

    2.10   Translation

    2.20   Interpretation

    2.30   Extrapolation

3.00   Application

4.00   Analysis

    4.10   Analysis of elements

    4.20   Analysis of relationships

    4.30   Analysis of organizational principles

5.00   Synthesis

    5.10   Production of a unique communication

    5.20   Production of a plan or proposed set of operations

    5.30   Derivation of a set of abstract relations

6.00   Evaluation

    6.10   Judgments in terms of internal evidence

    6.20   Judgments in terms of external criteria

SOURCE: From Benjamin S. Bloom, J. Thomas Hastings, and George F. Madaus, *Handbook on Formative and Summative Evaluation of Student Learning* (New York: McGraw-Hill, 1971), pp. 271–73.

the dual or triple purposes of a discussion. These purposes are: (1) to learn some information as a group and examine it critically; (2) to value one's own opinions and those of one's classmates; (3) to learn the skills of criticism, assessment, and synthesis. Once teachers recognize the purposes of questioning, they will be able to question more critically and to answer questions more thoughtfully and meaningfully.

Sigel and Saunders (in Cassidy, 148) suggest preschool-age children be asked questions that demand labeling ("What is this called?"), reconstructing previous experiences ("What did you have for breakfast this morning?"), proposing alternatives ("What is another way that you could go down the slide?"), resolving conflicts ("How can you both use the blocks at the same time?"), making comparisons, classifying, estimating, enumerating, synthesizing, evaluating ("Which painting do you like best?"), generalizing, and transforming. These are things children can do, but they need guidance in thinking about them and doing them well.

Some researchers have also noted that boys seem to be less reluctant to answer oral questions, even if they do not have an accurate notion of the answer. Similarly, girls with the right answer may be intimidated by oral questioning. Research is not conclusive here, and to make generalizations would be to stereotype unfairly. It may be useful to remember these tentative observations, however.

ORAL HISTORIES

Oral history is a method of collecting historical information and is a legitimate and useful way to study history. Through oral history, students can discern the differences between an objective and a personal point of view and weigh the value of each; they can see discrepancies in historical writings; and they can see how nonhistorians compose and present history. Oral history should not be a substitute for more conventional study, but a supplement.

By conducting interviews students gain a new perspective on history and become much more enthusiastic about the topics they are pursuing. Although oral history does not have to involve the interviewing of an older person, this will usually be the case with students, simply because of their age. For practice students could interview each other.

Oral histories are useful for studying community history and family histories and for improving interpersonal relations while developing social skills. As Mehaffy, Sitton, and Davis note: "oral history is useful in helping students find that 'the study' of history is everywhere around them." (1) The authors provide some useful reminders for teachers in regard to oral history:

- Oral history is not just a person with a tape recorder. One must plan and research *before* the interview. Questions should be prepared although not necessarily all used in a "lock step" manner.
- Oral history need not be transcribed to be useful. Many oral history programs, particularly those in Canada and the United Kingdom, do not transcribe.
- Classroom oral history need not be a BIG project. Realistically, we recommend that teachers should consider gaining experience with oral history in a rather highly focused study extending over a relatively short time.
- Oral history is not the final product of history. It is a *source* for history, not typically history itself. (1-2)

In describing this process in one project, Nelson and Singleton note that "after the project was completed and all the tapes were transcribed, students were asked to evaluate the project. Most of them agreed something was lost in the transcription. The voice with all of its inflections, hidden meanings, and verbal images contributed significantly to the meaningfulness of the project." (93)

Many preservice teachers have conducted oral history interviews, usually with older relatives. There is a range of topics to choose from, but interviewers are encouraged to stick to one topic rather than ramble through all imaginable areas of interest. Possible topics include the following:

The subject's early schooling

Economic differences in the subject's lifetime

Transportation and communication contrasts

Courtship and dating changes

Leisure activities long ago

Work and jobs

Many preservice teachers have a fear of conducting such interviews initially, but almost universally they find the experience valuable, both cognitively and emotionally. Many found that they could relate to their grandparents' experiences and how they felt as young adults. A woman who interviewed her grandmother made the following comment:

> I enjoyed talking with her. In fact we had a sixty-minute tape and neither of us had realized that an hour was up even after an hour and a half. . . . I learned a lot from my grandma for she has such a fantastic memory. . . .

Although oral history is a supplement, it often allows for in-depth examination of an event or process that may not be fully described in a textbook (see the boxes on pages 334–348).

Mehaffy and his colleagues ask and answer some important procedural questions for first-time interviewers:

1. What equipment do I need?
   A reel-to-reel recorder is best but a cassette tape recorder can be used if one remembers to (1) get the best equipment possible, (2) use high-quality 30-minute tapes, (3) use an external microphone, and (4) try to arrange an interview setting as quiet as possible.
2. Do I need a legal release?
   Not really, but it's not a bad idea since some people may wish to change something after it's recorded.
3. How do students learn to interview?
   - Learn the goals of the interview and the background of your subject as well as the events of the world at that time.
   - List questions, starting with lower-order ones and building to more evaluative questions.

- Practice in school.
- Send two-person teams to do interviewing to support each other.
- Test equipment before going to the interview and before beginning the interview. (5-7)

Neuenschwander adds a few tips:

1. Be an active listener.
2. Don't become so enamored of the interview that objectivity is lost.
3. Take notes during the interview. This can help with spelling questions as well as act as an outlet for nervousness.
4. Don't ask compound questions. (18-19)

Neuenschwander also reminds us that

An interview is actually nothing more than a purposeful conversation between two people . . . Although it is the oral historian who initiates the process and seeks to ask questions in such a way that the information obtained fits into historically meaningful patterns, it is the interviewee who must determine the shape of the interview.

Under such circumstances, no two interviews are ever identical even if the same narrator is interviewed on the same topics by two equally well-trained interviewers. . . . The degree of responsiveness and the quality of the information supplied by a willing narrator are thus determined by the knowledge, skill and personality of the interviewer. (15)

One student of mine noted that the oral history interview was valuable for a number of reasons.

In the case of my father, I learned a great deal about his elementary schooling in terms of the organization of the school day, subjects studied, teaching methods, classroom management, and extracurricular activities. I was a little disappointed that my dad couldn't remember more than he did, and I could tell that he was disappointed too. However, we did cover a wide range of topics, and I began to realize how much I don't know about my father and the past from which he comes. I see more clearly now that the past is made up of people, not dates, and that these people's daily lives are what makes up history. Thus, understanding their lives helps understanding history.

Another value came out of this that was totally unexpected. It was the opportunity for the exchange of ideas, viewpoints, and values between my father and me. It was very interesting to hear what he had to say about his education and education in general. I was anxious to try out my ideas on him, and what resulted was a fascinating conversation that revealed a great deal about our ideas on such important things as education.

This activity is a worthwhile activity for all people of any age. What you get out of it depends on how much you are willing to put into it. A better understanding of the past in some particular aspect is the least of which you can come away with, and this in itself is a treasure. (Bjorkbom)

THE DEPRESSION
ED JABLONSKI, SUSAN OLSEN, MARK BAKER

How was your family life affected by the Depression? What did you and your family do to make ends meet?

Well, things weren't as bad for us like in some other families. My dad was laid off from Barrett's [the copper mill], but he was a skilled worker. His job was masonry work. He would line the furnaces in the copper mill with a special kind of brick. He knew all there was to know about brick and cement work. When he got laid off he became sort of a handyman. He would do any kind of brick or cement work for people in our neighborhood and other places like Mayfair. He didn't make as much as he used to, but he made enough to get by. With less money coming in we had to scavenge more things instead of buying them. Me and my younger brothers would climb under the factory fences and swipe coal for heat. Instead of being able to buy food at the mom-and-pop store we had to raise our own. We traded some neighbors for a few chickens and ducks and mom got a vegetable garden going. Even though we would swipe some coal, we didn't always have enough to go around in the winter, so mom would take the duck feathers and make piajiinas, a sort of down blanket. They were really warm to sleep in at night. We also had to wear a lot of hand-me-down clothes. Either that or mom would make them herself. Those clothes lasted a heck of a lot longer than the clothes we used to buy at the store. We had to cut corners a lot, but we managed.

Another View

D: OK. The—Did the local people do anything for the people who were having financial trouble during the Depression?

F: The Depression was the end of what I consider the real American spirit where people took care of their own. Up until the Depression there was very little relief; if somebody was in need, his neighbors would help. Afterwards, it became a public job.

D: What would the neighbors do before this?

F: Bring in food or take care of any of the necessities or families would take care of their own.

D: OK. What government programs became available to the people in your community during the Depression?

F: Well, we had the relief agencies which really grew during that time. We had government work programs. The WPA was strong in our area.

D: What was the WPA?

F: Works Progress Administration— where they did construction work with picks and shovels instead of machinery to stretch out the work to give the people jobs.

D: Was this financially necessary?

F: It kept people going, but it also fostered the idea that the government will take care of us. I've seen WPA jobs that you could do in twenty min-

(continued)

(continued from previous page)

utes that would be a day's work for one of them.

D: Did a lot of people take advantage of this program?

F: Some did, but there were a group of coal miners in our town who could have sat around or scrounged any kind of jobs they could get. They could have worked for the WPA but maybe some of them were beneath them. I don't know. But in order to keep busy, they scrounged any materials they could find. Like the coal companies gave them pipe, other companies would give them wood, and they built three recreational parks. They had swings, sliding boards, see-saws, and pavilions all made from throwaway materials. Those three parks are still in existence, but not like they were during the Depression when everybody was working on them.

Another View
How did the Great Depression affect your family's life at this time?

It affected it very dramatically, of course, just like it did for everyone else, except the very rich. My father was a professor at the University of Chicago when the banks failed, all of our savings went with the banks. As you know, I guess, people got scared and went to the banks to get their money. We had some money in a customs savings bank, and my father delayed going because he didn't like to panic, and when he got there, the doors were closed. I think he got some of this money back years later; I think it came out to ten cents on the dollar, but whatever it was, there was no federal deposit insurance of any kind. We didn't have a large amount of money to lose, and we had a farm in Iowa, so we always had food. I believe my father's salary went down to around eighteen hundred dollars a year, and I don't know what the rent was, but we couldn't pay the whole thing. The fellow who owned the apartment building we lived in on the South Side of Chicago came around to collect the rent, and my father told him that we couldn't pay it all. So the guy asked him, "How much can you pay?" and he told him about forty dollars a month. He said, "Well, I'll take it." Of course, he couldn't throw everyone out who couldn't pay full rent, otherwise he would have nobody in the building.

There were many other side effects, of course, uh, my father was discharged from the university—fired. People in the lower schools of Chicago suffered terribly during this time. The board of education ran out of money and gave teachers worthless scrip instead of money. Teachers suffered grievously, since the merchants wouldn't accept this scrip. But, as a university professor who was fired, it adjusted the cost of our house to poverty, and we were relegated to simple meals for a while, as I well remember. I loved baseball, and I wanted a catcher's mitt, and I saved ten cents a week for what seemed like a hundred years. I finally got one for five dollars, and I still have it laying around somewhere.

ETIQUETTE, CONDUCT, MANNERS, FUN AND GAMES
KELLIE WEST, TANYA MCCOY, KATHLEEN BRINKMILLER, JOY MANTEGNA, LYN CECCHINI

D: What were some other signs of respect for authority or elders?

M: One very obvious thing was that men would always arise in the presence of a woman. Young women would also arise when being introduced to an older woman, or when she entered the room. In connection with this, there was much more hesitancy for a younger person to initiate a conversation with an elder. The respectful thing to do was to wait until spoken to. Also, in connection with addressing adults, first names were not used freely. For instance, in a doctor's office, a nurse or doctor would never have addressed an older man or woman as "Harry" or "Mabel." Women at that time were never addressed as Ms. The term was simply an unknown. Every woman was either Miss or Mrs. As mentioned in the reference to the house mother, in the North, it was just not common to say "sir" or "ma'm," but the overall tone was one of respect with an elder.

D: Did they use "sir" and "ma'm" in the South at that time?

M: Yes. [Pause] But my only awareness of it came from one or two people I knew from the South. I remember especially our senior year in high school when your dad transferred from Mississippi to Illinois, and said "sir" and "ma'm" to the teacher and we all laughed. We thought it sounded funny. Another thing he did

that we were not used to was to stand when the teacher called on him for an answer. After a few weeks, he did stop that, though.

D: Did you ever hear girls cuss?

M: Very, very seldom. In fact, I can only think of one person.

D: Was that frowned upon?

M: Yes.

D: Did men cuss often in the presence of ladies?

M: No.

D: In college classes, did people relax and prop their feet up?

M: No, not generally. Posture, like clothing, was more disciplined or modest.

Another View

T: So, did any strange things ever happen on these dates? Did you ever go anywhere strange?

D: Went to the drive-in, me and a girl, my brother and my cousin. Went to the drive-in in my '63 Ford with a trunk that opened by a handle near the front seat. We put them [brother/cousin] in the trunk so we didn't have to pay for them.

T: Oh, really?

D: We had to go to the back of the drive-in and I pulled the handle to let them out and the handle didn't work. They got stuck in the trunk and we had to take the back seat out to get them out of the trunk.

(continued)

(continued from previous page)

Another View

M: We played games out in the street. All the neighborhood kids got together to play "kick the can" or we'd play, "May I."

K: Is that like "Mother may I?"

M: Yeah.

K: How'd you play "kick the can?"

M: You just got a can and took sides and kicked it. And you'd try to get it over on their side and they'd try to kick it back to you. It was like I guess like football except you never tackled or nothing, you just kicked the ball. But you ran into each other to kick the can.

Another View

J: What kind of music did your band play?

D: I would call it a rock 'n' roll band.

J: What instrument did you play in that band?

D: I played the electric piano and the organ and the band that we had was a five-piece band in high school and it was called Johnny Dee and the Sounds and I guess our two claims to fame were going on the Ted Mack Amateur Hour when I was fifteen years old in New York. We drove in and went into the studio and it was taped so we were able to watch ourselves afterwards on T.V. and the song, I even remember the song that we did, the song was called, "Caravan" and the piano had a solo in that song. So I guess you could say I was one of the stars on the Ted Mack Amateur Hour. And then the other claim to fame was that we cut a demo, that's called a demo recording, where you go into New York and you record for a studio and the song that we recorded was "Honky Tonk" and that was a popular song in the fifties. So that took up a lot of time because it was a lot of practice at night, playing at teenage dances on Friday or Saturday night.

Another View

GF: We played fox-in-the-morning-and-geese-in-the-evening. And, ah. . . games where we would just . . . and then there was another game that was . . . that the boys played and I'm not sure what it was called, step ball I think somebody called it, because of all the houses having these cement steps in Pittsburgh. They would throw the ball against . . . one, there were two people they would, one would throw the ball against the step as hard as he could and then it would arch back over him and then the other person would try to catch it and that would be an out and if he didn't catch it then it would be a strike. And that went on a lot of the day. So we had a, I thought we had a very nice time during that, those days.

GS: Could you explain fox-in-the-morning, geese-in-the-evening? How is that played, or what are the rules?

GF: Well, I think it must be originally originated from England because a lot of the people were Scotch-Irish,

(continued)

(continued from previous page)

English-Scotch-Irish, including myself. My family was English-Scotch-Irish. Ah, fox-in-the-morning, geese-in-the-evening and rover, rover I dare you to come over and then one side would form a line in the middle of the road interlocking arms and then the other side would try to break through that line. And then sometimes they broke through and then other times they didn't. It was something like that. Then we also played a game that was a lot of fun and could take all day. One of those was run-sheep-run and again that probably originated in England. And, ah, one side would count off till the other side ran away, all over the, this could go all over the neighborhood. You set your boundaries though and then you had chalk and little strings and then you were supposed to chalk arrows as you went to leave clues and tie strings around telephone poles and so forth. But the game that I liked best was release-the-peddler. Now I think that that title must have been release-the-prisoner to begin with, because release-the-peddler doesn't really make sense. But again, you had two sides and you had a chalk square which we chalked in the alley, a big chalk square. And then one side ran away and the boundaries were more limited for this game. And then you hid anywhere you could like for hide-and-seek. Then the other side

would try and find you. Then when they would find a person, when they would touch you, then you had to go willingly with them to within about twenty-four feet of the square, or maybe it was more than that. And then you could struggle and that's where the fun began. Then you would start struggling like mad and trying to get away from the person or two people or three people even that were trying to drag you into the square. The minute your foot got over that chalk line you had to stay in the square and not struggle anymore. And then when the one team had captured everybody into the square they won the game. But there was a catch because if one person from your team could come around and sneak around when they were, the guards were not looking, they usually had a couple of guards by the square, and run into the square that would release all the prisoners. And that's how I happened to run into disaster[laughs] , because I was running into the square between houses in the back over the lawn and the people had put up a little wire to probably protect their lawn and I fell, tripped over that wire, and my head fell right down on that hard cement and I was knocked out for about, for a few minutes. [Laughs] But I still liked the game, we still played the game.

LIFE IN WARTIME
LESLIE DELP, MIRIAM ROTH-MURPHY, KEVIN REUSS

D: When you lived in the country when you were little . . . did it have a name?

F: It was a place called Hayes in Middlesex, and it was country . . . we lived in an old cottage . . . it was a couple of hundred years old . . . and it belonged to my mother's aunt and she let us live in a couple of rooms on one side of the cottage. It is difficult to imagine doing it now . . . the only form of heat was a fireplace in a small living room, and the kitchen consisted of just a wooden table, with no running water and no electric light out there . . . we had a gas stove and a gas light that you had to light at night if you wanted a light in the kitchen.

D: Were those conditions because of the location, or because you didn't have any money?

F: Well, both. My father worked in a factory. But because of the war, we wanted to get out of London, so we took whatever there was available to live in. My parents were pleased to be out of London when the bombs were dropping. We used to have a system in England . . . when the Germans came over . . . where there was a siren would go off and there would be this wailing sound and that would signify that the planes were coming over and that they were going to drop bombs . . . and although they didn't drop them very often in the area where we were, the planes used to go over where we were to get to London . . . and sometimes they would drop the bombs short and oc-

casionally there would be bombs dropped in our area. When the sirens sounded, we used to go out into the garden, right down into the back, and there would be this shelter build kinda half under the ground. They would dig a hole in the ground and line it with concrete and then they'd put corrugated iron over the top and pile dirt and stuff over the corrugated iron . . . whenever the siren sounded, which would often happen late at night, we'd all have to get up out of bed, in the dark, and come down the stairs, go out the back, into the garden, into the bomb shelter, and then we would try to get to sleep again in these little bunks, and then when the raid was over, they'd sound another, what they used to call the all-clear siren and then we'd get back up out of bed and go back . . . I don't really remember the details.

D: I guess it wasn't a very happy time then? I mean, did you play and stuff like that? Do you remember what you did, like play in any of the bombed-out houses?

F: The kids in London used to play in the bombed-out houses . . . there weren't that many bombed-out places in the country. We used to go visit relatives every now and again and there would be bombed-out places all around . . .

One thing about living in those times; you know, kids today have sodas and candies and ice creams and fruit, and stuff like that, but in the war

(continued)

(continued from previous page)

in England, you didn't have any of that. You know, I didn't see a banana until I was like ten or twelve years old; and we didn't have candy, you just couldn't get it. Everything was rationed.

Another View

M: Two French soldiers came to our house and informed us that they were arresting us because we were dirty Jews. They gave us five minutes to get on the back of a truck. My mother grabbed a few things like photographs and jewelry. Once we were aboard the truck, we had no idea where we were going. When we got to the prison, we were separated by sex. They didn't tell us why we were arrested. Ah . . . we were there for approximately three to four days. My personal feeling is that they needed to wait until they rounded up enough Jews to fill up a train. On the fourth day, they ordered us to get on a train to head to the concentration camp.

D: Did you know that you were headed to a concentration camp?

M: No, we did not know that we were going there. All I remember is that it was very cramped on the train. It was like riding in cattle cars. It was very uncomfortable.

D: How did you know when you had arrived at the camp? Do you remember what time of day it was?

M: Well, the train stopped and we were loaded onto trucks that took us to Gers[the name of the concentration camp]. I was much too young to remember what time of day it was. I do remember some of the characteristics of the camp. Ah . . . men and women were segregated from each other. Children under the age of twelve were placed with the parent of their sex. Children who were over the age of twelve were considered adults and could be separated from their parents. The camp was also divided alphabetically. My mother, sister, grandmother, and I were placed in K barrack. Our last name being Kann meant that we would have been placed in K barrack. Now, my cousin Leon, who was fourteen and considered an adult male, was placed in a K barrack for males. My father had been placed in a hospital unit due to the injury that he sustained during the First World War. He could not take the outdoor heat. The barracks resembled gigantic huts and housed fifty to sixty people. We were forced to sleep on straw mattresses. Now, I remember that it got extremely hot during the day because the Gers was located in the Pyrenees near the Spanish border. [She pauses to take a deep breath.] I remember that the camp had no running water. The bathrooms were outhouses and the sanitation was awful. Germs collected around the outhouses. Consequently, children were coming down with dysentery.

D: Did you and Aunt Renee come down with dysentery?

M: No. My mother would not let us play with the other children because she was afraid that we would get sick. You have got to remember that we did not have access to the kind of medications that are available now.

(continued)

(continued from previous page)

[She is whimpering.] The children were dying off daily. Now, I said that my father was placed in the hospital unit. Due to his injury from the First World War, he had epileptic seizures when he was exposed to extreme heat and had to be monitored for his condition. We were given brief visitation rights to see him. I don't really remember how often or for how long they were. But, Omi [her mother] had made friends with one of the camp guards who allowed us to visit Opi [her father] when there were no visitation rights. Oh, Opi made friends with a Spanish doctor and a cook in the hospital. The cook secretly got us additional food to eat. [She takes a breath.]

D: Did the Spaniards run the camp?

M: Well, the French utilized the Spaniards. The Spaniards had escaped the Franco regime and France did not know exactly what to do with them.

D: So how long were you in the camp?

M: About five months.

D: Now how did you escape?

M: Ah . . . well . . . my father made friends with a Spanish doctor in the hospital who convinced one of the guards to let us out in the middle of the night. Now, my father had kept a sum of money in his cane. He had a hollow cane! He gave the guard, who let us out, a sum of money. He let us out at about three A.M. We walked to the train station where we purchased train tickets to go to Lyon on the following day.

D: Did your family ever feel like you weren't going to get out of the camp?

M: Well, I was too young to remember, but my mother has told me since that

things got uglier each day. Every day Jews were hauled off and shipped back to Germany to go to the extermination camps. [She is crying.] A friend of my mother was forced to leave. My mother thought that she ended up in Auschwitz, but we will never know.

Another View

K: When did you start noticing the troops?

W: In 1945 as the Russian Army came closer and the German Army pulled back. That's when we really found out that it was very interesting for us children, you know because the German Army, you know the big trucks and we were retreating.

K: I imagine they were gas trucks.

W: Yes, they, the German Army was short on gasoline so a bigger truck would pull a smaller truck behind so the smaller truck wouldn't have to use the gasoline. Then it was actually pretty quiet and then in May 1945 Germany surrendered. And then first the Russian tanks came through and after that the plain soldiers with the horses and buggies and some of them on foot, some of them on bicycles.

K: And they were not good, not good at all?

W: Ah, they were mostly celebrating because the fighting was over and they did a lot of drinking, they were drunk and then they went after the women, to rape the women, and there was no help. You couldn't go anywhere to complain about it, that was just either hide or get raped.

WORKING
LAWRENCE GILLIGAN, PATTY LEGO, JENNIFER BELL

I: What do you do for a living?

E: Well, I'm presently retired, but I have held a lot of jobs in my life.

I: Well, what is one of the very first jobs you remember?

E: Let's see. I guess my very first job involved picking blueberries. My brothers, sisters, and I used to pick blueberries in the woods just outside our house on Dothan Street [Arlington, Massachusetts]. This was back around the time of the Depression. Our parents didn't have much money; neither did anyone at that time. Things were tight in terms of money—especially spending money. We used to pick blueberries all morning long and then sell them later on in the day. Most of the money went to our parents to pay for daily needs, and we usually got to keep a quarter.

I: Ok, I see. Well, do you remember any jobs that you just hated?

E: Ya, I remember one job that I had that only lasted a day. It was a sweatshop for paperwork. We all were given a typewriter and a stack of paper that had to be typed by the end of the day. And it wasn't a fancy typewriter that they have today, it was one of those manual ones that you really had to type the letters for it to work. I think it was one cent a page for the first seventy pages, then two cents each additional page. I just couldn't handle the way they were in that place, so I took my day's pay at the end of the day and left, and I never came back.

I: I guess that this wasn't your lifelong job, was it? What was your longest held job, and did you like it?

E: I was a professional dancer, and yes I loved my job. What this job entailed was dancing in various dance halls all over: Buffalo, Boston, Pittsburgh, Albany, Syracuse, Worcester, Cambridge—all over. I used to love to travel; it gave me a chance to get away for a while. Not that I didn't like being home with my mother and father, but I enjoyed traveling.

Another View

GD: What did you get paid?

GM: Twenty-five cents an hour. [Laugh] When you worked in the shops you only made forty-five cents an hour.

GD: How long did you work at the silk mill?

GM: I stayed there about a year. Then I went to Elmira, New York. I got a

(continued)

READING AND WRITING

Almost every preservice elementary school teacher takes a course in teaching reading. A variety of reading skills are needed to teach social studies. More than any other discipline, social studies is heavily dependent on the reading and comprehension of large quantities of information. A poor reader will invariably be a poor social studies student—all the more reason for the teacher of social studies to emphasize reading skills as much as possible.

(continued from previous page)

job down there and told them I was eighteen. My cousin was down there and needed some help with her baby. I worked in the knitting mills there and helped her at night. I was a folder. Do you know what a folder is? Well, it was in an underwear factory. The material came in big rolls. You laid it down and had to make sure that the leg would not be on a flaw in the material. I stayed there for about six months and then went to the knitting mills that made the material. That was in Horsehead Heights.

GD: What was your favorite job?

GM: The shops. That was 1900, and, when was the war? I worked there during the war. It was 1942. I know because my dad died in 1941 and I was really down in the dumps and when I heard they was hiring in the shops, I thought it would do me good to get out. That's when I went to work. I would pile the lumber. I was used to handling things fifty to a hundred pounds. I liked that job.

Another View

M: Have you witnessed discrimination in the workplace?

G: Yes, I have, especially at the bank. I feel discrimination occurs at banks because the majority of women employees are under the supervision of men. Women never get what men get in banking. For example, the bank hired a male college graduate with no experience for a high-paying loan office job even though women were in line for the spot. The hired man couldn't perform his expected task so they reassigned him to the position of a teller. However, they continued to pay him the high salary of a loan officer instead of the wages of the women tellers. I feel if you do the same work you should get the same pay.

M: What can you do about this discrimination?

G: Well, all you can do is inform the Labor Board with a complaint. They come to the premises of the employer. However, it is a long time before any action is taken. In the meantime, the employer pressures the complaining employee. Therefore the employee becomes discouraged and quits or is fired before the Board does anything about it. You can notify them of things to be done but they don't come back to see that it is done.

Two areas need to be examined concerning the comprehension of material: the student's ability and the reading level of the text. Text readability can be determined by a number of formulas—the Fry method, the Fogg method, the Raygor formula, the Dale-Chall formula, and so on.* Most of them rely on a mix-

---

* See the work by Dupuis and others cited in the references for a fuller discussion of these readability formulas.

SCHOOLING
SUZANNE WAGNER, SHAWN SHANER, RENEE SEMON, LAUREN STERKEL

G: I went to school in Thompsonville School and it was a one-room school house and when I first started we had eight grades. We had a central heating system—a pot belly stove! We had a boy and girl outhouse. We had a pump in the front of the school we used for drinking water, we had those collapsible tin cups and we had a big blackboard that went in front of the schoolhouse and we had a stage which the teacher used for drama performances. We started our school day with a school prayer, then the pledge of allegiance and the first graders were the first on the docket for Mrs. Horner who was my teacher for six years. She had to teach all eight grades so she had to divide her time, and the first graders started first. Even though you didn't try to listen, you heard everybody else's lessons as you were writing on your chalkboard, trying to do your ABCs.

S: So did she teach different lessons? Did she teach to groups, or how did it work?

G: Well, no, she taught, there may be only four or five children in one grade so she taught each grade as she went along, and there were some things like we all did writing and music together, and she had an organ that she played. And she had a story time that she had at the end of the classroom, we got there about 9:00 and left around 3:15. If we were very good she read us a story. But she had the usual reading, writing, arithmetic, history and geography and a little bit of everything.

S: Did you have much homework?

G: I don't remember having much homework in the elementary school, like when the other classes were being taught we had time to do our work in class so that it would be there and no one would forget, and that's when we did our homework. I don't think she had time to correct it, even if we did it.

Another View

M: Where did you live when you went to school?

G: Well, my family and I lived in a mining town and our town was close to the main town of that area. When I went to school we had to cross the river by walking over the railroad tracks. When it was real wet and lots of rain,

(continued)

ture of sentence length and number of syllables in randomly selected passages, although some also include vocabulary as a variable.

Student reading ability also can be determined through standardized tests, as well as cloze techniques, teacher observations, and directed reading activities. The reading abilities of students in one classroom may have a range of four or five years, which means the teacher must group the diverse readers ac-

(continued from previous page)

the bridge that we crossed would flood and the mothers would have to take the kids across unless the bridge was totally out or flooded over, then we went to school by truck.

Another View

R: What did your school look like?

J: It was a small one-room schoolhouse with a bell on top—just like in the movies you see. We had a coal stove that your grandmother used to stoke every morning. She'd walk to school with us, start the fire and make sure that everything was ready for the day. Then, when the school was over, she would sweep, make sure the fire was out and close the school. I'd help her.

R: Did she get paid for that?

J: Yes, she got paid, but I don't know how much.

Another View

GD: When did you move to Wyoming?

GM: Well, we still went to school in Colorado for a few years. My aunt Lucille was our teacher. She taught us in our ice house. Dad cut out a window in it and put desks in. We used old books from Commo. She taught us for four months. She passed us on the fifth grade. Here is when we moved to Wyoming. We were in fifth grade. We rode in the passenger train from Commo, Colorado, to Slater, Wyoming. It was about February. Got off at Slater and went in a lumber wagon to my mother's homestead where Willard lives now. [Willard is Grandma's oldest brother.]

GD: Where did you go to school there?

GM: We didn't go. I was like the teacher, mom didn't have time. So, we used some old books from Commo, Colorado, and we had school every day. Not very long, but we had it.

GD: When did you start going to a regular school?

GM: The next year they built a schoolhouse at one and three-quarters miles west of us. Ms. Hankins from Iowa was our teacher.

GD: Did you start studying social studies yet?

GM: Yes, we got our first social studies books. They were difficult books. Geography and history, it is like what they call social studies now. We started this in fifth grade and really strong in the seventh grade. There was only one teacher, who taught at this school. There was only my brothers, sisters, and I, plus about two other kids. We learned a lot here, especially about penmanship. [Here she went off on how they used to practice penmanship.]

cordingly and find a variety of materials that fit the students' abilities. These might include special texts for slow learners, trade books, or a mixture of print and nonprint media.

What reading skills need emphasis in social studies? There are at least these five areas: (1) vocabulary and concept development, (2) comprehension, (3) reference location skills, (4) map reading, and (5) critical evaluation skills.

COMMUNICATION AND POLITICS
BRIAN WILLIAMS, STACY GEIER

B: Where in Ireland did you live?

M: I lived in Dublin, the capital city, in a northern suburb of the city.

B: How was the communication in your hometown different from other areas in Ireland?

M: Dublin was a city, not as cosmopolitan as New York, but it was definitely a major city. It was small enough where you could meet someone if you were in the center city, which is unlikely here in the states. As far as transportation, they used buses or they walked from place to place. Because of this people were much more talkative. If you were to make eye contact with another person, they would tend to say "Dia dhuit," which in Irish means, "God be with you." Because it's a Catholic country, the response would be, "God and Mary be with you." If you knew someone, they would respond in fun, "God, Mary, St. Joseph and St. Patrick be with you." Friends tried to outdo the others' greeting by adding more and more saints. It is the tradition of the Irish to be very friendly and talkative.

B: Why has communication changed in Ireland?

M: I would have to say it is because of the television and movies and because the people can identify with problems in other countries.

B: How was the communication in your hometown different from other areas in Ireland?

M: There is a slight difference. Because Dublin is a city and a suburb of a city, there is more of a sense of keeping to your friends, but you still greeted your neighbors. In the country people would go door to door and visit, but that was not seen much in the city. Despite the talkativeness and friendliness, there is a definite reserve. Although we may communicate very easily on topics of interest, we as a nation, are not as open with communicating feelings. We tend to be embarassed talking about feelings and expressing emotions both in the city and the country. We do not make a big display of emotion and that is part of the Irish character. Showing feelings, like hugging or telling someone that you love them, would tend to embarrass the person.

(continued)

As already noted, social studies is largely dependent on new vocabulary and concepts. These must be understood largely through reading in order to gain further insight into the nature of social studies and worldly pursuits.

The following outline by Chapin and Gross suggests ways that teachers can help students improve their reading skills:

1. Help students to hear and see what they read.
   a. Use direct sensory experiences such as field trips to the local community.
   b. Use vicarious experiences such as visual and audio media, role playing, and simulated games.

(continued from previous page)
Another View

S: Did you vote for JFK?

D: Yes, I did. It was my first presidential election. You had to be twenty-one to vote then.

S: Why did you vote for him?

D: It was the thing to do at the time. He was almost the great hope for a new tomorrow. He was going to bring an end to the old folks presidents. He was a vibrant young politician taking over for Eisenhower, and Truman before him and Roosevelt before him.

S: Why did other people that you knew at the time vote for him?

D: It was the first time that the T.V. had a great impact on the way people viewed the candidates. The debates between Kennedy and Nixon made Nixon look very bad. It wasn't in what he said, but in how he looked in comparison. It was a close election, even with the debates, we sweated it out until the end. There were a lot of Catholics, too, which never held any water for me, but for a lot of people, it did.

S: Tell me what happened in your life when you found out Kennedy was shot?

D: I was at work. We didn't get a lot of information right away, we just heard that he'd been shot. It was hard to believe. The last time before that must have been McKinley. One hour later we found out that Kennedy was dead. This was even harder to believe. Throughout the company and the country, work came to a standstill. Everyone was just standing around talking about it. The company I worked for at the time was highly unionized, the union got the company to shut down that day. I don't remember what day of the week it was. The company shut down for the funeral also. Lots of people took it very hard. It must have been over a weekend because the young woman I was dating wouldn't go out. Everyone sat at home and watched T.V. coverage of the event. The funeral and everything was a big event on T.V. It was the only thing that was on. It was all televised. I remember watching T.V. with my mother and seeing Jack Ruby shoot Oswald live. It was unbelieveable, everyone saw it live. Not only was the president shot, but the other guy was shot on live T.V.

---

   c. Stimulate continued growth in listening, observing, and nonverbal communication.

   d. Show students the new vocabulary as it appears in magazines and newspapers and current events.

2. Use a small number of key social studies concepts or ideas. Don't aim for complete coverage of hundreds of people or technical terms. Choose concepts that are of greater importance or frequency in the social studies.

   a. Use short explanations and numerous examples to illustrate concepts.

   b. Repeat the use of new concepts in interesting contexts; students must hear and use the new words frequently.

IMMIGRATION
RON ZYDONIK

GS: Do you remember much of the boat ride?

GM: I know we landed at the lady of . . . statue, Statue of Liberty . . . ah . . . ah . . . Ellis Island.

GS: What did you have to do to get into the country? Did you have to do anything?

GM: Well, yeah. When you got off the boat, your hair got washed in kerosene. To make sure you didn't bring any lice over. They did that at Ellis Island. You go right into this building right off the boat. See years ago they did that, but not anymore.

GS: The immigration department?

GM: Yeah.

GS: What else?

GM: You had to have a vaccination for smallpox. See, that was quite a disease out at Europe at one time. They didn't want you bringing it over here. And you got a physical from the doctor. Then they took you to the depot . . . you had to have your tag on. Where you were going and what your name was. And as soon as you got on that train they shipped you off. But you had to stay at Ellis Island for three days until they got through with you, until they processed you. Most everyone had to stay three days 'cause I don't think they could process you in . . . all those people in one day. When my dad became a citizen, that automatically made me a citizen. But they would not give me a photostatic copy of the papers, but they gave me the number of the citizenship papers so I could get a job, because I had no birth certificate. Yeah. You go through a lot. When you came over to this country they check your credentials to see if you were ever a murderer or a crook, you know. But other than that, they don't do anything else.

---

    c. Pronounce names and places carefully.

    d. Show pictures of individuals and objects; use maps identifying places; in many cases spell out words on the chalkboard.

    e. Train students in glossary and dictionary usage. (41-42)

COMPREHENSION

Comprehension refers to the complex process of obtaining meaning from printed or spoken language. Reading specialists refer to literal and inferential comprehension, although at times these terms overlap. Barrett's "Taxonomy of Reading Comprehension" gives four levels of comprehension: literal, inferential, evaluative, and appreciative. As noted in Dupuis and others, Barrett's taxonomy "provides a useful hierarchy of comprehension levels parallel to Bloom's cognitive hierarchy." (29) The Dupuis work provides many useful comprehension strategies for teachers. The one reprinted above for *Goldilocks and*

COMPREHENSION QUESTIONS FOR READERS OF GOLDILOCKS AND THE THREE BEARS

1. Recognition or Recall of Details
   What did Goldilocks eat at the three bears' house?

2. Recognition or Recall of Sequence
   What did Goldilocks do after she sat in the three bears' chairs?

3. Inferring Cause and Effect Relationship
   Why did Goldilocks enter the three bears' house?

4. Predicting Outcomes
   Before the students are told the ending of the story, ask the following:
   What do you think will happen to Goldilocks when the three bears come home?

5. Judgments of Reality or Fantasy
   Could this story have taken place? Why or why not?

6. Judgments of Worth, Desirability, or Acceptability
   Was Goldilocks right to have entered the three bears' house? Why or why not?

7. Identification with Characters and Incidents
   How did you feel when the three bears found Goldilocks asleep in the little bear's bed?

SOURCE: Dupuis and Askov, p. 184.

the Three Bears makes use of Barrett's taxonomy. Similar strategies can be applied to other types of social studies reading materials.

REFERENCE LOCATION

Skills of reference location are vital to social studies research and understanding. These skills include the use of dictionaries, encyclopedias, newspapers, the card catalog, and specialized reference works like atlases and anthologies of key issues. Some good ideas include learning how to find information in books, teaching the use of map lists in reference works, learning to use various indexes and tables of contents, and noting copyright dates to give a historical perspective.

MAP READING

According to Askov and Kamm, there are three complex skills involved in map reading: representation, location, and measurement.

The representation skills concern the use of symbols in depicting information. The location skills refer to the use of grids and directions to describe places

HINTS FOR TEACHING LISTENING SKILLS

1. Check the amount of speaking that you do during a class. Are you talking too much? Requiring too much listening?
2. Have students record the amount of time they listen both in class and outside of class.
3. Give oral directions or announcements only once. Have other students repeat instructions if necessary.
4. Give listening tests; occasionally give oral quizzes.
5. Be a good model yourself in listening.
6. Tell your students what to listen for. With practice they can learn to listen for the main ideas without the assistance of lists of questions or written scripts.
7. Have students outline and compare their views of the major points of a speech the class has heard.
8. Have students look for speakers' different frames of reference.
9. Occasionally ask your students to rate their own listening skills.
10. Be sure that you as well as the students speak clearly enough to be easily heard.
11. Most important, have something for students that is worth listening to. Part of this job is for the teacher to arrange an interesting class.
12. Allow the student (initially) to communicate in a language he or she already knows. This is especially important for the culturally different. Utilize what happens in his outside environment to generate his willingness to listen in class.
13. As the students' language power increases with more adult contacts, bring more adult volunteers into the classroom.

SOURCE: Chapin and Gross, p. 58.

of objects, and the measurement skills pertain to the use of scale to determine distances between places and sizes of areas. (124)

A more detailed description of map and globe skills is provided in Chapter 11.

WRITING

Like reading, the ability to write is vital to the skillful expression of knowledge. Students often say that they hate to write and ask if there is an easy way to learn to write better. Writing is never easy, and the only way to improve writing skills is to practice them every day—that is, to compose something original every day. In social studies, students could write make-believe diaries or letters of historical figures, reports to the president as if they were cabinet members,

TABLE 12.4
Number of Vehicles Passing Clarke School Tuesday between 10:00 A.M. and 10:30 A.M.

Car	12
Truck	7
Motorcycle	3
Bus	2
Moped	2
Camper	1
Bicycle	1

SOURCE: Hawkins, p. 3.

newscasts, historical fiction, original myths or legends, life stories, family histories, career aspirations, travelogues, descriptions of their neighborhood or community, editorials, position papers, and so on. The depth, development, and content of such writing will depend on student ability.

LISTENING

This skill was discussed in Chapter 8. Some suggestions for teachers appear in the box on page 350.

GRAPHING

This skill has gone largely unnoticed in many classrooms in recent years. That is unfortunate, because graphs provide an alternative way to represent and comprehend data in a manner that may be more effectively understood by many students.

In his "How-to-Do-It" pamphlet, Hawkins describes the use and construction of the four most popular types of graphs (bar, picture, line, and circle graphs). These can be used at any grade level to clarify and illustrate data. Graphs are often used to present information more dramatically and to make large numbers understandable. "Relationships which are not readily grasped from tables of statistics or narratives can be shown and clarified." (Hawkins, 1) Note the contrast between Table 12.4 and Figure 12.9. Both the graph and the table give the same information, but the graph accentuates the differences across categories rather than just expressing them.

Although graphs can be very effective, they can also distort information through data manipulation, eye appeal, symbol use, and the use of illusion. Because graphs are so frequently used by newspapers, magazines, television, and textbooks, students should learn to detect bias in graphs as well as be able to read them.

FIGURE 12.9

Number of Vehicles Passing Clarke School Tuesday between 10:00 A.M. and 10:30 A.M.

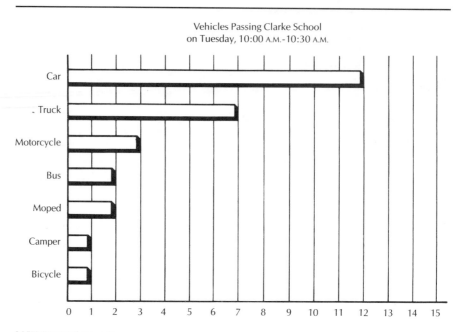

SOURCE: Hawkins, p. 3.

CRITICAL THINKING

This section addresses the ability of students to understand what they read enough that they can apply upper-level thinking skills to the matter at hand. This may involve decision making, which has been discussed in earlier chapters, or a hierarchical developmental perspective such as that proposed by Bloom or Barrett. In either case, critical evaluation is an extension of other types of skills discussed previously. Although it is sometimes viewed separately, it is not necessarily a separate and isolated reading skill in social studies.

Critical thinking is a complex of intellectual skills that are consciously, deliberately, and consistently applied by a thinker when he or she is confronted by a body of data from which a conclusion or solution must be derived, or by an agreement of a third party who wishes the thinker to accept a predetermined interpretation, point of view, or conclusion. (Hudgins et al., 330)

There has been increased attention to the idea of thinking and the teaching of thinking over the past five years. Many educators have conceded that emphasizing content without emphasizing why it is important or how students can deliberate on the issue has largely been a failure. Students have not learned the content or have learned it superficially and soon forgotten it. However, "a great deal of research in cognitive psychology shows that the more actively you process information, the more you retain it." (Berger)

Thinking skills programs, to be most successful, must not be taught in isolation, but with content. In addition, they should be taught in more than a single course, not just in social studies, for example. Nevertheless, it has been noted by some educators that social studies is the logical place to emphasize pupils' thinking skills, since such skills would seem to lead children toward a more active, intelligent, thoughtful role as adult members of a democratic society. (Raths et al., 61)

In *Teaching for Thinking,* Raths and his colleagues examine and identify some symptoms of human behavior that reflect inadequate experiences with thinking. These include impulsiveness, overdependence on the teacher, inability to concentrate, missing the meaning, dogmatic or assertive behavior, rigidity or inflexibility of behavior, extreme lack of confidence in one's own thinking, or an unwillingness to think.

There are cautions about this list, however. It is possible that a student may have physical or emotional problems that inhibit good thinking. A teacher should be aware of or alert to such problems before pressing students to "think better." A prerequisite for thoughtful work in a classroom is a feeling of security among the children. Thinking means, in a way, risk taking—testing the unknown. Children are not about to do that if the consequences of trying might be embarrassment or chastisement.

At least twelve thinking operations can be introduced and applied in all subject areas (Raths et al., 40–47). These include:

Comparing

Observing

Classifying

Imagining

Hypothesizing

Criticizing and evaluating

Identifying assumptions

Designing projects and investigations

Interpreting

Decision making

Summarizing

Problem solving

Here are examples of some of these operations as they apply to social studies. Raths and colleagues give more, and teachers will be able to think of their own applications.

COMPARING

Students might compare life in an urban or rural area of their state or life in their town with life in a town of comparable size in Italy or India.

IMAGINING

Students might imagine themselves as legislators or the president. What new laws would they propose? Or they might imagine what would happen if all guns were banned in the United States.

EXAMINING ASSUMPTIONS

When extensive road work is done, it is usually during the summer or in warm weather. What assumptions might one make about that? When citizens vote not to raise taxes to make major school building improvements, what might one assume about these citizens' views of education?

CRITICIZING AND EVALUATING

Ask students to criticize or evaluate the after-school day-care programs in their neighborhood or the political changes in the Eastern bloc nations.

DESIGNING PROJECTS AND INVESTIGATIONS

Some possible small-group projects might include an evaluation of the needs of citizens interviewed in the local shopping mall, the projected growth patterns of the community over the next 20 years, or the need for bike trails in the area.

QUESTIONS AND ACTIVITIES

1. If our world were not so complex, would there still be a need for a calendar? In other words, do you think people need calendars or clocks? What differences do they make in our lives?

2. What could be some other ways to keep track of time besides the changes in the moon and the sun?

3. Because the international date line is merely an imaginary standard, what might be the ramifications if there were no such standard? What difference would it make if the date line was located somewhere else in the world?

4. If you could rename the months, what might you call them and why?

5. On pages 316–317 it is noted that cultures measure time from different perspectives. In America time is measured from the birth of Christ. What are some other events or ways that other cultures might or do use to measure time?

6. How might one check to see if the information gathered in an oral history interview is accurate? Would the accuracy of the information make a difference?

7. Ask some local elementary school teachers how much writing their students do in social studies. If little writing is done, what are the reasons?

8. Almost any data can be expressed pictorially as well as in words. Think of data that you have encountered in your recent schooling. How might that information be organized graphically?

REFERENCES

Askov, E. and Kamm. *Study Skills in the Content Areas.* Boston, MA: Allyn and Bacon, 1982.

Barrett, T. C. "Taxonomy of Reading Comprehension." *Reading 360 Monograph.* Lexington, MA: Ginn, 1972.

Berger, J. "Classroom Focus Shifting to the Act of Thinking," *New York Times,* April 13, 1988, p. B10.

Bjorkbom, K. "Oral History Interview." Unpublished. March 26, 1984.

Cassidy, D. J. "Questioning the Young Child: Process and Function," *Childhood Education,* vol. 65, Spring, 1988, pp. 146–49.

Chapin, J., and R. Gross. *Teaching Social Studies Skills.* Boston, MA: Little, Brown, 1973.

Cornbleth, C. "Using Questions in Social Studies." NCSS How-to-Do-It Series, ser. 2, no. 4. Washington, DC: National Council for the Social Studies, 1977.

Dupuis, M., and E. Askov. *Content Reading in the Classroom.* Englewood Cliffs, NJ: Prentice Hall, 1982, p. 184.

Dupuis, M., E. Askov, J. Lee, and B. Badiali. *Reading and Writing in Content Classrooms.* Glenview, IL: Scott, Foresman, 1989.

Friedman, K. C. "How to Develop Time and Chronological Concepts." NCSS How-to-Do-It Series, ser. 1, no. 22. Washington, DC: National Council for the Social Studies, 1964.

Fromboluti, C. S., preparer. *Helping Your Child Learn Geography.* Washington, DC: U.S. Department of Education, 1990.

Gall, M. "The Use of Questions in Teaching," *Review of Educational Research,* vol. 40, December, 1970, pp. 707–21.

Hawkins, M. L. "Graphing: A Stimulating Way to Process Data." NCSS How-to-Do-It Series, ser. 2, no. 10. Washington, DC: National Council for the Social Studies, 1980.

Hudgins, B., M. Riesenmy, D. Ebel, and S. Edelman. "Children's Critical Thinking: A Model for Its Analysis and Two Examples," *Journal of Educational Research,* vol. 82, no. 6, October, 1988, pp. 327–38.

Lunstrom, J. "Reading in the Social Studies." In *Developing Decision-Making Skills,* P. Kurfman, ed. 47th NCSS Yearbook. Washington, DC: National Council for the Social Studies, 1977.

Mehaffy, G. L., T. Sitton, and O. L. Davis, Jr. "Oral History in the Classroom." NCSS How-to-Do-It Series, ser. 2, no. 8. Washington, DC: National Council for the Social Studies, 1979.

Nelson, M. R. "Clio, Calliope and Urania: Mythology in the Elementary Classroom," *Social Education,* vol. 42, no. 2, February, 1978, pp. 132–35.

Nelson, M. R., and H. W. Singleton. "Using Oral History in the Social Studies Classroom," *The Clearing House,* vol. 49, no. 2, October, 1975, pp. 89–93.

Neuenschwander, J. A. *Oral History as a Teaching Approach.* Washington, DC: National Education Association, 1976.

Piaget, J. *Construction of Reality in the Child.* New York: Basic Books, 1954.

Raths, L., S. Wasserman, A. Jonas, and A. Rothstein. *Teaching for Thinking.* 2nd ed. New York: Teachers College Press, 1986.

Rowe, M. B. "Wait-time and Rewards as Instructional Variables: Their Influence on Language, Logic, and Fate Control," *Journal of Research in Science Teaching,* vol. 11, no. 2, 1974, pp. 81–94.

Sanders, N. M. *Classroom Questions: What Kinds?* New York: Harper and Row, 1966.

Seefeldt, C. "History for Young Children" *Theory and Research in Social Education,* vol. 21, no. 2, Spring, 1993, pp. 143–55.

Thavenet, D. J. "Family History: Coming Face-to-Face with the Past." NCSS How-to-Do-It Series, ser. 2, no. 15. Washington, DC: National Council for the Social Studies, 1981.

Thornton, S., and R. Vukelich. "Effects of Children's Understanding of Time Concepts on Historical Understanding," *Theory and Research in Social Education,* vol. 16, no. 1, Winter, 1988, pp. 69–82.

Watkins, H. *Time Counts: The Story of the Calendar.* London: Neville Spearman Ltd., 1954.

Wilson, P. W. *The Romance of the Calendar.* New York: Norton, 1937.

Chapter Thirteen

FOCUSING
ON SPECIAL ISSUES

This chapter focuses on a number of special issues—controversial topics, law, global education, academic freedom, and censorship. All can be at times controversial. Controversy is not something most teachers strive to create. Often the mere suggestion of it is enough to deter some teachers from discussing or studying a topic. Nevertheless, the social studies curriculum often seems to be embroiled in controversy. So many things can become contentious, given the proper environment, that it is nearly impossible not to arouse emotion in someone at some time. The best one can do is try to keep the parameters of the controversy clear and controlled.

This chapter will present a number of issues that have aroused controversy in schools and will discuss how to deal with them most effectively. Ignoring the issues or proselytizing on them are not effective ways to deal with controversy. Rather, the teacher needs to predict the difficulty and deal with it in a forewarned manner. Planning, organization, and open communication are keys to diminishing controversy and censorship. Anticipation and preparation are vital in order to prevent the substance of controversial issues from being ignored in waves of emotional rhetoric. Before proceeding, consider what topics might be controversial in your school or classroom and consider why they might be controversial. The second part of the chapter looks at teaching about law and global education. Both law and global education fit well into integrated aspects of most elementary school units. Both law and global education are outreach based, that is, they extend beyond the classroom and demand a broader scope than other areas. In addition, they require the use of community resources. Ideally, these issues should be integrated into the social studies curriculum across disciplines and grade levels. But due to the limited material available, few teachers have taken this integrative approach. Thus the burden falls on the individual teacher.

The last part of the chapter considers academic freedom—what it is and what it is not. Without the freedom to draw upon his or her intellectual and pedagogical training, the teacher becomes didactic and potentially autocratic. Censorship is the issue central to academic freedom. Many teachers are unaware of censorship threats until they hit close to home. By then, however, it may be too late to inject sound logic in the face of emotionalism. This chapter offers both historical and contemporary views of censorship. Both generic problems and actual case studies are examined. The concluding section identifies some strategies that can be used by teachers and parents to minimize confrontation and maximize learning.

CONTROVERSIAL ISSUES

When I ask my new classes of preservice teachers to list some of the issues that they think might be too controversial for elementary school study, similar issues appear on their lists every year. Here are some examples:

sex education	fascism
birth control	nationalism
abortion	race relations
gun control	poverty
homosexuality	ecology
drugs	overpopulation
alcohol	nuclear energy
religion	student rights
economics	evolution
communism	women's rights

the former Soviet Union

People's Republic of China

ethnic studies

government control of our lives

the CIA and the FBI

big business oligopolies

child abuse

family structure in other cultures

isolationism

world interdependence

war

peace

immigration

values

This list is not exhaustive, nor is it unusual, but many young teachers already recognize the potentially controversial nature of these issues and, fearing difficulties, they self-censor. In fact, teacher self-censorship has been found to be the most prevalent form of censorship. (Nelson, 1983)

What constitutes a controversial issue? This question does not allow for an absolute answer. If it did, most people would recognize the potential explosiveness of certain issues and plan accordingly. Many controversies arise unexpectedly, leaving teachers and administrators virtually unprepared.

A simple (and tautological) response is that a controversial issue is one that arouses controversy or debate. That, of course, could be almost anything. Local concerns can make a seemingly nondescript issue into a lightning rod of tumult. The way a teacher handles an issue or how it relates to other school or national events may determine controversy.

As indicated in the previous list, any issue that involves sex is likely to provoke some parents. Issues that some churches have taken a specific position on—such as birth control, abortion, evolution, homosexuality, or religion itself—may also arouse comment.

Gross suggests seven criteria that might be considered in deciding whether to study an issue or topic (1–3).

1. Is this issue beyond the maturity and experiential level of the pupils?
2. Is this issue of interest to the pupils?
3. Is this issue socially significant and timely for this course and grade level?
4. Is this issue one which the teacher feels can be handled successfully from a personal standpoint?
5. Is this issue one for which adequate study materials can be obtained?
6. Is this issue one for which there is adequate time to justify its presentation?
7. Is this issue one that will clash with community customs and attitudes?

Gross goes on to note:

The teacher should become fully acquainted with the community in which he [or she] is employed. An understanding of power groups, strong religious and business forces, influential individuals, and the predominant racial and national backgrounds will be an invaluable aid in organizing a course of study and in choosing issues which might be studied. (3)

It is unlikely that many issues will be totally free of controversy based on Gross's criteria. If a teacher decides to reject any topics on the ground that it might arouse controversy, the alternative is a watered-down, fact-oriented, bland, but inoffensive curriculum in which state and national capitals, presidents, dates in history, and exports and imports are studied. In other words, we would have a curriculum that reflects the lowest level of Bloom's cognitive taxonomy (see Chapter 12).

Studying Population

To demonstrate how a seemingly innocuous issue can arouse controversy, we will consider population study. Here are just a few reasons why many people find the topic controversial:

- First, the study of population involves fertility rate. This may be anathema to some parents, even if the study is statistical. Some parents may see the study of statistics as clarification of fertility, illegitimate births, abortion, birth control, and the advocacy of any or all of these subjects.
- Second, mortality rate may lead to a study of death and comments on death in our society. This may be viewed as harmful to children's psyches.
- Third, migration study could lead to the question of the value of immigration. Some people wish to see immigration restricted in order to protect jobs and keep out foreigners, even though the parents may be the children or grandchildren of foreigners.
- Fourth, the study of world hunger or disease may be depressing and make children blame the United States for world hunger.

To avoid potential controversy, population study should be introduced in an integrated manner. Family study in the lower grades should be cross-cultural and include broader views of families—divorce, adoption, birth rates, and family mobility.

American or world history study could include population issues in an ancillary manner. For example, the United States was peopled mostly by immigrants. What about other nations? How did immigration affect birth and death rates in the United States? How have state population data changed over the past hundred years? The United Nations has been a strong advocate of world population control, and every administration has supported that effort. Former UN ambassador Jeane J. Kirkpatrick "reiterated the support of the Reagan Administration and the executive branch of government for the 'ongoing work' of [the] UN Fund for Population Activities." (*Popline,* 1)

Thus controversial issues can be studied if there is adequate preparation, introduction, and investigation. Even so, careful preparation will not necessarily protect teachers from infringement on their academic freedom and external attempts at censorship.

LAW-RELATED EDUCATION

Law-related education is concerned with giving students the opportunity to understand the pervasive role of the law in everyone's life. The intention is not to create a few junior lawyers, but to teach all students the skills needed to operate within the laws of our society. In his book *The Educational Imagination,* Eisner answers some questions that many teachers, students, and parents ask about the introduction of law-related education.

> What does a lay person need to know about the law to understand his or her rights, the basic ways in which our legal system works, the rights and obligations incurred in the signing of a contract? What does it mean to be arrested? What is the difference between a criminal and a civil suit? What is a tort and when has a crime been committed?
>
> . . . Students could be introduced to the study of law first because the problems that it poses are interesting and rich—there is much that could be related to their lives in a fairly direct fashion—and second because it is important for citizens to know something about the legal system under which they live so that at the very least they will be in a position to understand the obligations of a contract and the remedies for its violation. (104)

The goals of law-related education include the enhancement of citizenship, the acquisition of legal skills, and the attainment of social science knowledge that surrounds the field of law. Law-related education is considered fundamental by many teachers. According to Nelson (1978), "an understanding of our society's laws is a basic skill every bit as important as reading, writing and arithmetic." (9) Law affects all citizens every day by impressing constraints on almost all citizen actions. "Attaining the skills necessary to recognize and operate effectively within those constraints is a priority of the law-related education movement." (Nelson, 1978, 9)

A common classroom exercise, called a mind walk, may be used to illustrate the pervasiveness of the law in our lives. First, students are asked to describe their activities in a typical day. Next they are asked to hypothesize which of these activities are affected by legal constraints or legal protection. As a variation on this exercise, a teacher could present a list of situations and ask students to pick out the activities that have legal ramifications and explain those ramifications. A sample list of activities is shown in the box on pages 362–363. Each of these activities has legal implications that can be drawn out in class discussion.

For example, item 4, "Get dressed," has a number of legal implications. Laws against indecent exposure preclude any choice about being dressed before going out in public, although how one is dressed is generally a matter of taste, not law.

When sold, all clothing must have washing or cleaning instructions and the size displayed on a label. These are Federal Trade Commission (FTC) requirements. The clothing also cannot be treated with certain chemicals, like

---

MIND-WALK EXERCISE

Next to every daily activity, please make the following notations: Place an X in either the "yes" or "no" column if you feel that the law (as you understand that term) does or does not affect that particular activity. If your response is "yes," complete the next blank space by stating how the law affects the activity.

ACTIVITY	ANY LEGAL IMPACT?		
	YES	No	How?
1. Alarm clock awakens you. Turn on light.			
2. Use the bathroom.			
3. Wash face. Apply deodorant.			
4. Get dressed.			
5. Eat breakfast—cereal, milk, juice, and eggs.			
6. Brush teeth.			
7. Read paper. See ad for TV sets on sale at store.			
8. Get in car.			
9. Drive to work.			
10. Stop at store on lunch hour to buy TV. Told it is a discontinued model, but better TV sets are available on easy credit terms.			
11. Get paid. Go to bank, cash check, deposit some of it.			

(continued)

SOURCE: From Nelson, *Law in the Curriculum.*

some flame retardants, that may be cancer causing. This, too, is the result of FTC regulations.

If the examples given in the box are too abstract or difficult for primary grade children, a simpler mind-walk exercise is illustrated on page 365. Teachers can make up their own mind walks with the assistance of lawyers or paralegals.

Assistance from nonschool personnel should not be seen as an inconvenience or as evidence of a teacher's shortcomings. Effective law-related education requires extensive use of community resources. Teachers should not assume they have the legal expertise to answer all law questions accurately. An effective program makes learning about the law as much a teacher's as a student's responsibility. The teaching of law should not be seen as another foray into trivial facts and details. Conceptual understanding of the law is within reach of every rational man and woman.

(continued from previous page)

ACTIVITY	ANY LEGAL IMPACT?		
	YES	NO	HOW?
12. Stop at grocery store to buy yogurt, vegetables, chicken, canned soup, and canned tomatoes.			
13. Buy prescription at pharmacy.			
14. Stop at Sears, Roebuck and Co. Buy stuffed animal for nephew. Pay with charge card.			
15. Go home; discover you have no heat. Call landlord.			
16. Listen to radio while you prepare dinner in electric oven.			
17. Eat dinner.			
18. Avon lady calls. You ask her in, buy $25 worth of cosmetics.			
19. Landlord phones to say pipes have burst but heat is on the way.			
20. Watch television. Hear a noise near back door and call police.			
21. Police call is tape-recorded.			
22. Police arrive, find back door jimmied but suspect gone.			
23. After difficult evening, you bathe, wash hair.			
24. Turn out lights and go to bed.			

A number of legal resources are available in the community. These include not only attorneys and police officers but courthouse personnel (clerk, protonotary, judge, bailiff, recorder of deeds), local magistrates, wardens, and social welfare workers (parole officers, youth service workers, welfare case workers). Other law-related resource personnel are consumer advocates, building inspectors, FBI agents, bankers, people from the media, county or state associations of lawyers, spouses, real estate agents, law students, representatives of various federal or state regulatory agencies, sports personalities, and political officeholders.

A professional athlete and his agent can show how the law enters into an athlete's career, from knowing how to read a contract to planning for that after-sports future. Students will appreciate the great amount of legal work that goes into a commercial endorsement for a product like basketball shoes or breakfast cereal.

ELEMENTARY LEVEL ACTIVITIES

The content of law studies can be applied to almost any elementary social studies unit in the established curriculum. A separate unit on law education would convey to students that the law is something one studies for three or four weeks and then forgets. A separate introductory unit is fine as long as the legal concepts introduced are integrated into the rest of the social studies curriculum later on.

Many primary level materials on the law begin with the notion of rules. In his *Handbook of Basic Citizenship Competencies,* Richard Remy offers suggestions about presenting the rule concept to students:

> Students could imagine what school would be like if there were no rules (about running, raising one's hand, taking responsibility for one's supplies, etc.). Children draw pictures or write stories to show how they and other children and adults in the school would be affected by the imaginary situation. Pictures or stories can be discussed to identify the people affected and ways in which they were affected by the imagined condition. Children can then discuss the value of given rules. (26)

Another starter activity on this same topic involves the use of a cartoon movie called *Why We Have Laws—Shiver, Gobble, and Snore* or of the children's book by Marie Winn on which the film is based (see references). The cartoon centers on three friends who decide to form their own community to escape the tyrannical and capricious rules of their king. They decide to go live in a place where they can be free—where there are no rules. They find, however, that without rules they are constantly arguing and are unable to live peacefully. They decide that to be truly free and to live with others they must make rules. The film, incidentally, can be used at a variety of grade levels.

GRADE-LEVEL IDEAS AND ACTIVITIES

The primary grades seek to teach students certain academic basics as well as social and personal basics necessary to function comfortably in our society. The activities above focus on why rules are created in the first place. Another level of study might focus on how *fair* certain rules are. To illustrate this concept, Nelson (1978) describes a situation originally developed by Susan Dawson Archer.

> In a kindergarten classroom the youngsters are hotly debating a question of fairness in a modern version of "The Little Red Hen." Two youngsters wished to bake cookies with a neighbor who said that if they returned the next day they could, indeed, bake cookies. The next day one youngster returned at the appointed time, helped in the baking and cleaning up, then anxiously waited for the cookies to cool. At that point the other child ran up and said that he smelled cookies. The first child, Kim, protested that Kevin should not get any cookies because he failed to help in the baking or cleaning up. Kevin said that he had wanted to help, but he had to watch his little sister while his mother took his grandfather to the doctor, it had been a last-minute emergency.

MIND WALK FOR YOUNG CHILDREN

ACTIVITY	ANY LEGAL IMPACT?		
	YES	NO	HOW?
1. Wake up to alarm.			
2. Use bathroom, wash, brush teeth.			
3. Get dressed.			
4. Eat breakfast—cereal, milk, juice, and toast.			
5. Walk to school. Cross two busy streets.			
6. Enter school.			
7. Pledge to flag.			
8. Buy milk/lunch ticket.			
9. Receive reading instruction, use textbooks.			
10. Go to P.E. class.			
11. Work with paste and glitter in art.			
12. Play at sand table.			
13. Eat lunch.			
14. Walk home, watch *Sesame Street* on TV.			
15. Play with dolls (Mickey Mouse, Kermit the Frog).			
16. Play with pet dog in your yard.			

SOURCE: From Nelson, "Teaching Young Children About the Law."

Now the kindergarten students are attempting to determine what is a fair solution for all parties concerned. (6–7)

Rather than a debate, the teacher might choose to role-play the situation or use a values clarification strategy. In any case, the concept of fairness can be assessed even by kindergarten children.

Concepts such as fairness, leadership, responsibility, and authority can be demonstrated to children at various grade levels through activities in the classroom, the school yard, and other areas of the school. A school custodian could come to a primary grade classroom to explore the nature of leadership and responsibility from his or her perspective. Children could discuss with the custodian the nature of his or her work and leadership in the school. They could also learn how they can aid the custodian by picking up litter, storing equipment in the proper place, and wiping their feet before entering the building.

In the middle grades and upper elementary grades, students usually focus on more specific subject areas or on studying units that cut across disciplines. Almost every state recommends the study of state history and government at some point in these grades. Typically such courses deal with the familiar litany of names, dates, and places. There are other, more law-related possibilities, however.

> The question of rights and responsibilities in state history is frequently over-
> looked, e.g., in a fourth-grade class in Pennsylvania the students skip lightly
> over the treaties William Penn and others made with some of the Native Amer-
> ican Indian tribes . . . a teacher [could] use this topic to delve into the nature
> of a treaty, its legal status, and its consequences for the future. Students [could]
> then begin questioning the limitations of those treaties today and investigate
> other treaties between various countries. (Nelson, 1978, 14)

Other common subjects in the middle grades that lend themselves to law-
related education are U.S. history, world history, and regional cultural studies.
"To merely 'study' the government composition of a country without attempting to understand the cultural influence on its laws is to neglect the most important and universal factors of national identity." (Nelson, 1978, 14)

Science and society often merge in law-related issues. The creation of
more powerful nuclear bombs is obviously a result of scientific and technological advancement, but laws and treaties regulate the use and proliferation of
such weaponry. Environmental science issues are similarly regulated, as will be
discussed later in this chapter.

Law-Related Strategies

Several excellent law-related strategies are promoted by the Department of Education in Pennsylvania. These strategies are organized around three major
themes for all grade levels: understanding self and others, understanding society, and understanding safety and crime prevention. The purpose of these Justice Education Teaching Strategies (JETS) is

1. To promote and maintain positive student attitudes in behavior:
   To have students develop activities to affect value judgments.
   To give a more positive but realistic view of law and people who
   administer the law.
2. To assist students in understanding their rights and meeting their responsibilities to help insure the safety and welfare of self and others:
   To increase knowledge of civil and criminal law.
   To increase knowledge of procedures used by police and other
   criminal justice agencies.

The following activities are tied to the recommended competencies developed by the Pennsylvania Department of Education.

UNDERSTANDING SELF AND OTHERS

The first activity from "Understanding Self and Others" encourages students to examine their feelings of self and others with an emphasis on individual rights and responsibilities within the community.

ACTIVITY 1: SNOW FORT[1]

Purpose: Provided with case studies involving problems of personal and property rights, students are asked to propose and substantiate a solution.

Key question: What are rights?

1. Have children discuss what they think rights are. (Just claims of privilege, according to law.)
2. Have the students name some rights that they feel are important to themselves.

Procedure: Divide the class into small groups to discuss a situation in which rights are in dispute. The groups will need to decide what are the rights of the boys and what are the rights of the girls. Each group is to solve the problem in the fairest way possible.

- The boys have built a snow fort on the playground at school. The girls want to play in it. Who owns the snow fort? Who owns the snow? Who owns the playground?
- The playground is used by both boys and girls. Do the girls have a right to use the snow fort on the playground?
- The boys did all the work of building the snow fort. Does this give them the right to decide who should play in it?
- How would you decide? What do you think would be fair?

Teachers shouldn't be looking for one right answer here; they should seek solutions that students will defend and others will listen to (see the Magic Circle exercise in Chapter 4). If students want *technically* right answers, the school district owns the playground and the snow. Thus everyone (or no one) owns the fort. The boys have no legal right to decide on the use of the snow fort, but a representative of the school district (teacher, principal) may decide to consider the boys' efforts in building the fort should a dispute arise over its use. Such a dispute could be avoided if the concerned parties considered the interests of others as well as of themselves.

AUTHORITY AND UPHOLDING LAWS

Rules, laws, and authority are essential for establishing and maintaining order. Compliance with rules is often difficult when individuals perceive them as restrictions rather than as means to safety and harmony. The following activities

---

[1] From *Foundations of Justice,* ed. Robert Ratcliffe (Columbus, OH: Merrill Bell and Howell Co., 1975).

illustrate this aspect of the law in two different ways. The first activity, called "Can You?," encourages students to think about authority and its importance. The second activity, called "Evidence," from the Law in Action Series (1975), allows students to "demonstrate a willingness to assume responsibilities to cooperate and assist in upholding rules and laws."

ACTIVITY 2: CAN YOU?

Procedure: Distribute the worksheet shown in Figure 13.1. Have students check whether or not they can make each of the decisions listed for themselves. If not, they should name the person who makes that decision in the third column, under "Who does?"

Discussion of student responses could focus on why different people—students, parents, or some other authority—are responsible for making certain decisions. Why couldn't the students or parents make all the decisions? Family decision making will vary, and a teacher should simply note the differences rather than judge one or two modes of decision making as superior or inferior to others. Are there different levels of authority?

ACTIVITY 3: EVIDENCE

Procedure: Show students the picture in Figure 13.2 and have them answer the following questions:

1. What is happening?
2. Who could the people be?
3. Do people disagree about what is happening?
4. Why do you think people see things in different ways?

This exercise illustrates how our own perceptions and background influence how we view things. Thus our legal system is designed to use corroborative evidence as a criterion in assessing guilt or responsibility.

ACTIVITY 4: BAD HABITS

Purpose: For students to understand the nature of how habits form and to begin to see addiction to drugs as a severe example.

Key questions: Do any of you have a bad habit, that is, one that your parents or friends tell you is socially unacceptable or "uncool"?

The teacher could tell a brief story of a bad habit that he or she had and how difficult it was to break. This could be something like nail biting, saying "you know" a lot, or smoking.

Procedure: Have students work in groups of two or three and have each person relate a bad habit that he or she has. Each group should provide possible solutions (punishments, rewards, peer pressure, and the like) for breaking a bad habit.

FIGURE 13.1
Worksheet to Accompany Activity 2

Can You?

CAN YOU DECIDE FOR YOURSELF:	YES	NO	IF NO, WHO DOES
1. to go to school?			
2. what traffic laws to obey?			
3. what television shows to watch?			
4. how much to spend on clothes?			
5. whom you have as friends?			
6. how much Hershey bars cost?			
7. who your teacher is going to be?			
8. what library book to check out?			
9. what games to play after school?			
10. how to wear your hair?			

SOURCE: From Justice Education Teaching Strategies K–6, Pennsylvania Department of Education, p. 57.

FIGURE 13.2

Picture to Accompany Activity 3

SOURCE: Reprinted by permission from *Courts and Trials* by Linda Riekes and Sally Mahe;
Copyright © 1975 by West Publishing Company. All rights reserved. Page 62.

Large-group discussion can address the larger question of breaking any bad
habits, with the direction of the discussion aimed toward clarifying that not
starting a bad habit is easier to do than breaking one.

Drug use is discussed by the teacher within the context of a bad habit.
Some consequences are introduced, such as loss of a job, personal harm, and
family breakup.

THE LAW AND DRUGS

The continued escalation of drug use has pushed this issue to the forefront of
law-related education. Many law and health groups have cooperatively produced materials to enhance drug prevention throughout the community.
These resources are listed at the end of the chapter.

Conflict Resolution

The increased use of violence in and around schools has provided the major
impetus for schools to address conflict resolution. Some schools have begun
peer mediation programs; others have made greater classroom efforts to resolve conflicts. Steps in a typical mediation are offered in the box on page 365.
Many state LRE projects now offer training in Conflict Management. Project addresses are listed at the end of the chapter.

STEPS IN A TYPICAL MEDIATION SESSION

Step 1. Introduction

The mediator makes the parties feel at ease and explains the ground rules. The mediator's role is not to make a decision but to help the parties reach a mutual agreement. The mediator explains that he or she will not take sides.

Step 2. Telling the Story

Each party tells what happened. The person bringing the complaint tells his or her side of the story first. No interruptions are allowed. Then the other party explains his or her version of the facts.

Step 3. Identifying Facts and Issues

The mediator attempts to identify agreed-upon facts and issues. This is done by listening to each side, summarizing each party's views, and asking if these are the facts and issues as each party understands them.

Step 4. Identifying Alternative Solutions

Everyone thinks of possible solutions to the problem. The mediator makes a list and asks each party to explain his or her feelings about each possible solution.

Step 5. Revising and Discussing Solutions

Based on the expressed feelings of the parties, the mediator revises possible solutions and attempts to identify a solution that both parties can agree to.

Step 6. Reaching Agreement

The mediator helps the parties to reach an agreement that both can live with. The agreement should be written down. The parties should also discuss what will happen if either of them breaks the agreement.

Use the mediation outline above and the following conflict situations to role-play a typical conflict situation. In each conflict situation, two students should play the parts of the people in conflict. A third student should use the outline to mediate the dispute and develop an agreement.

Consumer Law

Additional aspects of law-related education include comparative law (with examples from various cultures), criminal law, prisons and punishment, juvenile law, contracts, torts or civil wrongs, and consumer law. This last area is popular with students and teachers because of their direct involvement in purchasing products and services. Students can, for example, examine toy ads and then purchase the products and put them to the test as shown on a television commercial. Despite their initial disappointment that the toys do not always perform as advertised, most students are pleased to become good consumers and to view advertising claims with skepticism.

One class of students with access to video equipment went even further in its toy investigation by recreating television commercials on film. The students then showed the film to other classes in the school as part of a school-wide campaign on consumer awareness.

Materials for studying consumer law are readily available, much of it excellent. The magazine *Zillions* published by Consumers Union is an excellent resource. Each issue examines some product in which children are interested in order to compare product claims versus facts. One month, for example, was "sports energy foods" like drinks and energy bars. Other articles focus on campaign ads, purchasing larger ticket items like stereos or televisions, toys, and sport products. There are also smaller interactive features and comic strip "adventures" in consumer purchases. For younger children—even many older ones—a good introduction to consumer education is the film *The Owl Who Gave a Hoot,* available from the National Audio Visual Center in Washington, DC. The cartoon illustrates a variety of illegal practices that consumers should be aware of in order to protect themselves.

A good book on consumer law is *Young Consumers* (from West Publishing, Law in Action series), a softcover book appropriate from the fifth (*maybe* the fourth) up to the ninth grade. It includes activities, thoughtful explanations, and community involvement projects.

Consumer law is often taught as a part of consumer education, with an emphasis on smart buying and budgeting as well as legal—and illegal—practices. *Where* consumer law is introduced in the curriculum is unimportant; what is important is that students learn consumer education in an integrated manner. Some basic consumer education competencies might focus on the function of the economic system, rights and responsibilities of the consumer, agencies that help consumers, credit use, business rights and responsibilities, the national consumer movement, and so on.

Consumer education is a convenient way to combine mathematics and social studies and to show the *applied* use of mathematics (see Chapter 12). For example, if a product is advertised as 20 percent off, students could find out how much a consumer saves by buying the product on sale. Of course, a good consumer realizes that one saves nothing if the product is either unnecessary or unwanted. Percentages, the metric system, sales tax calculations, cost per unit, and discounting are all mathematics-based functions that combine skills in math with consumer education.

Children can study how advertising influences purchases and how it is regulated by law. Good consumerism is achieved through practice, not just lip service. Students should go to the store and pretend to buy a few necessary products (butter, salad oil, and orange juice, for example) and then report their findings. What is the best buy? Are there other factors besides cost that enter into one's purchases, such as advertising, traditional family use, a neighbor's recommendation, personal taste, and packaging?

The study of law can be applied to almost any area. The key to implementing any justice education program, however, is the utilization of local justice personnel by the teacher.

Children can study how advertising influences purchases and how it is regulated by law.

GLOBAL EDUCATION

We live in a smaller world than ever before. What occurs in the Middle East affects the United States—not just eventually, but immediately, as we know from the Persian Gulf War and the conflicts in Bosnia. Television reporters broadcast the story on the news, newspapers cover it the next day, the stock market shows the effects, and the cost or availability of goods changes almost overnight. The tremendous changes in Eastern Europe, the former Soviet Union, Latin America, and South Africa also make the need for studying globally greater than ever. The world has changed and is still changing in the 1990s.

It would be nice if, by ignoring world problems, those problems would go away. It *would* be nice, but, unfortunately, this is not going to happen. World problems are American problems; ignoring them means ignoring their effect on American social and economic realities. Global education tries to put all of this in a manageable perspective for teachers and students. Again, integration is the best approach, and the possibilities are limitless. The 1982 "Position Statement on Global Education" by the National Council for the Social Studies states:

> The growing interrelatedness of life on our planet has increased the need for citizens to possess the knowledge and sensitivity required to comprehend the global dimensions of political, economic, and cultural phenomena. (36)

Those who advocate global education, however, have no axe to grind, as Collins and Zakariya note.

> Global education is not an ideology. It is a reflection of the fact that we are all members of a single human species being together on an ever more crowded and polluted planet. But recognizing our common citizenship in the world community does not mean that we must repudiate our national identities. (3)

Most global educators see global education as an extension, not a substitute, for nationalistic education. Being global does not mean that one is any less patriotic. Loyalty to one's country need not suffer because of global concerns. Being global, in fact, may make one a *better* citizen and thus might be seen as enhancing patriotism. H. T. Collins, quoting Thomas Shannon,[2] summarizes global education as follows:

> Global education is not a thinly disguised attempt to sell some vague form of "one-worldism" or "world-citizenship" to American schools. On the contrary, its purpose is to assure that our citizens are adequately prepared to function intelligently as decision-makers in the market-place and at the ballot box in their local communities, in their own states, and as citizens of the United States of America. (18)

---

[2] From Shannon's speech to the Association for the Advancement of International Education, February 1980, Anaheim, CA.

Global education is, not surprisingly, a perspective that goes beyond American borders. The Halton, Ontario, Global Education Group states that

> A Global Perspective is a way of thinking, a way of looking at life on this planet. Education for a Global perspective seeks to bring about a broader outlook in students, moving them from a local focus in their lives to a planetary view of life. (Halton Board of Education, 1994)

Exposure to global education may have a greater impact in elementary school, when young minds are being shaped, than in high school, after prejudices have intervened. Even the primary grades are not too early to begin a global education.

Recognizing this, some school districts have initiated "twinning" projects, in which an American school district and a foreign one exchange teachers and students for a period of time. The State College, Pennsylvania, School District has begun such exchanges with a school in England and one in France. Students as young as 10 have visited in their "twinned" district. There is also an exchange of letters, videotapes, and other material about life at school and at home.

As Marshall McLuhan has noted, the global village is everywhere. Television has made the world smaller, but without teacher guidance global events remain unconnected in a child's mind. It is naive to pretend that children are ignorant of world happenings, although they may be ignorant of the *significance* of such happenings, either to them or to the world at large. To lead students on such a path requires teachers who have also questioned the significance of world events.

A global education should address the following six elements:

1. Perspective Consciousness (a recognition that one's view of the world is not universally shared)
2. State of Planet Awareness (awareness of prevailing world conditions and developments such as population growth, economic conditions, intranation conflict, etc.)
3. Cross-cultural Awareness (the diversity of cultures, ideas, and practices around the world and how these compare)
4. Sense of Global Dynamics (an awareness of how the world's systems work and the extent to which they are interdependent)
5. Awareness of Emergent Human Goals (knowledge of various social movements that create goals and values that transcend national cultures and ideologies)
6. Awareness of Ethical Problems in the Global Context (knowledge of ethical questions and issues that derive from increased capacities for seeing, predicting, and manipulating global conditions such as distribution of the world's food, wealth, and other resources). (Lafayette, 3)

One of the greatest shortcomings of new teachers may be their general lack of knowledge of global concerns. Ideally, global education should begin before college. However, many preservice teachers may have to foster their own global education. Some good starting suggestions:

1. Subscribe to a large daily newspaper with its own staff of correspondents. Their perspectives may balance the wire service views or provide different details.

2. Watch television news for up-to-date coverage of global affairs. With the growth of 24-hour cable news shows, this has become easier.

3. Read an issues-oriented magazine—either a weekly news magazine or a monthly essay and commentary magazine.

4. Attend lectures and discussions on global issues. The most important aspect is not cognitive so much as affective, gaining an awareness of global issues and a concern with solving global problems.

5. Link up with various web sites in other nations to find differing points of view on various issues.

6. Get into the world. See how people live and think. Travel cheaply while you still can as a single, unattached adult.

Teaching Strategies

The NCSS "Position Statement on Global Education" recommends that teachers emphasize the following aspects of world affairs:

- That the human experience is an increasingly globalized phenomenon in which people are constantly being influenced by transnational, cross-cultural, multi-cultural, multi-ethnic introductions
- The variety of actors on the world stage (including multi-national corporations, church groups, scientific and cultural organizations, United Nations agencies)
- That humankind is an integral part of the world environment
- The linkages between present social, political, and ecological realities and alternative futures
- Citizen participation in world affairs (37–38)

Most global ideas can be applied to the existing curriculum. For example, according to the expanding-communities model (see Chapter 2), most first graders study the family. But rather than studying just the American family, or the Nigerian or Japanese family, a global approach would try to tie these families together through mutual problems or economic realities. Sam's father in Nigeria might work on a coffee plantation; as the price of coffee rises, people in the United States drink less coffee, causing Sam's father to be unemployed. A similar situation can be seen with American workers. Unemployment, hunger, disease, human dignity, energy production, pollution, and the threat of war are all global issues, not simply national concerns.

Johnson and Benegar provide some useful activities under three broad topics—global awareness, global interdependence, and cross-cultural understanding. The following activity, called "Globingo," examines the nature of the world and its decreasing size.

ACTIVITY 5: GLOBINGO

Purpose: To discover how class members are connected to the rest of the world and to speculate about further global connections.

Materials: "Globingo" worksheets (pages 378–379) and a large map of the world.

Procedure:

1. Distribute copies of the "Globingo" worksheet to all the students.
2. Allow 10 to 15 minutes for students to walk around the classroom looking for classmates who fit the various squares. It is important during this period that students ask one another questions rather than passively hand around the game sheets. Students should dig for the information they need. They should continue to try to fill up their game sheets even after they have scored one or more "Globingos." Try to keep the game going until every student has scored.
3. If students wish to carry this on further at lunch, or involve their families, postpone debriefing until a subsequent class period.
4. Ask students what they learned about one another in the process of filling in their "Globingo" squares.
5. On a large map of the world, help students locate all the nations identified by this activity. This can be done by pulling apart the squares on the game sheets and pinning them to the appropriate locations on a world map. Are students surprised at all the connections their class has with the rest of the world? Are there countries mentioned that no longer exist as such (for example, East Germany, Ifni, Rhodesia, and Trieste)?
6. Probe students to explain the reasons for all the connections they found in this activity. What caused these connections? In what ways do we learn more about the rest of the world? Travel? Newspapers? Trade among nations?
7. Ask students what they think the phrase "shrinking world" means. Do students think that they will become more connected to the rest of the world? In what ways?

A second area covered by Johnson and Benegar is global interdependence, which highlights the interconnectedness of peoples despite barriers of culture, time, and distance. Activity 6 focuses on global interdependence through gasoline consumption.

ACTIVITY 6: FILL 'ER UP

Purpose: To examine variations in the price of gasoline around the world; to speculate about driving habits, gasoline consumption, and energy conservation as a global trend; and to explore alternatives to automobile transportation. Students need *at least* two class periods for this activity, as well as preclass time.

"GLOBINGO" WORKSHEET

The object of "Globingo" is to fill in as many squares as possible with the names of class-mates who fit those squares. As soon as one row—horizontal, vertical, or diagonal—has been completely filled in, the student has scored "Globingo." The code key below ex-plains the letter-coded spaces on the game sheet. The name of the relevant country, as well as the student's name, should be recorded in each square. Each student may sign another classmate's sheet only *once,* even if more than one square could apply to that student.

Find some one who:

A. has traveled to some foreign country

B. has a pen pal in another country

C. is learning a foreign language

D. has a relative in another country

E. has helped a visitor from another country

F. enjoys a music group from another country

G. is wearing something that was made in another country

H. enjoys eating foods from other countries

I. can name a famous sports star from another country

J. has a family car that was made in another country

K. has talked to someone who has lived in another country

L. lives in a home where more is than one lan-guage is spoken

M. saw a story about another country in the newspaper recently

N. learned something about another country on TV recently

O. owns a TV or other appliance made in another country

P. has a parent or other relative who was born in another country

(continued)

SOURCE: Johnson and Benegar, pp. 131–37.

Materials: Provide worksheets with questions regarding the price of gasoline in various countries, a list of countries and their gasoline prices, a large world map, a world almanac and atlases, construction paper, crayons or markers, scissors, and thumbtacks or pushpins.

Procedure: Have students provide data on an auto model (such as the family sedan) and its approximate gas mileage. They should spend time figuring where they would get bet-ter mileage or alter their driving habits because of gasoline prices. More ideas regarding this activity are discussed by Johnson and Benegar.

The last major concept that Johnson and Benegar seek to enhance is cross-cultural un-derstanding—that is, the acceptance and understanding of other people, groups, and cultures in order to build increased global understanding. This is demonstrated in the following ac-tivity.

(continued from previous page)

A	B	C	D
name	name	name	name
country	country	country	country

E	F	G	H
name	name	name	name
country	country	country	country

I	J	K	L
name	name	name	name
country	country	country	country

M	N	O	P
name	name	name	name
country	country	country	country

ACTIVITY 7: INTERNATIONAL ROAD SIGNS[3]

Purpose: To encourage students to explore options for communication across cultural and language barriers by working with international road signs.

Materials: A handout (Figure 13.3) is needed for each child (without the answers at the bottom), as well as construction paper, scissors, and markers.

---

[3] From Johnson and Benegar, pp. 131–37.

FIGURE 13.3
International Road Signs to Accompany Activity 7

INTERNATIONAL ROAD SIGNS

1. _____   2. _____   3. _____

4. _____   5. _____   6. _____

7. _____   8. _____   9. _____

1. CHILDREN CROSSING
2. ROAD NARROWS
3. RAILROAD GRADE CROSSING
4. SLIPPERY ROAD
5. TELEPHONE
6. HOSPITAL
7. NO PARKING
8. TOILETS
9. ACCESS for the
   HANDICAPPED

Procedure:

1. Ask students to imagine that they are visiting another country whose language they do not speak or read. What problems might they face? What problems might a visitor to the United States face, particularly in everyday routine activities? If students do not mention road signs, point out that these signs are important for pedestrians and bikers to understand, as well as drivers, because they give directions to hospitals, phones, restrooms, and lodging. To accommodate these needs, international road signs were devised. This system uses standardized nonverbal symbols to convey information, instructions, and warnings. Although a message may also be stated verbally in the country's official language, the shapes and symbols of the signs provide sufficient information to people who are familiar with the international road sign communication system.

2. Divide the class into groups of four or five students, and give each group a copy of the handout. Tell the students to decide as a group what they think each sign means. Allow 15 to 20 minutes for this exercise.

3. Ask a spokesperson from each group to report the group's answers to the whole class. Did all the groups agree on the meaning of the signs? Did any sign have anyone stumped? Which seemed the easiest to figure out? Read the correct answers (written below the signs).

4. Ask the students what helped them to understand the meanings of the signs. Could they be as easily understood by people who speak a language other than English? Could all of them be universally understood all over the world? (If students do not mention it, point out that some symbols may not be understood if one has never seen such devices).

5. Distribute construction paper, scissors, markers, and other art materials, and ask each student to think of a message or rule and make a sign illustrating that message in a way people all over the world could understand. When all the signs are finished, attach a sheet of paper to each sign and post the signs around the room. During subsequent class periods, allow students a little time to look at each sign and guess what it means, writing their names and guesses on the attached sheet.

6. After a few days, tally the guesses and summarize the results. Which signs had the most correct guesses? Which signs were the hardest to understand? Ask the students to hypothesize about the possible results of acting on some of the wrong guesses. Can they suggest some general characteristics of signs that are easily understood?

Some Possible Rules

1. No eating or drinking in this store
2. Shirt and shoes required
3. Bridge out ahead
4. One way
5. Keep off the grass
6. Danger! Thin ice
7. No diving
8. Bus stop
9. Quiet, hospital zone

    10. No exit
    11. Closed for repairs
    12. Do not feed the animals
    13. Post office
    14. No littering

Activity 7 can be better appreciated when one has been forced to use such signs. The signs are sometimes a nuisance because one often has to guess what they mean, until one learns the international "language." In a foreign country, however, where the simplest endeavors like catching a bus, finding a telephone, mailing a letter, using a public toilet, and driving become tremendous hurdles, international signs are a blessing.

Additional Areas of Global Study

Several other areas of global education deserve to be mentioned. Among these are peace education, population study, environmental education, and human rights study. The latter two areas have both global and law-related impact.

PEACE EDUCATION

Peace education often includes the related issues of economic development, poverty, social justice, and environmental health, because it is primarily these issues that keep people from achieving real peace.

Most peace study in secondary schools focuses on the threat of war as a motivating, centralizing theme. Some curricula try to encourage world peace through a world government. This approach, however, ignores the fact that many nations have experienced peace without a strong central world government. Thus the assumption that this type of government is necessary for peace is another example of cultural blindness.

The concerns of peace can be studied as early as elementary school. One approach suggests the possibility of peace without conflict resolution. As previously noted, resolving conflict is both global and law-related. How do people in other cultures resolve their differences? How do Americans do so? In the United States, lawsuits are common and acceptable. This is not the norm, however. In some cultures a lawsuit is a sign of failure to compromise, and the two parties are less esteemed because of it.

If children grow up in a society that encourages compromise and discourages conflict, will such children be more reluctant to wage war and more eager to wage peace? Preliminary research seems to indicate that this might be the case. For example, in a small study of American and Icelandic 10- to 12-year-olds, Icelandic children were more eager to avoid conflict and would compromise much more willingly than American children. (Nelson, 1986)

PEACE EDUCATION

What is peace education? It is education that teaches students about the achievement and maintenance of peace. Peace is defined in a number of ways, however. One definition is negative, defining peace as the absence of war. Other definitions equate peace with justice and harmony.

Johan Galtung, a Norwegian who founded the Institute for Peace Education in Oslo in 1966, distinguishes between the two different conceptualizations of peace, but he expands these two definitions into a large taxonomy:

> The distinction between these two types of peace gives rise to a fourfold classification of relations between two nations: war, which is organized group violence; negative peace, where there is no violence but no form of interaction either and where the best characterization is "peaceful coexistence"; positive peace, where there is some cooperation interspersed with occasional outbreaks of violence; and unqualified peace, where absence of violence is combined with a pattern of cooperation.*

What form does peace education take in school? First, peace educators aim for awareness on the part of students—awareness of the goals of peace and the efforts that must be undertaken in "waging peace." These goals can be integrated with the curriculum, particularly in social studies. For example, in history class a teacher could devote less time to wars and more time to movements to avoid war.

Students could also study cultural perspectives on conflict resolution and discuss alternatives to war in the world. A unit on media could focus on the media's role regarding war and peace. For example, many people claim the Vietnam War was lost through television news—"The Six O'Clock War." The media's presence in South Africa has been officially blamed by that government for inciting more violence. What role should the media have during war and peacetime?

What can individuals do in the interest of peace? Students might try to work with other students by writing government officials encouraging peace efforts or through other, more original means. Educators for Social Responsibility (ESR) in Cambridge, MA, has developed curricular materials on this topic. At the early elementary level the program does not advocate formal discussion of peace issues, although it advocates that peace between children between children and parents, and between children and teachers should be explored and skills developed. At the upper elementary level, it advocates discussion of peace issues when children bring them up. Although this program may not be as advanced or developed as more aggressive peace educators would like, it does bring peace studies into the school.

---

*Johan Galtung. *Peace Research—Education—Action: Essays in Peace Research,* vol. 1 (Copenhagen: Christian Ejlers, 1975), p. 29.

THE WORLD SUMMIT FOR CHILDREN

In late September of 1990 the first World Summit for Children was held at the United Nations headquarters in New York City. Over 70 presidents and prime ministers from around the globe attended, including President George Bush of the United States, Prime Minister Margaret Thatcher of Great Britain, and Prime Minister Brian Mulroney of Canada.

The summit was called by six initiating countries (Canada, Egypt, Mali, Mexico, Pakistan, and Sweden) to try to provide better opportunities for the 1.5 billion children who will be born in the 1990s worldwide—the largest generation in the history of the world.

Children too often are last on the list of governmental priorities when countries allocate their budgets. Because of this, over 14 million children die *each year,* most from malnutrition and disease that could be prevented at very low cost. In addition, UNICEF (the United Nations Children's Fund) estimates that another 150 million are so malnourished that they are unable to reach their full mental and physical potential, thereby robbing the

world of the contributions of these children and making them an additional drain on their countries' resources.

From this concern comes UNICEF's "first call for children," making their concerns first in their countries' priorities in good times and in bad.

This is not the first time that concern has been expressed worldwide for children's rights, but earlier attempts were either not universally agreed to or not enforceable. The first statement on children's rights, in 1924 by the League of Nations, was weakened by the failure of the United States to join the League. In 1959 the United Nations adopted an expanded version of the League statement, the Declaration of the Rights of the Child, but the declaration had no means of enforcement.

In 1979 the UN began negotiating on the drafting of a convention on the rights of the child that would overcome the problems associated with previous statements. The negotiations were extremely complex and protracted because of the varying customs, habits, traditions, and

(continued)

ACTIVITY 8: HOW I MIGHT IMPROVE THE WORLD[4]

Procedure:

1. Ask class, "If you could offer one idea to make a more perfect world, what would it be?" These are all listed on the board and comments (objective, not put-downs) are made.
2. Show filmstrip, "The Best of All Possible Worlds" (Argus Communication, Niles, IL), a 96-frame story about a kind and fair god who wished to create a world free of pain and misery. Discuss definitions of a "perfect world."

[4] Adapted from Jill Monson in B. A. Reardon, *Educating for Global Responsibility.*

(continued from previous page)

laws that had to be wrestled with from all nations of the world. The question of how to determine if signatory nations were complying with the convention was also a difficult issue.

Finally, "on September 2, 1990, the United Nations Convention on the Rights of the Child came into effect as a binding law for those who have ratified it."* (The United States was not one of those signatory nations.)

The convention's 54 articles include:

The right of a child to live with his or her parents

The right to express an opinion in any matter or procedure affecting the child

The right to freedom of expression, thought, and religion

The right to protection from abuse or neglect

Safeguards for children who are up for adoption

The right to the highest level of health possible

The right to education, especially free and compulsory primary education by the state

Protection from harmful labor practices

Prohibition from torture, cruel treatment or punishment, and capital punishment

The mechanism by which the convention is to be implemented involves a UN monitoring committee that will receive reports from the ratifying nations on the steps being taken to meet the document's provisions. "Although the UN will not be able to penalize countries for flouting the convention's articles, nations will have to justify their behavior before the monitoring committee."[†] It was also hoped that the convention could be used in schools to familiarize students with the concept of legal rights.

---

*S. Dryden, "Children's Rights: First International Agreement," *International Herald Tribune,* Special Section, "Children in the 1990s," September 29–30, 1990.

†Dryden.

3. Each student writes a paper or draws a picture entitled "My Ideas for a Perfect World." Discussion ensues on what each of us can do now to make the world more perfect (don't tease younger siblings, clean up the school grounds, recycle, not use drugs, and so on).

4. Display papers and refer to them later in asking students how they are doing in making the world more perfect.

POPULATION STUDY

Population study is an integral part of global education. Many international groups focus on population study in an effort to reduce world hunger, disease, and strife. Some of these groups publish pamphlets, newsletters, charts and other useful educational materials.

- Population Reference Bureau (publishes *Popline Newsletter* and the *World Population Data Sheet*)
- Global Perspectives in Education (publishes *Intercom,* which focuses on many global issues)
- Zero Population Growth (publishes *Elementary Population Activities Kit*)

ENVIRONMENTAL EDUCATION

Environmental education is often considered a science, although this subject has tremendous social effects. Population, energy, natural resources, and pollution are some of the essential issues of environmental education.

Energy is more than the scientific process of generating power; it is a social issue as well. Should strip mining of coal be allowed? If so, is there an obligation to return the earth to its former state? What about mine runoff into streams used for drinking water? How much pollution from coal burning is acceptable? Whose responsibility is acid rain? Should safety be compromised in the interests of increasing the production of American energy and decreasing dependence on foreign sources?

Questions of this type incorporate values strategies (Chapter 4), group discussions (Chapter 6), role-play strategies (Chapter 8), and community resource study (Chapter 9). Similar questions can be used to address nuclear power, oil consumption, and hydroelectric power.

Pollution, natural resources, and national parks became controversial issues in the early 1970s and once again in the 1980s due to legislation implemented by James Watt, President Reagan's first secretary of the interior.

During President Bush's presidency, questions of global warming and acid rain were of even more concern to scientists worldwide. These are clearly issues that have great social (and thus social studies) impact. Because the debate is so current, teachers must use newspapers, news magazines, and scientific publications to stay current on these issues. President Clinton has fostered the creation of new National Wilderness Areas and Monuments, sometimes to the consternation of local residents. The conflict between environmentalists and "developers" is played out throughout the world; in the U.S., western states have been the most common sites because of the high percentage of open land, most of it owned or controlled by the federal government.

Often a professional journal will present important issues like these. For example, the March 1990 issue of *Social Education* has a special section on nuclear proliferation, including new nuclear nations, the connection between nuclear power and nuclear waste, and the environmental hazards of nuclear arms proliferation. The March-April issue of *Social Studies and the Young Learner* had a timely piece on the global problems of water pollution. (Simmons, 1994)

HUMAN RIGHTS STUDY

To many people, international human rights study is the most important of global issues. Anderson suggests introducing elementary students to the Declaration of Rights of the Child adopted and proclaimed by the United Nations (see pages 384–385). After reading and discussing the declaration, Anderson suggests that upper-grade children might keep "a daily log of the actions they personally take to ensure the rights of younger children . . . such as: 'I took my little brother to the dentist' or 'Helped my little sister with her homework.'" (54)

Anderson suggests several ways that teachers can design learning experiences that encourage children's respect for others:

1. Increase children's ability to empathize
2. Decrease children's egocentric perceptions
3. Decrease children's ethnocentric perceptions
4. Decrease children's stereotypic perceptions

She goes on to suggest ways to show how basic human needs are met and not met, cautioning that "it is important . . . to give a balanced view of deprivation so that children will not get the idea that Third World Countries have all the problems, while equity and justice reign over the rest of the globe." (56)

It is difficult to argue with Anderson's intentions of worldwide equity and justice, but we must recognize that some people will support equity and justice only if it does not cost them anything—financially, spiritually, or legally. Thus it is possible that human rights education might be opposed because it does not really affect people in the United States or because of the view that Americans should not interfere in the affairs of other countries.

This kind of attitude clearly opposes the interests of global education and other issues discussed in this chapter, which rely on the interactive nature of school, home, and community and of all countries. To live at peace in the world, this interdependent attitude must be emphasized. Specific data for the United States that underscore the abuse of children's rights are provided by the Children's Defense Fund. Table 13.1 is one illustration of that.

Worldwide there is increased attention to the plight of refugees. There are over 25 million refugees as of 1996, according to the United Nations High Commissioner for Refugees (UNHCR), with over half of them children. A number of useful publications with useful teaching and action ideas are available from the UNHCR and are listed at the end of the chapter.

ACADEMIC FREEDOM

Academic freedom refers to the teacher's right to teach what he or she deems appropriate, as well as the students' freedom to learn about such topics. This does not mean that a teacher can teach anything for any reason. There are court cases that provide some legal guidelines for determining academic

TABLE 13.1
Every Day in America

3	children die from abuse or neglect.
6	children commit suicide.
13	children are homicide victims.
16	children are killed by firearms.
87	infants die.
316	children are arrested for violent crimes.
403	children are arrested for drug abuse.
466	children are born to mothers who had late or no prenatal care.
788	children are born at low birthweight.
1,420	babies are born to teen mothers.
1,788	children are born without health insurance.
2,556	children are born into poverty.
3,356	children drop out of high school every school day.
3,533	children are born to unmarried mothers.
5,702	children are arrested.
8,523	children are reported abused or neglected.
100,000	children are homeless.
10 million	have no health insurance.
14.7 million	live in poverty.

SOURCE: Children's Defense Fund.

freedom. "[The] courts have held that academic freedom is based on the First Amendment and is fundamental to our democratic society. It protects a teacher's right to evaluate and criticize existing values and practices in order to allow for political, social, economic, and scientific progress." (Fischer et al., 120) In their book, *Teachers and the Law*, Fischer and his colleagues attempt to answer a series of questions related to academic freedom. For example, can a teacher be prohibited from discussing controversial issues? Most courts have ruled no, but it has been noted that a teacher has a duty to be "fair and objective in presenting his personally held opinions and to ensure that different views are presented." (121)

Can a teacher be punished for using a controversial teaching method that is not clearly prohibited? Not usually, but "when methods are inappropriate, when they are not supported by any significant professional opinion, or when they are clearly prohibited by reasonable school policy, they are not likely to be protected by academic freedom." (Nelson, 125) In both 1969 and 1974, the National Council for the Social Studies developed statements on academic freedom. Both are reprinted in Cox. The 1969 statement went as follows:

> Even though an individual teacher may not protest, it is the responsibility of
> the profession to remain alert to possible infringements upon academic free-

ACCURACY IN ACADEMIA

In 1985 a new group of self-appointed "watchdogs" was formed. The group, called Accuracy in Academia (AIA), was formed with the stated purpose of ensuring "balance and a livelier discussion." AIA was founded by Reed Irvine, a militant conservative, who also founded Accuracy in Media, a group whose purpose is to challenge perceived liberal bias in major news organizations.

AIA appoints student volunteers to surreptitiously monitor and report on professors at colleges around the country. The AIA's executive director, Lazlo Csorba III, believes that liberal biases dominate college campuses and says that AIA is acting to correct the imbalance. According to Csorba, "the issue is not whether any of these missionaries have a right to believe whatever they please. It is whether in advancing their sad doctrines they are engaging in scholarship or in ideological polemics."[1]

AIA's tactics and intentions have not been well received. American professors, educators, and journalists have been most outspoken in their distaste for the group's mission. A *USA Today* editorial noted:

> This public listing and chiding of professors is reminiscent of the era when the late Sen. Joe McCarthy destroyed careers of diplomats, government aides, artists, writers and actors by accusing them of Communist sympathies.
>
> And it has the distasteful aspect of recruiting students to spy in the lecture hall. The college classroom is the place where students who disagree with their professors have the right—and the obligation—to look them in the eye and challenge them. It is not the place where students should be encouraged to slink out and file a complaint with self-appointed thought police in Washington.[2]

AIA has not received the hoped-for support from the political right. William Bennett, then the U.S. secretary of education, called it "a bad idea" and noted that "a university is the place that can house people of different ideological persuasions . . . you don't make ideas safe for students, you make students safe for ideas."[3] The director of the conservative Committee for the Free World described the organization's approach as "wrongheaded and harmful" and urged it to "shut down the operation before it goes any further."[4]

Is this group a serious threat? Maybe not, but history has shown that censorship often begins with such "wrongheaded" actions. In addition, the restriction of academic freedom at colleges that people *choose* to attend is likely to lead to even greater restrictions in public elementary and secondary schools, where attendance is required.

Academic freedom is seriously threatened by groups like AIA as long as they have an audience or adherents to act on their recommendations.

[1] Les Csorba III, "Leftist Professors Are the Real Threat," *USA Today*, January 10, 1986, p. 8.

[2] "Campus Snitches Threaten Freedom," *USA Today*, January 10, 1986, p. 8.

[3] "Campus Snitches . . ."

[4] "Balance or Bias," *Time*, December 23, 1985, p. 57.

dom. Loss of academic freedom by one member of the profession diminishes the freedom of all. (Cox, 43)

And the 1974 statement noted:

Ultimately, freedom to teach and to learn will exist only if a continuing effort is made to educate all Americans regarding these important freedoms. Professional educators must set an example in their communities that illustrates their respect for schools and classrooms as a free marketplace of ideas as well as appreciation for the concerns of parents and other members of the Community who legitimately disagree. By showing our faith as educators in the clash of opposing viewpoints, we can hope to achieve a society that functions according to this precept. (Cox, 47)

The two statements complement each other. The NCSS continues to review periodically the status of academic freedom. The 1974 statement was more thorough and built on the previous one.

CENSORSHIP

Questions of academic freedom naturally lead to questions about censorship. Censorship is hardly a new concept. Beale (1941) describes the censorship of textbooks in the South during the 1850s:

Readers, speakers, and orators were the worst of all. They were used by younger children and their attacks were more subtle. *The American First Reader,* the *English Reader,* Mandeville's *Course of Reading . . .* , even Noah Webster's spellers were denounced as abolitionist propaganda. . . .

These repeated complaints of Southern slaveholders took effect in the form of greatly modified textbooks. Northern publishers could not afford to lose their Southern book trade.

Just as teachers experience censorship, so do textbook publishers.

Some publishers sent the Northern books south with merely the title page changed to give a Southern imprint, but this was likely to be discovered. Others carried two sets of books, one for Northern, the other for Southern trade, with objectionable passages all carefully deleted from the latter. Still others, and these the majority, omitted from all textbooks passages that would offend Southern sensibilities. (164)

Censorship also has been aimed at the study of evolution, at reference works in English, and at a number of novels.

One of the most developed cases of censorship involved the Rugg social studies textbook series, used in districts across the country in the 1940s. In a number of districts the books were banned outright, and in one they were burned in a community bonfire. The Rugg texts were attacked as anti-business and anti-American. Many of these protectors equated teaching students to think with anti-Americanism. According to the president of the Daughters of the Colonial Wars in Philadelphia:

They tried to give the child an unbiased viewpoint, instead of teaching him real Americanism. . . . All the old histories taught my country right or wrong. That's the point of view we want our children to adopt. We can't afford to teach them to be unbiased and let them make up their own minds. (*Time,* September 8, 1940, pp. 64-65)

Because of Rugg's prominence and the widespread use of his textbooks, the attacks were widely publicized and, as noted, often successful.

Another well-known controversy involved *Man: A Course of Study* (MACOS), materials that were developed for fifth graders in the late 1960s by the Education Development Corporation with National Science Foundation (NSF) funding. In the 1970s MACOS became a convenient punching bag for Arizona Congressman John Conlan, who quoted its material out of context. For example, Conlan claimed that the MACOS materials advocated female infanticide and the drinking of seal blood. In reality, the practices were presented in the cultural context in which they occurred, that is, in the life of the Netsilik people. The practices were never condoned, nor were they condemned. Through innuendo, Conlan managed to orchestrate a climate of fear, causing many schools to drop the MACOS materials. Embarrassed by the furor, Congress prohibited the NSF from receiving money for education projects for two years.

According to the American Library Association, textbook censorship cases skyrocketed 300 percent between November 1980 and 1983 (*People for the*

American Way); the number continued to increase between 1983 and 1995. A major force behind such censorship drives is the so-called moral majority.

Rossi characterizes the complaints of fundamentalist religious groups as remarkably similar—"that many social studies texts and materials undermine parental authority, invade family privacy, degrade our country and the Founding Fathers, promote communism, teach children to question values and advocate anti-Christian lifestyles." (254)

Much of the organized "new right" censorship has been under the leadership of Mel and Norma Gabler of Longview, Texas, and their Educational Research Analysts staff. The Gablers' frightening logic is revealed in this quotation from their handbook:

> As long as the schools continue to teach ABNORMAL ATTITUDES and ALIEN THOUGHTS, we caution parents not to urge their children to pursue high grades and class discussion because the harder students work, the greater their chances of brainwashing. (1)

It is ironic that the Gablers are so concerned with brainwashing, since their intent is to deny children the opportunity to think. "They are determined to prevent all young people from being exposed to any book, idea, or discussion that escapes the boundaries of their narrow view of the world." (*People for the American Way,* 4)

Many issues arouse the ire of "new right" groups, including evolution, values, communism, sex education, and literary or reference works that may allude to such ideas. Most of the evolution/creationism furor has been directed at secondary school biology textbooks, but it is not unlikely that social Darwinism could be discussed in secondary social studies classes and the basic premise of evolution in an upper elementary classroom. Thus the notion of evolution has been seen as controversial whether it appears in textbooks or in classroom discussion.

The evolution/creationism controversy of the 1920s was resurrected during the 1960s when "a group of scientifically trained fundamentalists began to reevaluate fossil evidence from the perspective of special creation as described in the Biblical record. . . . Faced with a formidable amount of evidence that supports the theory of evolution, the creationists try to demonstrate that such evidence is biased and incomplete, or that it can be reinterpreted to fit whatever conceptual system is convenient." (Nelkin, 263–64) Relying on pressure and intimidation, the creationists have managed to force changes in texts and teaching. Some states passed laws requiring the teaching of creationism to parallel evolution, although these have since been struck down as clearly unconstitutional because they violated the separation of church and state as specified in the Bill of Rights.

Since 1986, the American Anthropological Association has published a series of pamphlets on this topic in an effort to show that so-called scientific creationism cannot be reconciled with scientific fact. These pamphlets address evolution and the "battle" between evolution and creationism. A listing of these pamphlets is included in the references at the end of the chapter.

The concern with values education is based on the fear that students will have a choice in deciding their own values, rather than being told what to believe. Again the Gablers provide their rationale for this in a special report:

"Too many discussions and textbooks leave students to make up their minds about things," complains Norma Gabler, adding, "now that's just not fair to our children." Schools must teach "absolutes," say the Gablers. Why? "Textbooks mold nations. . . ."

Mel Gabler adds, "when a student reads in a math book that there are no absolutes, suddenly every value he's been taught is destroyed. And the next thing you know, the student turns to crime and drugs." (*People for the American Way,* 3)

Using a rationale reminiscent of the McCarthyism of the 1950s, many "new right" groups object to any discussion of communism, communist countries, or comparative economic or social systems. To inform or to educate is viewed as indoctrination. "If students learn too much about communism, they might become communists," runs this logic—the same logic used in prohibiting sex education or drug education in the schools. Ignorance is bliss; knowledge is dangerous. If this kind of logic prevailed, schools would be at risk for telling students about accidents in driver education, about volatility in chemistry, and about poisons when dealing with young children. "Mr. Yuk" could be an invitation to drink ammonia or furniture polish. Clearly, educators must resist this attack on learning. If not, small groups campaigning for their views will undermine educators and the entire public school system.

Censorship Cases

The most well known censorship cases in recent years have centered on the use or availability in schools of certain novels and reference works. In the 1979 case of *Zykan* v. *Warsaw* (the Indiana Community School Corporation and the Warsaw School Board of Trustees), high school students Brooke and Blair Zykan challenged the Warsaw school board's decision "to limit or prohibit the use of certain textbooks, to remove a certain book from the school library, and to delete certain courses from the curriculum" (*Zykan* v. *Warsaw*). The prohibited books included *Values Clarification, The Stepford Wives, Go Ask Alice, The Bell Jar,* and *Growing Up Female in America.* Courses deleted from the curriculum included Values Clarification, Black Literature, Gothic Literature, Folklore and Legends, Science Fiction, Shakespeare, and Creative Writing.

In 1979, the Indiana court ruled that school officials could make decisions regarding classroom texts, library books, and curriculum courses solely on the basis of personal, social, political, and moral beliefs. This, it was held, was not a violation of constitutionally protected academic freedom, and the case against the school board was dismissed. In 1982, however, the *Zykan* decision was contradicted by another case, *Pico* v. *Board of Education, Island Trees Union Free School District et al.,* in which a student sued the school

These books have been banned in various places by school boards.

board for barring certain books from the school library and from use in the school (see page 397).

In Girard, Pennsylvania, Studs Terkel, the author of *Working* (Avon, 1975), spoke to a school board seeking to ban his book. Similar instances of censorship have been reported in California, Idaho, Maine, Iowa, Oregon, Washington, and elsewhere, according to the National Coalition Against Censorship.

One argument offered for censorship is that a majority of the community supports it. This issue was addressed in an *amicus curiae* (friend of the court) brief in the *Island Trees* case filed by the National Council of Teachers of English, New York State English Council, National Council for the Social Studies, and Speech Communication Association:

> Nor does the asserted fact that a majority of Island Trees residents support the board make censorship any more tolerable. It is commonplace that majorities may oppose "liberal" books today and "conservative" ones tomorrow; in the process, they are not permitted to ban either. (12)

Thus attempts by some liberal groups to ban *Huckleberry Finn* because of its stereotypical treatment of blacks are no more justified than any other type of censorship.

A few years ago a school in Vermont denied students the opportunity to perform the play *Runaways,* by Elisabeth Swados, produced on Broadway in 1978. The play, about embittered, abused children, was deemed "inappropriate for the rural Vermont High School." (*New York Times,* February 21, 1984, A15) It was argued that the school board had not specified its reasons for banning the production and had made a "personal political decision," but the federal district court disagreed. Because the play was available to be read by students, the court ruled that the board was not suppressing the play's ideas and upheld the board's right to declare the play not suitable for the age groups for whom it would be presented. A similar case occurred in St. Louis, in which school officials blocked a presentation of the movie *Inherit the Wind,* a fictionalized account of the famous Scopes "monkey" trial, which challenged an old Tennessee law prohibiting the teaching of Darwin's theory of evolution.

In Empire, California, over 300 copies (all that the district owns) of "Little Red Ridinghood" were locked away in a storage room because the classic Grimm Brothers fairy tale recounts that the little girl took a bottle of wine to her grandmother. A district official was quoted as saying that the story condoned the use of alcohol.

In 1990, in Owensboro, Kentucky, the elementary school librarian was ordered to stop purchasing books by Judy Blume because the author used obscenities.

The debate has not significantly abated. Libraries have become the most common battleground. An innocently named group called Family Friendly Libraries has organized "a nationwide campaign to pressure librarians and boards of trustees to repudiate the 'infamous' Library Bill of Rights, the strongly anticensorship policy statement of the American Library Association." Instead this group urges libraries to *not* provide materials and information providing all points of view. Rather they urge libraries to "emphasize the 'superiority' of the traditional family." (National Coalition Against Censorship, 1)

A photography exhibition by the late Robert Mapplethorpe in 1990 was seen by some as a catalyst for these school decisions, even though the Mapplethorpe photography was displayed in museums, not schools. One sign in support of the exhibit at the Contemporary Arts Center in Cincinnati noted: "If you give artists freedom of expression, soon every American will want it."

Even phonograph records, tapes, and disks are not immune to such censoring. Because of the fear of Congressional labeling, most major record labels have now developed ratings systems similar to those that the film industry developed. These are warning labels, rather than restrictive labels that prevent the purchase of a tape or CD. Under some state laws, certain opera recordings would be unavailable to minors. A bill in Florida would ban the sale to minors of any recording containing lyrics about sexual activity, illegal drug or alcohol use, murder, or suicide. Such operas as *La Traviata, Faust, Carmen, Tosca,* and *Madame Butterfly* would all be restricted under such a law. (Blumner & Hosford) "So what?" one might ask, especially if one does not care for opera. The

TABLE 13.2
The V-Chip Television-Rating System

TV Y	ALL CHILDREN Program is suitable for all children. It should not frighten younger children.
TV Y7	OLDER CHILDREN Designed for children age 7 and older. Program may contain mild physical or comedic violence that may frighten children under 7.
TV G	GENERAL AUDIENCE Program is appropriate for all ages. It contains little violence, no strong language, and little to no sexual dialogue or situations.
TV PG	PARENTAL GUIDANCE SUGGESTED Program may contain limited sexual or violent material that may be unsuitable for younger children.
TV 14	PARENTS STRONGLY CAUTIONED Program may contain some material that many parents would find unsuitable for children under 14 years of age.
TV M	MATURE AUDIENCE ONLY Program is specifically designed to be viewed by adults and therefore may be unsuitable for children under 17.

restriction, however, would set a chilling precedent for the availability of other forms of art, literature, and music.

In late 1996 the television networks agreed to rate all their program offerings with one of six different ratings (see Table 13.2), but this did not satisfy many people who thought the ratings did not inform viewers of the characteristics of the shows that led to the rating. These critics wanted shows identified as having violence, strong sexual content, or nudity, similar to the ratings most of the pay-TV channels like Showtime and HBO offered for their programs. The network executives said that there were simply too many shows to rate swiftly and easily enough for broadcast, and Congress, which had been about to apply some sort of ratings system, accepted this rationale and the network rating system for a trial year. The federal mandate that new televisions have a so-called v-chip to allow access to certain shows to be restricted by parents may have a salubrious effect on children and television, but that will take a number of years to occur since the actual v-chip won't be installed in televisions until 1998, and it will take at least until 1999 to assess its effectiveness. (Kunkel, B4)

Much more slippery is what to do about access to controversial subjects on the Internet. A restrictive access regulation was rolled back in 1996, but many web sites that have nudity mandate that the user "sign" a pledge that he or she is at least 21 in order to access the site. This has not completely satisfied some critics and there is likely to be much more debate regarding restricting access to certain sites in some way, possibly with some analogue to the television v-chip.

THE CASE OF PICO V. ISLAND TREES BOARD OF EDUCATION

In 1975 the Island Trees, New York, Board of Education removed nine books from high school and junior high school libraries after they appeared on a list of "objectionable" books distributed by Parents of New York United. These books included *A Reader for Writers, Slaughterhouse Five, The Naked Ape, Down These Mean Streets, Best Short Stories by Negro Writers, Go Ask Alice, A Hero Ain't Nothing but a Sandwich, Soul on Ice,* and *The Fixer;* the board also restricted the use of *Black Boy.* According to *Civil Liberties,* the membership newsletter of the American Civil Liberties Union, the board called the books "anti-American, anti-Christian, anti-Semitic and just plain filthy."*

Five students, represented by the New York Civil Liberties Union, sued the board on the ground that their First Amendment rights had been violated. The federal district court in the eastern district of New York threw out the suit, but the U.S. Court of Appeals for the Second Circuit reversed that ruling, finding that First Amendment issues were involved in the case. The U.S. Supreme Court, in a 5-4 decision in June of 1982, upheld the Court of Appeals decision. Shortly thereafter, all the books were reinstated in the school library.

Associate Justice Brennan wrote the court's plurality decision and stated:

> We think that the First Amendment rights of students may be directly and sharply implicated by the removal of books from the shelves of a school library. . . . the State may not, consistently with the First Amendment, contract the spectrum of available knowledge. In keeping with this principle, we have held that in a variety of contexts the Constitution protects the right to receive information and ideas. . . . Our Constitution does not permit the official suppression of ideas.

Civil Liberties, July 1982, p. 8.

Strategies for Dealing with Censorship

It is obvious that academic freedom and censorship are not merely historical issues; they are of more importance today than ever before. Many teachers hope that if they ignore the controversies, they will go away, but, as we have seen, this has not happened. The acknowledged key to successful censorship battles is to be proactive rather than reactive. According to Stahlschmidt, censorship can take many forms. Precensorship, which occurs in the selection process, "becomes a problem when librarians (or teachers) are unduly influenced by the values of the community and ignore other criteria—often for the sake of avoiding controvers." (99) (See Nelson and Ochoa, 1987, for ideas on this.) Other forms of censorship are challenges that take place after a book has been selected. These may come from teachers, administrators, school or library staff, school board members, or even students. To lessen the likelihood of con-

HAZELWOOD SCHOOL DISTRICT V. CATHY KUHLMEIER

The journalism students of Hazelwood East High School in Missouri published a school newspaper, the *Spectrum.* A number of controversial topics such as teen marriage, drug abuse, and religious cults were examined in *Spectrum,* since the district's policy stated that there would be no restriction of "free expression or diverse viewpoints within the rules of responsible journalism."

In May 1983 the high school principal objected to two articles, one in which three pregnant students discussed their sexual experiences and birth control and a second in which a student described her reactions to her parents' divorce. The principal felt that in the first case the students could be easily identified, and he also thought the topics were inappropriate for the younger students in the school. In the second case, he felt that the parents

of the student should have been allowed to respond to the article. The principal, R. E. Reynolds, ordered the *Spectrum* adviser to cut out two pages of the newspaper, later explaining that there was not enough time to reedit the articles or change the layout and still get the newspaper out before the end of the school year. The *Spectrum* staff learned of the actions only when the paper was distributed.

Cathy Kuhlmeier and other student staff members of the *Spectrum* sued the school district, claiming that their First Amendment rights to freedom of the press had been violated. They argued that the *Spectrum* was a "forum for public expression," a place for students to express their opinions.

The district argued that the newspaper was a part of the school curriculum, and

(continued)

troversy or censorship, Donelson suggests the following guidelines. Although these were made up specifically for English teachers, they have general application as well.

First, each . . . department (or teacher) should develop its own statement of rationales for teaching a unit.

Second, each school should establish a committee that will recommend books for possible use by the department.

Third, each school should work hard to win community support for academic freedom and to win that support before censorship strikes.

Fourth, each school should try to communicate to the public what is going on in social studies classrooms and why. Teachers should send notes home before using potentially disquieting material to inform parents and ask about objections. Even then, it sometimes takes only one parent to raise problems. Principals should be informed before a teacher embarks on a "perilous" curriculum unit so that the principal will not be caught in the middle later.

Fifth, each school should establish and implement a formal policy to handle attempted censorship. School boards should be pressed for a policy on

(continued from previous page)

as such the principal could legally decide what was appropriate. In addition, the board said that he had acted properly in protecting the privacy rights of students and others involved in the articles.

In January 1988 the U.S. Supreme Court ruled 5-3 that "no violation of First Amendment rights occurred." It agreed with the school district that the newspaper was a "laboratory situation" for a journalism class, and thus was part of the school curriculum and subject to regulation by school officials in a "reasonable manner."

Justice William Brennan wrote the dissent, in which he asserted that the state's mandate "to inculcate moral and political values is not a general warrant to act as 'thought police' stifling discussion of all but state-approved topics and advocacy of all but the official position." He concluded his opinion by noting that "the young men and women of Hazelwood East expected a civics lesson, but not the one the Court teaches them today."

Student press associations and many journalism and civil liberties organizations denounced the decision as a violation of the students' right to free speech, but most school administrator groups hailed the decision. The executive director of the Gannett Center for Media Studies, E. E. Dennis, predicted a minimal impact as a result of the ruling. "The student press is already very timid. It was always a captive voice and now is more captive."*

See Supreme Court Decision 98 L Ed 2d 592; *New York Times* account of January 14, 1988.

*A. S. Jones, "School Officials Acclaim Decision as Appropriate Strengthening of Authority," *New York Times,* January 14, 1988, A26.

curriculum decisions *before* problems arise. In addition, a Book Challenge Review Committee should be established. This body should include a board member, a teacher, an administrator, a local business or community representative, a parent and, if local, a college faculty member. Again, this formal policy should be established *before* trouble arises.

Sixth, each school should expect its teachers to prepare rationales for any book to be taught in class. One should not be afflicted by misplaced martyrdom. If the material cannot be clearly justified for class use at one's grade level, the material should not be used. (163–65)

Should any accusations be made, Cox notes that

It is fundamental that all charges must be substantiated and that the burden of proof rests upon the accuser. The accused must be informed of all charges and evidence against him and be given full opportunity to respond. . . .

Academic freedom is neither easily defined nor can it always be protected . . . only continuing concern, commitment, and action by teachers, administrators, school boards, professional organizations, students and the citizenry can insure the reality of academic freedom in a changing society. (44)

As noted earlier, teachers can hope that they will never be involved in an academic freedom issue, but if they are, they should seek help from their professional organizations—the National Education Association, the American Federation of Teachers, and the National Council for the Social Studies. All have Academic Freedom Defense Funds. Civil liberties groups like the American Civil Liberties Union will also provide assistance in cases involving academic censorship.

QUESTIONS AND ACTIVITIES

1. What issues that have been in the news lately are too controversial for school discussion? Why?

2. Many countries where people go hungry have less and less land on which to grow food. Should this concern other countries or schoolchildren in other countries?

3. What are two laws that you wish did not exist? How could you go about getting them changed?

4. Our society is very litigious—Americans use the courts to settle disputes much more than most societies do. This is quite costly for taxpayers. Can you think of realistic alternatives to court action if people have disagreements?

5. Visit a local courthouse or magistrate's court session. Do you see justice administered in any particular or surprising manner?

6. What might happen if a teacher told a class of primary grade students that the only rules they had to follow in the classroom were those agreed upon by students?

7. Should there be different sets of laws for different types of people? If so, in what way should people be differentiated? If not, why do we have juvenile courts?

8. How far should consumer laws go in protecting society? We have laws that mandate seat belt use, but allow smoking in many places. Does this seem inconsistent?

9. Many people never travel more than 100 miles from their homes. Is global education or the study of international human rights a waste of their time?

10. If you could live anywhere outside the United States, where would it be? What would you want to learn about people there?

11. Should the notion of academic freedom protect a teacher who gives students information that is incorrect?

12. Should parents be allowed to decide what the schools should teach? If so, to what degree? If not, why not?

13. Would censorship of vulgar language keep students from using such language?

14. Ask an elementary school teacher or school district official what procedures are in place for dealing with censorship cases.

15. How do you feel about restricting children's access to the Internet? On what basis would you restrict access and how would you suggest such restrictions be done?

REFERENCES

Anderson, C. C. "Human Rights in Elementary and Middle Schools." In *International Human Rights, Society, and the Schools.* M. Branson and J. Torney-Purta, eds. NCSS Bul. 68. Washington, DC: National Council for the Social Studies, 1982.

Beale, H. K. *Are American Teachers Free?* New York: Scribner & Sons, 1936.

_____ *A History of Freedom of Teaching in American Schools.* New York: Scribner & Sons, 1941.

Becker, J. *Education for a Global Society.* Bloomington, IN: Phi Delta Kappa Educational Foundation, 1973.

Blumner, R. E., and C. Hosford. "Hear No Evil," *Civil Liberties* (American Civil Liberties Union newsletter), Spring 1990.

Collins, H. T. "East of Gibraltar, West of Japan: Questions and Answers About Global Education." In *Getting Started in Global Education: A Primer for Principals and Teachers.* H. T. Collins and S. B. Zakariya, eds. Arlington, VA: National Association of Elementary School Principals, 1982.

Collins, H. T., and S. B. Zakariya. *Getting Started in Global Education: A Primer for Principals and Teachers.* Arlington, VA: National Association of Elementary School Principals, 1982.

Cox, C. B. *The Censorship Game and How to Play It.* NCSS Bul. 50. Washington, DC: National Council for the Social Studies, 1977.

Donelson, K. L. "Censorship in the 1970s: Some Ways to Handle It When It Comes (and It Will)." In *Dealing with Censorship,* James E. Davis, ed. Urbana, IL: National Council of Teachers of English, 1979.

"Drama on Scopes Trial Is Banned from Class," *New York Times,* February 21, 1984, p. A13.

Eisner, E. W. *The Educational Imagination.* 3rd ed. New York: Macmillan, 1994.

Fischer, L., D. Schimmel, and C. Kelly. *Teachers and the Law.* New York: Longman, 1981.

Forum, the Newsletter of Educators for Social Responsibility. 23 Garden Street, Cambridge, MA 02138

Gabler, M., and N. Gabler. Handbook no. 1, 1974. Educational Research Analysts, P.O. Box 7518, Longview, TX 75610.

Gross, R. "How to Handle Controversial Issues." NCSS How-to-Do-It Series, ser. 1, no. 14. Washington, DC: National Council for the Social Studies, 1964.

Halton Board of Education. "A Guide to Education for a Global Perspective," Halton, Ontario, 1994.

Johnson, J., and J. Benegar. "Global Issues in the Intermediate School," *Social Education,* vol. 47, no. 2, February 1983, pp. 131–137.

Kunkel, D. "Why Content, Not the Age of Viewers, Should Control What Children Watch on TV," *The Chronicle of Higher Education,* January 31, 1997, pp. B4–5.

Lafayette, R. C. "Education Theory and Methods: International Teacher Education," Report no. SP026862. Bloomington, IN: Indiana University, 1985.

McLuhan, M. *Understanding Media.* 2nd ed. New York: McGraw-Hill, 1965.

"Mobilizing Community Groups for Law-Related Education." *Technical Assistance Bulletin* no. 3. Chicago: American Bar Association, Youth Education for Citizenship, n.d.

National Coalition Against Censorship, *Censorship News,* no. 60, Fall/Winter 1995. (NCAC, 2 West 64th St., New York, NY 10023)

National Council for the Social Studies. "Position Statement on Global Education," *Social Education,* vol. 46, no. 1, January 1982, pp. 36–38.

Nelkin, D. "Science Rationality and the Creation-Evolution Dispute," *Social Education,* vol. 46, no. 4, April 1982, p. 263–264.

Nelson, J. "Academic Freedom and Teacher Self-Censorship," *The Social Studies Professional,* September 1983.

Nelson, J., and A. Ochoa. "Academic Freedom and Censorship: A Special Section," *Social Education,* vol. 51, no. 6, October 1987.

Nelson, M. *Law in the Curriculum.* Bloomington, IN: Phi Delta Kappa Educational Foundation, 1978.

_____ "Teaching Young Children About the Law," *Childhood Education,* vol. 56, no. 5, April/May, 1980, pp. 274–277.

_____ "Perspectives of Icelandic and American Children Regarding Conflict Resolution," *Revista Cayey,* Fall 1986.

Palonsky, S., and J. Nelson. "Political Restraint in the Socialization of Student Teachers," *Theory and Research in Social Education,* vol. 7, no. 4, Winter 1980.

People for the American Way. Special Report. Washington, DC, 1983.

Pico v. Board of Education, Island Trees Union Free School District, U.S. Court of Appeals for the Second Circuit, 79-7690, November 20, 1979. *Amicus curiae* brief of National Council of Teachers of English, New York State English Council, National Council of Social Studies, and Speech Communication Association.

Popline, May 1982, vol. 4, no. 5. Population Institute, Washington, DC.

Reardon, B. A. *Comprehensive Peace Education.* New York: Teachers College Press, 1988.

Reardon, B. A., ed. *Educating for Global Responsibility.* New York: Teachers College Press, 1988.

Remy, R. *Handbook of Basic Citizenship Competencies.* Alexandria, VA: Association for Supervision and Curriculum Development, 1979.

Riekes, L., and S. Ackerly. *Courts and Trials.* Law in Action series. St. Paul, MN: West Publishing Co., 1975, 1980.

Rossi, J. "Introduction to the Growing Controversy over Book Censorship," *Social Education,* vol. 46, no. 4, April 1982, p. 254–255.

Simmons, D. "Thinking Globally, Acting Locally: Using the Local Environment to Explore Global Issues," *Social Studies and the Young Learner,* vol. 6, no. 4, March-April 1994, pp. 10–13.

Stahlschmidt, A. "A Workable Strategy for Dealing with Censorship," *Phi Delta Kappan,* vol. 64, no. 2, October 1982, pp. 99–102.

"Supreme Court Sends Island Trees to Trial," *Civil Liberties* (American Civil Liberties Union newsletter), July 1982, p. 8.

Toffler, A. *Future Shock.* New York: Bantam Books, 1970.

Totten, S., and M. Kleg, eds. "Nuclear Proliferation: Political Issues." Special section, *Social Education*, March 1990, pp. 133–163.

Why We Have Laws: Shiver, Goble, and Snore (film). Learning Corporation of America, Stephen Bosustow Productions, 1970.

Winn, M. *Why We Have Have Laws: Shiver, Gobble, and Snore.* New York: Simon and Schuster, 1972.

Young Consumers. Law in Action series. St. Paul, MN: West Publishing Co., 1986.

Zykan v. Warsaw, U.S. District Court for the Northern District of Indiana, South Bend Division, Civil Action File no. 579-68, December 3, 1979.

Additional References

A partial listing of pamphlets from the American Anthropological Association:

The Record of Human Evolution

Evolution v. Creationism: A Selected Bibliography

Anthropology and "Scientific Creationism"

Evolution

All are available at 25 cents each from:

American Anthropological Association
1703 New Hampshire Av. NW
Washington, DC 20009

Law-Related References

A number of national groups offer assistance in law education.

American Bar Association/Youth
Education for Citizenship Committee
Division for Public Education
American Bar Association
541 North Fairbanks Court
Suite 1500
Chicago, IL 60611-3314

Center for Civic Education
Law in a Free Society Project
5146 Douglas Fir Rd.
Calabasas, CA 91302

Constitutional Rights Foundation
601 South Kingsley Dr.
Los Angeles, CA 90005

Court TV
600 Third Ave.
New York, NY 10016

Educators for Social Responsibility
23 Garden St.
Cambridge, MA 02138

National Institute for Citizen Education in the Law
25 "E" St.
Washington, DC 20001

Phi Alpha Delta Law Fraternity
Public Service Center
P.O. Box 3217
Granada Hills, CA 91394-0217
(818)-368-8103
padpscla@aol.com

Center for Research and Development in Law Related Education (CRADLE)
Wake Forest University School of Law
Box 7206 Reynolda Station
Winston-Salem, NC 27109-7206

Drug Prevention Information

Schools Without Drugs
U.S. Department of Education
Washington, 1989
To obtain copies write to:
Schools Without Drugs
Pueblo, CO 81009

Drug Prevention Curricula: A Guide to Selection and Implementation
National Clearinghouse for Alcohol and Drug Information
P.O. Box 2345
Rockville, MD 20852

Schools and Drugs: A Guide to Drug and Alcohol Prevention Curricula and Programs
Crime Prevention Center
California Attorney General's Office
P.O. Box 944255
Sacramento, CA 94244-2550

Drug Video Program
Office of Public Affairs
U.S. Department of Education
400 Maryland Ave. SW
Washington, DC 20202

Refugee Materials from the United Nations Public Information Section

UNHCR by Numbers 1996 (and subsequent years)

Protecting Refugees: Questions and Answers

Refugee Children

AL   Janice Cowin
Alabama Center for Law and Civic Education
Cumberland School of Law
800 Lakeshore Dr.
Birmingham, AL 35229
205/870-2433
FAX 205/870-2673

AK   Majorie Menzi
State Department of Education
801 West 10th St.
Juneau, AK 99811-1878
907/465-8720
FAX 907/465-3396

AZ   Lynda Rando
Arizona Center for LRE, Ste. 1800
111 W. Monroe St.
Phoenix, AZ 85003-1716
602/340-7360
FAX 602/271-4930

Barbara Stafford
Executive Director

AR   Learning Law in Arkansas, Inc.
12201 Shawnee Forest Dr.
Little Rock, AR 72212
501/375-9335

CA   Todd Clark, Executive Director
Constitutional Rights Foundation
601 South Kingsley Dr.
Los Angeles, CA 90005-2319
213/487-5590

Joseph Maloney
Citizenship and LRE Center
9738 Lincoln Village Dr.
Sacramento, CA 95827-3302
916/228-2232

Charles Quigley, Executive Director
Center for Civic Education
5146 Douglas Fir Rd.
Calabasas, CA 91302-1405
800/350-4223
FAX 818/340-2029
center4civ@aol.com

Laura Dille
State Bar of California
Department of Public Education
555 Franklin St.
San Francisco, CA 94102-4456
415/561-8230
FAX 415/561-8861

Thomas Nazario
USF School of Law Street Law Project
2310 Fulton St.
San Francisco, CA 94117-1080
415/666-6832
FAX 415/666-6433
nazariot@usfca.edu

CO   James Giese, Executive Director
      Social Science Education
      Consortium
      Barbara Miller
      Colorado Legal Education Project
      Social Science Education
      Consortium
      P.O. Box 21270
      Boulder, CO 80308-4270
      303/492-8154
      FAX 303/449-3925

      Gayle Mertz
      Law Related Education Network
      905 Hartford St.
      Boulder, CO 80303-6315

CT   James Schmidt
      c/o Secretary of State
      Connecticut Consortium for
      Law/Citizenship
      30 Trinity St.
      Hartford, CT 06106
      203/566-33904
      FAX 203/523-5757

DC   Lee Arbetman
      National Institute for Citizen
      Education in the Law (NICEL)
      Judith Zimmer
      D.C. Center for Law in Education
      711 G St., S.E.
      Washington, DC 20003-2815
      202/564-6644
      FAX 202/546-6648

      Richard Roe
      Georgetown Law Center
      D.C. Street Law Project
      111 F St., N.W.
      Washington, DC 20001-2815
      202/662-9615
      FAX 202/662-9681
      roe@law.georgetown.edu

DE   Barry Townsend
      Deleware LRE Project
      Widener University School of Law
      4601 Concord Pike,
      P.O. Box 362
      Wilmington, DE 19803-1406
      302/429-1860
      FAX 302/323-2955

FL   Annette Pitts
      The Florida LRE Association
      1625 Metropolitan Circle, Ste. B
      Tallahassee, FL 32308-1587
      904/386-8223
      FAX 904/386-8292
      abpflreaed@aol.com

GA   Anna Boling
      Carl Vinson Institute of Government
      The University of Georgia
      201 Milledge Ave.
      Athens, Ga. 30601-3803
      706/542-6223
      FAX 706/542-9301

HI   Sharon Kaohi
      Hawaii Friends of Civic/Law Related
      Education
      189 Lunalilo Home Rd., 2nd Fl.
      Honolulu, HI 96825
      808/396-5390
      FAX 808/548-5390
      sharon.kaohi@notes.kl2.hi.us

      Jaylene Sarcedo
      Hawaii State Bar Association
      Young Lawyers Association Division
      Penthouse—9th Fl.
      1136 Union Mall
      Honolulu, HI 96813-2711
      808/537-1868
      FAX 808/521-7936

ID   Lynda Clark, LRE Coordinator
      Idaho Law Foundation
      525 W. Jefferson
      P.O. Box 895
      Boise, ID 83701-0895
      208/334-4500
      FAX 208/334-4515

IL   Ronald Banaszak
      Special Committee on Youth Educa-
      tion for Citizenship
      American Bar Association
      541 N. Fairbanks Court
      Chicago, IL 60611-3314
      312/988-5735
      FAX 312/988-5032
      rbanaszak@staff.abanet.org

      Carolyn Pereira
      Constitutional Rights Foundation

Chicago
407 S. Dearborn, Ste. 1700
Chicago, IL 60605-1111
312/663-9057
FAX 312/663-4321
crfc@wwa.com

Donna Schechter
Commission on Law Related Education for the Public Illinois State Bar Association
Illinois Bar Center
424 S. Second St.
Springfield, IL 62701-1704
217/525-1760
FAX 217/525-0712

IN   Robert Leming
Indiana Program for LRE
Indiana University
2805 E. 10th St. Ste. 120
Bloomington, IN 47408-2601
812/855-0467
FAX 812/855-0455
rleming@indiana.edu

IA   Timothy Buzzell
Iowa Center for LRE
Drake University Law School
Offerman Hall, Rm. 194
27th and Carpenter
Des Moines, IA 50311
515/271-3205
FAX 515/271-3966

KS   Ron Keefover
Kansas Judicial Center
Office of Judicial Administration
301 S.W. 10th Ave.
Topeka, KS 66612-1507
913/296-4872
FAX 913/296-7076
ronk@spress.com

Art Thompson
Kansas Bar Association
1200 Harrison
P.O. Box 1307
Tokeka, KS 66601-1037
913/234-5696
913/296-7076

KY   Bruce Bonar
Model Laboratory
Eastern Kentucky University
Richmond, KY 40475
606/622-3766
FAX 606/622-1020

Deborah Williamson
Kentucky LRE
Administrative Office of the Courts
100 Millcreek Park
Frankfort, KY 40601-9230
502/573-2350
FAX 502/695-1759

LA   Maria Dooley
Louisiana Center for Law and Civics
Louisiana State Bar Association
601 St. Charles Ave., 2nd Fl.
New Orleans, LA 70310-3404
504/619-0129
FAX 504/566-0930

ME   Janice Berry
Maine State Bar Association
124 State St.
P.O. Box 788
Augusta, ME 04332-0788
207/622-7523
FAX 207/633-0083

Pamela Anderson
University of Maine, School of Law
246 Deering Ave.
Portland, ME 04102-2837
207/780-4159
FAX 207/780-4239
pamelaa@usm.maine.edu

MD   Rick Miller
University of Baltimore
Citizens Law-Related Education Program
1420 N. Charles St.
Baltimore, MD 21201-5779
410/837-6760
FAX 410/837-6762

MA   Nancy J. Kaufer
Massachusetts Bar Institute LRE
20 West St.
Boston, MA 02111-1218
617/338-0571
FAX 617/542-8315
kaufer@massbar.org

Joan Kenney
Massachusetts Supreme Court
Public Information Office
Old Court House, Rm 218
Boston, MA 02110
617/557-1114
FAX 617/742-1807

MI   Linda Start
Center for Civic Education
Oakland Schools
2100 Pontiac Lake Rd.
Waterford, MI 48328-2735
810/858-1947
FAX 810/858-4661

MN   Jennifer Bloom
University of Minnesota
Minnesota Center for Community
Legal Education
340 Coffey Hall
1420 Eckles Ave.
St. Paul, MN 55108-1030
612/625-9231
FAX 612/624-7713
jdb@fourh.mes.umn.edu

MS   Melanie Henry
Mississippi State Bar
643 N. State St.,
P.O. Box 2168
Jackson, MS 39225-2168
601/948-4471
FAX 601/355-8635

Linda Kay
Mississippi State Department of Education, Social Studies
604 Walter Sillers Bldg.
550 High St.
Jackson, MS 39205-0771
601/359-3791
FAX 601/382-7436

MO   Millie Aulbur
The Missouri Bar Association
P.O. Box 119
326 Monroe St.
Jefferson City, MO 65102
314/635-4128
FAX 314/635-2811
mobar@mail.cdmnet.com

Linda Riekes
St. Louis Public Schools
Law and Citizenship Education Unit
5183 Raymond
St. Louis, MO 63113-1616
314/361-5500
FAX 314/361-3589

MT   Linda Peterson
Office of Public Instruction, Academic and Professional Service
State Capitol
P.O. Box 202501
Helena, MT 59620-2501
406/444-5726
FAX 406/444-3924
lpeterson@opl.mt_gov

NE   Janet Hammer
Supreme Court of Nebraska
P.O. Box 98910
1220 State Capitol,
Lincoln, NE 68509-8910
402/471-3205
FAX 402/471-2197

Tom Keefe
LRE, Nebraska State Bar Association
P.O. 81809
635 S. 14th St.
Lincoln, NE 68508-2701
402/475-7091
FAX 402/475-7098

NV   Phyllis Darling
Nevada Center for Law-Related Education
Clark County School District
601 N. Ninth St.
Las Vegas, NV 89101-2505
702/799-8468
FAX 702/799-8452

NH   Holly Belson
New Hampshire Bar Association
112 Pleasant St.
Concord, NH 03301
603/224-6942
FAX 603/224-2910

NJ   Sheila Boro
New Jersey Bar Foundation
1 Constitution Square
New Brunswick, NJ 08901-1500
908/937-7519
FAX 908/828-0034

James Daley
New Jersey Center for Law-Related
Education
103 McQuaid Hall
Seton Hall University
South Orange, NJ 07079
201/761-9394
FAX 201/761-7642
gardner@lanmail.shu.edu

NM   Michelle Giger
Center for Civic Values
LRE Project
P.O. Box 2184
Albuquerque, NM 87102-2505
505/764-9417
FAX 505/242-5179
ccv@technet.um.org

NY   James J. Carroll
Project LEGAL
Syracuse University
732 Ostrom Ave.
Syracuse, NY 13210-2942
315/443-4720

Gregory Wilsey
Law, Youth and Citizenship Program
New York State Bar Association
One Elk St.
Albany, NY 12207
518/474-1460
FAX 518/486-1571
lyc@nysba.org

Thomas J. O'Donnel
Project P.A.T.C.H.
Northport-East Northport UFSD
110 Elwood Rd.
Northport, NY 11768-3455
516/262-6874
FAX 516/262-6635
patch@li.net

Mary Hughes
Kings County District Attorney's
Office
Project Legal Lives
Municipal Bldg.
Brooklyn, NY 11201
718/250-2000
FAX 718/250-8723

NC   Jan Agostino
Center for Research and Develop-
ment of LRE (CRADLE)
Wake Forest University School of
Law
Reynolda Station
P.O. Box 7206
Winston-Salem, NC 27109-7206
800/437-1054
FAX 910/759-4591

Doug Robertson
North Carolina Department of Public Instruction
116 W. Edenton St.
Raleigh, NC 27603-1753
919/715-1877
FAX 919/715-1897

ND   Deborah Knuth
State Bar Association of North
Dakota
P.O. Box 2136
Bismarck, ND 58502-2136
701/255-1404
FAX 701/224-1621

OH   David Naylor
College of Education, University of
Cincinnati
608 Teachers College
Cincinnati, OH 45221-0001
513/556-3563
FAX 513/556-2483

Bud Dingwall
Ohio Center for LRE
1700 Lake Shore Dr.
P.O. Box 16562
Columbus, OH, 43216-6562
614/487-2050
FAX 614/486-6221

OK   Michael H. Reggio
Oklahoma Bar Association, LRE Program
P.O. Box 53036
1901 N. Lincoln Blvd.
Oklahoma City, OK 73152
405/524-2365
FAX 405/524-1115
mreggio@aardvark.ucs.uoknor.edu

OR   Marilyn Cover
Classroom Law Project
6318 S.W. Corbett St.
Portland, OR 97201
503/245-8707
FAX 503/245-8538
mcover@lclark.edu

PA   David Keller Trevaskis
Law, Education, and Participation
(LEAP)
Temple University School of Law
1719 N. Broad St.
Philadelphia, PA 19122-2504
215/204-8593
FAX 215/204-5455
dtrevask@thunder.ocis.temple.edu

PUERTO RICO
Dr. Federico Matheu
General Education Council
Department of Education
Munoz Rivera Ave.
268 Banco Poular, 21st Fl.
Hateo Rey, Puerto Rico 00919
809/764-0101
FAX 809/764-0820

RI   Claudette Field
Rhode Island Legal/Educational
Partnership Program
255 Westminster St., 4th Fl.
Providence, RI 02903-3414
401/277-6831
FAX 401/277-6839
ccfield@eworld.com.org

Joyce L. Stevos
Program and Staff Development
Providence School Department
797 Westminster
Providence, RI 02903-4018
401/456-9126
FAX 401/456-9252

Theresa Watson
Ocean State Center for Law and Citizenship Education
80 Washington St., Rm. 302
Providence, RI 02903-1819
401/277-5233
FAX 401/277-5263
twatson@uriacc.uri.edu

SC   Cindy Coker
South Carolina Bar, LRE
P.O. Box 608
Columbia, SC 29292-0608
802/252-5139
FAX 803/799-4118

SD   Robert Wood
University of South Dakota, South
Dakota LRE
Delzell Education Center
414 E. Clark St.
Vermillion, SD 57069-2307
605/677-5832
FAX 605/677-5438

TN   Judith Cannizzaro
Metro Nahville Public Schools, Social Studies
2601 Bransford Ave.
Nashville, TN 37204-2811
615/259-8660
FAX 615/259-8734

Suzanne Stampley
Tennessee Bar Association, LRE
3622 West End Ave.
Nashville, TN 37205-2403
625/883-7701
FAX 615/297-8058

TX   Rhonda Haynes
Department of LRE, State Bar of
Texas
P.O. Box 12487
Austin, TX 78711-2487
512/463-1463
FAX 512/475-1904

UT   Nancy N. Mathews
Utah State Office of Education, Department of LRE
250 East 5th S.
Salt Lake City, UT 84111-3204
801/538-7742
FAX 801/538-7769

Kathy Dryer
State of Utah LRE Project
645 South 200th E.
Salt Lake City, UT 84111-3834
801/322-1802
FAX 801/531-0660

VT   Jean Blacketor
Vermont LRE
2 Sugar Maple Lane
Keene, NH 03431-5200
603/357-9928
nedcaron@together.org

VA   Joyce Davis
Virginia Institute for Law and Citizenship Studies
Virginia Commonwealth University
1015 W. Main St.
P.O. Box 842020
Richmond, VA 23284-2020
804/828-1940
FAX 804/828-1323

WA   Margaret Fisher
Office/Administrator for Courts
950 Broadway Plaza
Tacoma, WA 94802-4405
360/705-5295
FAX 360/586-8869

WV   Thomas R. Tinder
West Virginia State Bar Association,
Citizenship/LRE Program
2006 Kanawha Blvd. E.
304/558-9126
304/558-2467
stamm@technet.wvbar.org

WI   Dee Runaas
State Bar of Wisconsin, LRE
402 W. Wilson St.
P.O. Box 7158
Madison, WI 53707-7158
800/728-7788
FAX 608/257-5502
drunaas@wisbar.org

WY   Donald Morris
Wyoming LRE Council
717 Frontier Park Ave.
Cheyenne, WY 82001
307/632-8013
donaldr.morris,104232,3342@compuserve.com

Tony Lewis
Wyoming State Bar Association
P.O. Box 109
Cheyenne, WY 82003-0109
307/632-9061
FAX 307/632-3737

Drug Prevention Information

Schools without Drugs
U.S. Department of Education
Washington, 1989
To obtain copies write to:
Schools Without Drugs
Pueblo, CO 81009

Drug Prevention Curricula: A Guide to Selection and Implementation
National Clearinghouse for Alcohol and Drug Information
P.O. Box 2345
Rockville, MD 20852

Schools and Drugs: A Guide to Drug and Alcohol Prevention Curricula and Programs
Crime Prevention Center
California Attorney General's Office
P.O. Box 944255
Sacramento, CA 94244-2550

Drug Video Program
Office of Public Affairs
U.S. Department of Education
400 Maryland Ave. S.W.
Washington, DC 20202

Chapter Fourteen

EVALUATING ALL OF US

While teaching in Chicago, I noticed that my students would grow edgy as report card week loomed ahead. Their common question, in informal conversation or in classroom conferences, was, "How'm I doin'? What'm I goin' to get?" My standard response was, "Don't *you* know?"

These sixth-graders had been told precisely what their grades would be based on; they had the same data as the teacher. Yet the students still wanted to know what grades they would receive. They weren't just seeking reassurance; they were honestly in the dark regarding the process of evaluation.

Since then I have formulated a number of hypotheses that have proved correct over the years:

1. Students are often not informed by their teachers about the process of evaluation and the figuring of grades.

2. Grades are often altered by teachers on the basis of comportment. That is, if the teacher does not appreciate students' conduct, their grades are lowered as a result. Conversely, teachers raise the grades of students who have exemplary conduct.

3. As a result of (1) and (2), students see their grades as almost unrelated to what has gone on in class during the previous nine weeks. Grades are a great mystery that some students *never* understand.

4. Evaluation is almost always summative rather than formative, despite what teachers may claim.

The evaluation *process* is often ignored for the evaluation product. This chapter will examine both and will provide examples of various methods that can be used to enhance the evaluation process.

Evaluation can be summative or formative, norm referenced or criterion referenced, depending on one's purpose. Evaluation reflects a philosophy of education. Without this, a teacher drifts from task to task, with purpose becoming subservient to activity. Measurement and grades are not synonymous with evaluation; they are just types of evaluation.

This chapter will consider evaluative instruments, including tests, quizzes, checklists, and anecdotal records as well as the process of portfolio compilation. Less formal evaluation can be carried out through personal conferences, the solicitation of student comments (test review process), the examination of creative writing, artwork, or role play, or via learning-center work.

Teacher evaluations are also part of the evaluation process. Self-evaluation, student evaluation, and peer evaluation should be used to complement the old and fallacious notion that student performance is a direct result of teacher performance alone.

Evaluation is not wholly objective. To give each student the best chance to perform well, the teacher should gather data of various types and use these to improve students' performances. Evaluation should be part of an ongoing improvement process, not just a game to catch students unawares. Ideally, an evaluation should allow students to demonstrate what they know, not merely what they do not know.

Teachers should initiate the broader artistic approach to evaluation to balance the strict scientific approach. To accomplish this requires an open attitude on the part of teachers, parents, administrators, *and* students.

WHAT EVALUATION MEANS

Evaluation in education is the process by which we assess what has occurred or is occurring in a classroom or school setting. According to Eisner, evaluation in education has five functions: (1) to diagnose, (2) to revise curricula, (3) to compare, (4) to anticipate educational needs, and (5) to determine if objectives have been reached.

Too often educators are exclusively concerned with the last function. Functions 2, 3, and 4 are more programmatic in scope than individual, though they need not be. The diagnostic function seems vital to the setting of objectives, yet, surprisingly, many teachers set objectives only with content in mind, rather than students. Thus the tail wags the dog. This does not mean that teachers totally ignore the diagnostic function. They often "read" their students' reactions to determine if knowledge is being absorbed (are their expressions confused, bored, glazed, eager, comprehending?) or draw a conclusion from the questions students ask during or after an explanation. Nevertheless, the diagnostic function is far less common than that of assessing the achievement of objectives.

During the 1980s there was concern over knowledge acquisition in connection with student test scores on content tests. In the 1990s, however, there was a growing realization that producing students who score well on content-based tests did not lead to the kind of students who could think, even if they scored well on tests. Thus there arose a concern about producing better *tests* to measure better *thinking.* The status of testing was summed up by Ernest Boyer, president of the Carnegie Foundation for the Advancement of Teaching: "Most of our current efforts at assessment have been woefully inadequate, fragmented, and even destructive." (Leslie and Wingert, 56)

Now there are calls for tests that include oral exams, written essays, and student exhibits of work or portfolios. There is much more to evaluation than testing, and both parents and school people are beginning to understand that.

Formative and Summative Evaluations

Evaluations are usually either formative or summative in intent. Summative evaluations refer to the time-based achievement of particular objectives. For example, if a unit is four weeks long, students are commonly assessed on completion of the unit. If the students perform poorly on the summative evaluation but a month later have command of the unit material, it does not matter. If they do well on the summative evaluation but forget all the material in two weeks, this would not be detrimental to the evaluation.

Formative evaluations are more process oriented. The teacher assesses students during a unit, for example, and then redirects them to study certain areas until they achieve a level of mastery. The time that this process takes will vary from student to student, but the teacher is concerned with the *achievement* of some objective, not the *appearance* of such achievement.

Many schools are not set up to encourage formative evaluation. Teachers do not provide alternative learning modes for reinforcing unfamiliar concepts or content. If students do not grasp the material, they are instructed to reread the chapter or redo the report. Alternatives like learning centers, cross-age tutoring, independent research, and teacher-student conferences are ways to help students understand the various forms in which knowledge can be presented. One method does not always work for all students.

Many parents are not especially enamored of formative evaluation. This is not because parents necessarily like summative evaluation, but because they find it more understandable. When a teacher reduces learning to simplistic numbers and letters, parents often think it is useful. Formative evaluations produce much better data, but their conclusions are less exact. Because parents were evaluated summatively when they were in school, they may prefer to have their children assessed in the same manner.

Even in cases where there is no grading, parents are less accepting of summative procedures. At a progressive elementary school in California, for example, the details of each child's performance were revealed during frequent parent-teacher conferences. After parents had heard what their child was accomplishing in various areas, they would frequently ask, "But how's he doing?" The teacher would then begin to reiterate the areas of accomplishment, but the parents would interrupt with, "Yes, yes, but *how* is he doing? What's his grade?" When reminded that grades were not given at this school, the parents, reply would be, "I know that, but if you *did,* what would he get?"

Norm-Referenced versus Criterion-Referenced Assessment

Norm-referenced tests are the most common type of formal testing. Their intent is to compare the achievement of a local group or individuals with that of a national sample of students of the same age or grade. Testing conditions are standardized to make the comparisons more valid. Despite this standardization, such tests are almost inherently unfair to various groups of students, in particular the socioeconomically poorest ones. Most of these tests are written by people with a particular view of what is important, and who make assumptions about students' backgrounds. Students with little access to a variety of books and magazines, with rural rather than urban or suburban backgrounds, or who are nonwhite rather than white will almost always rank lower on such tests. As Dupuis and her colleagues note:

> If a teacher thinks of student evaluation only in terms of norm-referenced tests in which students' performance is compared to age and grade peers in a national norming sample, teaching can be very discouraging indeed, especially if one teaches students from lower socioeconomic level neighborhoods. Achievement on norm-referenced measures is so closely related to family background that it simply does not reflect specific learning gained in a particular class. (302)

In criterion-referenced testing, students are compared not to their peers but to themselves, in terms of a set of objectives. When students master the objective, they need no further work related to that objective. However,

> criterion-referenced tests must not . . . be used simplistically; mastery attained at one point in time will not necessarily be retained if opportunities are not provided for application and practice. Therefore, objectives should be

written to achieve a spiraling effect so that skills are reviewed at each successively higher level with greater complexity and difficulty. (Dupuis et al., 49)

Thus a criterion-referenced instrument allows students to reach class goals, individual goals, or both, depending on the teacher's intention or use of the instrument. Too often teachers equate evaluation or assessment strictly with tests and measurement. Callahan et al. summarize the relationship as follows:

> Measurement is concerned with quantitative data about specific behaviors. Examples of measurement include tests and the statistical procedures used to analyze the results. Thus, measurement is a descriptive and objective process, one that is relatively free from human value judgements.
>
> Assessment includes this objective data from measurement, but it also includes other types of information, some of which are more subjective, such as anecdotes in a student's record, teacher observations and ratings of student performance. (405)

In other words, tests are only one way to evaluate students. Evaluation should be based on a much broader range of information.

TYPES OF EVALUATIVE INSTRUMENTS

Tests are the most common type of summative evaluation instrument used in schools. They are not necessarily the best tool, however. The purpose of tests and the extent to which they are used reflect one's philosophy of education and schooling. Most tests are not especially revealing, particularly those that ask students to recall large amounts of data. However, many teachers feel that this is an accurate measure of learning. To assess the validity of a test, teachers should ask the following three questions (Callahan et al., 405):

1. Does the instrument adequately sample the content intended?
2. Does it measure the cognitive, affective, and psychomotor skills that are important to the unit of content being tested?
3. Does it sample all the instructional objectives of the unit?

The latter point is vital, since many tests assess areas not presented as unit objectives. The objectives and evaluation, however, should be linked. If one sets an objective, then it must be assessed in some manner. If not, how is it possible to know whether the objective has been achieved? Although this may seem obvious, many preservice and in-service teachers fail to evaluate students on unit objectives.

Objective Tests

There are many types of tests and test questions. Most are either essay or so-called objective tests. An objective test is almost never truly objective, however, as most teachers have only their own views of the material in mind. The answer called for often reflects the teacher's subjective opinion. Similarly, the teacher decides how many and what type of questions will be asked concerning each area studied. Most student responses cannot be clarified on an objective test.

Many times students lament that they studied hard for an objective test but the teacher asked the wrong questions. This is not a cruel attempt at humor; rather, it is often true. Many teachers see an evaluation as a way of revealing what students do *not* know rather than what they know. In one sense, evaluations allow students to show off. Tests should be a positive, not a negative, experience. Most teachers can design a test that will baffle a third grader. The trick is to devise instruments that will challenge students to do as well as they can, to show as much as they can.

The major drawback of objective tests is that they mostly measure lower-level learning (see Bloom's taxonomy, Chapter 12). A test that is exclusively objective is bound to be a "What don't they know?" type of evaluation because there is only one right answer, with no variations accepted or possible.

Objective tests include multiple choice, true-false, short answer, matching, and fill-in types of questions. According to Ellis, "elementary students who lack the capability to develop an essay that conveys their true understandings of a topic are often able to demonstrate their understandings by discriminating among alternate answers." (220)

Because we have all taken objective tests, this discussion will focus on suggestions regarding their use, rather than on unneeded descriptions of the types of questions.

TRUE/FALSE STATEMENTS

The statements used in this type of test should be entirely true or entirely false. A variation is the *modified* true-false test, in which the student is allowed to change one of several underlined words to make the statement true. When writing a true-false test:

- Write statements clearly to avoid ambiguities.
- Include only one idea or thought in a true-false item.
- Try to develop ideas or thoughts that require more than just simple recall of knowledge.
- Avoid using statements taken directly from textbooks.

Here is a poorly written example:

T F Native Americans came to this country before Columbus arrived.

Since this country was not in existence until 1776, some students could see the statement as false, which was not the intention. Geographic description would be better than a political reference. A better wording:

T F Native Americans came to the North American continent long before the arrival of Europeans.

Calvin and Hobbes   by Bill Watterson

MULTIPLE-CHOICE TESTS

The questions in a multiple-choice test can measure more than just knowledge. It is possible to include items that measure comprehension, application, or even higher levels of understanding such as analysis. Unlike in true-false tests, guessing is substantially reduced, although not eliminated. When writing a multiple-choice test:

- Keep all answer choices about the same length and on the same vocabulary level.
- Avoid "all of the above" or "none of the above" statements. They require less higher-level thinking and are often confusing. If four good alternatives cannot be found, the question should be discarded.
- State the problem or question clearly in the introduction; state the choices as briefly as possible.

A poorly written example:

The Constitution guarantees all citizens:

A. the right to vote

B. the right to free speech

C. the right to strike

D. the right to take arms against an unjust ruler

E. all of the above

The *intended* answer is B, but the question is not as easy as it seems. D is considerably longer and may be an undue distracter for some students. A might seem right, but that depends on whether the Bill of Rights and the other amendments are included in the definition of "the Constitution." Avoiding these pitfalls by defining terms clearly and not having excessively long or lame choices like "all of the above" would give a better picture of what students actually understand.

MATCHING QUESTIONS

Tests of this type can be used to illustrate an understanding of the relationship between people and places, geographic names and locations, dates and events, people and ideas, and so on.

- Make one of the two lists longer so that the process of elimination does not give students an answer. If the lists are uneven, students are not doomed to miss two answers when they miss one.
- When setting up matching questions, place both sets of items on the same page, preferably side by side, so that students can view all the possibilities together.
- Keep directions clear and specific and response items short.
- Make relationships obvious so that students do not waste time pondering the lists.

These questions can mislead easily. Consider the following:

Match the People with the Most Appropriate Country

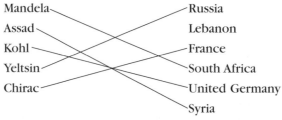

Match People and Governmental Agencies

Albright	Treasury
Daley	United Nations
Cohen	State
Reno	Defense
Richardson	Justice
	Senate

The correct answers are shown, but other answers could easily be justified and would be counted wrong. In the first set, Assad *could* be justified as matching with Lebanon. In the second set, Cohen could be matched with both Defense and Senate since he is a former Senator. Albright has been both American Ambassador to the United Nations and Secretary of State. Which answer is correct? With this type of question, space could be included for a brief explanation of why particular pairs are matched. This takes more than guesswork and allows the teacher to understand the student's deliberations more clearly.

FILL-IN QUESTIONS

These tests can be tricky, because students often fill in a correct answer that is not what the teacher wanted. For example, "King Richard the Lionhearted of England was imprisoned in _____" could be completed with a location or a country, but if the student responded with a date or a building it would still be correct. When writing fill-in questions:

- Design items so that there is clearly only one correct response.
- Design items to sample more than knowledge. Statements taken directly from textbooks should not be used.
- Provide sufficient space for students' answers. If more than a single word is expected, make that clear.

Essay Tests

Essay questions allow teachers to find out much more about what students know—rather than what they do not know—as well as whether they can present their ideas in a logical and coherent manner. Unfortunately, if students are poor spellers, grammarians, or writers, this may be interpreted as indicating that they do not know the material. As mentioned in chapters 3 and 12, reading and writing skills are needed in all subject areas. However, if some students are not yet equipped with the proper tools to handle an essay test, there is no point in giving them one.

Essay questions should focus on main ideas, not details, and should allow students to "color in the picture" as needed. The questions should aim to elicit high-level responses from students, rather than just knowledge or comprehension. Evaluative essay answers demand personal reflection and defense. If these skills have not been encouraged by the teacher in class discussion or small-group work, the resulting answers can be disappointing. Again, this may not indicate students' inability as much as their wariness.

A teacher should provide choices on essay questions. Certain phrasing may confuse students. Allow them to select responses whereby they can show off. Again, students should be able to show what they do know rather than what they do not know.

On an essay test, make the questions interesting and list the criteria for evaluating student answers.

Checklists and Anecdotal Notations

Checklists provide an alternative to the test or quiz that can be used to indicate mastery of certain skills or material. Using the checklist method, a teacher observes students at work, examines their assignments, and notes their contributions in class discussion. While gathering data, the teacher notes the progress of each student in several areas, indicating which students need more work in certain areas and which do not. Checklists can

TABLE 14.1
Map Skills: Directions and Symbols

| | DIRECTION | | | SYMBOLS | | |
	KNOWS CARDINAL DIRECTIONS	KNOWS INTERMEDIATE DIRECTIONS	CAN USE LATITUDE AND LONGITUDE	RECOGNIZES LAND/ WATER COLORS	UNDERSTANDS PICTORIAL SYMBOLS	UNDERSTANDS ABSTRACT SYMBOLS	USES KEYS AND LEGENDS
Larry	✓	P	O	✓	P	O	O
Maria	✓	✓	O	✓	✓	P	P
John	✓	✓	O	✓	P	O	O
Andre	✓	✓	O	✓	✓	P	O
Sherwyn	✓	✓	P	✓	✓	✓	P
Don	✓	✓	✓	✓	✓	✓	✓
Theresa	✓	✓	P	✓	✓	✓	P
Kathy	✓	✓	✓	✓	✓	✓	✓
Wendy	✓	✓	✓	✓	✓	✓	✓
William	✓	✓	O	✓	P	P	P
June	✓	✓	P	✓	✓	✓	✓
Margaret	✓	✓	P	✓	✓	✓	✓
David	✓	✓	P	✓	✓	✓	P
Anna	✓	✓	O	✓	✓	P	P
Evelyn	✓	P	O	✓	✓	P	P
Gregory	✓	✓	O	✓	✓	✓	P
Bernice	✓	✓	O	✓	✓	P	O
Ramon	✓	✓	P	✓	✓	✓	P
Janet	✓	✓	✓	✓	✓	✓	✓
Yolanda	✓	✓	O	✓	P	O	O
Duane	✓	✓	O	✓	✓	✓	P
Reynaldo	✓	✓	P	✓	✓	✓	P
Chester	✓	✓	P	✓	✓	✓	✓

Key: ✓ = mastery; P = progressing; O = no progress made, or has not begun.

thus be designed as diagnostic or summative instruments. A sample check-list for map skills is shown in Table 14.1.

Many schools encourage the use of anecdotal records in assessing students' comportment. Such records also can be useful in assessing cognitive, affective, and psychomotor achievement. Observations of students both in and out of class can generate much useful data, as Ellis points out:

> In social studies, students spend a considerable amount of time in group work and other activities that are difficult to reduce to paper-and-pencil expression. For both on-going and summative evaluative purposes, a teacher needs to be a descriptive researcher observing the behavior of his or her students. Valuable data can be gathered on pupil progress in this fashion. (210)

Observational notes can be taken during an observation and expanded on at lunch, after school, or while students are at a special activity like physical education. Playground observations may help a teacher discern if the citizenship claims students make in class are really practiced. For example, if a student talks of fair play in a sociodramatic episode, does that student practice it with others on the playground? If not, the implications of such a statement may not have been truly internalized.

When one observes without a checklist, it allows for more to be seen because there is no concern with scoring a particular event. A teacher may observe some very surprising actions that would have gone unnoticed under the tighter structure of a checklist. Obviously there are times for both checklists and anecdotal notation.

NONINSTRUMENTAL EVALUATIONS

As just noted, informal evaluations provide a whole different perspective on students and student abilities. They can be just as meaningful even when they lack specific objectives if teachers have the growth and assessment of their students in mind. There are many types of qualitative evaluation. A few of the most successful and rewarding types are discussed below.

ARTWORK AND CREATIVE WRITING

Creative work often indicates what students are learning and thinking about in social studies. Student drawings can indicate an understanding of chronology, geography, or social relations. The advantage here is that the student feels no pressure to look for the right answer. For example, during a unit on anthropology the teacher might request his or her second graders to draw some aspect of the lives of the first humans. A student depicts a family group in a cave with a telephone and a dinosaur lurking outside. The teacher can compliment the student's artistry but note that the chronology is inappropriate. Dinosaurs were long gone by the time humans arrived, and telephones, of course, were not common in cave life. Thus the picture becomes a useful diagnostic instrument. The teacher can see what the child understands regarding early humans as well as what concepts need more development (Figure 14.1).

In the same manner, creative writing assignments can give clues to student-acquired knowledge. An assignment like "What do you think Lee and Grant talked about at Appomattox?" could reveal whether students are cognizant of what the weather is like in Virginia in April, what events were most important in causing the Civil War, and what factors led to the ultimate defeat of the Confederacy. All this information could come from an assignment that did not have these as its specific objectives.

FIGURE 14.1

A picture like this one can be used to evaluate mastery of chronological concepts. Since cave dwellers, dinosaurs, and televisions did not exist at the same time, the student who drew this possesses some chronological misconceptions.

PERSONAL CONFERENCES

For students who do not express themselves well in writing or do not perform well on tests that require large amounts of reading, the personal conference is a useful method. Five minutes of interactive discussion with a student on a personal basis is as useful as a half-hour test. After the student responds to a question, the teacher can seek further clarification and a defense of ideas. The student can also volunteer information not precisely called for. A written test negates this interactive shaping of responses. Personal conferences can be held on an irregular basis as well as when other students are studying or reading silently. Here is how one third grader responded in a conference:

TEACHER: What are some of the largest industries in Japan?
STUDENT: Oh, cars, TVs, radios, cameras, fishing, steel.
TEACHER: Good. You said fishing. What separates that from the others that you mentioned?
STUDENT: Well, it is done in the water.
TEACHER: Yes, what else?

Parent-teacher conferences provide personal and direct feedback in the evaluation of students.

STUDENT: It's easier, I mean, it's not like a factory. People just go out and fish and that's that.

TEACHER: Why is there a lot of fishing in Japan?

STUDENT: What do you mean?

TEACHER: We studied life in Switzerland and they didn't fish. Why do the Japanese fish?

STUDENT: Because Japan is a bunch of islands. There are fish all around. Switzerland isn't near the ocean.

TEACHER: Looking at the globe here, can you guess other countries that might fish?

STUDENT: Mmm. England, Iceland, America, Mexico, Peru?

Clearly this interview reveals more about the student's understanding of the interaction of economy and geography than any written test could easily provide.

ROLE PLAY

Another method that can be used to evaluate a student's understanding of time and space is historical or cultural role play. Fifth graders who dramatize

Thomas Jefferson talking to Alexander Hamilton or Benjamin Franklin reveal their understanding of the ideas that motivated these men. What did they feel strongly about? Of course, teachers could simply ask students, but they would run the risk that students were looking for what the teacher thought was right. A more detailed discussion of role play can be found in Chapter 8.

VIDEOTAPING

Another evaluative instrument that may be available to teachers in some schools is videotaping. The teacher should ask another school employee to operate the video camera—preferably a handheld one, to allow for a variety of angles. Although students will initially be curious and may not behave naturally, subsequent tapings should be more realistic.

After the teacher has reviewed the tape and analyzed it, it can be used again, so a new one need not be purchased for each session. What should one look for in a videotape? Under normal circumstances, a teacher's attention is limited to a few students at a time. The video camera may reveal working patterns in the classroom that the teacher may not have noticed. Small work groups may be less inhibited without the teacher listening, even if a camera is present. Thus the camera can reveal cognitive, affective, and psychomotor abilities previously unknown to the teacher.

STUDENT STATEMENTS

Student assessment of learning experiences is also useful in evaluations. Ellis refers to these as "I learned" statements, which may be either oral or written:

> Their purpose is merely to give students a chance to self-select one or more of the things they learned during a class session, an investigation, or perhaps a series of lessons. Students who can write can save their daily evaluations and use them as study material for a test or other evaluation. For younger learners, "I learned" statements can be written on the board or on a large sheet hung in the room. (208)

TEST PREPARATION

One of the most profitable evaluations involves the assessment of students as they prepare for tests. This can be done diagnostically (that is, formatively) or summatively if combined with the actual test or quiz to be given. During this type of evaluation, students may be more relaxed—that is, less pressured—and a teacher has the opportunity to find out the areas in which students need more work.

Often teachers choose to evaluate diagnostically before a unit begins by giving an instrument similar to the quiz they plan to use at the end of the unit. Through this pre-test, which should utilize all types of questions, teachers can see what weaknesses and strengths the class and individual students have. This alerts the teacher to changes that should be made in the material to be covered. For example, if almost all class members seem to exhibit knowledge and understanding of the major similarities and differences between Canada and the United States, the teacher might choose to spend more teaching time on the implications of such characteristics. For the few students who do not display such knowledge, the teacher could provide some individualized work to bring these students near the class level of content understanding.

Tests used diagnostically may indicate that much of the unit content is superfluous. If so, why bother redoing it? Or such diagnoses may indicate that the necessary foundation for dealing with the unit content is *not* present. Why push forward, then, essentially aiming students toward failure or frustration?

One useful way to implement this method is to schedule a review day with the class two days prior to a test or quiz. The students should prepare written questions for this review—a minimum of five per student. After the questions are handed in to the teacher, they become the focus of the review discussion time. The teacher selects a question to ask and, after receiving an answer, asks the students, "Why is this a good question? What does it reflect about what we studied? Could it be reworded to better reflect important aspects of our lessons? Does the answer to this question raise other good questions?"

From such questions, students get an understanding not only of the content of their materials but of the structure of knowledge and the intent of the teacher's evaluation. Students may begin to see that evaluation is concerned more with understanding why certain answers are *better* than with just providing those answers.

As a variation on this method, the teacher could tell the students that part of their grade on the exam will come from their own questions. The teacher could then weigh the questions handed in as part of the exam (10 to 15 percent) and actually use the best questions. This is not just a way to save the teacher's time; it also reveals what students think is important. If a majority of the class is missing the point, maybe the formal exam should be deferred. The usual test or quiz review consists of answering teacher-prepared questions. This activity has other evaluative purposes. For example, some students may reveal that they are not prepared for summative evaluation. If it is obvious that some students will not do well on the quiz, why press on with it? Some teachers might feel that if one exam is postponed students might never prepare for future exams. Such thinking assumes that the teacher's role is one of adversary. If that is so, it means that very little learning is occurring and the process of schooling becomes a sham.

Again, test preparation should focus on more than just the answers to the questions; it should also determine why such answers are important, how we know they are important, and how this can be confirmed. Some students may see all this clearly and express that insight well. These same students may do poorly on the written exam. This may reveal that they are poor readers or writers, or just have "test-itis." The student's command of the material during test preparation should be weighed against a poor performance on the test itself and evaluated accordingly. Is this fair if other students do not get the same break? Of course it is, if one is not so driven by grades and grading policies. Some people become so obsessed with grades that they actually begin to believe that grades are truly accurate and will determine a student's success in life. There is no research to support this. Evaluation should allow students to show what they know. Would it be so awful if all one's students did well?

One last method of evaluation is a variation on the spelling bee. Here, two teams answer questions, with one point given for each correct answer. Or, instead of using teacher-generated questions, the teacher could use student-generated questions. In this case, participants would score one point for each question used and two points for the correct answer. Unlike a spell-down, in which participants sit down after giving an incorrect response, a student could sit down after he or she got two or three questions right. This would allow the teacher to better assess which students needed more work. Questions selected for the last participants could get progressively easier so that these students could also get to show what they *do* know.

PORTFOLIO CREATION AND ASSESSMENT[1]

The use of portfolios has grown dramatically since the early 1990s. In compiling a portfolio, a student selects a variety of his or her best work that serves to illustrate the capabilities and performance of that student. The use of portfolios is one component of what some educators refer to as authentic assessment, that is, in providing a more accurate picture of what a student actually knows or can do.

The selection of materials for the portfolio is an important act; the portfolio should not merely be a "work folder" with all the papers, tests, or activities that the student has done included in it. Rather, the portfolio should have both organizational and critical rationales. The student should be able to explain why each piece that she or he has selected is representative of some aspect of growth in the student's learning. These materials should be organized around some themes or goals that the student and the teacher agree upon, such as growth in basic numerical skills, place-location skills, written communication, or personal understanding. Through the use of the portfolio students can demonstrate what they know, what they are capable of doing, and how they have grown intellectually or in ability over a period of time.

The portfolio should include some student work done in class, project work done at home and in school, teacher comments on the student's work, photos of materials created, and a reflective statement from the student. A good rule of thumb regarding the amount of evidence to include could be the following:

---

[1] My thanks to Professor Tom Dana for his suggestions and ideas for this section.

- One piece is not enough
- Everything is too much
- Keep adding pieces *as long as they add value*

TEACHER EVALUATIONS

Teaching is an interdependent act. Although this chapter mainly addresses student evaluation, teacher evaluation is equally important.

How does one evaluate one's own teaching? Many feel that the teacher's performance is a function of student performance: if students do well, it is because one has taught well. They believe that the converse is also true: poor student performance means poor teaching. This simplistic view of teaching, however, ignores student self-motivation, parental encouragement, access to materials outside of class, and other student responsibilities. In fact, this view is educational reductionism at its worst.

In New York State, for example, successful schools and teachers are determined by student performances on the state-administered and standardized Regents examinations. Because teachers and schools wish to be deemed successful, they interrupt the standard curriculum one month before the Regents exams so that a month of studying can be devoted to the exams. Other states and districts have similar types of exams. This kind of evaluation of teachers is fine if one has good students—but an anathema if one does not. Although the teacher is probably the key to successful learning, teacher performance cannot be measured by student performance on standardized tests. In elementary schools the tests are usually given in reading and mathematics. Thus searching for meaningful student performance in social studies through tests is futile.

EVALUATION BY STUDENTS

Evaluation of a teacher's performance by students may provide insight for the teacher. Surprisingly, elementary school students are usually more honest than high school or college students in assessing the teacher. In college, students often use the anonymous evaluation to blame the teacher for not evaluating them better. Elementary school students are generally not as grade conscious and have fewer hostilities toward their teachers. Thus student evaluation may be quite useful if it is solicited in a clear manner and permits students to respond clearly. A simple but useful student assessment is shown in the box on page 428. The assessment is simple, but it provides some clues as to what students learn from their teachers. Question 6 provides clues for personalizing future work.

EVALUATING ONESELF

Although self-evaluation is difficult, it should be done by teachers. We all have our own perceptions of how well we teach. The assessment should be made

---

EVALUATING A FOURTH-GRADE UNIT

1. The best part of this unit was:

    _____

    _____

    _____

2. The worst part of this unit was:

    _____

    _____

    _____

3. If your little brother or sister was going into fourth grade and asked about this unit, what do you think you might tell him or her?

    _____

    _____

    _____

4. Were there any activities in the unit that you might like to do again? Yes _____ No _____ If yes, what were they? _____

5. Did your teacher let you study things that you like or just things that the teacher likes?

    _____

    _____

    _____

6. What things do you like to read about?

    _____

    _____

    _____

---

not long after class has ended. Taking 15 minutes to write an assessment of one's own performance can be helpful in many ways. First, it encapsulates the day's activity. Second, it is therapeutic—writing down one's thoughts can be very comforting, especially after a tough day. Third, it indicates what direction one's teaching is going and what needs to be improved as well as what seems to be well done.

If it is possible to videotape a classroom session or two, teachers should use this method to evaluate their own performances. The camera will reveal whether teachers listen to their students, whether they are too task oriented or too easily distracted, whether they talk to all students or just a few. These are just some of the ways that videotape can be used to evaluate oneself.

EVALUATION BY OTHER TEACHERS

Peer evaluation is often ignored by teachers out of fear. Rather than exploring their collegial relationships, many teachers fear that someone else will see them teach and lose respect for them. But peers can be useful critics: they are no threat, they understand the problems the teacher is facing, and they can be honest in the hope of receiving useful reciprocal feedback. Eisner encourages this educational criticism, noting that

> The nonspecialized use of educational criticism within classrooms, schools, and school districts might contribute to the kind of community among staff, students, and parents that would help make schools the kind of supportive and humane places that they can and should become. (244)

In conclusion, evaluation is as much an artistic endeavor as a scientific one; one's biases will always be present. Thus it is expeditious to try to gather evaluative data in as many different ways as possible. Brubaker offers the following guidelines for evaluation (64-67):

- Evaluation is a philosophical dispute with oneself concerning what one thinks is important.
- Try, insofar as it is possible, to recognize your biases as an evaluator and distance yourself from them while engaged in the evaluation process.
- Those involved in the evaluation process should be clear as to the fact that measurement is one kind of evaluation but should not be used synonomously with the term "evaluation."
- Try, insofar as it is possible, to accept the person being evaluated where he or she is as the starting point and convey belief in the person's demonstrated abilities as well as potential for further growth.
- Evaluate on a periodic basis with the time frame clear to all.

These guidelines were developed for supervisory evaluation of teachers, but they have generic application as well.

The process of evaluation should be clearly understood by the teacher. Why are certain data being gathered? What do they show? Is there a better or alternative way for gathering such data? Does the evaluation show what students know or just what they do not know? Examinations in social studies classes should reflect these questions.

An essay exam is perhaps the best approach to evaluations. Essay questions usually ask for students to demonstrate their understanding of the material and their ability to analyze and evaluate the concepts by applying what they have learned to new learning situations.

Although this kind of examination may be fair to give, it may be unfair to assess because there is often no one way to answer an essay question. It is sometimes hard to convince students that there are no right answers. The goal is to present one's beliefs as rational arguments that will hold up under scrutiny. This is the nature of the assessment process in the school setting and the world outside. To assume that objective tests eliminate bias is to create a world of unreality, one that is shattered upon leaving the warmth of the school setting.

QUESTIONS AND ACTIVITIES

1. Are objective tests really objective? Could they be made so?

2. What might happen if schools gave no grades? What if colleges gave no grades?

3. How could students in primary grades engage in self-evaluation?

4. What dangers might there be in self-evaluation?

5. How useful would peer comments be in an evaluation?

6. In many countries there is open admission to college and the nation subsidizes college costs. Is this system realistic for the United States to consider?

7. Why do many teachers and parents prefer to use the grading system commonly found in schools?

8. If a teacher told a class that all students would receive A's if they all achieved the teacher's goals for them, how might the students react? How might you react?

9. Ask some elementary school teachers how they evaluate their students.

10. If students work on a project together, how should they be evaluated and graded?

REFERENCES

Brubaker, D. L. *Curriculum Planning.* Glenview, IL: Scott Foresman, 1982.

Callahan, J. F., L. H. Clark, and R. Kellough. *Teaching in the Middle and Secondary School.* 5th ed. Englewood Cliffs, NJ: Merrill, 1995.

Dupuis, M. M., J. W. Lee, B. J. Badiali, and E. N. Askov *Reading and Writing in Content Classrooms.* Glenview, IL: Scott Foresman, 1989.

Eisner, E. W. *The Educational Imagination.* 3rd ed. New York: Macmillan, 1994.

Ellis, A. *Teaching and Learning Elementary Social Studies.* 5th ed. Boston: Allyn and Bacon, 1995.

Leslie, C., and P. Wingert. "Not as Easy as A, B or C," *Newsweek,* January 8, 1990, pp. 56–58.

Sanders, N. M. *Classroom Questions—What Kinds?* New York: Harper and Row, 1966.

Appendix

SOURCES FOR UNIT INITIATION AND DEVELOPMENT

The following lists provide the names and addresses of groups that can be useful in the development of unit topics. Included are trade groups, professional organizations, foreign embassies or consulates, and some nonprofit institutes. The addresses are current as of 1997. Most of the groups listed will provide information and materials free of charge, but that may not always be the case. Requests for materials should be accompanied by a cover letter explaining why you wish the requested material and how you intend to use it. A follow-up letter of thanks detailing what you did with the material and, if possible, photographs of students using the material or a letter of thanks from students should also be sent.

Additional addresses may be found in the *Encyclopedia of Associations* (33rd ed., 1997) and the *National Trade and Professional Associations of the United States* (32nd ed., 1997).

PROFESSIONAL GROUPS

American Anthropological Association
4350 N. Fairfax Dr., Ste. 640
Arlington, VA 22203

American Association for the
Advancement of Science
1333 H St. NW
Washington, DC 20005

American Bar Association
750 N. Lake Shore Dr.
Chicago, IL 60611

American Geographical Society
156 Fifth Ave., Ste. 600
New York, NY 10010-7002

American Historical Association
400 A St. SE
Washington, DC 20003

American Library Association
SO E. Huron St.
Chicago, IL 60611

American Political Science Association
1027 New Hampshire Ave. NW
Washington, DC 20036

American Psychological Association
750 First St. NE
Washington, DC 20002-4242

American Sociological Association
1722 N. St. NW
Washington, DC 20036

National Coalition of Educational Activists
P.O. Box 679
Rhinebeck, NY 12572-0679

National Council for the Social Studies
3501 Newark St. NW
Washington, DC 20036

National Education Association
1201 16th St. NW
Washington, DC 20036

Phi Delta Kappa
408 N. Union Ave.
P.O. Box 789
Bloomington, IN 47402-0789

NONPROFIT ORGANIZATIONS

African American Institute
833 United Nations Plaza
New York, NY 10017

African Wildlife Foundation
1717 Massachusetts Ave. NW
Washington, DC 20036

Alcoholics Anonymous World Services
475 Riverside Dr.
New York, NY 10163

American Automobile Association
AAA Dr.
Heathrow, FL 32746

American Civil Liberties Union
132 W. 43rd St.
New York, NY 10036

American Peace Society
1319 18th St. NW
Washington, DC 20036-1802

Amnesty International USA
322 8th Ave.
New York, NY 10001

Asia Foundation
P.O. Box 193223
San Francisco, CA 94119-3223

B'nai B'rith International Headquarters
1640 Rhode Island Ave. NW
Washington, DC 20036

Common Cause
1250 Connecticut Ave NW
Washington, DC 20036

Council of Better Business Bureaus
4200 Wilson Blvd. Ste. 800
Arlington, VA 22203-1804

Gerontological Society
127S K St. NW, Ste. 350
Washington, DC 20005

Human Rights Campaign Fund
101 14th St. NW, Ste. 200
Washington, DC 20005

League of Women Voters
1730 M St. NW
Washington, DC 20036

National Association of the Deaf
814 Theyer Ave.
Silver Spring, MD 20910

National Audubon Society
700 Broadway
New York, NY 10003

National Coalition to Ban Handguns
100 Maryland Ave. NW
Washington, DC 20002

National Rifle Association
11250 Waples Mill Rd.
Fairfax, VA 22030

National Wildlife Federation
8925 Leesburg Pike
Vienna, VA 22184

Population-Environmental Balance
2000 P St. NW, Ste. 210
Washington, DC 20036

The Population Institute
107 2nd St. NE
Washington, DC 20002

Sierra Club
730 Polk St.
San Francisco, CA 94109

Wilderness Society
900 17th St. NW
Washington, DC 20006-2596

TRADE GROUPS

Advertising Council
261 Madison Ave., 11th Fl.
New York, NY 10016-2303

Agriculture Council of America
927 15th St. NW, Ste. 800
Washington, DC 20005-2304

American Bakers Association
1350 Eye St. NW, Ste. 1290
Washington, DC 20005-3005

American Bankers Association
1120 Connecticut Ave. NW
Washington, DC 20036

American Dairy Association
O'Hare International Center
10255 W. Higgins Rd.
Rosemont, IL 60018-5616

American Donkey and Mule Society
2901 N. Elm St.
Denton, TX 76201

American Forest and Paper Institute
1111 19th St. NW
Washington, DC 20036

American Forests
1516 P St. NW
P.O. Box 2000
Washington, DC 20005

American Fur Merchants Association
224 W. 30th St., 2nd Fl.
New York, NY 10001-4905

American Honey Producers Association
P.O. Box 584
Chesire, CT 06410

American Horse Council
1700 K St. NW, Ste. 300
Washington, DC 20006

American Iron and Steel Institute
1101 17th St. NW
Washington, DC 20036-1700

American Meat Institute
P.O. Box 3556
Washington, DC 20007

American Peanut Research and Education
Society
376 Ag Hall
Oklahoma State University
Stillwater, OK 74078

American Petroleum Institute
1220 L St. NW
Washington, DC 20005

American Sheep Industry Association
6911 S. Yosemite St.
Englewood, CO 80112-1414

American Ski Federation
207 Constitution Ave. NE
Washington, DC 20002

American Society of Travel Agents
1101 King St.
Alexandria, VA 22314

American Soybean Association
540 Maryville Centre
P.O. Box 419200
St. Louis, MO 63141

Automotive Information Council
13505 Dulles Technology Dr.
Herndon, VA 22071-3415

Beer Institute
122 C St. NW, Ste. 750
Washington, DC 20001-2109

Bicycle Manufacturers Association
of America
3050 K St. NW, Ste. 400
Washington, DC 20007

Dude Ranchers' Association
P.O. Box 471
La Porte, CO 80535

Edison Electric Institute
701 Pennsylvania Ave. NW
Washington, DC 20004-2696

Farmers Educational and Cooperative
Union of America
11900 E. Cornell Ave.
Aurora, CO 80014-3194

General Aviation Manufacturing
Association
1400 K St. NW, Ste. 801
Washington, DC 20005

Gold Institute
1112 16th St. NW, Ste. 240
Washington, DC 20036

Institute of Scrap Recycling Industries
1325 G St. NW, Ste. 1000
Washington, DC 20005

International Association of Amusement
Parks and Attractions
1448 Duke St.
Alexandria, VA 22314

International Ice Cream Association
1250 H St. NW, Ste. 900
Washington, DC 20005

Motion Picture Association of America
1600 Eye St. NW
Washington, DC 20006

National Association of Broadcasters
1771 N St. NW
Washington, DC 20036

National Cattlemen's Association
P.O. Box 3469
Englewood, CO 80155

National Confectioners Association of the
U.S.
7900 Westpark Dr., Ste. A320
McLean, VA 22102

National Corn Growers Association
1000 Executive Pkwy, Ste. 105
St. Louis, MO 63141

National Cotton Council of America
P.O. Box 12285
Memphis, TN 38182-0285

National Glass Association
8200 Greensboro Dr., 3rd Fl.
McLean, VA 22102

National Mining Association
1130 17th St. NW
Washington, DC 20036-4677

National Soft Drink Association
1101 16th St. NW
Washington, DC 20036

Petroleum Marketing Education Foundation
1901 Fort Myers Dr., Ste. 1200
Arlington, VA 22209

Silver Institute
1112 16th St. NW, Ste. 101
Washington, DC 20036

The Soap and Detergent Association
472 Park Ave. S.
New York, NY 10016

Travel Industry Association of America
1100 New York Ave. NW, Ste. 450
Washington, DC 20005

Wire Service Guild
133 W. 44th St.
New York, NY 10036

FOREIGN EMBASSIES IN THE UNITED STATES

AFGHANISTAN
2341 Wyoming Ave. NW
Washington, DC 20008

ALBANIA
1511 K St. NW, Ste. 1000
Washington, DC 20005

ALGERIA
2118 Kalorama Rd. NW
Washington, DC 20008

ANDORRA
2 United Nations Plaza, 25th Fl.
New York, NY 10017

ANGOLA
1050 Connecticut Ave. NW, Ste. 760
Washington, DC 20036

ANTIGUA-BARBUDA
3216 New Mexico Ave. NW
Washington, DC 20016

ARGENTINA
1600 New Hampshire Ave. NW
Washington, DC 20009

ARMENIA
2225 R St. NW
Washington, DC 20008

AUSTRALIA
1601 Massachusetts Ave. NW
Washington, DC 20036

AUSTRIA
2343 Massachusetts Ave. NW
Washington, DC 20008

BAHAMAS
2220 Massachusetts Ave. NW
Washington, DC 20008

BAHRAIN, STATE OF
3502 International Dr. NW
Washington, DC 20008

BANGLADESH
2201 Wisconsin Ave. NW
Washington, DC 20007

BARBADOS
2144 Wyoming Ave. NW
Washington, DC 20008

BELGIUM
3330 Garfield St. NW
Washington, DC 20008

BELIZE
2535 Massachusetts Ave. NW
Washington, DC 20008

BENIN, PEOPLE'S REPUBLIC OF
2737 Cathedral Ave. NW
Washington, DC 20008

BOLIVIA
3014 Massachusetts Ave. NW
Washington, DC 20008

BOSNIA and HERZEGOVINA
1707 L St. NW, Ste. 760
Washington, DC 20036

BOTSWANA
3400 International Dr.
Washington, DC 20008

BRAZIL
3006 Massachusetts Ave. NW
Washington, DC 20008

BRUNEI DARUSSALEM
2600 Virginia Ave. NW
Washington, DC 20037

BULGARIA
1621 22nd St. NW
Washington, DC 20008

BURKINA FASO
2340 Massachusetts Ave. NW
Washington, DC 20008

BURMA (UNION OF MYANMAR)
2300 S St. NW
Washington, DC 20008

BURUNDI
2233 Wisconsin Ave. NW
Washington, DC 20007

CAMBODIA
4500 16th St. NW
Washington, DC 20011

CAMEROON, REPUBLIC OF
2349 Massachusetts Ave. NW
Washington, DC 20008

CANADA
501 Pennsylvania Ave. NW
Washington, DC 20001

CAPE VERDE, REPUBLIC OF
3415 Massachusetts Ave. NW
Washington, DC 20007

CENTRAL AFRICAN REPUBLIC
1618 22nd St. NW
Washington, DC 20008

CHAD
2002 R St. NW
Washington, DC 20009

CHILE
1732 Massachusetts Ave. NW
Washington, DC 20036

CHINA, PEOPLE'S REPUBLIC OF
2300 Connecticut Ave. NW
Washington, DC 20008

COLOMBIA
2118 Leroy Pl. NW
Washington, DC 20008

COMOROS (temporary)
336 E. 45th St. 2nd Fl.
New York, NY 10017

CONGO, PEOPLE'S REPUBLIC OF THE
4891 Colorado Ave. NW
Washington, DC 20011

COSTA RICA
2114 S St. NW
Washington, DC 20008

CROATIA
2343 Massachusetts Ave. NW
Washington, DC 20008

CYPRUS
2211 R St. NW
Washington, DC 20008

CZECH REPUBLIC
3900 Spring of Freedom St. NW
Washington, DC 20008

DEMOCRATIC REPUBLIC OF THE CONGO
1800 New Hampshire Ave. NW
Washington, DC 20009

DENMARK
3200 Whitehaven St. NW
Washington, DC 20008

DJIBOUTI
1156 15th St. NW, Ste. 515
Washington, DC 20005

DOMINICA
3216 New Mexico Ave. NW
Washington, DC 20016

DOMINICAN REPUBLIC
1715 22nd St. NW
Washington, DC 20008

ECUADOR
2535 15th St. NW
Washington, DC 20009

EGYPT
3521 International Court NW
Washington, DC 20008

EL SALVADOR
2308 California St. NW
Washington, DC 20008

EQUITORIAL GUINEA
1511 K St. NW, Ste. 405
Washington, DC 20005

ERITREA
1708 New Hampshire Ave. NW
Washington, DC 20009

ESTONIA
2131 Massachusetts Ave. NW
Washington, DC 20008

ETHIOPIA
2134 Kalorama Rd. NW
Washington, DC 20008

EUROPEAN UNION
2300 M St. NW
Washington, DC 20037

FIJI
2233 Wisconsin Ave. NW
Washington, DC 20007

FINLAND
3301 Massachusetts Ave. NW
Washington, DC 20008

FRANCE
4101 Reservoir Rd. NW
Washington, DC 20007

GABON, REPUBLIC OF
2034 20th St. NW
Washington, DC 20009

GAMBIA, THE
1155 15th St. NW, Ste. 1000
Washington, DC 20005

GEORGIA, REPUBLIC OF (temporary)
1511 K St. NW, Ste. 424
Washington, DC 20005

GERMANY, FEDERAL REPUBLIC OF
4645 Reservoir Rd. NW
Washington, DC 20007

GHANA
3512 International Dr. NW
Washington, DC 20009

GREECE
2221 Massachusetts Ave. NW
Washington, DC 20008

GRENADA
1701 New Hampshire Ave. NW
Washington, DC 20009

GUATEMALA
2220 R St. NW
Washington, DC 20008

GUINEA
2112 Leroy Pl. NW
Washington, DC 20008

GUINEA-BISSAU
918 16th St. NW, Mezzanine Ste.
Washington, DC 20006

GUYANA
2490 Tracy Pl. NW
Washington, DC 20008

HAITI
2311 Massachusetts Ave. NW
Washington, DC 20008

THE HOLY SEE (The Vatican)
Apostolic Nunciature
3339 Massachusetts Ave. NW
Washington, DC 20008

HONDURAS
3007 Tilden St.
Washington, DC 20008

HUNGARY
3910 Shoemaker St. NW
Washington, DC 20008

ICELAND
1156 15th St. NW, Ste. 1200
Washington, DC 20005

INDIA
2107 Massachusetts Ave. NW
Washington, DC 20008

INDONESIA
2020 Massachusetts Ave. NW
Washington, DC 20036

IRELAND
2234 Massachusetts Ave. NW
Washington, DC 20008

ISRAEL
3514 International Dr. NW
Washington, DC 20008

ITALY
1601 Fuller St. NW
Washington, DC 20009

IVORY COAST (COTE D'IVOIRE)
2424 Massachusetts Ave. NW
Washington, DC 20008

JAMAICA
1520 New Hampshire Ave. NW
Washington, DC 20036

JAPAN
2520 Massachusetts Ave. NW
Washington, DC 20008

JORDAN
3504 International Dr. NW
Washington, DC 20008

KAZAKSTAN
3421 Massachusetts Ave. NW
Washington, DC 20008

KENYA
2249 R St. NW
Washington, DC 20008

KOREA (SOUTH)
2450 Massachusetts Ave. NW
Washington, DC 20008

KUWAIT
2940 Tilden St. NW
Washington, DC 20008

KYRGYSTAN
1511 K St. NW
Washington, DC 20005

LAOS PEOPLE'S DEMOCRATIC REPUBLIC
2222 S St. NW
Washington, DC 20008

LATVIA
4325 17th St. NW
Washington, DC 20011

LEBANON
2560 28th St. NW
Washington, DC 20008

LESOTHO
2511 Massachusetts Ave. NW
Washington, DC 20008

LIBERIA, REPUBLIC OF
5201 16th St. NW
Washington, DC 20011

LITHUANIA
2622 16th St. NW
Washington, DC 20009

LUXEMBOURG
2200 Massachusetts Ave. NW
Washington, DC 20008

MACEDONIA
3050 K St. NW, Ste. 210
Washington, DC 20007

MADAGASCAR
2374 Massachusetts Ave. NW
Washington, DC 20008

MALAWI
2408 Massachusetts Ave. NW
Washington, DC 20036

MALAYSIA
2401 Massachusetts Ave. NW
Washington, DC 20008

MALI
2130 R St. NW
Washington, DC 20008

MALTA
2017 Connecticut Ave. NW
Washington, DC 20008

MARSHALL ISLANDS
2433 Massachusetts Ave. NW
Washington, DC 20008

MAURITANIA
2129 Leroy Pl. NW
Washington, DC 20008

MAURITIUS
4301 Connecticut Ave. NW, Ste. 441
Washington, DC 20008

MEXICO
1911 Pennsylvania Ave. NW
Washington, DC 20006

MICRONESIA
1725 N St. NW
Washington, DC 20036

MOLDOVA
2101 S St. NW
Washington, DC 20008

MONGOLIA
2833 M St. NW
Washington, DC 20007

MOROCCO
1601 21st St. NW
Washington, DC 20009

MOZAMBIQUE
1990 M St. NW, Ste. 570
Washington, DC 20036

NAMIBIA
1605 New Hampshire Ave. NW
Washington, DC 20009

NEPAL
2131 Leroy Pl. NW
Washington, DC 20008

NETHERLANDS, THE
4200 Linnean Ave. NW
Washington, DC 20008

NEW ZEALAND
37 Observatory Circle NW
Washington, DC 20008

NICARAGUA
1627 New Hampshire Ave. NW
Washington, DC 20009

NIGER
2204 R St. NW
Washington, DC 20008

NIGERIA
1333 16th St. NW
Washington, DC 20036

NORWAY
2730 34th St. NW
Washington, DC 20008

OMAN
2535 Belmont Rd. NW
Washington, DC 20008

PAKISTAN
2315 Massachusetts Ave. NW
Washington, DC 20008

PALAU
2000 L St. NW, Ste. 407
Washington, DC 20036

PANAMA
2862 McGill Terr. NW
Washington, DC 20008

PAPUA-NEW GUINEA
1615 New Hampshire Ave. NW, 3rd Fl.
Washington, DC 20009

PARAGUAY
2400 Massachusetts Ave. NW
Washington, DC 20008

PERU
1700 Massachusetts Ave. NW
Washington, DC 20036

PHILIPPINES
1600 Massachusetts Ave. NW
Washington, DC 20036

POLAND
2640 16th St. NW
Washington, DC 20009

PORTUGAL
2125 Kalorama Rd. NW
Washington, DC 20008

QATAR
4200 Wisconsin Ave. NW
Washington, DC 20016

ROMANIA
1607 23rd St. NW
Washington, DC 20008

RUSSIA
2650 Wisconsin Ave. NW
Washington, DC 20007

RWANDA
1714 New Hampshire Ave. NW
Washington, DC 20009

SAINT CHRISTOPHER (ST. KITTS)
and NEVIS
3216 New Mexico Ave. NW
Washington, DC 20016

SAINT LUCIA
3216 New Mexico Ave. NW
Washington, DC 20016

SAINT VINCENT and THE GRENADINES
3216 New Mexico Ave. NW
Washington, DC 20016

SAUDI ARABIA
601 New Hampshire Ave. NW
Washington, DC 20037

SENEGAL
2112 Wyoming Ave. NW
Washington, DC 20008

SEYCHELLES
820 2nd Ave., Ste. 900F
New York, NY 10017

SIERRA LEONE
1701 19th St. NW
Washington, DC 20009

SINGAPORE, REPUBLIC OF
3501 International Pl. NW
Washington, DC 20008

SLOVAKIA
2201 Wisconsin Ave. NW
Washington, DC 20007

SLOVENIA
1525 New Hampshire Ave.
Washington, DC 20036

SOLOMON ISLANDS
820 2nd Ave., Ste. 800
New York, NY 10017

SOUTH AFRICA
3051 Massachusetts Ave. NW
Washington, DC 20008

SPAIN
2375 Pennsylvania Ave. NW
Washington, DC 20037

SRI LANKA
2148 Wyoming Ave. NW
Washington, DC 20008

SUDAN
2210 Massachusetts Ave. NW
Washington, DC 20008

SURINAME
4301 Connecticut Ave. NW
Washington, DC 20037

SWAZILAND
3400 International Dr. NW
Washington, DC 20008

SWEDEN
1501 M St. NW
Washington, DC 20005

SWITZERLAND
2900 Cathedral Ave. NW
Washington, DC 20008

SYRIA
2215 Wyoming Ave. NW
Washington, DC 20008

TANZANIA, UNITED REPUBLIC OF
2139 R St. NW
Washington, DC 20008

THAILAND
1024 Wisconsin Ave. NW
Washington, DC 20007

TOGO
2208 Massachusetts Ave. NW
Washington, DC 20008

TRINIDAD and TOBAGO
1708 Massachusetts Ave. NW
Washington, DC 20036

TUNISIA
1515 Massachusetts Ave. NW
Washington, DC 20008

TURKEY
1714 Massachusetts Ave. NW
Washington, DC 20008

TURKMENISTAN
2207 Massachusetts Ave. NW
Washington, DC 20008

UGANDA
5911 16th St. NW
Washington, DC 20011

UKRAINE
3350 M St. NW
Washington, DC 20007

UNITED ARAB EMIRATES
3000 K St. NW, Ste. 600
Washington, DC 20007

UNITED KINGDOM
3100 Massachusetts Ave. NW
Washington, DC 20008

URUGUAY
1918 F St. NW
Washington, DC 20006

UZBEKISTAN
1746 Massachusetts Ave. NW
Washington, DC 20036

VENEZUELA
2409 California Ave. NW
Washington, DC 20008

VIETNAM
1233 20th St. NW, Ste. 501
Washington, DC 20036

WESTERN SAMOA
820 2nd Ave., Ste. 800D
New York, NY 10017

YEMEN
2600 Virginia Ave. NW, Ste. 705
Washington, DC 20037

YUGOSLAVIA
2410 California St. NW
Washington, DC 20008

ZAMBIA
2419 Massachusetts Ave. NW
Washington, DC 20008

ZIMBABWE
1608 New Hampshire Ave. NW
Washington, DC 20009

TOLL-FREE TELEPHONE NUMBERS

Many people do not write or realize that phoning may cut some time off the receipt of material. AT&T has an 800 directory that costs about $11. One should be strongly considered for purchase for any elementary school. Almost every state bureau of travel and tourism has an 800 number. Call 800 information, 800-555-1212 or 888-555-1212, to obtain numbers. Some examples of other 800 numbers that illustrate the breadth of the 800 directory:

United Airlines
800/241-6522

Philippine Airlines
800/435-9725

North Carolina Aquarium Society
800/832-3474

Harry and David Fruits & Gifts Catalog
800/547-3033

Pacific Trading Cards
800/551-2002

Holiday Inns
800/465-4329

Paradise Island (Bahamas)
800/321-3000

WORLD URBAN CENTERS (BASED ON ESTIMATES FOR THE METROPOLITAN AREA FOR THE YEAR 2000)

1.	Mexico City	31,616,000
2.	Tokyo-Yokohama	26,130,000
3.	São Paulo	26,045,000
4.	New York	22,210,000
5.	Calcutta	19,660,000
6.	Rio de Janeiro	19,380,000
7.	Shanghai	19,155,000
8.	Bombay	19,065,000
9.	Beijing	19,064,000
10.	Seoul	18,711,000

COUNTRIES WITH THE LARGEST PERCENTAGE OF THEIR ENERGY COMING FROM NUCLEAR POWER (1990 DATA)

1.	France	74.5%
2.	Belgium	60.1%
3.	Hungary	51.4%
4.	South Korea	49.1%
5.	Sweden	45.9%

LARGEST NATIONAL LANDS IN THE UNITED STATES

1.	Yellowstone (ID, MT, WY)	2,220,000 acres
2.	Death Valley (CA, NV)	2,049,000 acres
3.	Lake Mead (AZ, NV)	1,469,000 acres
4.	Glen Canyon (AZ, UT)	1,194,000 acres
5.	Grand Canyon (AZ)	1,179,000 acres
6.	Glacier National Park (MT)	1,013,000 acres

INDEX

ACKNOWLEDGEMENTS

Page 7: © The Bettman Archive; 10: © The Granger Collection, New York; 18: © Louise Russell; 31: National Air and Space Museum/Smithsonian Institution; 39 left: © Spencer Grand/The Picture Cube; 39 right: © Frank Siteman/The Picture Cube; 41: © Robin Sachs; 51 left: © Robert Pacheco/EKM-Nepenthe; 51 right: © Jean-Claude Lejeune/Stock, Boston; 53: © Louise Russell; 55: © Joel Gordon, 1976; 58: © Peter Vandermark/Stock, Boston; 65: © Naismith Memorial Basketball Hall of Fame; 79: © UPI/Corbis-Bettman; 95: © Donald Dietz/Stock, Boston; 102: Johnnie Walker/The Picture Cube; 131: © The Jacob A. Riis Collection, Museum of the City of New York; 133: © EKM-Nepenthe; 140: © Peter Menzel/Stock, Boston; 141: © AP/Wide World Photos; 143: © The Bettman Archive; 145: © Woolaroc Museum, Bartlesville, OK; 207: © Bob Daemrich/Stock, Boston; 215: © Alan Carey/The Image Works; 217: © Elizabeth Crews; 223: © The Picture Collection, The New York Public Library; 231: © Elizabeth Crews; 235: © Monkmeyer Press Photos; 241: © Peter Menzel/Stock, Boston; 245: © Louise Russell; 256: © Robin Sachs; 270: © Robin Sachs; 274: © Robin Sachs; 277: © Photofest; 290: © NASA; 307: © NASA; 317: © The Bettman Archive; 319: © Culver Pictures; 373: Courtesy of Power Wheels; 391: © Reuters/Corbis-Bettman; 394: © Robin Sachs; 423: © Louise Russell.